Hands-On Domain-Driven Design with .NET Core

Tackling complexity in the heart of software by putting DDD principles into practice

Alexey Zimarev

BIRMINGHAM - MUMBAI

Hands-On Domain-Driven Design with .NET Core

Commissioning Editor: Richa Tripathi
Acquisition Editor: Chaitanya Nair
Content Development Editor: Rohit Singh
Technical Editor: Gaurav Gala
Copy Editor: Safis Editing
Project Coordinator: Vaidehi Sawant
Proofreader: Safis Editing
Indexer: Tejal Daruwale Soni
Graphics: Alishon Mendonsa
Production Coordinator: Nilesh Mohite

First published: April 2019

Production reference: 1300419

Published by Packt Publishing Ltd.
Livery Place
35 Livery Street
Birmingham
B3 2PB, UK.

ISBN 978-1-78883-409-4

www.packtpub.com

To my wonderful family: my wife Olga, our sons Denis and Miklail, and our Siberian husky Taiga. Thank you for your patience and for giving me time and space to complete this big work. Without your support, this book would have never been published.

To my friend and colleague Sérgio Silveira Vaqueiro. We learned a lot from each other and I am very happy to have an opportunity to work with you. Nearly all the code in this book is based on the code we've prepared for the Hands-on Event Sourcing workshop that we deliver together.

`mapt.io`

Mapt is an online digital library that gives you full access to over 5,000 books and videos, as well as industry leading tools to help you plan your personal development and advance your career. For more information, please visit our website.

Why subscribe?

- Spend less time learning and more time coding with practical eBooks and Videos from over 4,000 industry professionals

- Improve your learning with Skill Plans built especially for you

- Get a free eBook or video every month

- Mapt is fully searchable

- Copy and paste, print, and bookmark content

Packt.com

Did you know that Packt offers eBook versions of every book published, with PDF and ePub files available? You can upgrade to the eBook version at `www.packt.com` and as a print book customer, you are entitled to a discount on the eBook copy. Get in touch with us at `customercare@packtpub.com` for more details.

At `www.packt.com`, you can also read a collection of free technical articles, sign up for a range of free newsletters, and receive exclusive discounts and offers on Packt books and eBooks.

Contributors

About the author

Alexey Zimarev is a software architect with a present focus on domain models, **Domain-Driven Design (DDD)**, event sourcing, message-driven systems and microservices, coaching, and mentoring. Alexey is also a contributor to several open source projects, such as RestSharp and MassTransit, and is the organizer of the DDD Norway meetup.

About the reviewers

Marcin Budny is a software developer with over a decade of experience in designing and building systems. He specializes in getting to the bottom of things and finding the worst-case scenarios. Mostly focused on the .NET ecosystem, he likes to venture into other territories to steal good ideas.

Marcin works mostly with Poland-based companies that cooperate with partners around the globe. That has resulted in a broad spectrum of challenges that he has had to face, which he has now turned into topics to share with his local software development community.

In this book, Marcin debuts as a reviewer.

Nick Tune is the coauthor of two books, *Patterns, Principles and Practices of Domain-Driven Design* (Wrox) and *Designing Autonomous Teams and Services* (O'Reilly), and frequently writes about technical leadership at NT.Coding().

Packt is searching for authors like you

If you're interested in becoming an author for Packt, please visit `authors.packtpub.com` and apply today. We have worked with thousands of developers and tech professionals, just like you, to help them share their insight with the global tech community. You can make a general application, apply for a specific hot topic that we are recruiting an author for, or submit your own idea.

Table of Contents

Preface

This book will help you solve complex business problems by understanding users better, finding the right problem to solve, and building lean, event-driven systems to give your customers what they really want. You will be taken through the fundamentals of **Domain-Driven Design** (**DDD**) principles and how it can be applied using modern tools such as EventStorming, Event Sourcing, and CQRS. Through this book, you will learn how DDD applies directly to various architectural styles, such as REST, reactive systems, and microservices. You will empower teams to work flexibly with improved services and decoupled interactions.

Who this book is for

This book is for .NET developers who have an intermediate level understanding of C#, and for those who seek to deliver value, not just write code. An intermediate level of competence in JavaScript will be helpful for the UI chapters.

What this book covers

Chapter 1, *Why Domain-Driven Design?*, covers the concepts of problem and solution spaces, requirements specifications, complexity, knowledge, and ignorance. These topics have a significant impact on how and what we deliver.

Chapter 2, *Language and Context*, deep dives into the importance of language and explains Ubiquitous Language.

Chapter 3, *EventStorming*, explores one of the most popular techniques for domain modeling and goes through some practical tips on how to organize useful workshops between domain experts and developers.

Chapter 4, *Designing the Model*, goes deeper into the modeling process, with more of a focus on artifacts that can help us to start writing code and deliver initial prototypes as soon as possible.

Chapter 5, *Implementing the Model*, forms the basis for our domain model implemented in code. We will go through different styles of performing the behavior in domain entities and also write some tests.

Chapter 6, *Acting with Commands*, shows how to implement commands, and how commands are the glue between our domain model and the world outside it. We will learn how to make our model useful by letting people interact with it.

Chapter 7, *Consistency Boundary*, takes a closer look at entity persistence, and its scope will be our focus. We will learn what types of consistency we need to deal with and how important it is to understand consistency boundaries.

Chapter 8, *Aggregate Persistence*, takes a deep dive into the topic of aggregate persistence. We will find a way to store our domain objects in a database and see our application working for the first time.

Chapter 9, *CQRS - The Read Side*, covers the read side of CQRS and explains what the read models are. You will learn how to use Ubiquitous Language for queries and see how to implement CQRS with one database.

Chapter 10, *Event Sourcing*, shows how events can be used to persist the state of an object, instead of using traditional persistence mechanisms. We will cover the concept of event streams and see how streams relate to aggregates. We will use the Event Store to persist our aggregates in streams and load them back.

Chapter 11, *Projections and Queries*, takes you through the challenges of querying the Event Sourced system and solving these challenges by using separate read models and projections.

Chapter 12, *Bounded Context*, makes you familiar with the concept of Bounded Contexts. We will identify contexts in our project and separate the system into pieces. We will also learn about the Context Map, which shows the landscape of Bounded Contexts for the entire system and their relationships.

Chapter 13, *Splitting the System*, gives practical advice about identifying Bounded Contexts and implementing more than one context in the sample application. This chapter is available as an online chapter at: https://www.packtpub.com/sites/default/files/downloads/Splitting_the_System.pdf.

To get the most out of this book

In order to follow the instructions in this book, you need to have intermediate-level understanding of C#. Other requirements are mentioned at the relevant instances in the respective chapters.

Diagrams for this book are created using Miro, an online collaboration tool, and `draw.io`, the free online service for creating diagrams and wireframes. The line style and the font are used intentionally, to embrace the temporal nature and usefulness of all models and diagrams

Download the example code files

You can download the example code files for this book from your account at `www.packtpub.com`. If you purchased this book elsewhere, you can visit `www.packtpub.com/support` and register to have the files emailed directly to you.

You can download the code files by following these steps:

1. Log in or register at `www.packtpub.com`.
2. Select the **SUPPORT** tab.
3. Click on **Code Downloads & Errata**.
4. Enter the name of the book in the **Search** box and follow the onscreen instructions.

Once the file is downloaded, please make sure that you unzip or extract the folder using the latest version of:

- WinRAR/7-Zip for Windows
- Zipeg/iZip/UnRarX for Mac
- 7-Zip/PeaZip for Linux

The code bundle for the book is also hosted on GitHub at `https://github.com/PacktPublishing/Hands-On-Domain-Driven-Design with .NET Core`. In case there's an update to the code, it will be updated on the existing GitHub repository.

We also have other code bundles from our rich catalog of books and videos available at `https://github.com/PacktPublishing/`. Check them out!

Download the color images

We also provide a PDF file that has color images of the screenshots/diagrams used in this book. You can download it here: `https://www.packtpub.com/sites/default/files/downloads/9781788834094_ColorImages.pdf`

Conventions used

There are a number of text conventions used throughout this book.

`CodeInText`: Indicates code words in text, database table names, folder names, filenames, file extensions, pathnames, dummy URLs, user input, and Twitter handles. Here is an example: "Mount the downloaded `WebStorm-10*.dmg` disk image file as another disk in your system."

A block of code is set as follows:

```
html, body, #map {
 height: 100%;
 margin: 0;
 padding: 0
}
```

When we wish to draw your attention to a particular part of a code block, the relevant lines or items are set in bold:

```
[default]
exten => s,1,Dial(Zap/1|30)
exten => s,2,Voicemail(u100)
exten => s,102,Voicemail(b100)
exten => i,1,Voicemail(s0)
```

Any command-line input or output is written as follows:

```
$ mkdir css
$ cd css
```

Bold: Indicates a new term, an important word, or words that you see onscreen. For example, words in menus or dialog boxes appear in the text like this. Here is an example: "Select **System info** from the **Administration** panel."

Warnings or important notes appear like this.

Tips and tricks appear like this.

Get in touch

Feedback from our readers is always welcome.

General feedback: Email `feedback@packtpub.com` and mention the book title in the subject of your message. If you have questions about any aspect of this book, please email us at `questions@packtpub.com`.

Errata: Although we have taken every care to ensure the accuracy of our content, mistakes do happen. If you have found a mistake in this book, we would be grateful if you would report this to us. Please visit `www.packtpub.com/submit-errata`, selecting your book, clicking on the Errata Submission Form link, and entering the details.

Piracy: If you come across any illegal copies of our works in any form on the Internet, we would be grateful if you would provide us with the location address or website name. Please contact us at `copyright@packtpub.com` with a link to the material.

If you are interested in becoming an author: If there is a topic that you have expertise in and you are interested in either writing or contributing to a book, please visit `authors.packtpub.com`.

Reviews

Please leave a review. Once you have read and used this book, why not leave a review on the site that you purchased it from? Potential readers can then see and use your unbiased opinion to make purchase decisions, we at Packt can understand what you think about our products, and our authors can see your feedback on their book. Thank you!

For more information about Packt, please visit `packtpub.com`.

Why Domain-Driven Design? 1

The software industry appeared back in the early 1960s and has been growing ever since. There have been predictions that one day all software will be written and software developers will no longer be needed, but this prophecy has never become reality, and the growing army of software engineers is working hard to satisfy the continually increasing demand.

However, from the very early days of the industry, the number of projects that were delivered very late and massively over budget, plus the number of failed projects, was overwhelming. The 2015 CHAOS report by the Standish Group (`https://www.projectsmart.co.uk/white-papers/chaos-report.pdf`) suggests that from 2011 to 2015, the percentage of successful IT projects remained unchanged at a level of just 22%. Over 19% of projects failed, and the rest experienced challenges. Although the report might set somewhat controversial expectations for project success, it still paints a picture that is familiar to many. These numbers are astonishing. Over four decades, a lot of methods have been developed and advertised as silver bullets for software project management, but there has been little or no change in the number of successful projects.

One of the critical factors that define the success of any IT project is understanding the problem that the system is supposed to solve. We are all very familiar with systems that do not solve the problems they claim to answer or do it very inefficiently. Both the SCRUM and XP software development methodologies embrace interacting with users and understanding their problems.

The term **Domain-Driven Design (DDD)** was coined by Eric Evans in his now-iconic book *Domain-Driven Design: Tackling Complexity in the Heart of Software* published by Addison-Wesley back in 2004. More than a decade after the book was published, interest in the practices and principles described in the book started to grow exponentially. Many factors influenced this growth in popularity, but the most important one is that DDD explains how people from the software industry can build an understanding of their users' needs and create software systems that solve the problem and make an impact.

In this chapter, we will discuss how understanding the business domain, building domain knowledge, and distinguishing essential complexity from accidental complexity can help in creating software that matters.

The objective of this chapter is to explore the following topics:

- Problem space versus solution space
- What went wrong with requirements
- Understanding complexity
- The role of knowledge in software development

Understanding the problem

We rarely write software to just write some code. Of course, we can create a pet project for fun and to learn new technologies, but professionally we build software to help other people to do their work better, faster, and more efficiently. Otherwise, there is no point in writing any software in the first place. It means that we need to have a *problem* that we intend to solve. Cognitive psychology defines the issue as a restriction between the current state and the desired state.

Problem space and solution space

In their book *Human Problem Solving*, Allen Newell and Herbert Simon outlined the problem space theory. The theory states that humans solve problems by searching for a solution in the *problem space*. The problem space describes the initial and desired states, as well as possible intermediate states. It can also contain specific constraints and rules that define the context of the problem. In the software industry, people operating in the problem space are usually customers and users.

Each real problem demands a solution, and if we search properly in the problem space, we can outline which steps we need to take to move from the initial state to the desired state. This outline and all the details about the solution form a *solution space*.

The classic story of problem and solution spaces, which get completely detached from each other during the implementation, is the story of writing in space. The story goes that in the 1960s, space-exploring nations realized that the usual ballpoint pens wouldn't work in space due to the lack of gravity. NASA then spent a million dollars to develop a pen that would work in space, and the Soviets decided to use the good old pencil, which costs almost nothing.

This story is so compelling that it is still circulating, and was even used in the TV show *The West Wing*, with Martin Sheen playing the US president. It is so easy to believe, not only because we are used to wasteful spending by government-funded bodies, but mostly because we have seen so many examples of inefficiency and misinterpretation of real-world issues, adding enormous unnecessary complexity to their proposed solutions and solving problems that don't exist.

This story is a myth. NASA also tried using pencils but decided to get rid of them due to the production of microdust, tips breaking, and the potential flammability of wooden pencils. A private company called Fisher developed what is now known as a **space pen**. Later, NASA tested the pen and decided to use it. The company also got an order from the Soviet Union, and pens were sold across the world. The price was the same for everyone, $2.39 per pen.

Here you can see the other part of the problem space/solution space issue. Although the problem itself appeared to be simple, additional constraints, which we could also call **non-functional requirements**, or, to be more precise, operational requirements, made it more complicated than it looked at first glance.

Jumping to a solution is very easy, and since most of us have a rather rich experience of solving everyday problems, we can find solutions for many issues almost immediately. However, as Bart Barthelemy and Candace Dalmagne-Rouge suggest in their article *When You're Innovating, Resist Looking for Solutions* (2013, Harvard Business Review `https://hbr.org/2013/09/when-youre-innovating-resist-1`), thinking about solutions prevents our brain from thinking about the problem. Instead, we start going deeper into the solution that first came to our mind, adding more levels of detail and making it the most ideal solution for a given problem.

There's one more aspect to consider when searching for a solution to a given problem. There is a danger of fixating all your attention on one particular solution, which might not be the best one at all but it was the first to come to mind, based on your previous experiences, your current understanding of the problem, and other factors:

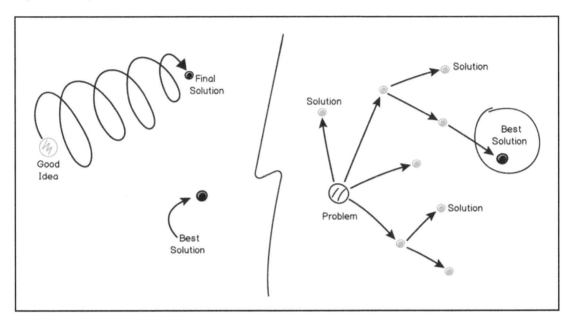

Refinement versus exploration

The exploratory approach to find and choose solutions involves quite a lot of work to try out a few different things, instead of concentrating on the iterative improvement of the original *good idea*. However, the answer that is found during this type of exploration will most probably be much more precise and valuable. We will discuss fixation on the first possible solution later in this chapter.

What went wrong with requirements

We are all familiar with the idea of requirements for software. Developers rarely have direct contact with whoever wants to solve a problem. Usually, some dedicated people, such as requirements analysts, business analysts, or product managers, talk to customers and generalize the outcomes of these conversations in the form of functional requirements.

Requirements can have different forms, from large documents called a **requirements specification** to more **agile** means such as user stories. Let's have a look at this example:

> *"Every day, the system shall generate, for each hotel, a list of guests expected to check in and check out on that day."*

As you can see, this statement only describes the solution. We cannot possibly know what the user is doing and what problem our system will be solving. Additional requirements might be specified, further refining the solution, but a description of the problem is never included in functional requirements.

In contrast, with user stories, we have more insight into what our user wants. Let's review this real-life user story: *"As a warehouse manager, I need to be able to print a stock-level report so that I can order items when they are out of stock."* In this case, we have an insight into what our user wants. However, this user story already dictates what the developers need to do. It is describing the *solution*. The real problem is probably that the customer needs a more efficient procurement process, so they never run out of stock. Or, they need an advanced purchase forecasting system, so they can improve throughput without stockpiling additional inventory in their warehouse.

We should not think that the requirements are a waste of time. There are many excellent analysts out there who produce high-quality requirements specifications. However, it is vital to understand that these requirements almost always represent the understanding of the actual problem from the point of view of the person who wrote them. A misconception that spending more and more time and money on writing higher-quality requirements prevails in the industry.

However, lean and agile methodologies embrace more direct communication between developers and end users. Understanding the problem by all stakeholders, from end users to developers and testers, finding solutions together, eliminating assumptions, building prototypes for end users to evaluate—all these things are being adopted by successful teams, and as we will see later in the book, they are also closely related to DDD.

Dealing with complexity

Before writing about complexity, I tried to find some fancy, striking definition of the word itself, but it appeared to be a complex task on its own. Merriam-Webster defines the word **complexity** as the quality or state of being complex and this definition is rather obvious and might even sound silly. Therefore, we need to dive a bit deeper into this subject and understand more about complexity.

In software, the idea of complexity is not much different from the real world. Most software is written to deal with real-world problems. Those problems might sound simple but be intrinsically complex, or even wicked. Without a doubt, the problem space complexity will be reflected in the software that tries to solve such a problem. Realizing what kind of complexity we are dealing with when creating software thus becomes very important.

Types of complexity

In 1986, the Turing Award winner Fred Brooks wrote a paper called *No Silver Bullet – Essence and Accident in Software Engineering* in which he made a distinction between two types of complexity—essential and accidental complexity. Essential complexity comes from the domain, from the problem itself, and it cannot be removed without decreasing the scope of the problem. In contrast, accidental complexity is brought to the solution by the solution itself—this could be a framework, a database, or some other infrastructure, with different kinds of optimization and integration.

Brooks argued that the level of accidental complexity decreased substantially when the software industry became more mature. High-level programming languages and efficient tooling give programmers more time to work on business problems. However, as we can see today, more than 30 years later, the industry still struggles to fight accidental complexity. Indeed, we have power tools in our hands, but most of those tools come with the cost of spending the time to learn the tool itself. New JavaScript frameworks appear every year and each of them is different, so before writing anything useful, we need to learn how to be efficient when using the framework of choice. I wrote some JavaScript code many years ago and I saw Angular as a blessing until I realized that I spend more time fighting with it than writing anything meaningful. Or take an example of containers that promised us to bring an easy way to host our applications in isolation, without all that hassle with physical or virtual machines. But then we needed an orchestrator, and we got quite a few, spent time learning to work with them until we got Kubernetes to rule them all and now we spend more time writing YAML files than actual code. We will discuss some possible reasons for this phenomenon in the next section.

You probably noticed that essential complexity has a strong relation to the problem space, and accidental complexity leans towards the solution space. However, we often seem to get problem statements that are more complex than the problems themselves. Usually, this happens due to problems being mixed with solutions, as we discussed earlier, or due to a lack of understanding.

Gojko Adžić, a software delivery consultant and the author of several influential books, such as *Specification by Example* and *Impact Mapping*, gives this example in his workshop:

> *"A software-as-a-service company got a feature request to provide a particular report in real time, which previously was executed once a month on schedule. After a few months of development, salespeople tried to get an estimated delivery date. The development department then reported that the feature would take at least six more months to deliver and the total cost would be around £1 million. It was because the data source for this report is in a transactional database and running it in real time would mean significant performance degradation, so additional measures such as data replication, geographical distribution, and sharding were required.*
>
> *The company then decided to analyze the actual need that the customer who requested this feature had. It turned out that the customer wanted to perform the same operations as they were doing before, but instead of doing it monthly, they wanted it weekly. When asked about the desired outcome of the whole feature, the customer then said that running the same report batched once a week would solve the problem. Rescheduling the database job was by far an easier operation that redesigning the whole system, while the impact for the end customer was the same."*

This example clearly shows that not understanding the problem can lead to severe consequences. We as developers love principles like DRY. We seek abstraction that will make our code more elegant and concise. However, often that might be entirely unnecessary. Sometimes we fall to the trap of using some tool or framework that promises to solve all issues in the world, easily. Again, that never comes without a cost. As a .NET developer, I can clearly see this when I look at the current obsession with dependency injection among the community.

True enough, Microsoft finally made a DI container that makes sense, but when I see it being used in a small console app just to initialize the logger, I get upset. Sometimes, more code is being written just to satisfy the tool, the framework, the environment, than the code that delivers the actual value. What seemed to be the essential complexity in this example turned out to be a waste:

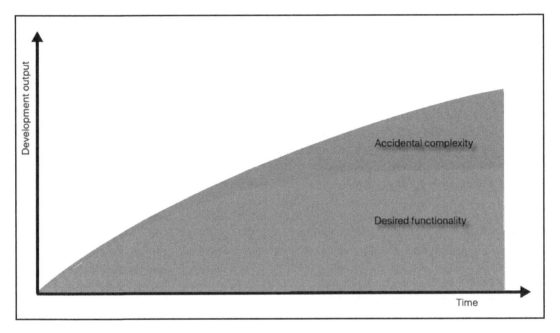

Complexity growth over time

The preceding graph shows that with the ever-growing complexity of the system, the essential complexity is being pushed down and the accidental complexity takes over. You might have doubts about the fact that accidental complexity keeps growing over time when the desired functionality almost flatters out. How could this happen, definitely we can't spend time only creating more accidental complexity? When systems become more prominent, a lot of effort is required to make the system work as a whole and to manage large data models, which large systems tend to have. Supportive code grows and a lot of effort is being spent to keep the system running. We bring cache, optimize queries, split and merge databases, the list goes on. In the end, we might actually decide to reduce the scope of the desired functionality just to keep the system running without too many glitches.

DDD helps you focus on solving complex domain problems and concentrates on the essential complexity. For sure, dealing with a new fancy front-end tool or use a cloud document database is fun. But without understanding what problem are we trying to solve, it all might be just waste. It is much more valuable to any business to get something useful first and try it out than getting a perfect piece of state-of-the-art software that misses the point entirely. To do this, DDD offers several useful techniques for managing complexity by splitting the system into smaller parts and making these parts focus on solving a set of related problems. These techniques are described later in this book.

The rule of thumb when dealing with complexity is—embrace essential, or as we might call it, domain complexity, and eliminate or decrease the accidental complexity. Your goal as a developer is not to create too much accidental complexity. Hence, very often, accidental complexity is caused by over-engineering.

Categorizing complexity

When dealing with problems, we don't always know whether these problems are complex. And if they are complex, how complex? Is there a tool for measuring complexity? If there is, it would be beneficial to measure, or at least categorize, the problem's complexity before starting to solve it. Such measurement would help to regulate the solution's complexity as well, since complex problems also demand a complex solution, with rare exceptions to this rule. If you disagree, we will be getting deeper into this topic in the following section.

In 2007, Dave Snowden and Mary Boone published a paper called *A Leader's Framework for Decision Making* in Harvard Business Review, 2007. This paper won the **Outstanding Practitioner-Oriented Publication in OB** award from the Academy of Management's Organizational Behavior division. What is so unique about it, and which framework does it describe?

The framework is **Cynefin**. This word is Welsh for something like *habitat,* accustomed, familiar. Snowden started to work on it back in 1999 when he worked at IBM. The work was so valuable that IBM established the Cynefin Center for Organizational Complexity, and Dave Snowden was its founder and director.

Cynefin divides all problems into five categories or complexity domains. By describing the properties of problems that fall into each domain, it provides a *sense of place* for any given problem. After the problem is categorized into one of the domains, Cynefin then also offers some practical approaches to deal with this kind of problem:

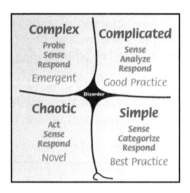

Cynefin framework, image by Dave Snowden

These five realms have specific characteristics, and the framework provides attributes for both, identifying to which domain your problem belongs, and how the problem needs to be addressed.

The first domain is Simple, or Obvious. Here, you have problems that can be described as *known knowns*, where best practices and an established set of rules are available, and there is a direct link between a cause and a consequence. The sequence of actions for this domain is *sense-categorize-response*. Establish facts (sense), identify processes and rules (categorize), and execute them (response).

Snowden, however, warns about the tendency for people to wrongly classify problems as *simple*. He identifies three cases for this:

- **Oversimplification**: This correlates with some of the cognitive biases described in the following section.
- **Entrained thinking**: When people blindly use the skills and experiences they have obtained in the past and therefore become blinded to new ways of thinking.
- **Complacency**: When things go well, people tend to relax and overestimate their ability to react to the changing world. The danger of this case is that when a problem is classified as simple, it can quickly escalate to the chaotic domain due to a failure to adequately assess the risks. Notice the *shortcut* from Simple to Chaotic domain at the bottom of the diagram, which is often being missed by those who study the framework.

For this book, it is important to remember two main things:

- If you identify the problem as obvious, you probably don't want to set up a complex solution and perhaps would even consider buying some off-the-shelf software to solve the problem, if any software is required at all.
- Beware, however, of wrongly classifying more complex problems in this domain to avoid applying the wrong best practices instead of doing more thorough exploration and research.

The second domain is Complicated. Here, you find problems that require expertise and skill to find the relation between cause and effect, since there is no single answer to these problems. These are *known unknowns*. The sequence of actions in this realm is *sense-analyze-respond*. As we can see, *analyze* replaces *categorize* because there is no clear categorization of facts in this domain. Proper analysis needs to be done to identify which good practice to apply. Categorization can be done here too, but you need to go through more choices and analyze the consequences as well. That is where previous experience is necessary. Engineering problems are typically in this category, where a clearly understood problem requires a sophisticated technical solution.

In this realm, assigning qualified people to do some design up front and then perform the implementation makes perfect sense. When a thorough analysis is done, the risk of implementation failure is low. Here, it makes sense to apply DDD patterns for both strategic and tactical design, and to the implementation, but you could probably avoid more advanced exploratory techniques such as EventStorming. Also, you might spend less time on knowledge crunching, if the problem is thoroughly understood.

Complex is the third complexity domain in Cynefin. Here, we encounter something that no one has done before. Making even a rough estimate is impossible. It is hard or impossible to predict the reaction to our action, and we can only find out about the impact that we have made in retrospect. The sequence of actions in this domain is *probe-sense-respond*. There are no right answers here and no practices to rely upon. Previous experience won't help either. These are *unknown unknowns*, and this is the place where all innovation happens. Here, we find our core domain, the concept, which we will get to later in the book.

The course of action for the complex realm is led by experiments and prototypes. There is very little sense in creating a big design up front since we have no idea how it will work and how the world will react to what we are doing. Work here needs to be done in small iterations with continuous and intensive feedback.

Advanced modeling and implementation techniques that are lean enough to respond to changes quickly are the perfect fit in this context. In particular, modeling using EventStorming and implementation using event-sourcing are very much at home in the complex domain. A thorough strategic design is necessary, but some tactical patterns of DDD can be safely ignored when doing spikes and prototypes, to save time. However, again, event-sourcing could be your best friend. Both EventStorming and event-sourcing are described later in the book.

The fourth domain is Chaotic. This is where hellfire burns and the Earth spins faster than it should. No one wants to be here. Appropriate actions here are *act-sense-respond*, since there is no time for spikes. It is probably not the best place for DDD since there is no time or budget for any sort of design available at this stage.

Disorder is the fifth and final realm, right in the middle. The reason for it is that when being at this stage, it is unclear which complexity context applies to the situation. The only way out from disorder is to try breaking the problem into smaller pieces that can be then categorized into those four complexity contexts and then deal with them accordingly.

This is only a brief overview of the categorization of complexity. There is more to it, and I hope your mind gets curious to see examples, videos, and articles about the topic. That was the exact reason for me to bring it in, so please feel free to stop reading now and explore the complexity topic some more. For this book the most important outcome is that DDD can be applied almost everywhere, but it is of virtually no use in obvious and chaotic domains. Using EventStorming as a design technique in complex systems would be useful for both complicated and complex domains, along with event-sourcing, which suits complex domains best.

Decision making and biases

The human brain processes a tremendous amount of information every single second. We do many things on autopilot, driven by instinct and habit. Most of our daily routines are like this. Other areas of brain activity are thinking, learning, and decision-making. Such actions are performed significantly more slowly and require much more power than the automatic operations.

Dual process theory in psychology suggests that these types of brain activity are indeed entirely different and there are two different processes for two kinds of thinking. One is the implicit, automatic, unconscious process, and the other one is an explicit conscious process. Unconscious processes are formed over a long time and are also very hard to change because changing such a process would require developing a new habit, and this is not an easy task. Conscious processes, however, can be altered through logical reasoning and education.

These processes, or systems, happily co-exist in one brain but are rather different in the way they operate. Keith Stanovich and Richard West coined the names implicit system, or **System 1** and explicit system, or **System 2** (*Individual difference in reasoning: implications for the rationality debate*? Behavioral and Brain Sciences 2000). Daniel Kahneman, in his award-winning book *Thinking Fast and Slow* (New York: Farrar, Straus and Giroux, 2011), assigned several attributes to each system:

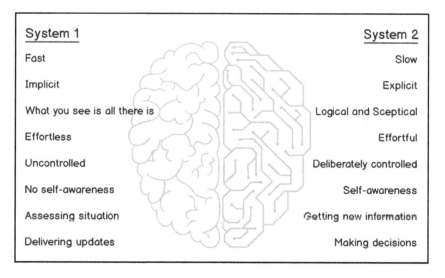

System 1	System 2
Fast	Slow
Implicit	Explicit
What you see is all there is	Logical and Sceptical
Effortless	Effortful
Uncontrolled	Deliberately controlled
No self-awareness	Self-awareness
Assessing situation	Getting new information
Delivering updates	Making decisions

System 1 and System 2

What does all this have to do with DDD? Well, the point here is more about how we make decisions. It is scientifically proven that all humans are biased, one way or another. As developers, we have our own ways of solving technical problems and of course we're ready to pick up the fight when being challenged by the business about the way we write software to solve their problems. At the other hand, our customers are also biased towards their ways, they probably already were earning money without our software or, they might have some other system created twenty years ago by ancient Cobol programmers and it somehow works, so they just want a *modern* or even *cloud-based* version of the same thing. The point I am trying to make here is that we should strive to mitigate our biases and be more open to what other people say and still not fall into a trap of their own biases. It was not without a reason for Google People Operations team to create the *Unconscious Bias @ Work* workshop to help their colleagues to become aware of their biases and show some methods to deal with them.

The Cynefin complexity model requires us to at least categorize the complexity we are dealing with in our problem space (and also sometimes in the solution space). But to assign the right category, we need to make a lot of decisions, and here we often get our System 1 responding and making assumptions based on our biases and experiences from the past, rather than engaging System 2 to start reasoning and thinking. Of course, every one of us is familiar with a colleague exclaiming *yeah, that's easy!* before you can even finish describing the problem. We also often see people organizing endless meetings and conference calls to discuss something that we assume to be a straightforward decision to make.

Cognitive biases are playing a crucial role here. Some biases can profoundly influence decision-making, and this is definitely System 1 speaking. Here are some of the biases and heuristics that can affect your thinking about system design:

- **Choice-supportive bias***:* If you have chosen something, you will be positive about this choice even though it might have been proven to contain significant flaws. Typically, this happens when we come up with the first model and try to stick to it at all costs, even if it becomes evident that the model is not optimal and needs to be changed. Also, this bias can be observed when you choose a technology to use, such as a database or a framework.
- **Confirmation bias**: Very similar to the previous one, confirmation bias makes you only hear arguments that support your choice or position and ignore arguments that contradict the arguments that support your choice, although these arguments may show that your opinion is wrong.
- **Band-wagon effect**: When the majority of people in the room agree on something, this *something* begins to make more sense to the minority that previously disagreed. Without engaging System 2, the opinion of the majority gets more credit without any objective reason. Remember that what the majority decides is not the best choice by default!

- **Overconfidence**: Too often, people tend to be too optimistic about their abilities. This bias might cause them to take more significant risks and make the wrong decisions that have no objective grounds but are based exclusively on their opinion. The most obvious example of this is the estimation process. People invariably underestimate rather than overestimate the time and effort they are going to spend on a problem.
- **Availability heuristic**: The information we have is not always all the information that we can get about a particular problem. People tend to base their decisions only on the information in hand, without even trying to get more details. This often leads to an over-simplification of the domain problem and an underestimation of the essential complexity. This heuristic can also trick us when we make technological decisions and choose something that has *always worked* without analyzing the operational requirements, which might be much higher than our technology can handle.

The importance of knowing how our decision-making process works is hard to overestimate. The books referenced in this section contain much more information about human behavior and different factors that can have a negative impact on our cognitive abilities. We need to remember to turn on System 2 in order to make better decisions that are not based on emotions and biases.

Knowledge

Many junior developers tend to think that software development is just typing code, and when they become more experienced in typing, get to know more IDE shortcuts, and know frameworks and libraries by heart, they will be ninja developers, able to write something like Instagram in a couple of days.

Well, the reality is harshly different. In fact, after getting some experience and after deliberately spending months and maybe years in death-marches towards impossible deadlines and unrealistic goals, people usually slow down. They begin to understand that writing code immediately after receiving a specification might not be the best idea. The reason for this might already be apparent to you if you have read all the previous sections. Being obsessed with solutions instead of understanding the problem, ignoring essential complexity and conforming to biases—all these factors influence us when we are developing software. As soon as we get more experience and learn from our own mistakes and, preferably, from the errors of others, we will realize that the most crucial part of writing useful, valuable software is the knowledge about the problem space, for which we are building a solution.

Domain knowledge

Not all knowledge is equally useful when building a software system. Knowing about writing Java code in the financial domain might not be very beneficial when you start creating an iOS app for real-estate management. Of course, principles such as clean code, DRY, and so on are helpful no matter what programming language you use. But knowledge of one domain might be vastly different from what you need for another domain.

That is where we encounter the concept of domain knowledge. Domain knowledge is knowledge about the domain in which you are going to operate with your software. If you are building a trading system, your domain is financial trading, and you need to gain some knowledge about trading to understand what your users are talking about and what they want.

This all comes to getting into the problem space. If you are not able to at least understand the terminology of the problem space, it would be hard (if not impossible) to even speak to your future users. If you lack domain knowledge, the only source of information for you would be the **specification**. When you do have at least some domain knowledge, conversations with your users become more fruitful since you can understand what they are talking about. One of the consequences of this is building trust between the customer and the developer. Such trust is hard to overestimate. A trusted person gets more insight and mistakes are forgiven more easily. By speaking the *domain language* to *domain experts* (your users and customers), you also gain credibility, and they see you and your colleagues as more competent people.

Obtaining domain knowledge is not an easy task. People specialize in their domains for years, they become experts in their domains, and they do this kind of work for a living. Software developers and business analysts do something else, and that particular problem domain might be little known or completely unknown when they need to obtain domain knowledge.

The art of obtaining domain knowledge is through effective collaboration. Domain experts are the source of ultimate truth (at least, we want to treat them like this). However, they might not be. Some organizations have fragmented knowledge; some might just be wrong. Knowledge crunching in such environments is even harder, but there might be bits and pieces of information waiting to be found at the desks of some low-level clerks, and your task is to see it.

The general advice here is to talk to many different people from inside the domain, from the management of the whole organization, and from adjacent domains. There are several ways to obtain domain knowledge, and here are some of them:

- Conversations are the most popular method, formalized as meetings. However, conversations often turn into a mess without any visible outcome. Still, some value is there, but you need to listen carefully and ask many questions to get valuable information.
- Observation is a very powerful technique. Software people need to fight their introversion, leave the ivory tower and go to a trading floor, to a warehouse, to a hotel, to a place where business runs, and then talk to people and see how they work. Jeff Patton gave many good examples in his talk at the DDD Exchange 2017 (`https://skillsmatter.com/skillscasts/10127-empathy-driven-design`).
- Domain Storytelling, a technique proposed by Stefan Hofer and his colleagues from Hamburg University (`http://domainstorytelling.org/`), advocates using pictograms, arrows, and a little bit of text, plus numbering actions sequentially, to describe different interactions inside the domain. This technique is easy to use, and typically there is not much to explain to people participating in such a workshop before they start using it to deliver the knowledge.
- EventStorming was invented by Alberto Brandolini. He explains the method in his book *Introducing EventStorming* (2017, Leanpub), and we will also go into more detail later in this book when we start analyzing our sample domain. EventStorming uses post-it notes and a paper roll to model all kinds of activities in a straightforward fashion. Workshop participants write facts from the past (events) on post-its and put them on the wall, trying to make a timeline. It allows the discovery of activities, workflows, business processes, and more. Very often, it also uncovers ambiguities, assumptions, implicit terminology, confusion, and sometimes conflicts and anger. In short—everything that the domain knowledge consists of.

Avoiding ignorance

Back in 2000, Philip Armour published an article called *Five Orders of Ignorance* (Communications of the ACM, Volume 43 Issue 10, Oct. 2000), with the subtitle *Viewing software development as knowledge acquisition and ignorance reduction.* This message very much correlates with Alberto's quote from the previous section, although it is somewhat less catchy but by no means less powerful. The article argues that increasing domain knowledge and decreasing ignorance are two keys to creating software that delivers value.

The article concentrates on ignorance and identifies five levels of it:

- The zero ignorance level, which authors call *the lack of ignorance,* is the lowest. On this level, you have no ignorance because you have most of the knowledge and know what to do and how to do it.
- The first level is the *lack of knowledge.* It is when you don't know something, but you realize and accept this fact. You want to get more knowledge and decrease your ignorance to level zero, so you have channels to obtain the knowledge.
- The second level also called the *lack of awareness,* is when you don't know that you don't know. Most commonly, this occurs when you get a specification that describes a solution without specifying which problem this solution is trying to solve. This level can also be observed when people pretend to have competence they do not possess, and at the same time are ignorant of it. Such people might be lacking both business and technical knowledge. A lot of wrong decisions are made at this level of ignorance.
- The third level is the *lack of process.* On this level, you don't even know how to find out about your lack of awareness. Literally, you don't have a way to figure out you don't know that you don't know, which sounds like inception, but that's exactly what it is. It is tough to do anything on this level since apparently there is no way to access end users, even to ask if you understand their problem or not, in order to get down to level two. Essentially, with the lack of process, it is nearly impossible to find out if the problem you're trying to solve even exists. Building a system might be the only choice in this case, since it will be the only way to get any feedback.
- The fourth and last level of ignorance is meta-ignorance. It is when you don't know about the five degrees of ignorance.

As you can see, ignorance is the opposite of knowledge. The only way to decrease ignorance is to increase understanding. A high level of ignorance, conscious or subconscious, leads to a lack of knowledge and a misinterpretation of the problem, and therefore increases the chance of building the wrong solution:

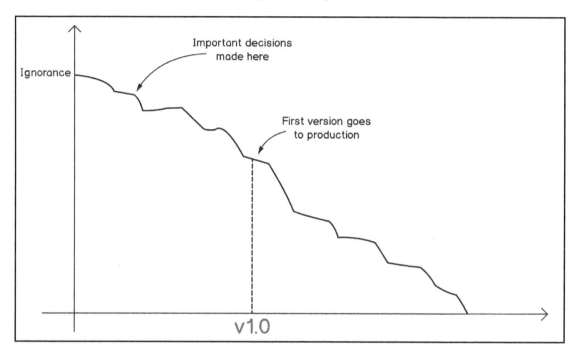

Ignorance is highest at the earliest stages

Eric Evans, the father of DDD, describes the upfront design as *locking in our ignorance*. The issue with the upfront design is that we do it at the beginning of a project, and this is when we have the least knowledge and the most ignorance. It has become the norm to make most of the important decisions about the design and architecture of the software at the very beginning of a project when there is virtually nothing to base such decisions on. This practice is quite obviously not optimal.

In the article *Introducing Deliberate Discovery* (`https://dannorth.net/2010/08/30/introducing-deliberate-discovery/`), Dan North suggests that we realize our position of being on at least the second level of ignorance when we start any project. In particular, the following three risks need to be taken into account:

- A few *unpredictable bad things* will happen during the project.
- *Being unpredictable*, these *things* are unknown in advance.
- *Being bad*, these *things* will negatively impact the project.

To mitigate these risks, Dan recommends using *INTRODUCING DELIBERATE DISCOVERY*, that is, seeking knowledge from the start. Since not all knowledge is equally important, we need to try to identify those sensitive areas where ignorance is creating the most impediments. By raising knowledge levels in these areas, we enable progress. At the same time, we need to keep an eye on new troublesome areas and resolve them too; and this process is continuous and iterative.

Summary

In this chapter, we briefly touched on the concepts of problem and solution spaces, requirements specifications, complexity, knowledge, and ignorance. Although at first, these topics don't seem to be directly related to software development, they have a significant impact on how and what we deliver.

Don't fall into the trap of thinking that you can deliver valuable solutions to your customers just by writing code and that you can deliver faster and better by typing more characters per second and writing cleaner code. Customers do not care about your code or how fast you type. They only care that your software solves their problems in a way that hasn't been done before. As Gojko Adžić wrote in his sweet little book about impact mapping (*Impact Mapping: Making a Big Impact With Software Products and Projects*, 2012, published by Provoking Thoughts), you cannot only formulate user stories like this:

- As a *someone*
- To *do something*
- I need to *use some functionality*

Your user, *someone*, might be already doing *something* by executing *some functionality* even without your software: using a pen and paper, using Excel, or using a system from one of your competitors. What you need to ensure is that you make a difference, make an impact. Your system will let people work faster, more efficiently, allow them to save money or even not to do this work at all if you completely automate it.

To build such software, you must understand the problems of your users. You need to crunch the domain knowledge, decrease the level of ignorance, accurately classify the problem's complexity, and try to avoid cognitive biases on the way to your goal. This is an essential part of DDD, although not all of these topics are covered in the original *Domain-Driven Design: Tackling Complexity in the Heart of Software* by Eric Evans, although known by the DDD community as the *Blue Book*.

In the next chapter, we will do a deep dive into the importance of language and discover the definition of Ubiquitous Language.

Further reading

Here is a list of information you can refer to:

- *A Leader's Framework for Decision Making*, Snowden D J, Boone M E. (2007), Harvard Business Review 2007 November issue
- *Thinking, Fast and Slow* (First edition), Kahneman, Daniel (2011), New York: Farrar, Straus, and Giroux
- *Impact Mapping: Making a Big Impact With Software Products and Projects*, Adžić, G. (2012), Provoking Thoughts.

Language and Context 2

In the previous chapter, we discussed the importance of language briefly. In the software industry, we developed this naïve perception that the only languages that matter are programming languages. That's why we often speak complete gibberish and our colleagues from other departments, or our customers, have a hard time understanding what we're trying to say. This issue is mutual because many lines of business have developed their jargon, which other people might not completely understand.

In this chapter, we're going to go deeper into the importance of language and go through several examples of mockups and code. We'll also get into the concept of language in a context and introduce the Ubiquitous Language, one of the most critical aspects of **Domain-Driven Design (DDD)**.

In this chapter, we'll go deeper into the following topics:

- Ubiquitous Language
- Why language is important
- Making implicit explicit
- Language in context
- Expressing behavior

Ubiquitous Language

It isn't a coincidence that the website of Eric Evans, the author of the original DDD book, is located at `http://domainlanguage.com`. Fundamental concepts of DDD, such as Ubiquitous Language and Bounded Context, are both based on the idea of language. It might sound strange to those who haven't spent many years developing software because, for less experienced developers, the only language that's important is a programming language. We learn to program usually by studying some concepts and applying them to practice using one of the programming languages. We think that we can translate a human language into a programming language, and this is the essence of our work. There's some degree of truth there indeed. However, this is by far not the essential part of the developer's daily routine.

Two people can understand each other only if they can speak the same language. It doesn't necessarily need to be verbal; it might very well be sign language or the language of music. But both interlocutors need to share the same understanding of this universal language. Otherwise, there will be trouble. Not only do they need to speak the same language, but this language must be in one context. There's a whole book called *American and British English: Divided by a Common Language?* by Paul Baker, which describes how different the same language became after being split by the ocean for a long enough time.

In this section, we'll look deeper into the importance of language and the context in which these concepts are crucial for successful software projects.

Domain language

Nearly every industry has developed a particular language that only people from that industry fully understand. Some of those words spread out to the world, like the automotive world, which enriched our language with terms such as gearbox, ignition, combustion engine, and even body shop. The last term is ambiguous when being looked at outside of the domain. But as soon as the domain is specified, it becomes clear that we don't mean a beauty product boutique, nor a software outsourcing company, but a place where car bodies are being repaired after accidents.

Of course, the automotive industry isn't unique in this sense. Other industries have developed their terms, and their language might be much less known and more cryptic for outsiders.

One of the examples of such an industry is, of course, the software industry. When two programmers discuss implementation details of some reasonably complex systems, non-programmers around them don't understand much of this conversation and usually get bored. Lack of understanding always results in a lack of interest:

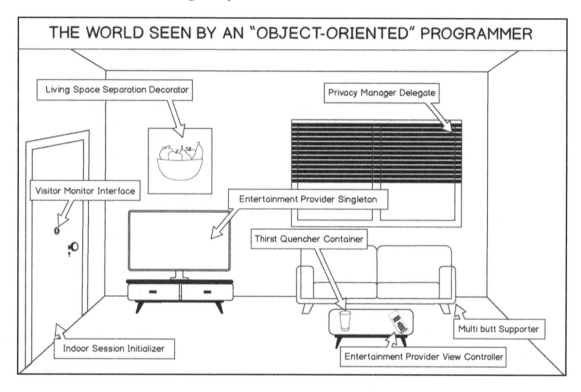

The world, as seen by a programmer (based on the original work by Manu Cornet)

The software industry is, in a sense, unique because it tends to serve a variety of business problems within any other industry. Almost everything today requires or wishes for some degree of automation, and this means software. This also means that people from the business will come to their developers or external software companies and try to express their problems using their language. When this language isn't understood correctly, issues arise.

Functional requirements, written by dedicated professionals who are neither business people nor software developers, have been seen as the holy grail of successful software. Each time we reach an undesired outcome after the software is delivered to an unhappy customer, we blame requirements. We say—next time, we'll write better requirements and more detailed specifications and explain what developers need to do down to every single small detail. It can quickly become a blame game when everyone is pointing fingers to each other and no one is willing to be responsible for anything.

In addition to the points we were discussing in `Chapter 1`, *Why Domain-Driven Design?* (in the *What went wrong with requirements?* section), one additional aspect is worth mentioning here. It's the language. Requirements not only focus on the solution and hide problems, but requirements also tend to **translate** business language to more technical language, which is seen as **developer-friendly**. In reality, this works more like a broken telephone. The more levels of translation that are being added to the transmission line, the less relevant information reaches the receiver without being disturbed beyond recognition.

One more aspect of such a *translation* is that it slows down communication. If developers require more information from the business but are unable to understand what the business means when they speak, the involvement of translators becomes unavoidable. Usually, these are the same people that write requirements, but not always. I've heard enough examples when only people such as enterprise architects are allowed to talk to customers; then, they translate their understanding to business analysis, who then throw requirements over the wall to poor developers, which are then literally lost in translation.

That's why understanding the business is significant for people who are working to create a good solution for real business problems. Being able to understand the business and communicate without a need for translations and translators not only shortens the communication time but also substantially improves the quality of such communication.

At the same time, we all know that business people, who usually play the customer role for the systems we create, are overall much less available as we would like them to be. You might end up having just a few session with people who actually possess the crucial information that you must obtain in order to make the system do what it should do. Sometimes they are even unwilling to take discussions with developers. It might be related to some personal issues, negative experience from the past or unconscious fear of looking silly in front of the bund of nerds.

In such cases, having a dedicated person, which is trusted by the business and speaks their language really helps. Our aim would be to ensure that this person is also trusted by the development team. You can call this role as a business analyst or a product owner, it doesn't really matter. The best people I know in this role are able to speak to everyone in their language, like the high-degree translators that work with world leaders behind their backs, being able to translate from one language to another without losing the meaning of things. At the same time, the best approach is still to avoid such a translation altogether.

For example, London City bankers are notorious for hiring developers who have already been exposed to banking and have ideally worked in the City before. They value their time and want to shorten the time spent on communication and discussions. Therefore, someone who has exposure to their language and shows a decent level of understanding of their business and their language is valued higher than someone else who might be a better developer but needs to be trained and get to know the language before really starting to work on real-life tasks.

Jargon terms are usually hard to grasp for outsiders since words that are being used are often everyday use words, but have an entirely different meaning. Some examples from the aforementioned financial domain are as follows:

- **Call**: Short for a **call** option, this is a demand for payment of lent or unpaid capital
- **Security**: To attest the credit, the right to property, or the ownership of stocks or bonds that are related to tradable derivatives, this certificate is used
- **Swap**: Among two borrowers, if each of them gain access to the required funds or a fixed interest is changed to floating, it's considered as swap

Learning the domain language is crucial to establish effective communication between domain experts and developers.

Sample application domain

Throughout this book, we'll be developing a sample application to practice our gained knowledge and skills. In this section, you'll get an introduction to the business domain, and more details will be added later throughout this book.

The domain that we're going to be working on is selling stuff online for private individuals. We'll be building an application to publish classified ads and something that might be necessary to support this type of activity.

If you aren't familiar with the terminology, think about a bunch of stuff you have in your storage room or in the basement, which you would be delighted to remove. You can publish a small ad online, and other people might buy things that you no longer need. You can also give stuff away for free. Examples of such services are websites such as eBay, Craigslist, Gumtree, Marktplaats (the Netherlands), and FINN.no (Norway).

Making implicit explicit

When we start working on a new system, we need to learn a lot. We discussed the paradox of ignorance in Chapter 1, *Why Domain-Driven Design?*, and you might remember that the highest level of ignorance and thereby the lowest level of knowledge is when we make a lot of decisions about the future system.

We not only suffer a lack of knowledge about the business domain we're trying to solve problems for—we're also forced to work in an environment with a high level of ambiguity. Before we learn about the domain language, we use our understanding, which is often based on assumptions.

Imagine a situation where you come to a meeting with domain experts at the beginning of the project. They try to explain their problem, and you slowly begin to study their language and, at some point, you think you got the idea and more or less know what to do. Here, it's important to remember what we were going through in the previous chapter when we discussed cognitive biases and their influence on decision making. The first and the most obvious risk is that **what you see is all there is (WYSIATI)**, or availability heuristics. You apply your limited knowledge to past experiences and then get the feeling of understanding. At this point, we're usually asked to make estimates and logically we fail, since biases play a trick on our minds and give the illusion of understanding.

At such meetings, we often agree on something. Then, everyone leaves the room to meet again and maybe discuss some specifications or even prototypes after a couple of weeks. Time passes by, we're still in the same room, and no one is pleased since, to our mutual dissatisfaction, we find out that we agreed on completely different things. Everyone had a picture in mind, and all those pictures were different.

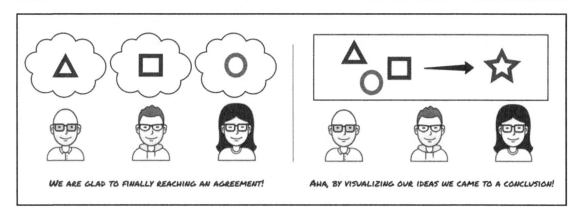

We agree on different things if we don't visualize

People spend hours arguing about things they thought are different but are the same. People also agree on something that they don't share a common understanding about, and this never goes well.

To fix this, we need to remove assumptions. We need to make *implicit* things *explicit*.

Look at this sample form from a real-life HR management system. Here, an employee can request sick leave:

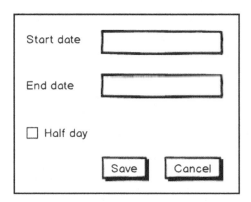

Sick leave registration form

Here, we can see a typical structure, which is created by a programmer. We could even imagine a SQL table where the data that's entered into this form gets stored. It most probably has the `StartDate`, `EndDate`, and `HalfDay` columns and the employee `id`. Notice that there's a **Save** button here too, which is very common to find in forms like this.

But despite the fact that this form might look okay, let's think a little bit more about what we see here. After spending a bit of time analyzing this form, we could see the following issues:

- The **Start date** is ambiguous. It might be the date when sick leave is registered, or it might also be the date when the employee didn't come to work because they got sick.
- The **End date** is even more ambiguous because it might represent the last day of the sick leave, or the day when the employee came back to work.
- **The Half day** might apply to both of those fields, but there's no clear indication of what it means.
- Finally, the **Save** button gives us no clue about what will happen next. There might be just a record in a table, and we need to tell someone to look at it, or there might be an approval process that gets started automatically. Does the employee need to call or send an email to the line manager after filling out this form?

As you can see, even in such a small form with two fields, one checkbox, and two buttons, many things are implicit. If we imagine the code behind this form, all those implicit and ambiguous concepts could be found there as well. I already mentioned a table that has columns that represent those fields in the form. All properties in the domain model classes, data model objects, and other code artifacts are equally implicit. Everything there demands an explanation, such as *this date means the day when an employee came back to work,* and without such an explanation. Things like reports could be just plain wrong.

Compare it with another example, also taken from a real-life HR management system, which was made by a competitor:

The sick leave registration form that makes sense

In this form, the fields make much more sense for regular people who don't need to solve puzzles or read the help to understand what to enter in these fields. Things that were made *implicit* in the first sample are *explicit* here. Everything, from naming individual fields to calls for actions, has a better meaning. We could also imagine that, behind this form, we can find code like this:

```
SickLeaveApplication.Handle(new SendSickLeaveForApproval
{
    EmployeeId = context.User.EmployeeId,
    DateRegistered = request.DateRegistered,
    FirstDayNotAtWork = request.FirstDayNotAtWork,
    LeftDuringWorkday = request.LeftDuringWorkday,
    CameBackToWork = request.CameBackToWork,
    CameBackAfterLunch = request.CameBackAfterLunch
});
```

This code expresses the same meaning and terminology as the user interface. So, not only will the end user have an easy time filling out this form, but also a fellow developer would be happy reading this code, where the intent is clearly expressed and all the concepts are explicit.

Another aspect of making implicit explicit is to create domain concepts that are visible in the code. In the preceding code, the `SendSickLeaveForApproval` command exhibits a precise domain concept in the code.

Domain language for classified ads

Our developers were discussing the flow of publishing classified ads. They went through the creation process and got to the point where the user clicks the **Publish** button. Together, with the domain expert, they discovered that ads couldn't be published immediately since an ad could contain malicious content. They decided to put in some approval process, which should take place after the user clicks **Publish** and the ad becomes visible on the website.

Developers quickly decided to create a property for their `ClassifiedAd` domain class, called `Status`. It should be an enum, which indicates different stages of the review and publication process. It could also be reused later for statuses that aren't yet known. Since they want to have behavior in their domain model, they added the `UpdateStatus` method to the class, which looks like this:

```
public class ClassifiedAd
{
    private ClassifiedAdStatus _status;
```

```
public void UpdateStatus(ClassifiedAdStatus newStatus)
{
    _status = newStatus;
    DomainEvents.Publish(
        new ClassifiedAdStatusUpdated(_id, newStatus));
}
}
```

Now that the method also publishes a domain event, other parts of the system can subscribe to this event and do some other vital actions.

 We will spend more time with domain events and commands later in this book. For now, the sample code uses domain events in the code to closely resemble events and commands we were using in the EventStorming chapter.

So, after the user clicks **Publish**, the following would happen:

```
ad.UpdateStatus(ClassifiedAdStatus.Published);
```

After the review is complete, the ad would be activated, like so:

```
ad.UpdateStatus(ClassifiedAdStatus.Activated);
```

It might seem acceptable. Our `ClassifiedAd` class is a state machine, where instances of this class move from one status to another through the life cycle of the ad. However, we already miss the intent. Our language becomes weird—instead of saying that we want to *publish* the announcement, we *update the status*. Instead of *activating* the ad, we *update the status* again!

Even if it all seems to work after some more behavior is added to the system, code like this will start to appear:

```
public void UpdateStatus(ClassifiedAdStatus newStatus)
{
    if (newStatus == ClassifiedAdStatus.Published
        && (string.IsNullOrEmpty(_title)
            || _price == 0 || string.IsNullOrEmpty(_text))
        throw new DomainException(
            "Ad can't be activated because some mandatory fields are
empty");

    if (newStatus == ClassifiedAdStatus.Activated
        && _status == ClassifiedAdStatus.ViolationReported)
        throw new DomainException("Reported ads can't be activated");

    if (newStatus == ClassifiedAdStatus.Deactivated
```

```
        && _status != ClassifiedAdStatus.ViolationReported)
        throw new DomainException("Only a reported ad can be deactivated");

    _status = newStatus;
    DomainEvents.Publish(new AdStatusUpdated(newStatus));
}
```

That isn't the code we expect to see in such a simple method. It takes too much responsibility, and the logical blocks in this method barely relate to each other. But things get worse when it gets to the domain event handling:

```
public void Handle(ClassifiedAdStatusUpdated @event)
{
    // controlling the ad visibility based on it's reported status
    if (_status == ClassifiedAdStatus.ViolationReported
        && @event.Status == ClassifiedAdStatus.MaliciousContentDetected)
        CommandDispatcher.Send(
            new UpdateAdVisibility(@event.Id, false));
}
```

The number of flow control operators is growing, and most of the behavior is now being driven by status updates, something that, in the beginning, was considered to be a small and concise operation on a single property of the domain object. The intent of this update operation is dissolved, and each call needs to be carefully controlled for side effects. The risk of damaging an existing behavior when adding new features is now genuine.

Discussions with domain experts also lost some meaning. Instead of using phrases such as *if the malicious content is detected, we hide the ad and inform our moderation group*, it becomes *and then we query all ads with the status equals* MaliciousContentDetected *and use the notification service to deliver a message to all users that have moderation rights*. The meaning of the language gets lost behind technical gibberish, mixed with generalized words such as **status** and **message**.

The team decides to refactor the code and use proper domain language instead. So, this is what they came up with:

```
public class ClassifiedAd
{
    private ClassifiedAdStatus _status;

    public void Publish()
    {
        _status = ClassifiedAdStatus.Published;
        DomainEvents.Publish(new ClassifiedAdPublished(_id));
    }
}
```

Now, we can also refactor the domain event handling to something like this:

```
public void Handle(ClassifiedAdPublished @event) =>
    CommandDispatcher.Send(new ShowClassifiedAd(@event.Id));
```

Then, to handle cases with malicious content, we can write the new event handler:

```
public void ReportViolation(User reportedBy, string reason)
{
    _violationReports.Add(reportedBy, reason);
    DomainEvents.Publish(new ViolationReported(reportedBy, reason));
}

public void Handle(ViolationReported @even) =>
    CommandDispatcher.Send(new InformModerators(@event.Id, @event.Reason));

public void Handle(MalicionsAdDetected @event) =>
    CommandDispatcher.Send(new InformModerators(@event.Id, @event.Reason));
```

Our small example also shows that the domain language can't be built by making a glossary with nouns. A misconception about collecting a lot of nouns in an extensive list and calling it a domain language definitely exists. But this isn't a happy path, and usually, it leads to something called an anemic model, which is considered an anti-pattern. Classes in anemic models only have properties, and properties are always named by nouns. But a no less important part of every domain is the behavior. Nouns express what the domain operates with, but verbs describe what's being done. Without verbs, our domain tends to be a set of magic actions when properties change values without any particular reason. But our preceding code clearly expresses the domain behavior by introducing verbs as part of the domain language. These verbs are precise, show the intent, and describe actions. They're used both in imperative style for activities and in the past tense when describing the history when we publish domain events from our code.

In the preceding example, we not only improve our code and brought a better understanding of what it does and what concepts are being present there, but we also discovered some new terms and concepts that our domain model would benefit from. We can start using this terminology when talking to domain experts and see whether they understand it. Sometimes, they might give developers strange looks, trying to understand their excitement because they knew this *new* concept already—its part of *their language*, and it was just never expressed in conversations between business and development people. Such breakthroughs not only make the code better and closer to the actual business model but also improve communication between developers and domain experts.

By making implicit things explicit, not only do we discover missing concepts in our code, but we also put them into our domain model. This part is essential because the language is used across the whole range of models—business and mental models, conceptual and visual models, and domain models in diagrams and code. This pattern of using the same concept and, in general, the same language across multiple levels of models in the system is called **Ubiquitous Language**.

Language and context

In the introduction of this chapter, we already touched on the topic of linguistic differences in the same language. If one language is divided by some boundary, be it a geographical, national, or professional area, it starts to split. We used British and American English as an example before, but of course, there are more examples like this. Dutch language spoken in Belgium is often even referred to as a separate language, Flemish because it sounds different, but mainly because, for everyday objects and actions, different words are being used. The same can be observed for languages that evolve within professional groups where people develop jargon, and we've looked at some examples of this too.

These examples were presented here to demonstrate how important it is to define the precise meaning of words. Avoiding confusion is indeed one of the goals in order to find and identify Ubiquitous Language.

It's important to realize that Ubiquitous Language is only valid within a context. A different context is defined by a different language. There's a misconception that Ubiquitous Language is called *ubiquitous* because it's the single language for the whole business, organization, or domain. That isn't the case. It's ubiquitous not horizontally, but vertically. Each context might have its own language, but all layers in this context share one Ubiquitous Language—meetings with the business, models, code, tests, UI concepts, data structures, and so on.

Let's have a look at the classic example of the term **Product** being used in different contexts of the e-commerce domain:

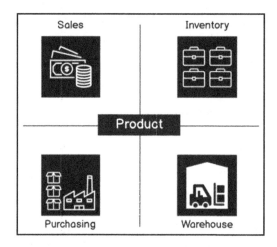

Product in different contexts

Although we're operating in the same domain, clearly the term **Product** has a somewhat different meaning in each of the identified contexts:

- **Sales**: For the salespeople, product means the sales price and maybe the margin. It's where the company earns money, and other properties of the product aren't that important.
- **Purchasing**: If we buy a product to resell, we're mostly interested in the purchase price, how many items of a given product the supplier has in stock, and how fast they can be delivered.
- **Inventory**: We're mainly interested in how many items we have in stock. If a specific item is out of stock, this context can keep the estimated date when it will be back in stock. Here, we probably also define some internal properties of the product, such as the item number.
- **Warehouse**: It needs to manage the space that's required to store products, so people in this context need to know when product batches arrive when shipments to customers take place, how products are packaged, and where they are stored.

As you can see, although we have a popular term, such as **Product**, different departments in the same domain or organization really have very little shared interest and have more in-depth knowledge in their subset of properties of something that otherwise could be considered the same object.

Another good example would be the term **policy** in the insurance domain. It's a bit less well-known for people that don't work in insurance but, in general, we understand that people that sell insurance to us are mostly interested in money and in getting new customers. So, for them, the policy means new sales and money. When it comes to approvals, if we take vehicle insurance as an example, policy implies risk. Even after a policy is sold, there's a chance that the risk assessment department could request additional documentation and, after some internal checks, reject the policy. And finally, when it comes to the point of handling a claim on the existing policy, for the claim handling department, it's a cost since the insurance company loses money.

Both examples demonstrate that, even for the same domain, there's a different context where language changes and sometimes changes significantly. What happens if we keep using the same meaning of words across contexts? Well, things become much less explicit. The degree of ambiguity increases with each new context that we fail to identify and separate. It leads to unclear models and, as a result, to obscure code, where we need to clarify what we mean exactly when we use this and that word.

Mixing different contexts in one working environment also leads to something called **context switching**. In *Quality Software Management: Systems Thinking*, Gerald Weinberg suggested that an increasing number of projects that one individual works on leads to significant productivity loss due to context switching:

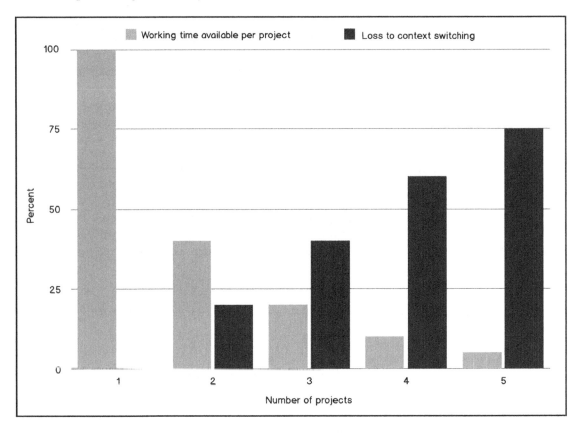

Productivity loss due to context switching

Adding one more project to current tasks means 20% productivity loss. Hence, when the number of contexts reaches five, the amount of time spent on the actual work becomes tremendously low. Most of the time is then spent figuring out in which context the current task belongs.

It's not only valid for the project. You might know from experience that, for larger projects where generalization prevails over precision and unambiguity, the phenomena of context switching effects the performance just as much. In our **product** example, if we were to put all of the properties of different logical views of the product in one place, working with such an object would involve some additional effort of trying to understand which part of the product we're working on at the moment. So, despite this still being one thing, the hidden context switching and productivity will suffer.

Assuming that centralization and generalization are good things, many software systems create so-called God classes, such as `Customer` or `Product`, which contain all possible properties for all possible views of a physical object. In addition to context switching, there are more downsides to such an approach.

One is obviously that not all properties need to have value during a specific life cycle of such an object in the system. For example, the phased-out product has no features that are related to sales whatsoever. But since we have one class for everything, we must assign empty values to all of these properties. Such an approach leads to a high degree of confusion since we hardly understand why these properties are vacant—either there's a mistake in the system, or this is just a typical situation due to the object's state.

Another issue is that, inevitably, such classes attract a lot of dependencies. You've probably seen data models, which sometimes mimic **domain models**, where the whole complex system has one large SQL database where tables have many cross-references. We could imagine that things such as `Product` can be referenced by `Order`, `ShoppingCart`, `Catalogue`, `Invoice`, `PurchaseInvoice`, `Return`, `CreditNote`, and so on. The model becomes tangled and very hard to maintain. Sometimes, it gets worse because referential dependencies are sometimes plain wrong. For example, it isn't correct to show an updated product description on some order from the past. The order should contain a snapshot of the purchased product as it was at the moment of purchase.

We've identified enough reasons for us to be cautious when it comes to forgetting about context when seeking language. Ubiquitous Language is always unambiguous, explicit, and context-specific. As soon as you sense or observe that the meanings of words start to change between different parts of the system, this should trigger an alarm in your head that you are probably crossing context boundaries.

Context emerges when discussing users. Developers love to think of people as users. This term is so ambiguous that it's almost guaranteed that we switch between different contexts when talking about users.

Getting back to our sample domain, the team developers discussed how their users would rate their deals. They thought that it could be useful if people could give a rating to each other, helping to build trust in the community. During the conversation, some of them noticed that they use the words *user, those who sell, seller, those who buy,* and *buyer* interchangeably. When the generic term *user* was used, it almost always required clarification: what role this user plays at that particular moment. At the same time, when they named their users as *buyers* and *sellers*, there was no ambiguity, and no further clarification was required.

After noticing this, the group decided that they discovered new elements of Ubiquitous Language and started to use these terms. It was a good insight that saved them a lot of time when they discussed models and removed ambiguity in code.

At the same time, splitting people into *sellers* and *buyers* in the authorization part of the system made no sense at all. These were just *users*, and they can log in to the system and do some operations, such as update their profile, without any clear distinction of whether they're going to sell or buy on the site. It was another context when the word *user* wasn't ambiguous and was explicit.

Later, they discovered another distinction for users when they modeled the back office system. There, users started to take roles, and again ambiguity was there until they identified these roles and began to use terms such as *administrator, support assistant,* and *reviewer*. A new context was discovered, and a new model emerged for that context, which was separated from other contexts by the meanings of words.

Summary

In this chapter, we discussed the importance of language in system design and how precise and unambiguous terminology brings clarity. We also have a shared understanding of the domain for business people and developers. We also looked at how different industries use the same words to express different concepts and what consequences this has on domain modeling.

The code sample in this chapter showed how unclear language could make the implementation more complicated and less understandable. By introducing better language to the code, we made it much clearer and shorter and more concise. We made some implicit concepts more explicit, and it helped to get a better understanding of the business and improved the code quality. We also discovered many verbs that became part of the language, which is an essential addition to a glossary of nouns that are often seen as the only important part of the domain model.

This chapter introduced the term *Ubiquitous Language,* which was coined by Eric Evans. We emphasize the fact that the ubiquity of the language isn't in its wideness but in its precision, and the fact that it's being used for all artifacts of the software development process—from initial discussions, through modeling and design, to code and tests.

We looked at how words change their meaning between different contexts and how context switching can negatively impact productivity. Using our sample domain, we went through a couple of examples of how contexts are being discovered during the modeling process and in conversations between developers and domain experts.

In the next chapter, we'll explore one of the most popular techniques for domain modeling and go through some practical tips on how to organize useful workshops between domain experts and developers.

3
EventStorming

Discovering domain terminology is essential, and this terminology becomes a part of the Ubiquitous Language. However, the process of discovery can be rather lengthy and not always successful. When we discuss how the business works and what problems we are going to solve by writing software, too often the conversation comes down to discussing the features that the business is keen to implement. A set of features, of course, can be called **software**, but it does not necessarily form a system. Furthermore, to build a comprehensive solution for a particular problem, more system-level thinking is required.

 Thinking in systems is only briefly covered in this book. To know the subject better, please refer to great books on this topic like the classic *An Introduction to General System Thinking* by Gerald Weinberg and *Thinking in Systems* by Donella H. Meadows, et al.

But who is going to tell us how the business operates as a system? Whom shall we talk to, and what format should this conversation take? We will uncover issues like these and try to find some answers in this chapter.

In this chapter, we will cover the following topics:

- What is EventStorming?
- The practical aspects of EventStorming
- How to facilitate a workshop yourself
- Deciding what to do after the workshop ends

EventStorming

In previous chapters, we learned how important it is to understand the actual problem. We also went deeper into the concept of Ubiquitous Language and explained that it is not only a glossary of terms but also the system's behavior described in words.

It remains unclear how to start the knowledge crunching and how to intensify our communication with domain experts to understand the problem space better and get a proper overview of what are we going to build.

Very often, we see that developers get to know the domain in the form of requirements. We have already been through this topic, and by now you should realize that requirements have their flaws. So, you want to improve your knowledge by talking directly to domain experts and organizing a workshop or meeting with them. Some people come, and you have a conversation for two or three hours; a lot of things get discussed, a lot of new insight comes to the surface, but there is a minimal outcome in the form of any modeling artifact. Sure, you could start drawing UML diagrams, but what business person would understand them? You could take notes to find out that you need a round or two of clarification workshops because there are too many vague and implicit concepts that form the foundation of your future system, and this makes it very hard to understand.

There are a few fundamental issues we need to be solved here:

- Provide visibility during the discussion. This should remove assumptions when many people are discussing the same thing with different terms. It also eliminates some of the ambiguity and brings it to the surface for further exploration.
- Have a modeling language that people understand. UML is not an option, and the usual boxes and arrows have no real notation, so people can get confused and start spending time trying to clarify the meaning of things.
- Involve many people simultaneously. In traditional meetings, only one person can effectively deliver the message, while everyone else needs to shut up and listen. As soon as many people start talking at the same time there is no conversation anymore. But, assuming people with different interests and backgrounds are present in one session, they might show a lack of interest and get bored.
- Find a way to express terms, behavior, model processes, and decisions, not features and data.

Back in 2013, Alberto Brandolini formulated a method that he called **EventStorming**, where he tried to address these issues. We are going to learn about this method in this chapter.

Modeling language

The basic idea behind EventStorming is that it gives a straightforward modeling notation that is used to visualize the behavior of the system in a way that everyone can understand. This approach creates visibility, increases engagement, and involves people who would otherwise be anxious about any participation in a modeling session at all, or putting anything on a whiteboard if they attend.

Considering behavior as the central aspect of the domain knowledge, the whole EventStorming exercise is about finding out how the business works. In general, we could postulate that each system at any given moment of time is found in a particular state. This state can change when actors that interact with the system do something. Actions of those actors cause the system to change state, so we can see that something has happened and now we need to deal with a new situation.

Let's look at a simple example of someone paying their bill using internet banking:

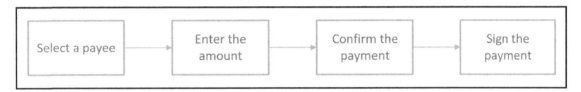

The sequence of events for payment processing (simplified)

As you can see here, from the person's point of view, the amount of money in their account decreased, the payment is complete, and the bill is considered paid and can be thrown away. From the recipient's point of view, however, the bill is considered paid when they get the money and can match this payment with an open bill by using an invoice number or some magic payment reference that was mentioned on the bill and the payment.

Each action performed by actors in these systems made some state transitions. The payment order was created and signed. The amount was deducted from the payer's account. The amount was then added to the payee's account. The bill was marked as paid. All these operations became *facts of life*, and, unless we have a time machine, we cannot reverse them. If the payee discovers that the bill has already been paid, they cannot just reverse everything. They need to send the money back by initiating a new payment.

These facts are known as **domain events**. It is the most basic and also the most important concept that EventStorming deals with. It is why it is called EventStorming. The idea of domain events is not alien to anyone. Facts of life are something that people can quickly grasp. They are something that happened; not something that someone wanted to do; not a feature; not a form or a button. Each domain event represents a fact, a change in the system we are trying to model.

Therefore, the first part of our modeling language is to create the concept of domain events. Each concept in EventStorming is represented as a sticky note of a specific color. The color is essential because, as we go along and bring more thoughts to the model, we need colors to consistently represent the same ideas across the model to avoid confusion.

The original suggestion of Alberto is to use orange sticky notes to represent domain events. The simplest possible model could look like this:

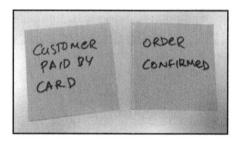

Start small and go from there

These are two domain events that occurred in sequence—first, a customer paid using a credit or debit card; then their order was confirmed. We can identify this as an e-commerce domain. There is nothing special about sentences written on sticky notes, except one crucial rule—events must have a subject (noun) and a predicate (verb). The verb must be in the past tense, indicating that something has happened and it became a fact.

If we get back to the bill payment example, we could try figuring out what events we would find there:

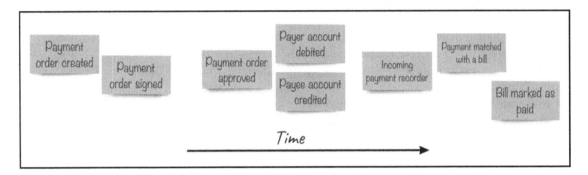

Events are placed on the timeline

There are a couple of things that you might immediately notice. The first is that domain events follow a timeline. It is quite logical because facts represent subsequent changes in the system and therefore happen in a particular order. For example, the payment is not approved before it is signed. Some things can happen in parallel, such as debiting and crediting accounts at the same time, as soon as the payment order is approved, which might mean that the bank is confident that the payer has enough funds to complete the payment.

The second thing is that we do not have only one system here. Indeed, we are modeling the whole process, but there are at least three parts that we can clearly distinguish—the user-facing internet bank, which creates and signs payment orders; the banking back office, which completes the transaction; and the payee's own payment-to-bill matching system that, by the way, could be completely manual.

Visualization

As we can see, our simple model already provides quite a lot of value to people involved in the workshop. Not only did we try to identify what happens during the process of a bill being paid, but we put the whole flow on a timeline and were able to roughly identify parts of the process that can happen in different physical systems.

Visualization is one of the most powerful aspects of any modeling technique, and EventStorming is not an exception. As soon as we put something on our model, we can reason about it instead of just pronouncing words and waving hands.

When people see what is considered to be the whole picture, some might start asking *what if* questions. *What if* there is not enough money in the account? *What if* the bill reference number is wrong? *What if* the payee account is not correct? What if, what if, what if? It then appears that our simple process is not that simple at the end of the day. Remember the availability heuristic, **WYSIATI** (short for **What You See Is All There Is**)? We base our initial understanding on a simplified view of the world. Everything works as it should; there are no exceptions and no edge cases, people behave and don't plan to make mistakes, with or without intentions to do so. It might come as a surprise, but the real world is a bit more complicated. Most of the time the number of edge cases; exceeds what is considered to be a regular flow of events. All these edge cases and potential exceptions become much more visible when things are visualized and brought to light for everyone to observe.

There is one issue here, which can do a disservice to those who are trying their best to create a proper events model. You could imagine that such a workshop happens in a meeting room. Usually, people sit around a table and talk. As we have already suggested, this is not how EventStorming works. We expect people to move around the room and be actively engaged in conversations, which might happen simultaneously at different sides of the room. So, we need some space. But this is not all the space we need. Have a good look at the preceding simple process model. Although we all could agree that we just modeled the happy path and no edge cases and exceptions are covered, the real-life process is way more complicated; this diagram already takes some horizontal space. Now, imagine real-world scenarios being modeled like this. Indeed, a traditional two-three meter whiteboard would do a disservice for you.

Imagine your model like this:

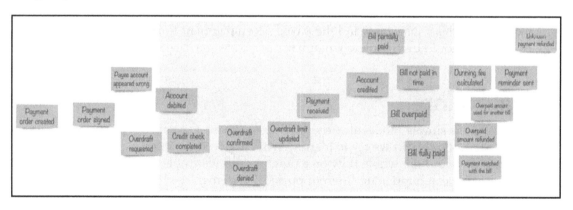

For a reasonably complex system you need a bigger space

Here in the middle is your whiteboard. But the model is not that small. As Alberto says, *my problem is bigger!*

What happens when there is not enough space left on a whiteboard? People treat the space left as a sacred resource. It becomes precious, and people start saving space. Some events become **not important** and therefore not put on the whiteboard. Some ideas become secondary and not worth looking at. All in all, the modeling discussion suffers to save some whiteboard space.

It is normal, and this is how our brain works. If we see some limit, no matter how silly or artificial it will look in retrospect, we will feel its physical presence and will also set up our activities accordingly. If you have a limited modeling space, prepare to get a limited model. So, beware of this issue and provide as much modeling space as you can for participants of any modeling session and of EventStorming meetings in particular. We will get some more specific advice in the next section.

Facilitating an EventStorming workshop

This section provides practical advice and shares some real-life experience for you as a facilitator of an EventStorming workshop. Remember that you do not need to **sell** DDD in your organization before doing EventStorming. This rather simple but very effective technique can help even if you have no plans to do DDD in your project. It will help you to build an understanding of the domain, for which you plan to create some software. It also creates a better relationship between developers and their potential users, since they will be openly discussing the problems that users have and showing empathy to these problems, while simultaneously seeking solutions.

Who to invite

For the workshop, you will always need to have two types of people—people with questions and people with answers.

People with questions are developers and architects. Surprisingly, developers rarely attend any sessions that directly involve the potential users of the software they plan to develop. We touched upon this topic when we discussed the separation between problem space and solution space in `Chapter 1`, *Why Domain-Driven Design?*. So again, having developers at these workshops is essential. Another group of people that some might expect to be those with answers, but who, in reality, have more questions are business analysts or requirements analysts, or whatever are they are called in your organization. Admittedly, they spend quite a lot of time together with potential users and customers, but usually, during the EventStorming workshop, they get new insights since this exercise is not one-to-one but for a group.

This group needs to study the information about the domain that is already available (general understanding, perhaps requirements or specifications if they have already been made) and prepare questions.

People with answers are usually those who we call **domain experts**. But remember that they do not know all the details, and they also can have an illusion of knowledge. This is why you need as many of them as you can get in the workshop since these people are usually not easy to gather together in one room because of their busy schedule. This indirectly suggests that these people are generally quite high in the organizational hierarchy, but not necessarily. You need to aim at getting the most people from each department. You should search for those who know how things are done instead of those who only know how things should be done, based on some fictitious descriptions and standards.

Both *people with questions* and *people with answers* groups would need to prepare for the workshop by formulating their questions better. Thinking about what issues need to be solved and being more specific about these issues, might help during the workshop. The preparation part doesn't only apply for developers. In the end, it is the business who needs their problems to be solved, so it would be helpful for them to be aware of their own needs and to have enough materials to be able to communicate these needs to the group of techies that supposedly will address those needs by writing code.

Preparing the space

Very often you can observe people coming to a workshop held in a regular meeting room to find out that there is no whiteboard, the projector does not work, and the presenter has a video output socket that is incompatible with the video equipment in the room. Such things are all very frustrating because they take a lot of time to fix, leaving less time for the actual work. What's even worse, it's not just one person whose time is wasted on this kind of issue. Everyone in this room is effectively blocked from doing anything and has to wait. Sometimes it is best to cancel the meeting in order not to lose any more time.

This is the situation you want to avoid, and EventStorming workshops have some specific requirements that need to be addressed in advance, to avoid such confusion.

Materials

Well in advance, when you have agreed on a date and time when people with questions will finally meet people with answers, start preparing documents immediately.

The most important material is your future modeling space. Remember, your problem is way bigger than any whiteboard you can find in any meeting room (except maybe the one you designed to hold EventStorming sessions, but I doubt you have one). It means you will have to use walls as the modeling space. Sticky notes do not stay well on walls, except walls made of glass. You will also want to remove your model from the wall afterward in order not to frustrate people who use the room after you.

Therefore, you will need a paper roll. For guerilla-style EventStorming, you might use a simple paper roll from IKEA, the original purpose of which is to provide unlimited painting space for children. But it is too narrow, and the best option is to acquire a plotter paper roll. These rolls are wider (usually about one meter wide), longer, and made from higher quality paper.

The next thing is to have something that you can use to fix the paper to the wall. You might need to inspect the wall's surface in the room where you plan to hold the workshop and try different fixing methods. Ensure that you have little or no obstacles for the paper roll, so the wall should not have paintings, holes, doors, or windows.

Of course, you need a lot of sticky notes. And I mean a lot. You never know how many domain events people are going to write, and the last thing you want to experience is when people start reconsidering events because there are no more sticky notes left. Stickies are cheap, and ideas are expensive, so take care to bring enough stickies to capture all ideas. You will need different sizes and colors; we will go through the color notation later in this chapter:

This is the least you will need

The final part is stationary. It is too often forgotten as something that's obvious, and then you are left with a handful of highly paid, very busy people in the room and only one working pen. It can be very frustrating. So, buy enough permanent markers, preferably black, not very thin and not very thick. Ideally, you need one marker pen per person and some to spare.

The room

Now, the place. EventStorming cannot be done when people are sitting. Quite the opposite—they need to stand and walk freely around the whole space. This is why the traditional meeting room set up with a large table in the center and lots of chairs around it does not work. So, the first thing you will need to ensure is that the walls where you plan to put the paper roll have enough space between them for people to move freely. Ideally, all chairs need to be removed, or at least moved to one place, far from the modeling space.

There should be some place where all the stationery will be placed. Therefore you will need at least a small table somewhere in the corner. Also, it is helpful to have the notation visible, so people use specific colors for specific concepts. Using different colors for one concept is very confusing and should be avoided.

EventStorming sessions are usually very intense and involve a lot of movement, thinking, and talking, and sometimes arguing. It is often fun but can be exhausting. So, as a facilitator, you need to keep the sugar level high and throats soothed. Prepare some snacks, drinks, and fruit—this helps. People also respect this kind of treatment and get a feeling of being invited to a special event.

The workshop

So, now space is prepared, and you need to call people into the room. When you get them coming to your session, use the tips in this section to keep an eye on the time and make the session more productive. We will also be going through some tips on how to observe and interpret human behavior, and how to make the meeting constructive.

Timing and scheduling

Plan at least two hours for one session. It might not feel enough (and this is usually true), but it is tough for people to be productive for a more extended period in such an environment. A more extended workshop will exhaust discussions and create a feeling of going in circles. That might be the case just because almost everything that can be discussed has already been considered and put on the wall. Therefore, resist the urge to plan more extended workshops, such as whole-day sessions.

The first hour is usually very intense, but after that, you will see the energy levels dropping. Let people rest for ten minutes, have a coffee, and eat the fruit you got for them. Often, participants will keep chatting in small groups about what has been discussed, so their brains will still be processing the information, but in a more relaxed way. After a break, new insights are usually uncovered. Also, you will need to apply different techniques step by step, and a break after the first hour will give you an excellent opportunity to do something different from what you were doing during the first part of the workshop. We will discuss these techniques later in this chapter.

The beginning

The beginning of an EventStorming session with people who have never done it before can be quite awkward. You, as a facilitator, explain the rules and give people pens and stickies, then put up the first element of the notation:

The first element in the notation

After this is done, there will be this moment of silence and uncertain movements in the crowd. No one knows what to do, and people are usually uncomfortable with doing something they aren't familiar with. It becomes especially obvious if such activity needs to be performed in front of the crowd:

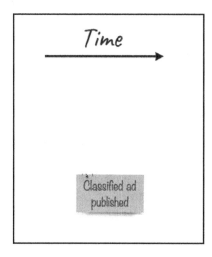

The random event in the middle—the icebreaker

This moment requires the facilitator to break the ice. It is not hard to do. When you organize such a session, you already know something about the organization and the domain. That allows you to imagine a domain event, or two, or more. Putting this on the wall is exactly what people need to learn by example. The whole thing is not hard to do, but without an example, people don't feel safe and secure. So, as a facilitator, you will need to put the first sticky note on the wall, or a few of them. Try making it relevant, or you can intentionally make them very silly, expecting people to react with laughter and sarcasm, fixing your error. Of course, the first reaction that you get is people speaking out loud what they think needs to be put on the wall, without taking any action at all and expecting you to write things down. This is how *traditional* meetings are done—people talk, and someone hopefully is taking notes. Resist this. As soon as you see someone explaining what you need to write on the next sticky or telling you that the stuff on the wall is wrong, just give them a pen and a stack of sticky notes. They will start writing. They will produce. They will discuss. Then, your job will be to observe and to guide, in case people get stuck.

There are at least two techniques that I know of about how to start the workshop by putting the first sticky note on the wall. The first comes from Alberto Brandolini. He says that you can put anything you want anywhere you want, but not at the start. Starting at the *beginning* is something you want to avoid. It is very natural for us as human beings to seek structure, and in our view, each process starts and ends somewhere. So, logically speaking, we need to start at the beginning. The only issue here is that there is no beginning. First, we always spend a lot of time and energy discussing where the process starts, without producing anything. Second, there will be something before any identified start, guaranteed. Therefore, put the first sticky somewhere in the middle and work from there. Stuff that happens before that event will go to the left, and things that occur after, to the right:

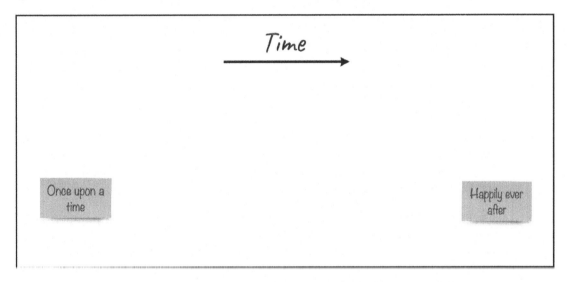

Now fill all the space in between

Dan North mentioned another technique in his talk at DDD Exchange 2016. On one sticky he writes **Once upon a time** and puts it close to the left side of the paper roll, but not at the edge. On the second sticky, he writes **Happily ever after** and puts it close to the right side of the paper roll, but again, not at the edge. You need these gaps on both sides because, as mentioned earlier, there will be definitely something earlier than **Once upon a time** and later than **Happily ever after**, and you will need space to put it there. As you can see, you need to have exactly zero knowledge about the domain to produce these two stickies, and it works quite efficiently. People get a sense of time, and with something already on the wall with space in between for them to fill, it sparks their imagination.

During the workshop

As a facilitator, your role is not to rule, but to observe and guide. The fewer rules you will set and enforce, the better your workshop is going to be. After the ice-breaking, some people will start putting stuff on the wall, and other people will start asking questions. At this stage, there are a few things to keep in mind:

- People tend to ask the facilitator questions, as they see them as the meeting organizer and therefore as a person who has more information and authority. As a facilitator, direct them and their questions to other people in the room, in particular to those people with answers, whom you have invited.

- There will be some confusion about domain events, especially if your audience are not native English speakers and the term **domain event** can be seen as technical (it isn't). As a result, there might be some who keep putting up stickies with features they desire to have (such as payment processing or a shopping cart), or imperative actions (such as process payment or register customer). It is the facilitator's job to prevent this and explain once again that, at this stage, the goal is to describe the flow of domain events, which are the facts of life and cannot be undone, removed, or changed.

- Apart from what has been mentioned earlier, there are no real mistakes or errors that people can make, at least at the level of notation. Do not try to de-duplicate events or generalize, do not discourage people from doing stuff by saying they are doing something incorrectly.

Usually, these three tips help to drive the workshop from the organizational point of view. But since we are dealing with people, there are always some behavioral and personal aspects. Several things usually happen that are essential for the facilitator to observe and sometimes intervene.

First, be prepared for complex discussions. If there are no discussions, then either the domain is too simple, or you got the wrong people, or there is something else that prevents people from speaking up. Disputes are inevitable since every person in the room has their point of view on the domain. Even developers quickly form their opinions after they understand the initial idea, or maybe read the specification. The critical thing here is that developers need to ask questions. There should be no assumptions about what happens and how it happens. It is the facilitator's job to encourage developers to participate since some of them are introverts and don't really like being in an open discussion. But since our goal is to give developers a better understanding of the domain, they need to participate.

Try to pay attention to edge cases. People always prefer to model the happy path, when no exceptions and errors occur. We always need to keep in mind that one event is a consequence of some other event under certain conditions. Yes, there could be some straight flows, but they aren't commonplace, especially if we are talking about business. For example, *payment processed* can logically lead to *order paid*, then *order shipped*, and then *order delivered*. But what if the payment has failed? What if the payment amount does not cover the full order total (partial payment)? What if goods aren't available in stock, although we think that they are? What if the parcel is lost in transit? All these things can and will happen. For developers, they might seem complicated, and usually, they don't know how to deal with these situations other than throwing an exception. But the business often has procedures in place to fix most of these situations, and these fixes can and should be modeled.

Second, discussions about edge cases will almost certainly create some ambiguity and uncertainty because not all exceptions are covered by business processes, or the people that you have available for the workshop don't deal with such situations. If there are several domain experts in the room, they might disagree and argue with each other. For your short workshop, such circumstances are counterproductive. Therefore, if you observe that some heated discussion is taking place, or at some point, there are too many puzzled faces and no one can bring clarity to something, you can identify a hotspot. At this point, you need to introduce one more element to the notation. Hotspots are usually marked by bright sticky notes; for example, Alberto proposes bright pink. So, you might have something like this on the wall:

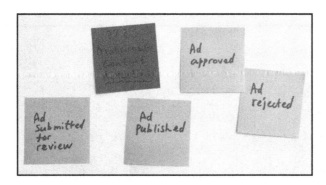

Bright colors help to bring attention

Identifying and characterizing hotspots allows you to postpone decisions and cut off arguments, effectively letting the group to move forward and not get stuck. You might find your wall full of hotspots by the end of the workshop, and this is entirely normal. It indicates that people that you have invited either need to come to some agreement about handling some situations, or you need to speak to someone else and collect missing information. Hotspots deserve close attention, but it should be after the workshop has finished. Try to cut off unproductive discussions and going in circles by putting up a pink sticky and asking people to move on.

The third thing to keep in mind is that, when you have a few domain experts who specialize in different parts of a larger domain, you will observe them grouping together by functional specialization area, forming islands or clouds of events that barely connect to other islands produced by other groups. It is very interesting to observe and essential to catch since you might be witnessing the first draft of your context map. We will discuss context maps later in the book. Do not discourage people from doing this, and go with the flow. Pay attention to how these islands interconnect. Usually, a minimal number of events belong to more than one group of domain events.

Then finally, there is a chance that your business works with organizations and systems that are out of your control. Such entities can be called **external systems** and need to be put on the model. There are domain events that can go to such systems, and you might also receive some events from external systems. That introduces the new element in your notation, and in Alberto's color scheme external systems are visualized using large pastel pink sticky notes:

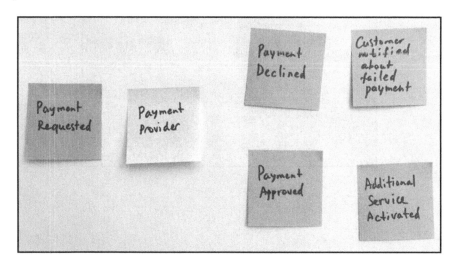

Payment provider is an external system

Remember about the unlimited modeling space and ensure that people do not try to save space because there is not much space left. Reorganize events to make more space or, preferably, put more paper on the wall. Remember that paper is cheap and knowledge is precious. You don't want to lose understanding because someone is saving space on paper.

When people run out of ideas, and there will be some awkward moments of silence. You might need to ignite the fire again by offering to look at the model from a different perspective. There are at least two relatively easy ways to enrich the model by adding something that's missing. First, ask people to traverse the timeline backward. Very often, something that was considered not significant was not put on the wall, but this thing is essential for the next thing to happen. For example, someone might have forgotten that a packing list needs to be produced before the order is shipped. Another technique is to identify where the business creates value. Trivially, try following the money. Very often, developers get into discussing fancy nice-to-haves and forget that the business needs to earn something to pay their salary.

Finally, as mentioned before, keep the time in mind and have at least one break per hour. Keep your promise and don't go overboard; don't keep people for longer than they have planned to stay. If you followed my advice and bought some fruit and drinks, some might even want to continue, but it is up to them to decide whether your workshop should take longer than expected.

After the workshop

When time is up, most probably you'll have a long paper roll with a lot of sticky notes in different colors. A lot of time and effort has been spent producing it, and this paper roll is often seen as a precious artifact. However, this is not exactly the case. You might want to keep evidence of what you have discussed and modeled, and especially the list of hotspots. But the main takeaway is the knowledge that developers and other participants just gained and will take to the bank. More domain knowledge and less ignorance are the most important, albeit invisible, artifacts of the EventStorming session.

That does not mean that you will throw away the paper roll. People that do it for the first time might see such action as a sign of disrespect. Keep the roll, take panoramic, pictures and send it to everyone. Yes, most probably you will never open the roll again. It is much more productive to create all these events from scratch should you need to do it again. People already know, and it will be even more beneficial for them to refine the model this way. But, for the sake of safety, keep the roll somewhere safe for a couple of weeks:

Keep them, but you'll probably never look at them again

Remember to plan follow-up sessions to discuss hotspots. Usually, smaller groups might need to participate. Sometimes you will need to invite someone else because of the questions you have got. You might not need to repeat what has already been done and concentrate on discussing the issues you have discovered. Indeed, using EventStorming in such discussions is beneficial and will enrich the model.

In the next chapter, we will also discuss how to perform the design-level EventStorming, which is a bit more technical and can only be done on a smaller functional area of the domain. The outcome of such a session can be taken straight to your issue tracker.

Our first model

Now let's try to practice and do an imaginary EventStorming session for our sample application domain. It is not easy to imagine how it would go since the most crucial aspect of any EventStorming workshop is the people and how they behave. We definitely cannot reproduce it here in writing, but we can imagine some discussions that can take place and the event flow that is produced.

We will be going through a fictitious EventStorming session, where a classified ads application will be discussed. A facilitator, let's call her Ann, has invited the following people to the workshop:

- John, the company owner. He believes that the system will be the market leader due to its simplicity and unique features.
- Mary is the UX (user experience) designer, and she has done some research on existing systems and has talked to some potential users.
- Nick and Eve are full-stack developers.
- Ian executes the back office, dealing with finances and ensuring that the company is doing well.

It is time for the planned session, and people stream into the meeting room, trying to locate chairs, but there are none. There are two small tables in the room—on one they find some fruit and drinks; on the other one lies a bunch of sticky notes of different colors and a lot of marker pens, enough for a crowd double the size. Two walls are decorated with a long sheet of paper, about seven meters in length. There is also a flipchart and a whiteboard. People look a bit puzzled, and now it is time to provide some clarity:

"Welcome to our first, but hopefully not last, EventStorming workshop," says Ann. *"We will be exploring how our company would like the business to run, and by the end of this session, everyone in this room should have a shared understanding of what we want to do.*

"To do this, we will describe what happens on our side when customers use our services," continues Ann, *"And we will be using sticky notes for that. To start with, we will just put up statements of fact, also known as domain events, on the wall. Imagine how stuff flows through the business, and when something happens, write a couple of words in the past tense on a sticky note and put it on the wall."*

Ann writes the word *legend* on the flip chart and puts up an orange sticky note with the words *something happened—domain event* in the middle. Then she draws a horizontal arrow on top of the paper sheet on the wall and writes *time* underneath. *"Since one fact follows another fact, they form sequences, or processes, which don't happen simultaneously, but in order, one after another. Therefore, we try to arrange these events on a timeline,"* she explains.

People in the room seem to get it, and Ann gives everyone a pile of sticky notes and a pen. Still, everyone seems reluctant to do anything and instead look at each other and feel a bit uncomfortable and nervous like they are afraid of doing something wrong. Then John says, *"Well, the best place to start is the start. What would be the first thing that happened? Maybe when a customer registers with us."* Such uncertainty triggers a discussion that goes nowhere. There is still not a single sticky note placed on the wall. Noticing this, Ann writes **Classified Ad Published** on a sticky and puts it somewhere in the middle.

A single sticky note on the wall sparks a discussion on what the primary element in the system should be called—would this be a *classified ad*, or just an *ad*, or something else? People start putting things that seem to happen before an *ad* is published, such as **Ad created** and **Ad updated**. After a glimpse, Mary expresses skepticism about these terms, since ads aren't updated. There are multiple independent properties of the ad, which change differently. For example, uploading a picture is done separately, then the ad title is updated. Changing the ad category can be restricted, and updating the price could trigger some interesting behaviors, such as informing people who have subscribed to a feed of classified ads for which the price recently decreased.

At the same time, John starts to discuss some advanced features, such as seller and buyer ratings, and eventually, they find out that, on the other part of the wall, there are no buyers or sellers, but *users*. This term seems to have meaning when talking about authentication and profiles but does not help during the selling and buying process.

At this moment, the wall looks like this:

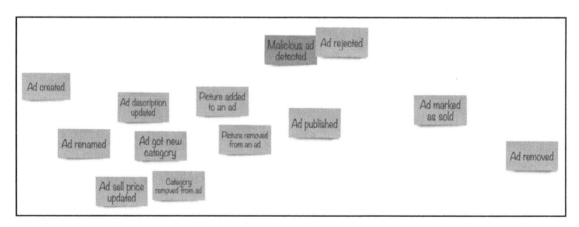

First model

Some work is done, and people need a little break to consume all the goodies that Ann has prepared for them, and to reflect on what has been discussed and discovered.

After the break, they continue.

Eve and John start to discuss the approval process, which was completely missing before. It seems that there is a large percentage of potentially fraudulent and generally malicious classified ads that are placed on competitor's sites, and all of them have some prevention mechanisms. Those who don't bother doing any reviewing at all quickly lose their credibility and trust, and are pushed out of business. But our company has no personnel to keep up with reviewing all ads manually, so the discussion keeps going in circles. Ann notices this and puts a bright pink sticky note on the wall that says *malicious ads detection*. *"We seem to need this, but we aren't sure how,"* she says. *"Let's just put it here as a reminder and get back to it later when we have discussed the rest."* The discussion on this topic then stops and constructively continues towards evolving the process before and after the detection takes place.

At this point, the third element is added to the notation:

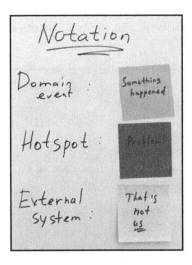

Final notation for the Big Picture workshop

Ian wasn't very active in the discussion and was walking around nodding and sometimes making a grimace of dissent. When Ann asked him what is wrong, Ian impatiently replies, *"No one has even thought about how are we going to earn any money. Without earning anything we will not survive. We don't have that much investment, and we better get some revenue as soon as we can."* That sends a small shockwave through the team, and people start thinking about how they forgot to bring the money aspect to the picture. Then, John explains the original idea that the essential service is free, but some additional services, such as placing an ad at the top of the search results, showing larger pictures, and so on, will be offered for a small fee. He also explains that the free service is only available for private individuals, and if a company wants to sell something via the website, they need to have an exclusive agreement. Plus, he continues, selling cars and real estate should be an entirely different thing, since it requires advanced integration and some safety measures, and these services will never be free.

This new information sparks discussions, and after a short while everyone agrees that for the first version they need to target the largest audience and the most straightforward possible service. It means that they will only offer free ads with a couple of options, which should create the primary revenue stream.

We're now at the end of the workshop, and the wall is covered in sticky notes. Here is what they produced:

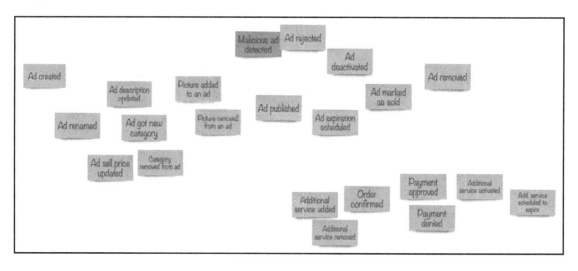

Final big picture model

As we can see, the session uncovered several points that were either unknown or assumed by others but were never made clear. Here are some examples:

- There is no such thing as *ad updated*, but rather a *picture uploaded* and *price decreased* and so on, which are more precise and trigger different logic.
- There are different contexts where a person is known as a *user* and at the same time as a *seller* or *buyer*. The link between those contexts isn't stable, which might be an indication that these are at least different entities.
- The **minimal viable product** (**MVP**) shrank to the bare minimum of free ads with small paid additions. Everything else will come later on.
- Features such as seller and buyer ratings and smart suggestions are nice to have but do not bring immediate value to the users.
- There will be, however, a strong need for some malicious content detection system, since manual reviewing will work for an insufficient period, if we consider the expectations of the number of ads to be published per day.

Developers got a much better understanding of what the business expects the system to do, and how their UX expert wants it to look. They made many adjustments and original ideas, and everyone seems to be on the same page. The ignorance level is much lower than before, and the risk of developers being busy solving the wrong problem is significantly mitigated.

Summary

In this chapter, we have learned what EventStorming is, and why every team would benefit from organizing such a workshop with domain experts, that is, to gain domain knowledge and decrease ignorance. We also looked at some practical tips on how an EventStorming session can be arranged and facilitated.

The final part of this chapter is about the model for our sample business. We discussed the business flow, identified many events and some hotspots, gaining a significant amount of insight into what kind of system we are going to build during this book.

We have briefly touched on the behavioral aspect of EventStorming, but there is more to it, which we cannot cover in this book due to the broad nature of this topic. Check out the next section to find references to Alberto Brandolini's work, and study the referenced materials to learn more about people, their biases and behaviors, and why software development is a learning process.

In the next chapter, we will look deeper into the modeling process, with more of a focus on artifacts that can help us to start writing code and deliver initial prototypes as soon as possible.

The EventStorming community has a lot of discussions about using the technique in distributed teams or when end users aren't directly available to participate in such sessions. Alberto points out that the body language is extremely important to get an overall feeling of how the session goes and to identify the roles of the participants in the session and in the business. In my view, that is true, but we often deal with situations when such a session is nearly impossible to organize. For distributed systems, I would personally recommend using online real-time tools, like Miro, which I used to create many diagrams for this book. It allows for people to participate in modeling sessions wherever they are located.

For SaaS businesses, the issue might be even harder because there's no single group of users that can be trusted to represent the whole user base. However, even with such a scenario, it is often possible to identify a group of the most engaged customers and invite them to be a part of your team. Not only you get great insights about how they use your system and how they want it to be improved, but also you get great free publicity by the word of mouth. People overall respect openness and greatly appreciate when their voice is heard by developers.

Further reading

Here is some information you can refer to:

- *EventStorming* (EventStorming.com)—the place to get more information and links
- *Introducing EventStorming*, Brandolini A. (2017), Leanpub (https://leanpub.com/introducing_eventstorming)

4
Designing the Model

Many think of domain models as data models. You can easily see this by searching for the `domain model` on Google—all the things you find are data diagrams or class diagrams. Although class diagrams sometimes contain some useful behavior (methods), even this does not happen that often. However, since the complexity of business is rarely in its data, we need to realize that behavior is an integral part of a domain model.

Big Picture EventStorming helps us to understand the whole business or a part of it, but we need to take it further to get to the implementation. Design-level EventStorming is just that—we look at the part of the system that is most interesting for us and dive deeper into it, discovering more events and new flows.

In this chapter, we will cover the following topics:

- What does the domain model represent?
- Patterns and anti-patterns
- Design-level EventStorming

Domain model

As we discussed in Chapter 1, *Why Domain-Driven Design?*, the software we design and implement has only one primary purpose—to solve a domain problem. Understanding the problem space or the business domain is crucial for the journey of finding proper solutions and satisfying users with the systems we make. When we get more understanding about the domain using techniques such as Big Picture EventStorming, as discussed in the previous chapter, we need to go a bit deeper and try visualizing our knowledge using visual artifacts that other people would understand and will be able to reason about. In short, we need a **model**.

What does the model represent?

There are many different things described by the word **model**. When we say **model**, we can think of a scale model of a car, a ship, or even a house. Such models represent real-life objects on a different scale and also demonstrate a substantially different level of detail. Some models could be quite abstract, such as a model of a building complex. Other models, however, can give a more detailed view of what they represent, such as scale models of cars, which are often very accurate. But most of the time, such models are also missing some of the important features of real cars, such as the engine, the gearbox, and sophisticated electronics.

So, models represent some artifact of the real world, but with a narrow purpose. How much space the building will occupy and how high the whole complex will be, for example, are often just enough for a rough model, during the first review stage of the building project. Models do not intend to replicate real life. Instead, they represent some particular aspects of real life at a certain level of detail, depending on the purpose of the model.

A map of a city's transport lines is a great example. In any generic map, you can see that it shows the transport links, all stations, and changes. It also indicates some essential geographical aspects, such as relative distance to the sea or on which side of the river the stations are located.

At the same time, such map does not show the distance between stations and has no direct resemblance to real geographical locations. To find exactly where stations are located in the city, or how much time you would need to spend traveling from one station to another, you would need another map.

This example demonstrates that a particular model could represent some useful aspect of real life, but could ignore other elements as they are not necessary. This does not mean that those neglected aspects aren't important at all, just that they are not crucial to that particular problem space. Thus, the transport links map solves the problem of orientation for public transport users, and it does it well. But it does not solve the problem of navigating on the street, and it doesn't need to because it serves a different purpose.

As such, domain models in software also need to represent those aspects of the business domain that are essential to solving the problem in question. It is sometimes very tempting to put everything we know and, to go further on this slippery path, everything we could assume about the business domain, in our model. But it would add unnecessary complexity to the model and won't help to solve the problem. Even worse, putting too many irrelevant details in the model might broaden the implementation scope and mystify the intention that the business people had in mind when specifying the problems they wanted to solve.

Going back to `Chapter 1`, *Why Domain-Driven Design?*, if the business domain and the particular problems we have to solve are in our problem space, the domain model is purely in our solution space. We will be modeling our solution, and those models will be our domain models.

Anemic domain model

The term **domain model**, although it already existed, was widely acknowledged after it was mentioned in Martin Fowler's book *Patterns of Enterprise Application Architecture* by Addison Wesley, 2003. Here is how Fowler defines the term in his book (`https://martinfowler.com/eaaCatalog/domainModel.html`):

> *"Domain model: An object model of the domain that incorporates both behavior and data."*

This definition is quite short and concise. And still, somehow, it got it very wrong if you look at the various links on Google if you search for `domain model`. If you have done the same as I did and searched for the phrase, you've found out that the majority of found images, and most of the links, lead to something that we can consider as data models or entity models. Such models visualize entities, data fields with types and relations between entities. In the best cases, links are attributed by domain terminologies such as *attends* or *consist of*, and in some rare cases, we can find class diagrams that show some methods.

What we see in the case of entity or data models are so-called **anemic models**. As the term suggests, such models only express the system state and know nothing of how this state changes and what operations are done in the system. Usually, if you look at the implementations of these systems, you will find that everything the system does is some manipulation of data. New entities are created, new relations are made, and fields in entities are changed. That's all.

There are a couple of reasons why anemic models became popular. First, guidelines to visualize domain models in UML suggest that things that are envisioned are **conceptual classes**. These classes represent real-world entities and their properties. In UML, such models include items (entities) with attributes (fields), their associations (relations), and actors. Hence, there is no place for behavior in conceptual classes. The next reason is that the idea of conceptual classes somehow got lost, and these UML models became the only domain models, where domain behavior was considered insignificant.

Getting back to Fowler, in the bliki article about anemic models (`https://martinfowler.com/bliki/AnemicDomainModel.html`), he clearly defines this way of modeling systems as an anti-pattern. In addition to the previous description, anemic models often tend to be implemented entirely by database operations. Models that consist of objects with relations closely resemble relational models, and therefore relational databases are most frequently used to persist such objects. The association between an anemic domain model and its state in the database is so tight that they become siblings and cannot be distinguished from one another.

Very often, if you find a system with an anemic model as the domain model, you will have a hard time understanding what the system does since all you see in the code is SQL and calls to run it. And if you ask people who work with the system about where you can find the implementation of their model, they will most probably point directly to the database. There is also an opinion that anemic domain models are useful in cases where the application has little or no behavior, and such a model serves perfectly fine as a persistence model. I would argue that in such cases, there is no reason to call it a domain model. Data models are perfectly fine since they serve the purpose of persistence. However, there is no real justification for presenting data models as domain models, since these are two different things.

Functional languages and anemic models

There is one more thing worth mentioning here. There are discussions in the functional programming communities about whether the models they design are anemic too. This is because, in functional programming, the use of classes is not mandatory and sometimes not even possible. Even when it is possible, it is not natural to use classes because functions and functional composition can solve many problems more easily. I would argue that if the behavior is still modeled and implemented as functions, such a model is not anemic. It might not directly fit the original definition, but 2003 was the time of dominance for object-oriented programming languages, so it was natural to use the term **object model**. However, the key here is in the combination of data and behavior, and definitely, when using a rich type system combined with clearly defined functions that express intent, such a model is indeed not anemic.

What to include in the domain model

As we mentioned earlier, a domain model's objects represent data and the behavior of the domain. By writing *objects*, I don't mean anything related to object-oriented languages, but rather the essence they represent. The implementation of a domain model is also shaped by the programming language that is used, so that such objects can be records, structs or, in fact, objects. Because this book is about using C# to implement **Domain-Driven Design (DDD)**, we will be using classes and objects to implement our domain models.

Even when we are equipped with the notion of polymorphism, we can combine data and behavior inside our classes. This does not directly mean that our domain model will include such classes. Everything that is part of the domain implementation is also part of the domain model. There is no better documentation for the domain model than the code that implements such a model.

Behavior and data in the model are interconnected. The behavior of the model has no other meaning than to manipulate the model's data, and since the data represents nothing else than what the model is interested in and operates on, such data is also known as the **state**. The state is the data that describes what our system looks like at a particular moment in time. Every behavior of the model changes the state. The state is that thing we persist to the database and that we can recover at any time before applying a new behavior.

This can be illustrated with a simple example:

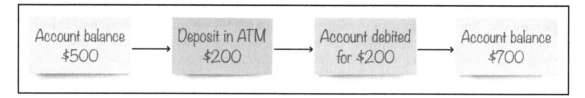

State transition is triggered by an action, causes a reaction

Here, you can see the account balance as a piece of state. When we apply a behavior, the state changes. This is called a **state transition**. Each domain model behavior causes a transition in the domain model state. Everything that documents how the domain state changes should be a part of the domain model.

Design considerations

As we've seen before, in object-oriented languages, we often see classes that use the power of polymorphism to keep the behavior close to the state. In functional languages, though, the state is usually maintained separately, since the behavior can be represented as functions that manipulate instances of record types that represent the state.

Logically, things such as communication protocols, user input validation, and persistence implementation are not seen as part of the domain model. These are technical and infrastructure concerns. A good rule of thumb here is that the whole domain model should be testable without involving any infrastructure. Primarily, in your domain model tests, you should not use test harnesses and mocks.

If you look at the onion architecture, the hexagonal architecture, and clean architecture principles, you will find that they have one thing in common. The center of any application is the **Domain**:

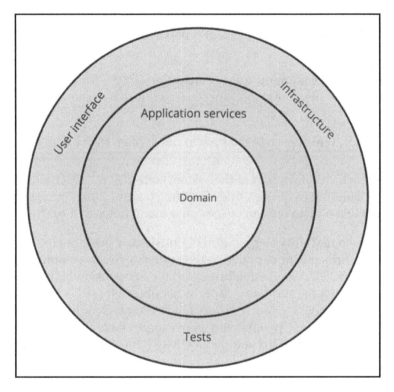

Onion architecture

Application services and **Infrastructure** are kept outside and form layers around this core of the system. Unlike a layered architecture, which has dependencies going down from the UI layer to the data layer, we can see that the **Domain** is the center of everything, and everything depends on it. Such a change, although it could be recognized as a small adjustment, has a very significant impact. Instead of everything depending on the data layer, which makes the database the master of all, the focus shifts to the domain, making the domain model the most significant part of the system.

CQRS

In addition to the previously discussed ways to design domain models as polymorphic classes using object-orientation and using functions operating with instances of record types for some functional languages, there is a different way to express state transitions inside the domain. With this, I mean the CQRS patterns, which was coined by Greg Young a decade ago.

The term originated from **command-query separation (CQS)**, formulated by Bertrand Meyer, which states that object methods are separated into two categories. These categories are as follows:

- Commands, which mutate the system (most often the object) state and return `void`.
- Queries, which return part of the system state and do not change the state of the system. This makes queries side effect free (except things such as logging) and idempotent so that they can be executed many times and get the same result.

Command-query responsibility segregation (CQRS) takes this principle outside of an object. It is the same principle but applied to the system level. Development of this pattern took a few years, from 2007, when Greg presented the early vision of it on the InfoQ conference, to 2010, when the summary paper was published (`https://cqrs.files.wordpress.com/2010/11/cqrs_documents.pdf`). It also took Google a few years to recognize the acronym. A few years back, people who were eagerly looking for CQRS got a suggestion from Google saying **Did you mean CARS?**, but today the pattern is widely known and praised.

Separating commands and queries on the system level means that any state transition for the system can be expressed by a command, and such a command should be handled efficiently, optimized to perform the state transition. Queries, on the other hand, return data derived from the system state, which means that queries can be executed differently and can be optimized for reading the state or any derivative of the state if such a derivative exists.

Such separation is beneficial in scenarios when there is a clear imbalance between writes to the database and reads from the database. A typical business or consumer-oriented application is massively imbalanced toward reads. However, stereotypical implementations are optimized for writes, using normalized relational databases, where writes can be performed rather efficiently but reads require numerous joins and extensive filtering:

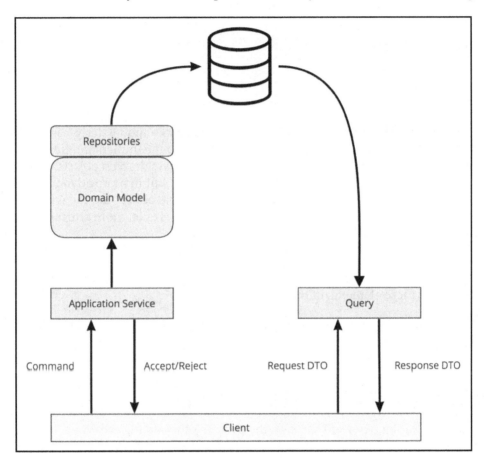

CQRS with a single database

In the simplest scenarios, CQRS can be implemented just by using database-mapped domain objects to execute operations on a domain model that mutate the system state (usually, it is done using ORM tools) and using direct SQL queries with joins across multiple tables to retrieve the system, completely ignoring the domain model class hierarchy. It leads to great optimization of reads and at the same time rightfully increases awareness of the state persistence mechanism. While this method is entirely legitimate, you should realize that, in this case, queries need to be either adequately abstracted from the data persistence layer, or be designed outside of the domain model.

In more complex scenarios, we could have not only two different *clients* to manipulate the same domain entities, but also split these entities apart. We will be looking closely at such techniques later in this book when we discuss event sourcing.

You might be wondering why CQRS made it into the domain model design section of the book, instead of being explained in the part that belongs to the implementation. The reason for this is that CQRS makes commands and queries first-class domain objects. Domain events should always be seen as first-class domain objects, but in more advanced CQRS implementation models, domain events play the crucial role of keeping the whole system consistent, and therefore the role of domain events becomes even more critical.

This is why CQRS is mentioned right here, for us to realize that we should not only include classes with properties and methods for our domain model, but things like commands, queries, and domain events belong to the model just as much, and we will be looking at how to model all these elements in the next section.

My final note is that EventStorming is valuable, regardless of whether or not you use CQRS for your implementation.

Design-level EventStorming

In the previous chapter, we went through the process of modeling the whole business using Big Picture EventStorming. We mainly discussed domain events and later added hotspots and external systems.

In this section, we will be looking to model at a more detailed level, using richer notation, to move closer to the actual implementation of the model in code.

Getting deeper knowledge

Let's go back to the moment when we finished the Big Picture EventStorming workshop. The team spent a couple of hours discussing essential topics:

- What processes does the business run?
- What kind of objects participate in these processes?
- What facts can we record about the system behavior?
- Who does what?
- What essential terms do we need to learn and use?

Discussions about these points produced a diagram with a lot of orange sticky notes representing facts of life, which we call **domain events**. There are also some pink sticky notes to be found here and there, indicating hotspots—things that need attention, further clarification, or cause worry. Usually, this means missing knowledge.

All these things bring the team somewhat closer to the actual implementation, but they don't feel like start coding just yet. The team members need to go deeper into the design and gain more specific knowledge about what actions can be performed in the system, and by whom.

This is a topic for another type of EventStorming workshop—design-level EventStorming. Let's look closer at how such a workshop can be organized.

Preparation for the workshop

For more detailed EventStorming workshops, you need more or less the same things as for a Big Picture workshop:

- Paper roll or any other type of unlimited modeling space
- Sticky notes of different colors; we'll get to the notation later on
- Enough permanent markers

Of course, the essential ingredient is to have the right people. But now, we are getting deeper into the details, so it is essential to choose one area to explore, and finding such a space is often a non-trivial task, which we will discuss later in this chapter. So, the right people would be those who will be busy writing the code, someone who is responsible for that part of the system as a product owner, and domain experts in the chosen area. As you can see, we can limit our group to fewer people than the Big Picture session.

Both options—limiting the scope and limiting the number of people—allow us to discuss the design in a much higher level of detail, have one single discussion thread, and have everyone express their thoughts and ask questions.

Extended notation

Since EventStorming is language and technology agnostic, we cannot model things such as classes, fields, methods, or functions. Instead, we need to use more universal concepts. We already discussed such thoughts in the CQRS section, and there we saw that we can express the behavior in our domain model not just as a list of methods, but as the execution of commands. Commands express the user's intent. The domain model then gets its state transitioned, and new events are produced, recording the purpose and the state transition. Queries represent what users want to see on their screens to take decisions and execute other commands. So, this provides some elements for the design session that are not related to any specific programming language or technology.

Commands

Commands and events are not bound to any language or technology. They also describe the system's behavior very well, using Ubiquitous Language and expressing the intent of our users.

Therefore, we include commands in the notation for the design-level EventStorming. Commands express the intent of the users that interact with the system, so applying commands to our system would naturally produce state transitions and result in events being emitted inside our domain model. If we use blue sticky notes for commands, the regular flow of command processing will look like this:

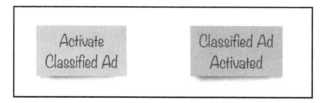

The command triggers the state change

Note that we have no arrows connecting sticky notes. The flow is determined solely by placing them together in chronological order. First, we ask the system to do something, and when the operation is accepted and performed, the system transitions its state and emits new events.

Avoid using arrows in your modeling space in general, since they create spatial locking for your sticky notes, which you will stop moving around because arrows are drawn on paper or a whiteboard and cannot be moved. Such locking lowers down the modeling dynamics and prevents experimentation.

Read models

The next new concept we will bring to our model is the read model. The read model is something that our users look at before asking the system to do something. It could be any screen in our application, such as a form, a dashboard, or a report. Any such screen contains a set of elements with a limited number of element types. Usually, we can classify elements as follows:

- The information shown as text and images
- Form elements such as input boxes, check boxes, and radio buttons
- Action buttons
- Navigation

When navigation elements naturally move users from one screen to another, action buttons are used to send commands to the system. Informational elements and form elements are something that our users look at before deciding what to do. What is shown inside these elements is defined by read-models. For the purpose of modeling, we could assume that our read models are screens in the system, so we can identify what information we need to combine and show to the user.

To demonstrate this, let's look at the following example:

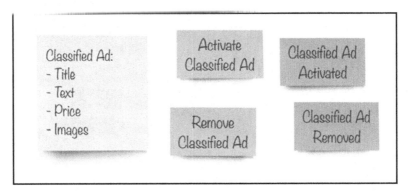

Read model, commands, and events

So, the green sticky note here represents the read model for a classified ad. From there, the user can do specific actions: publish the ad or remove it. Executing one of these commands will result in an event being published by the domain model.

Users

Most of the time, commands in our system are executed by people who use the system—by users. When designing the model, we often need to understand who is running which command, just because not all commands are allowed to be executed by everyone. We might define different user roles, such as *administrator*, *manager*, *reviewer*, and so on, and somehow visualize them, along with their ability to execute specific commands. You might also find it useful to identify personas and use them in addition to, or instead of, roles. It is particularly helpful if you expect one person to perform different roles in the system or when you are modeling an existing system in which you know specific people and their particular duties, and using their names directly in the model will bring clarity and understanding to everyone involved.

Visually, we can use smaller sticky notes with a person figure, drawn as the UML actor symbol. You might call your users **actors** too, but in UML, actors aren't necessary users. In EventStorming, we want users to be visualized differently, so we use larger pale magenta sticky notes to show external systems, as we discussed in the previous chapter.

Let's put some users into our model:

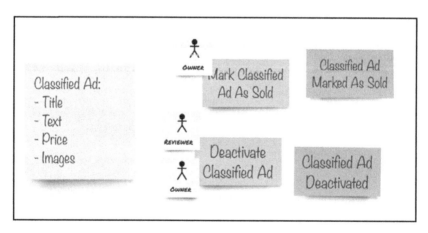

Users are those who trigger commands

I used a different read model, which can be used by two different types of users. Here, the **Classified Ad** owner can mark it as sold. But both the owner and someone who has the role of **Reviewer** can deactivate the ad.

Policies

The last elements we will be using in the design-level session is policy. As we learned, previously actions in the system are represented by commands. Users can execute actions by sending commands. When a command is processed, the system changes its state and emit events. This is the initial reaction of the system on the user's action. But, when we publish events, we also let other elements of our domain model, that were previously unaware of the command being executed, know that something happened. This is very useful in order to not execute all work linked to a certain action at once. Ideally, we should limit the amount of work we do to process a command to the absolute minimum. Technically, such atomic operations can be represented as one transaction. It might very well be that some other operations also need to be executed as the result of the domain model state transition, but we don't need to wrap these actions in one transaction and force the user to wait until all such work is done. This is exactly where we need policies. Policies subscribe to domain events, and when a policy receives some domain events it is interested in, it will check the event content and potentially send another command to the system to complement the work. There might be numerous policies reacting to the same event type, doing all kinds of post-processing in an asynchronous fashion, while the user gets control back after the original command has been executed.

We can express a policy in our modeling space like this:

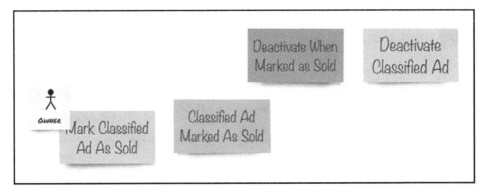

Policies might trigger commands based on events

Looking at this model, we can transcribe it like this—*when the owner of a classified ad marks it as sold, the system should also deactivate this ad.*

As you can see, a policy can react to domain events and issue commands, based on certain conditions. Such behavior is called **reactive behavior**, and systems that actively use this pattern can be referred to as **reactive systems**.

 Please note that the term "reactive" became ambiguous during recent years. The *Reactive Manifesto* postulates the definition for a "reactive system", which is different from what I mean in this book.

All together now

To sum up, we can draw a conceptual picture of all the elements that were introduced in this section, like this:

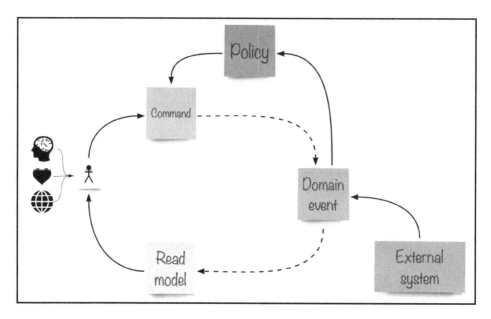

The picture that explains (almost) everything—Alberto Brandolini

The transcription for this picture would be—the user, using information from the system, represented as the read model, and information from the outside world, feelings, and the thoughts of the user, send operation requests to the system, known as **commands**, which might result in a system state change that produces domain events. Domain events can trigger policies, which might issue new commands, based on the information received in those events and the system's state. External systems could also produce domain events. The system's state change results in reading models being updated as well, so the user can receive new information from the system and the cycle repeats.

This diagram can describe the majority of systems out there, and you might imagine that it is not only applicable to software systems. The picture also maps very nicely with CQRS and this, I believe, makes the CQRS pattern so useful. Some might argue that CQRS adds accidental complexity to the system due to implementation efforts. However, when done correctly, it adds more clarity to the models because it directly implements the **separation of concerns** (**SoC**) principle (*On the role of scientific thought* by Edsger W. Dijkstra, 1974), and in general makes the system easier to build and maintain.

Modeling the reference domain

In this section, we are going to design a part of the reference domain using the tools we have covered in this chapter.

Our team is getting together again to discuss a part of the system in more detail. They have decided that the classified ad life cycle is their core domain at the first stage and that the section related to additional services and payments will be implemented later due to their investor's decision to gain users before monetizing the application.

It is important to realize that such decisions cannot be solely made by developers, and it is vital to involve all stakeholders in the decision-making process.

First things first, and we need to quickly review the events that were identified as part of the classified ad life cycle. Our team gets to work, but quickly reaches the point where they get this on the wall:

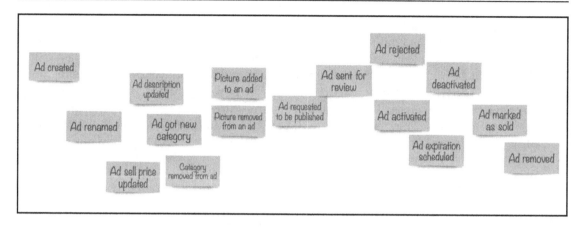

The first round of the session—domain events only

As you can see, this model is a little bit different from the final model from the previous chapter. Every time the team discusses the model, some changes occur because team members get a better understanding of the domain.

The next thing they do is add some commands that result in events that are already present on the model. In many cases, commands demonstrate the direct intent of users to do something that directly results in events. These commands are the most obvious ones that come to the model first.

Sometime later, the model looks like this:

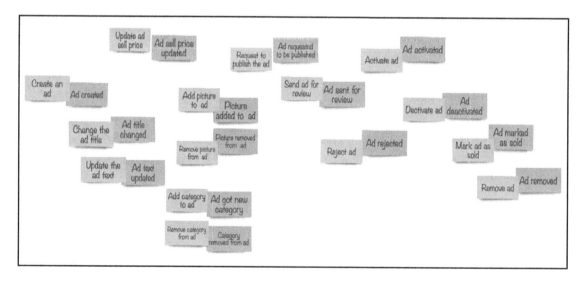

Events and commands

The team then agrees that most commands are executed by users, but then a discussion sparks about who the user is. Technically, everyone who uses the system is a user. But different people can do different things, and something that is allowed to be done by administrators cannot be done by regular users. This is obvious, but from there, the team identifies the need to separate people by what they do. Of course, one person can always play different roles, but in this concrete example, most operations are done by one type of user—those who want to *sell* things. Naturally, the role is identified as a *seller*. After making this discovery, the model starts to go into more detail:

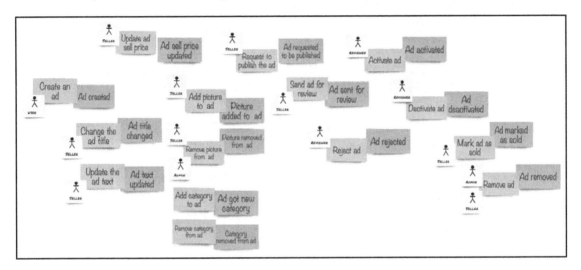

Events, commands, and actors

As you can see, along the way, more roles are identified and assigned to commands. For example, an ad cannot be approved or rejected by the seller; this makes no sense. Someone from inside the service needs to do this work and either allow the ad to be published or deny publication for one or another reason.

Interestingly enough, since the discussed context is only covering the ad life cycle, there is no buyer involved. So, the team keeps interchangeably using the words **owner** and **seller**. For the sake of consistency, they lean toward using the term **seller** but remember that all words in the Ubiquitous Language are context-specific. And the reason why we do not have the **buyer** here is that, as far as the team is currently concerned, they will only deal with buyers in some other parts of the system, meaning another context. Preliminarily, they identify that buyers would participate in conversations about buying agreements and terms, and in the escrow context, should this be required. Also, the team keeps thinking about mutual reviews and, naturally, both sellers and buyers will participate in this activity.

Then, thoughts start to roam around events that appear for different reasons. One of those events is **Ad deactivated**. The seller might click the **Deactivate** button when looking at an ad, or an ad might be rejected for publication by the reviewer. The discovery is made that the `Deactivate Ad` command can be executed by both the seller and by the system itself when a **policy** to deactivate rejected ads is triggered. Adding policies to the model results in some more details:

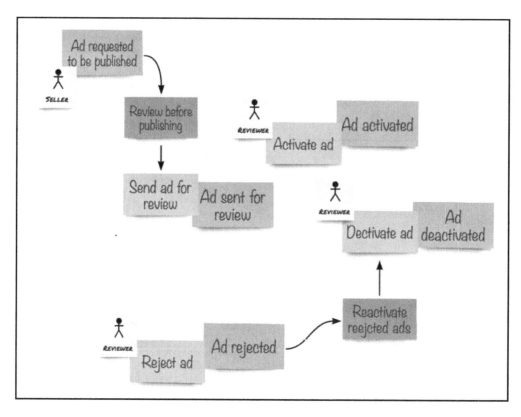

Part of the model with policies

Finally, the team went through some commands that require specific information to be displayed to allow users to make decisions and execute them as commands. Not everywhere can such clarity be reached during the first iteration, and in such cases, the team needs to postpone making any decisions to a later stage. It is more important to make progress and move on than chase too granular a model, which will never be perfect anyway.

For example, when adding a category to the ad, sellers must be able to choose from the list of existing categories using some advanced techniques such as type-ahead search. And for reviewers, it is helpful not only to see the ad's content but also get more details about the seller who authored the ad. A combination of factors, such as the seller's experience of the platform, the number of previously published ads, the number of currently published ads, and finally, the current ad content, can provide clarity for reviewers, helping them to distinguish malicious ads from legitimate ones.

When working with read models, there are a lot of opportunities for developers to work together with UX experts, UI designers, and other people, since real models are natural parts of the UI. But commands should not be forgotten either since they are the handlers that make the system do something useful. Without commands, the whole system would just be a collection of static pages, since there would be no way to change the system's state and execute any behavior. The entire UI of any system is a collection of read models with command executors attached to them as buttons and other action-triggering elements.

You might also think about *task-based UI*, a useful approach to designing UI elements in such a way that leads users to make simple, atomic, and precise operations. In our example, we used task-based UI too because our sellers change the ad price separately from the ad title simply because these operations are substantially different. The idea of task-based UI is very much aligned with CQRS and command handling. It's no surprise that the most information about this technique can be found in Greg Young's articles related to CQRS, such as this one: `https://cqrs.wordpress.com/documents/task-based-ui/`.

Summary

In this chapter, we identified the domain model and agreed that the model represents some part of real life, which is targeted to solve some specific problem. We also discussed the importance of behavior and that it is an essential part of the model that is often overlooked and even ignored.

Along the way, we introduced the CQRS pattern. It separates commands as something to be done inside the model and that represent behavior, from queries that have the only purpose of retrieving state.

Then, we got more elements for the EventStorming modeling technique in order to model detail in more depth, moving toward something that we can start implementing in code. We recognized that these new elements match well with the CQRS paradigms.

Finally, we went through the modeling session of our sample domain and got more insight into how the core part of the system should work, so we are now prepared to convert this knowledge into code. That is what we will be doing in the next chapter.

Further reading

For more information is a list of resources you can refer to:

- *Introducing EventStorming*, Brandolini A. (2017), Leanpub (https://leanpub.com/introducing_eventstorming)
- *Microsoft Inductive User Interface Guidelines*, Microsoft Corporation, 2001 (https://msdn.microsoft.com/en-us/library/ms997506.aspx)
- *Task-Based UI* (https://cqrs.wordpress.com/documents/task-based-ui/)

Implementing the Model 5

In previous chapters, we went through a different level of knowledge crunching and domain analysis. We used EventStorming as our primary tool, so, as a result of our efforts, we got plenty of paper rolls, with lots of colorful sticky notes on them. But how can we make some working code from it? That is a good question, and this is precisely what we will start doing when moving along in this chapter.

By the end of this chapter, we will have a basis for our domain model implemented in code. We will go through different styles of performing the behavior in domain entities and also write some tests.

The following topics will be covered:

- Create a project for the domain model
- Add domain objects to the new project
- What the entities and value objects are
- How to ensure that the domain model is always in a valid state

Technical requirements

This chapter will provide guidelines to do some hands-on work. To follow up with that, you will need to have the following tools:

- .NET Core 2.2.203 or higher (`https://www.asp.net/`)
- Visual Studio 2017 or higher (`https://www.visualstudio.com/vs/`), or JetBrains Rider (`https://www.jetbrains.com/rider/`)

There is no particular requirement on a platform since .NET Core, and the tooling is available almost everywhere. Throughout this book, I will be using Rider on macOS. Initial screenshots will be from Visual Studio 2017 for Windows since most readers would be using this IDE. Some dialog boxes vary significantly between Visual Studio for Windows, Visual Studio for Mac, and Rider.

I will be using some features of C# 8.0 in the code, so it is necessary to use **.NET Core SDK 2.2.203** or higher.

I assume that you are familiar with the tool that you are using and with the .NET Stack in general, so you know how to create projects, build them and execute applications in different environments.

Starting up the implementation

In this section, we will create a new project and add a domain project to it.

Since we plan to implement a web application, we will consider this from the beginning and will use a web application template. We will also add some projects to host different parts of our system and tests.

If you aren't familiar with tools for .NET, you can always check Mapt, the extensive library of Packt books and video courses, and use materials from there to improve your skills. In this book, we assume that readers have an adequate level of knowledge of C# and the tools to develop applications using .NET.

Creating projects

We will start with an empty project. You need to create a .NET Core web application and don't forget to enable the creation of a Git repository so it can keep a history of your changes.

We would expect our system to get more substantial, but we start small. Let's call the solution `Marketplace`, and our first project would be called just that. The type of project to create is an **ASP.NET Core Web Application**. This project is our startup, which will be executed by the .NET runtime. You need to choose the **Empty** project type for the new Web API project because we won't be using Razor or SPA (single page application) templates.

We already discussed that the domain model should not have dependencies on infrastructure. In general, it should not have references to anything but standard language types, itself, and some set of base classes and interfaces, if necessary. To enforce this, let's create a separate project where we will put all our domain objects. Add one more project to the solution and call it `Marketplace.Domain`. This project will not be executed by itself, so the project type should be **Class Library (.NET Standard)** and don't forget to change the framework for it to **netstandard2.0** (or later). The **.NET Standard** is the default for class libraries, but feel free to use ASP.NET Core target framework as well if you aren't planning to use your library in the legacy .NET Framework applications.

Then, we need to add one more project for unit tests. You can do it by adding a project to your solution, which would be called `Marketplace.Tests`. The project type is a unit test project, and type is **xUnit** since we will be using xUnit.net testing framework for our tests in this book. The xUnit.NET test project is one of the default test project templates of the ASP.NET Core SDK. Remember to add a reference to the `Marketplace.Domain` project to the test project, since we'll be mostly testing our domain code.

The solution should now look like the following screenshot:

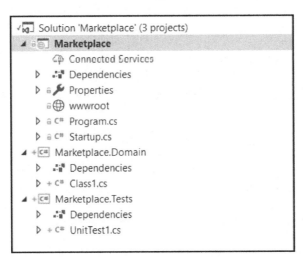

A glimpse of the solution structure

It makes sense to remove the `wwwroot` and `Properties` folders, `Class1.cs` and `UnitTest1.cs` files, since we will create new classes from scratch and we do not need empty folders to hang around.

The framework

We will need somewhere to place *this set of base classes and interfaces* mentioned in the previous section. We might dispute whether these things are required at all. They are not required to start a simple `Hello World` style project, but, as we go along, we will need to create more abstractions.

Also, we will need some components that will allow our domain model to work with things like database, message bus, web server, and so on. According to onion architecture principles, these are **adapters**. Our project, in the end, will need to have a collection of adapters for all pieces of infrastructure that are being used.

You might rightfully ask—are we going to build a framework? Aren't frameworks considered evil and shouldn't they be avoided? Well, we should take everything with a grain of salt and having a set of useful abstractions for our domain object and infrastructure would greatly help us while moving along. Also, we definitely will need to build some of the adapters, and although these can be separated in their own libraries, which will connect to our abstractions (hence ports and adapters), for the reason of simplicity, we will put most of these things in one project, and this project will be called `Marketplace.Framework`. You can choose any other name for this project if you don't like the name `Framework`, but in this book, we will be referencing it a lot, so I hope you don't get confused.

Most of the abstractions and implementations in this framework would be production ready by the end of this book. And unlike third-party frameworks, you keep full control of what is inside it and how it works, so this should make it a milder evil, even if you don't like frameworks at all.

Many DDD practitioners keep reciting the mantra *you don't need DDD framework*, and this is partially true, but people always need to have some baseline for their applications to speed up the development. We use the .NET Framework, built by Microsoft, rather than creating all these classes from scratch for every project. When we get to the point of having a set of useful abstractions and components in our framework, we can use it, or something similar to it, in some other project and be entirely in control.

So, to finish up this section, add a class library project to the same solution. The framework for it should be **netstandard2.0** (or later), just as it was for the `Marketplace.Domain` project. Call this new project `Marketplace.Framework`

Transferring the model to code

Since we aren't doing a `Hello World` exercise, we won't be using the executable project for a while. Instead, we will concentrate on writing things inside the domain project, adding some practical classes and interfaces to the framework projects, and writing tests.

First, we need to identify which building blocks our implementation will be based on. These building blocks are often referenced as **Domain-Driven Design** (**DDD**) tactical patterns, as opposed to DDD strategic patterns. Some even say that tactical patterns can be ignored in favor of strategic patterns. Although I agree that Ubiquitous Language, Bounded Context, and Context Map are the essential parts of DDD, I still believe that some tactical patterns are useful and bring clarity and common language for the implementation. This book is not a collection of tactical DDD patterns, and relevant concepts will only be used when necessary to implement the model.

Entities

Let's get back to our EventStorming session and look at part of our model, shown as follows:

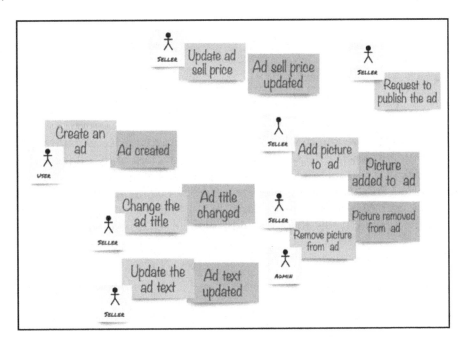

The core domain modeled with sticky notes

There is a repetition in all those commands. Can you see it? All those commands are being executed on something that is called a **Classified Ad**. Also, if you recall all those conversations with domain experts, our team members frequently referred to this term when talking about the business in general, and also about the model.

Mainly, we have an entity here. Entities represent unique objects of the same type. In addition to classified ads, we might expect our system to hold information about sellers and buyers, and those might be entities too, apart from being just roles in the system. It is because we need to identify those people, so we need to have something unique, like username or email address, to understand who is who. The same is valid for a classified ad. Imagine ads like the following:

Draft sketch of the user interface

Both ads are the same if we ignore who is selling and for what price. But, most probably, these are two different objects. Because of the mass-production of IKEA, there is a significant chance that multiple similarly used objects are being sold at the same time, but for us, those objects are different. It is because we are not using object properties, like model and size, to find out if two objects are identical. In our system, these objects will be represented in two different classified ads and will have separate identities.

Identities

We mentioned a username or email as an identity of users in the system, but what can be used as an identity for objects? In real life, many objects are already identified. The most common identity is an item serial number. Complex objects like smartphones, TV sets, computers, and cars have unique identifiers that help manufacturers to know in what configuration these objects were produced, and therefore, they can provide better support. Also, due to the significant price of such objects, they are usually tracked individually.

However, when we talk about our system, most of the time we need to use our own identity. The only important rule, really, is that all entities need to be uniquely identified. There are a few ways to get such an identity, and you might already be familiar with some. Probably the most frequently used method to get unique identities today (later referenced as **IDs**) is to use unique database keys. It is because most systems out there are data-oriented and designed with persistence-first in mind. Such a system will not work without persisting stuff to a particular database. Such a method has at least one definite advantage—such IDs are usually numeric and incremental, so it is straightforward to dictate such an ID over the phone. But the most significant disadvantage comes from the ID source—the database must be present to get such an identity, even if later in the flow, the system will decide not to accept the object and drop it instead, so it never gets persisted. Most of the experienced developers have seen weird constructs in the code where an empty or dummy row is being inserted into some table to get an object ID, and later, such a row either needs to be populated with real values or removed. Such an approach creates a whole load of issues, and we will not be using it.

Instead, we will use generated unique IDs. Because we would prefer not to use any infrastructure to create our IDs, we will use one reliable method and identity type—a **globally unique identifier (GUID)**, more commonly known as a **universally unique identifier** (UUID). Such an ID can be generated using the current time and some information about the computer, where it is produced. There is a very high probability that such an ID is globally unique. When using GUIDs, we can generate identities for objects before touching any infrastructure and therefore, for example, create references to an object that only exists in memory.

Classified ad entity

As we have understood from our EventStorming model, we most probably need an entity to represent a classified ad. It seems to be one of the central concepts of our system. We spent a great deal of time discussing our model with domain experts, and this term kept coming up in the conversation. It is a perfect indicator that we have identified some vital domain concept also, because we keep getting a repeated pattern when one command results in one event, and we keep having a *classified ad* as an object.

Entities are represented in code as objects, and, therefore, we need a class so we can create instances of such a class. Here is our first attempt to create a class to represent a classified ad:

```
namespace Marketplace.Domain
{
    public class ClassifiedAd
    {
        public Guid Id { get; private set; }

        private Guid _ownerId;
        private string _title;
        private string _text;
        private decimal _price;
    }
}
```

You might feel puzzled about this class, and you'd be right to question this kind of entity implementation. It looks like a property bag, and the only difference with a **DTO** (short for **data transfer object**) here, is that this class only has one property, and all other details are represented by private fields. This class will compile, but it is practically unusable because even the single public property can only be set from inside the class, but we have not exposed any way of doing this.

However, despite being useless, this implementation demonstrates two essential principles that we need to keep in mind while going further. First, all entities need to have an ID, and it must be accessible from outside the entity. Second, since we are using an object-oriented language, we shall try to encapsulate as much as we can, and keep our internals safe, and preferably invisible to the outside world.

To be able to instantiate this class correctly, let's create a constructor that will at least allow us to set the entity id:

```
using System;

namespace Marketplace.Domain
{
    public class ClassifiedAd
    {
        public Guid Id { get; }

        public ClassifiedAd(Guid id)
        {
            if (id == default)
                throw new ArgumentException(
                    "Identity must be specified", nameof(id));
            Id = id;
        }

        private Guid _ownerId;
        private string _title;
        private string _text;
        private decimal _price;
    }
}
```

The following things are added here:

- Since we only set the Id property value in the constructor, we can make it a read-only property.
- When creating an instance of ClassifiedAd, we must supply id, because there is no parameterless constructor.
- The supplied id must be valid. Otherwise, the constructor will throw an argument exception.

Right here, we enforced the rule that our entity can only be created giving a valid set of arguments (currently only one), and any created entity of the given type will be, by definition, legitimate. You might be concerned that a classified ad without some human-readable attributes, like title and price, is in fact not correct, but this concern is not technical. The business might decide that this is indeed a valid entity.

Adding behavior

The next thing for us to do is to figure out what we can tell our entity to do. Remember, we need to design (and implement) behavior-first. The only reason for us to add those `private` fields to the entity was actually to support the behavior. As we discussed before, each action that is performed in the system amends the system state, and those `private` fields represent just that—state. But again, encapsulation being enforced, we shall not allow manipulating the entity state by changing property values from outside the entity; this will lead us to the dusty land of CRUD. Let's see how we can breathe life into the entity:

```
namespace Marketplace.Domain
{
    public class ClassifiedAd
    {
        public Guid Id { get; }

        public ClassifiedAd(Guid id)
        {
            if (id == default)
                throw new ArgumentException(
                  "Identity must be specified", nameof(id));

            Id = id;
        }

        public void SetTitle(string title) => _title = title;

        public void UpdateText(string text) => _text = text;

        public void UpdatePrice(decimal price) => _price = price;

        private Guid _ownerId;
        private string _title;
        private string _text;
        private decimal _price;
    }
}
```

We have added three straightforward methods, and you might feel a bit disappointed because these are property setters (not even glorified). But, what we do here is express the idea of using Ubiquitous Language in code, and transfer words from sticky notes (commands in this case) to methods.

Of course, this is just a start. In the following section, we will look deeper into our entity implementation, and find out how methods that express behavior can become more useful.

Ensuring correctness

In the previous section, we were checking the entity constructor parameter to be valid to ensure the newly created entity object is also correct. We applied a constraint, which does not allow creating a new entity without specifying the valid parameter value. By doing this, we are guarding our domain model against getting objects that aren't valid. It is one of the essential functions of the domain model as such, and since we are embracing *the behavior-first* approach, this type of code needs to be a part of the domain model implementation and not outsourced to external layers, like UI or application service layer. Of course, since our domain model is the system core, it takes a few hops for data to move from the user interface to domain objects. It is a valid approach to do a preliminary quality check on the data that tries to enter the domain model before it does. It improves the user experience due to much faster feedback. However, the ultimate control is always performed inside the domain model itself, since it shall never come to an invalid state.

Constraints for input values

You may have recognized some flaws in the entity implementation in the previous section. There are quite a few of them at the moment, but let's look at the most obvious one. What is sorely missing here is the owner ID. It is hard to believe we can allow having ads without anyone owning them. How in this case will we understand who can modify the content of such ads? Plus, we already have the _ownerId field in this class. So, let's add one more parameter to the constructor to enforce this constraint:

```
public ClassifiedAd(Guid id, Guid ownerId)
{
    if (id == default)
        throw new ArgumentException(
          "Identity must be specified", nameof(id));
    if (ownerId == default)
        throw new ArgumentException(
          "Owner id must be specified", nameof(ownerId));

    Id = id;
    _ownerId = ownerId;
}
```

 From this moment on, we will not list the whole class, but just a part of it that is being changed.

We have not only added one more parameter but also added one more check. So now, our entity is guaranteed to be valid after it is created, since the client must supply both the ad ID and the owner ID.

The code that creates a classified ad entity would look like the following:

```
public void CreateClassifiedAd(Guid id, Guid ownerId)
{
    var classifiedAd = new ClassifiedAd(id, ownerId);
    // store the entity somehow
}
```

Notice that we are adding more parameters to the entity constructor, and the constructor itself grows since we add more checks for these parameters. In the end, it is not very easy to understand what is going on, because many rules are mixed in one large chunk of code. Also, it is quite evident that we are not checking core complex rules, which involve multiple properties of the entity. In our case, all we control is that each parameter has a value. This approach is not wrong but is also not ideal. Instead, we can check the validity of such values, even before reaching the entity constructor, using **value objects**.

Value objects

Value object pattern is not unique to DDD, but it probably became most popular within the DDD community. It probably happened due to such characteristics of value objects as expressiveness and strong encapsulation. Fundamentally, value objects allow declaring entity properties with explicit types that use Ubiquitous Language. Besides, such objects can explicitly define how they can be created and what operations can be performed within and between them. It is a perfect example of making implicit, explicit.

Let's look closer at what a value object is, by creating one in our code. Before, we were taking the `ownerId` parameter in the entity constructor, and checking it to have a non-default GUID. What we want here is a user ID, since we know that the ad owner is one of our users, because people need to be registered in the system before creating classified ads. It means that we can embrace the type system and make implicit more explicit by using a new type called `UserId`, instead of using `Guid`.

Let's create a new class in the `Marketplace.Domain` project and call it `UserId`. The initial code for this class would look like the following:

```
using System;

namespace Marketplace.Domain
{
```

```
public class UserId
{
    private readonly Guid _value;

    public UserId(Guid value)
    {
        if (value == default)
            throw new ArgumentNullException(
                nameof(value), "User id cannot be empty");
        _value = value;
    }
}
```

As you can see, we moved the assertion that the identity value is not an empty GUID, to the `UserId` constructor. It means that we can change our entity constructor to the following:

```
public class ClassifiedAd
{
    public Guid Id { get; }
    private UserId _ownerId;

    public ClassifiedAd(Guid id, UserId ownerId)
    {
        if (id == default)
            throw new ArgumentException(
                "Identity must be specified", nameof(id));

        Id = id;
        _ownerId = ownerId;
    }
    // rest of the code skipped
}
```

Our entity has no check for the `ownerId`, since, by receiving the argument of type `UserId`, we guarantee that the value is valid. Of course, we do not check here if the supplied GUID points to a valid user, but this was not our intention, at least for now.

However, we still have one more check for the argument validity in the entity constructor. Let's make the entity `id` type a value object too by adding a `ClassifiedAdId` class with the following code:

```
using System;

namespace Marketplace.Domain
{
    public class ClassifiedAdId
```

```
    {
        private readonly Guid _value;

        public ClassifiedAdId(Guid value)
        {
            if (value == default)
                throw new ArgumentNullException(
                    nameof(value),
                    "Classified Ad id cannot be empty");
            _value = value;
        }
    }
}
```

Now our constructor has no checks at all, and it still makes a valid entity:

```
public class ClassifiedAd
{
    public ClassifiedAdId Id { get; }
    private UserId _ownerId;

    public ClassifiedAd(ClassifiedAdId id, UserId ownerId)
    {
        Id = id;
        _ownerId = ownerId;
    }
    // rest of the code skipped
}
```

As we move to the application layer, where our entity would be constructed, we could imagine that calls to the constructor would look like this (assuming that id and ownerId are of type Guid):

```
var classifiedAd = new ClassifiedAd(new ClassifiedAdId(id), new
UserId(ownerId));
```

The preceding code clearly says that we are sending the classified ad ID first, and the owner ID second to the entity constructor. When we use Guid as the type for both parameters, if we accidentally change the order of parameters, our application would still compile, but of course, our entities will be constructed incorrectly, and the whole system would break somewhere deep down the execution pipeline. Strongly typed parameters of value object types force the compiler to engage type checking, and if we messed up arguments, the code won't compile.

But value objects aren't just wrapper types around primitive types. As we learned before, entities are considered equal if their identities are the same. Value objects are different since their equality is establishing by value, hence the pattern name. A classical example of a value object is money. If we take two €5 banknotes, they represent two different entities, since they are in fact two distinctly different objects, and even have unique numbers printed on them. But for payment, both are entirely identical, since they have the same value of €5.

But how do we represent it in code? Let's create the `Money` class and give it a try:

```
namespace Marketplace.Domain
{
    public class Money
    {
        public decimal Amount { get; }

        public Money(decimal amount) Amount = amount;
    }
}
```

Now, let's write a simple test to check whether two objects of the `Money` type are equal if the amount is equal:

```
using Marketplace.Domain;
using Xunit;

namespace Marketplace.Tests
{
    public class MoneyTest
    {
        [Fact]
        public void
        Money_objects_with_the_same_amount_should_be_equal()
        {
            var firstAmount = new Money(5);
            var secondAmount = new Money(5);
            Assert.Equal(firstAmount, secondAmount);
        }
    }
}
```

Of course, this test fails because a class instance is a reference object, and two instances of the same class are different objects, no matter what their properties and fields contain. We can conclude that neither the `Money` class nor our `UserId` and `ClassifiedAdId` classes can represent value objects.

To make the `Money` class closer to proper value object type, we need it to implement the `IEquatable` interface. The class instance will need to be compared with instances of the same type, so we need `Money` to implement `IEquatable<Money>`. If you add this interface to the class, in Rider, and in Visual Studio with Resharper, there will be an option to generate the necessary code automatically using the **Generate equality to members** refactoring suggestion:

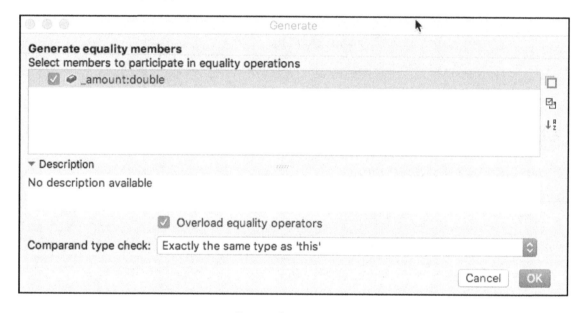

Generate equality members in Rider

Therefore, if the **Overload equality operators** option is enabled, code for implicit equality operators will also be created. So, the code for our Money class will look like the following:

```
using System;

namespace Marketplace.Domain
{
    public class Money : IEquatable<Money>
    {
        public decimal Amount { get; }

        public Money(decimal amount) => Amount = amount;

        public bool Equals(Money other)
        {
            if (ReferenceEquals(null, other)) return false;
            if (ReferenceEquals(this, other)) return true;
            return Amount.Equals(other.Amount);
        }

        public override bool Equals(object obj)
        {
            if (ReferenceEquals(null, obj)) return false;
            if (ReferenceEquals(this, obj)) return true;
            if (obj.GetType() != this.GetType()) return false;
            return Equals((Money) obj);
        }

        public override int GetHashCode() => Amount.GetHashCode();

        public static bool operator ==(Money left, Money right) =>
        Equals(left, right);

        public static bool operator !=(Money left, Money right) =>
        !Equals(left, right);
    }
}
```

If we run the same test now, it will pass, because, when we call Assert.Equals(firstAmount, secondAmount), the preceding code will compare the values of the _value field for both instances when these values are the same. Because we also created code for implicit equality operators, we can use comparisons like if (firstAmount == secondAmount) in our code.

Now, imagine we need all this code for each value object type we create. Yes, with some nice auto-magic from Resharper, we can generate this code very quickly, and then hide it in a region, which will always be collapsed. But, if we decide to add one more attribute to the value object, we will need to reopen this region and add this new attribute in several places.

We can reduce the amount of boilerplate code, and provide the ability for equality comparison methods to be dynamic, by using a base class. There are at least two ways to create such a base class. One includes using reflections to discover all fields in the implementation type, and use all of them for equality purposes. Another method involves creating an abstract method that needs to be overridden in each implementation to provide specific values that are used for equality. While the first method allows writing less code since all fields are automatically discovered and used, the second method allows us to choose which attributes will be used for equality.

In one of the next versions of C#, which might already be available when you read this book, the new feature will be introduced that is called **record types**. On a high level, record types will be similar to F# records. Using record types, declaration of value objects would become very short, and all boilerplate code for equality (and more) will be generated by the compiler.

For example, declaring the Money type earlier would be done in one line like this:

```
public class Money(double amount);
```

Throughout this book, I use classes, which are reference types, unlike structs, which are value types. It means that those value objects aren't completely following the immutability principle. We, however, will try to do as much as we can to ensure that these objects cannot be changed freely, but using the assignment operator for the object instance will only assign the reference to the original object, which is different for value types.

Using the abstract base class in the Marketplace.Framework project, we can now refactor the Money class to the following:

```
using Marketplace.Framework;

namespace Marketplace.Domain
{
    public class Money : Value<Money>
    {
```

```
        public decimal Amount { get; }

        public Money(decimal amount) => Amount = amount;
    }
}
```

As you can see, all the boilerplate code is now moved to the base class, and we get back to essentials. The test, however, still passes because of the proper equality implementation in the base class.

So far, we have only had straightforward rules in value objects, but when we work with money, we should be adding one useful check. Rarely, if we talk about money, we mean a negative amount. Yes, such amounts exist in accounting, but we are not building an accounting system. In our domain, classified ads need to have a price, and the price cannot be negative, as our domain expert explained. So, we can represent this rule in a new value object, shown in the following code:

```
using System;

namespace Marketplace.Domain
{
    public class Price : Money
    {
        public Price(decimal amount) : base(amount)
        {
            if (amount < 0)
                throw new ArgumentException(
                    "Price cannot be negative",
                    nameof(amount));
        }
    }
}
```

Thus, despite our base, Money class still allows its amount to be negative or zero; the price will always be positive and, as a result, valid in our domain.

Speaking about immutability, we must ensure that there are no methods that our value objects expose, which allow changing field values inside these objects. If we want to do some operation on a value object instance, it needs to produce a new instance of the same type, but with a new value. By doing this, we ensure that the original object will retain its value.

Let's look at the `Money` example and add some useful operations to it, keeping immutability in mind:

```
using Marketplace.Framework;

namespace Marketplace.Domain
{
    public class Money : Value<Money>
    {
        public decimal Amount { get; }

        public Money(decimal amount) => Amount = amount;
        public Money Add(Money summand) =>
            new Money(Amount + summand.Amount);
        public Money Subtract(Money subtrahend) =>
            new Money(Amount - subtrahend.Amount);
        public static Money operator +(
          Money summand1, Money summand2) => summand1.Add(summand2);

        public static Money operator -(
          Money minuend, Money subtrahend) =>
            minuend.Subtract(subtrahend);
    }
}
```

If we have a sum of €1 coin and two €2 coins, the total value is €5. If we compare it with a banknote of €5, its value is the same. Since we aren't interested in shape, size, and weight of those monetary instruments and we are only interested in value, we can conclude that those two have equal value. Our preceding new `Money` class lets us express this statement in the test code, which will be green when we run it.

```
[Fact]
public void Sum_of_money_gives_full_amount()
{
    var coin1 = new Money(1);
    var coin2 = new Money(2);
    var coin3 = new Money(2);
    var banknote = new Money(5);
    Assert.Equal(banknote, coin1 + coin2 + coin3);
}
```

Now, we can finally rewrite our identity classes to proper value object implementations:

```
public class ClassifiedAdId : Value<ClassifiedAdId>
{
    private readonly Guid _value;
    public ClassifiedAdId(Guid value) => _value = value;
```

```
    }

public class UserId : Value<UserId>
{
    private readonly Guid _value;
    public UserId(Guid value) => _value = value;
}
```

Now, let's have a more in-depth look at more advanced ways to instantiate value objects and entities.

Factories

Now, we can implement more value objects that will be used for other fields in our entity. Remember, we have three methods in the entity that expressed its basic behaviour—`SetTitle(string)`, `UpdateText(string)`, and `UpdatePrice(double)`. The easiest one to deal with would be the last one since we already have a value object type for it—`Price`. Let's focus on the other two methods and see what constraints we can implement using value objects instead of plain strings for ad title and text.

The complete value object class for the classified ad title could look like this:

```
using System;
using Marketplace.Framework;

namespace Marketplace.Domain
{
    public class ClassifiedAdTitle : Value<ClassifiedAdTitle>
    {
        public static ClassifiedAdTitle FromString(string title) =>
            new ClassifiedAdTitle(title);
        private readonly string _value;

        private ClassifiedAdTitle(string value)
        {
            if (value.Length > 100)
                throw new ArgumentOutOfRangeException(
                    "Title cannot be longer that 100 characters",
                    nameof(value));

            _value = value;
        }
    }
}
```

Let's go through it to understand how it works.

First, we use our abstract `Value<T>` base class to remove the boilerplate code, just as we did before in the identity and `price` value objects. Then, skipping the `static` method, you can see the `private` value field, again, like in other value objects we have created before. However, then we have a private constructor, which accepts a regular string argument. Inside the constructor, we enforce the constraint that the ad title cannot be longer than `100` characters. It will not allow us to spread such checks to other parts of the application. You might ask the question—why is the constructor `private` in this case? It is because we might have different sources of data for the title string, and, before calling the constructor, we might need to take some additional operations. It is not done in the preceding code snippet just yet, but we will add such functionality later. The next question would be—how do we construct new instances of this class if the constructor is `private`? It is where the **factory** pattern becomes useful.

Factories are functions that are used to create instances of domain objects, which are, by definition, valid. Factory functions can execute some logic to construct valid instances, and such logic could be different per factory. It is why we would expect to have multiple factory methods in one value object class, although this is not a requirement. Factories also help to make implicit things more explicit by using proper naming. In our `ClassifiedAdTitle` class, we only have one factory, which converts the string to the value object instance. It is quite clear what it does and what kind of argument it accepts.

Let's see how we can use factories to handle different use cases. Imagine that we get a requirement for ad title to support `Markdown` partially. In fact, we only need to support italic and bold. We do need to validate the existing factory argument since any string is a valid `Markdown` string anyway. But, if we can get input from some online editor that can only produce pure HTML, we can do a conversion in a new factory function:

```
public static ClassifiedAdTitle FromHtml(string htmlTitle)
{
    var supportedTagsReplaced = htmlTitle
        .Replace("<i>", "*")
        .Replace("</i>", "*")
        .Replace("<b>", "**")
        .Replace("</b>", "**");
    return new ClassifiedAdTitle(Regex.Replace(
        supportedTagsReplaced, "<.*?>", string.Empty));
}
```

I have to admit that this function is not perfect because it is insufficient in the number of tags it handles. It also cannot correctly handle HTML tags that are written using capital letters. But it is good enough for demo purposes to give you an idea of what kind of logic can be included in factory functions.

Now, let's move to the `Price` class and see if it can create some factories and apply more rules to it. Since `Price` inherits from `Amount`, we can look to make the `Amount` class more strict:

```
using System;
using Marketplace.Framework;

namespace Marketplace.Domain
{
    public class Money : Value<Money>
    {
        public static Money FromDecimal(decimal amount) =>
            new Money(amount);
        public static Money FromString(string amount) =>
            new Money(decimal.Parse(amount));
        protected Money(decimal amount)
        {
            if (decimal.Round(amount, 2) != amount)
                throw new ArgumentOutOfRangeException(
                    nameof(amount),
                    "Amount cannot have more than two decimals");
            Amount = amount;
        }

        public decimal Amount { get; }

        // Public methods go here as before
    }
}
```

As you can see here, `Money` class now has a `protected` constructor, which cannot be called from outside, except inherited classes like `Price`. The constructor now checks if the amount argument has more than two decimal points, and throws an exception if this is the case. Finally, we have two factory functions that create instances of `Money` from decimal or string arguments. Most probably, we will receive strings from the API so we can try parsing them inside the factory. It will, of course, throw the decimal parsing exception should the given string not represent a valid number.

We are checking if an amount of money has two decimal places, and usually, this is what we need to do. However, bear in mind that not all currencies support two decimals. For example, the Japanese Yen must have no decimals at all. Amounts in Yen are always round. You'd probably be surprised to know that Omani Rial supports three decimal places, so if you plan to deliver your application in Oman, you should not use the Money class from this book, or at least change the rules.

Always check if rules that you apply are valid on all markets that you plan to support. Things like currencies, date and time formats, people names, bank accounts, and addresses can have surprisingly large varieties across the globe, and it is always worth checking if you are applying rules that make sense.

Now, let's imagine that our application needs to support different currencies. I mean that currency information would also need to be included in this value object. After adding it, we get code like this:

```
using System;
using Marketplace.Framework;

namespace Marketplace.Domain
{
    public class Money : Value<Money>
    {
        private const string DefaultCurrency = "EUR";

        public static Money FromDecimal(
          decimal amount, string currency = DefaultCurrency) =>
            new Money(amount, currency);

        public static Money FromString(
          string amount, string currency = DefaultCurrency) =>
            new Money(decimal.Parse(amount), currency);

        protected Money(decimal amount, string currencyCode = "EUR")
        {
            if (decimal.Round(amount, 2) != amount)
                throw new ArgumentOutOfRangeException(
                    nameof(amount),
                    "Amount cannot have more than two decimals");

            Amount = amount;
            CurrencyCode = currencyCode;
        }
```

```
public decimal Amount { get; }
public string CurrencyCode { get; }

public Money Add(Money summand)
{
    if (CurrencyCode != summand.CurrencyCode)
        throw new CurrencyMismatchException(
            "Cannot sum amounts with different currencies");

    return new Money(Amount + summand.Amount);
}

public Money Subtract(Money subtrahend)
{
    if (CurrencyCode != subtrahend.CurrencyCode)
        throw new CurrencyMismatchException(
            "Cannot subtract amounts with different currencies");

    return new Money(Amount - subtrahend.Amount);
}

public static Money operator +(
    Money summand1, Money summand2) =>
        summand1.Add(summand2);

public static Money operator -(
    Money minuend, Money subtrahend) =>
        minuend.Subtract(subtrahend);
}

public class CurrencyMismatchException : Exception
{
    public CurrencyMismatchException(string message) :
        base(message)
    {
    }
}
}
```

First, we passed currency information to the constructor and both factory methods. By default, factories will use EUR if no currency is specified. We also keep currency information inside the class. Second, Add and Subtract methods started to check if both operands have the same currency. In case currencies of operands don't match, these methods throw an exception.

We also added a domain-specific exception that explicitly tells us that operations on two instances of Money cannot be completed because they have different currencies.

Imagine how many bugs such simple technique can prevent in a multicurrency system, where developers too often forget that monetary value for the same decimal amount can be drastically different, depending on which currency this amount of money is issued? For example, one US Dollar is roughly equal to 110 Japanese Yen and adding 1 to 110, in this case, won't give you the right result.

One thing that remains uncovered with our Money object is that we can supply any string as currency code and it will be accepted. As you might imagine we can have this failure very easily:

```
var firstAmount = Money.FromDecimal(10, "USD");
var secondAmount = Money.FromDecimal(20, "Usd");
var thirdAmount = Money.FromDecimal(30, "$");
```

Looking at the Money class code, we can quickly conclude that no operations can be performed on combinations of these objects. firstAmount + secondAmount will crash because our class will decide that they have different currencies. The thirdAmount is utterly invalid because the Dollar sign is not a valid currency code, but our class still accepts it. Let's see what can we do to fix it.

To be able to check the currency code validity, we either need to keep all valid country codes inside the code of our value object class or use some external service to do the check. The first option is self-contained, so we will not have any dependencies for the value object class. However, by doing this, we will inject a somewhat alien concept to the value object code, which we will need to change each time something happens in the world of finances. One might argue that new currencies do not appear every day, but at the same time, Eurozone has been expanded during the last few years, and each time a new country starts using Euro, their old currency disappears, and this needs to be taken into account. These factors are utterly external to our system, and it would not be smart to create such an easy-to-forget time bomb in our code.

Domain services

We can go for a dependency on some external service, but we know that domain models should not have external dependencies, so how do we solve this issue? We can use a pattern called **domain service**. In DDD, domain services can perform different kinds of tasks, and here, we will look into one type of them.

Our domain service needs to check if a given country code is valid. The `Money` class will get it as a dependency, so we need to declare the domain service inside our domain model. Because we do not want to depend on anything on the outside of our domain model, we should not put any implementation details inside the domain model. It means that the only thing we are going to have inside the domain project is the domain service interface, shown in the following code:

```
namespace Marketplace.Domain
{
    public interface ICurrencyLookup
    {
        CurrencyDetails FindCurrency(string currencyCode);
    }

    public class CurrencyDetails : Value<CurrencyDetails>
    {
        public string CurrencyCode { get; set; }
        public bool InUse { get; set; }
        public int DecimalPlaces { get; set; }

        public static CurrencyDetails None = new CurrencyDetails {
            InUse = false};
    }
}
```

The new interface will not just check if a given currency code can be matched with some currency. Since we already discussed that different currencies might have a different number of decimal places, the service will return an instance of `CurrencyDetails` class with this information included. If there is no currency found for the given code, the service will return `CurrencyDetails.None` constant.

It is very common in C#, that if a function is expected to return an instance of a reference type, it also can return null to indicate that there is no valid result that the function can produce. Although, at first, this approach might seem easy, it creates massive problems. Our code becomes full of null checks because we suspect that every function can return null, so we must trust no one to avoid `NullReferenceException`. Null has a specific null-type, and it is too easy to assign null to something that should never be null.

Sir Charles Antony Richard Hoare, better known as Tony Hoare, introduced null references to the Algol programming language back in 1965. He remembers doing this **because it was so easy to implement**. Much later, at the QCon conference in London in 2009, he apologized for null reference saying *I call it my billion dollar mistake*.

Video: `https://www.infoq.com/presentations/Null-References-The-Billion-Dollar-Mistake-Tony-Hoare`.

In most functional languages, the null reference does not exist, because it can easily break the functional composition. Instead, optional types are being used. In the preceding code snippet, we use a similar technique to return a pre-defined value that indicates that there is no currency found for a given code. This constant has the proper type and proper name, and we should never check the function output for null.

To mitigate the null reference issue, Microsoft decided to allow explicit declaration of nullable reference types. By default, reference types will be assumed as non-nullable. This feature will remain until the next version of C#, and you can get more details about the proposal here: `https://github.com/dotnet/csharplang/blob/master/proposals/nullable-reference-types.md`.

When the interface is there, we can change our value object like to look like the following:

```
using System;
using Marketplace.Framework;

namespace Marketplace.Domain
{
    public class Money : Value<Money>
    {
        public static string DefaultCurrency = "EUR";
        public static Money FromDecimal(
          decimal amount, string currency,
            ICurrencyLookup currencyLookup) =>
            new Money(amount, currency, currencyLookup);

        public static Money FromString(string amount, string currency,
            ICurrencyLookup currencyLookup) =>
            new Money(decimal.Parse(amount), currency, currencyLookup);

        protected Money(decimal amount, string currencyCode,
          ICurrencyLookup currencyLookup)
        {
            if (string.IsNullOrEmpty(currencyCode))
```

```csharp
                throw new ArgumentNullException(
                    nameof(currencyCode),
                    "Currency code must be specified");
        var currency = currencyLookup.FindCurrency(currencyCode);
        if (!currency.InUse)
            throw new ArgumentException(
                $"Currency {currencyCode} is not valid");
        if (decimal.Round(
            amount, currency.DecimalPlaces) != amount)
            throw new ArgumentOutOfRangeException(
                nameof(amount),
                $"Amount in {
                 currencyCode} cannot have more than {
                    currency.DecimalPlaces} decimals");

        Amount = amount;
        Currency = currency;
    }

    private Money(decimal amount, CurrencyDetails currency)
    {
        Amount = amount;
        Currency = currency;
    }

    public decimal Amount { get; }
    public CurrencyDetails Currency { get; }

    public Money Add(Money summand)
    {
        if (Currency != summand.Currency)
            throw new CurrencyMismatchException(
                "Cannot sum amounts with different currencies");

        return new Money(Amount + summand.Amount, Currency);
    }

    public Money Subtract(Money subtrahend)
    {
        if (Currency != subtrahend.Currency)
            throw new CurrencyMismatchException(
                "Cannot subtract amounts with different currencies");

        return new Money(Amount - subtrahend.Amount, Currency);
    }

    public static Money operator +(Money summand1, Money summand2)
        => summand1.Add(summand2);
```

```
        public static Money operator -(Money minuend, Money subtrahend)
            => minuend.Subtract(subtrahend);

        public override string ToString() => $"{
            Currency.CurrencyCode} {Amount}";
    }

    public class CurrencyMismatchException : Exception
    {
        public CurrencyMismatchException(string message) :
            base(message)
        {
        }
    }
}
```

There are a couple of new things going on here, listed as follows:

- We give the value object a dependency on the currency lookup domain service. Since we are using the interface, our domain model still has no external dependencies.
- Since we are not using the null reference to indicate that there is no currency found for the specified code, we do not use null checks. Instead, we check if the returned currency is valid or not. Since the CurrencyDetails.NotFound constant has its InUse property set to false, we will throw an exception just as we would do for any currency that exists, but is not in use.
- We do not use two as the maximum number of decimal places. Instead, we get this number from the currency lookup, so our value object becomes more flexible.
- For our public methods, we need a simplified constructor, since these methods control that both operands have the same (valid) currency. Because we only trust our internals to use this constructor, it needs to be private. Both Add and Subtract methods use this constructor.
- Added ToString override to be able to see the human-readable value of the value object, for example, in test results.

Our Money value object is still very much testable since we can supply a fake currency lookup:

```
using System.Collections.Generic;
using System.Linq;
using Marketplace.Domain;

namespace Marketplace.Tests
```

```
{
    public class FakeCurrencyLookup : ICurrencyLookup
    {
        private static readonly IEnumerable<CurrencyDetails>
        _currencies =
            new[]
            {
                new CurrencyDetails
                {
                    CurrencyCode = "EUR",
                    DecimalPlaces = 2,
                    InUse = true
                },
                new CurrencyDetails
                {
                    CurrencyCode = "USD",
                    DecimalPlaces = 2,
                    InUse = true
                },
                new CurrencyDetails
                {
                    CurrencyCode = "JPY",
                    DecimalPlaces = 0,
                    InUse = true
                },
                new CurrencyDetails
                {
                    CurrencyCode = "DEM",
                    DecimalPlaces = 2,
                    InUse = false
                }
            };

        public CurrencyDetails FindCurrency(string currencyCode)
        {
            var currency = _currencies.FirstOrDefault(x =>
              x.CurrencyCode == currencyCode);
            return currency ?? CurrencyDetails.None;
        }
    }
}
```

With this implementation in place, we can refactor the tests for Money as follows:

```
using System;
using Marketplace.Domain;
using Xunit;
```

```
namespace Marketplace.Tests
{
    public class Money_Spec
    {
        private static readonly ICurrencyLookup CurrencyLookup =
            new FakeCurrencyLookup();
        [Fact]
        public void Two_of_same_amount_should_be_equal()
        {
            var firstAmount = Money.FromDecimal(5, "EUR",
            CurrencyLookup);
            var secondAmount = Money.FromDecimal(5, "EUR",
            CurrencyLookup);

            Assert.Equal(firstAmount, secondAmount);
        }
        [Fact]
        public void Two_of_same_amount_but_differentCurrencies
        should_not_be_equal()
        {
            var firstAmount = Money.FromDecimal(5, "EUR",
            CurrencyLookup);
            var secondAmount = Money.FromDecimal(5, "USD",
            CurrencyLookup);

            Assert.NotEqual(firstAmount, secondAmount);
        }


        [Fact]
        public void FromString_and_FromDecimal_should_be_equal()
        {
            var firstAmount = Money.FromDecimal(5, "EUR",
            CurrencyLookup);
            var secondAmount = Money.FromString("5.00", "EUR",
            CurrencyLookup);

            Assert.Equal(firstAmount, secondAmount);
        }

        [Fact]
        public void Sum_of_money_gives_full_amount()
        {
            var coin1 = Money.FromDecimal(1, "EUR", CurrencyLookup);
            var coin2 = Money.FromDecimal(2, "EUR", CurrencyLookup);
            var coin3 = Money.FromDecimal(2, "EUR", CurrencyLookup);
            var banknote = Money.FromDecimal(5, "EUR", CurrencyLookup);
            Assert.Equal(banknote, coin1 + coin2 + coin3);
```

```
}

[Fact]
public void Unused_currency_should_not_be_allowed()
{
    Assert.Throws<ArgumentException>(() =>
        Money.FromDecimal(100, "DEM", CurrencyLookup)
    );
}

[Fact]
public void Unknown_currency_should_not_be_allowed()
{
    Assert.Throws<ArgumentException>(() =>
        Money.FromDecimal(100, "WHAT?", CurrencyLookup)
    );
}

[Fact]
public void Throw_when_too_many_decimal_places()
{
    Assert.Throws<ArgumentOutOfRangeException>(() =>
        Money.FromDecimal(100.123m, "EUR", CurrencyLookup)
    );
}

[Fact]
public void Throws_on_adding_different_currencies()
{
    var firstAmount = Money.FromDecimal(5, "USD",
    CurrencyLookup);
    var secondAmount = Money.FromDecimal(5, "EUR",
    CurrencyLookup);

    Assert.Throws<CurrencyMismatchException>(() =>
        firstAmount + secondAmount
    );
}
[Fact]
public void Throws_on_substracting_different_currencies()
{
    var firstAmount = Money.FromDecimal(5, "USD",
    CurrencyLookup);
    var secondAmount = Money.FromDecimal(5, "EUR",
    CurrencyLookup);

    Assert.Throws<CurrencyMismatchException>(() =>
        firstAmount - secondAmount
```

```
            );
        }
    }
}
```

You can see here that we are testing some positive and some adverse scenarios to ensure those valid operations are correctly completed, and also, those invalid operations aren't allowed to be executed.

Entity invariants

We have gone through using value objects to protect invalid values from being even used as parameters for entity constructors and methods. This technique allows moving a lot of checks to value objects, provides nice encapsulation, and enables type safety. Then, when we create a new entity or execute some behavior using entity methods, we need to do some more checks. Since we can be quite sure that all parameters already contain valid individual values, we need to ensure that a given combination of parameters, current entity state, and execute behavior, is not going to bring the entity to some invalid state.

Let's look at what complex rules we have for our classified ad entity. To find such rules, we can use some sticky notes from our detailed EventStorming session in Chapter 3, *EventStorming*, and put them on a chart like this:

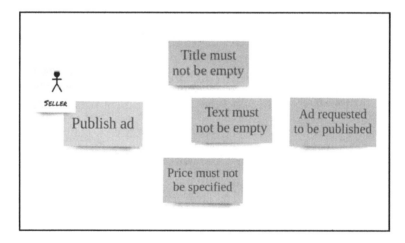

Analyzing constraints for a command

We put the command to the left side, the event to the right side, and try to find out what could prevent our command being executed in a way that produces the desired outcome (the event). In our case here, we need to ensure that, before an ad can be put to the review queue, it must have a non-empty title, text, and price. By using value objects alone, we cannot guarantee that our entity state is correct as a whole. The entity state validity can change depending on what state the entity has at a particular moment of its life cycle. Only when a given command is being executed, we need to check if these constraints are satisfied. It is what we can call an invariant for this entity—an ad that is in a pending review cannot have an empty title, an empty text, or zero price.

There are at least two ways to ensure that our entity never gets to an invalid state. The first and most obvious way is to add checks to the operation code. We have no method to request the ad to be published, so let's add it and make some changes related to the fact of using value objects for entity state as well:

```
namespace Marketplace.Domain
{
    public class ClassifiedAd
    {
        public ClassifiedAdId Id { get; }

        public ClassifiedAd(ClassifiedAdId id, UserId ownerId)
        {
            Id = id;
            OwnerId = ownerId;
            State = ClassifiedAdState.Inactive;
        }

        public void SetTitle(ClassifiedAdTitle title) => Title = title;

        public void UpdateText(ClassifiedAdText text) => Text = text;

        public void UpdatePrice(Price price) => Price = price;

        public void RequestToPublish()
        {
            if (Title == null)
                throw new InvalidEntityStateException(this, "title
                cannot be empty");
            if (Text == null)
                throw new InvalidEntityStateException(this, "text
                cannot be empty");
            if (Price?.Amount == 0)
                throw new InvalidEntityStateException(this, "price
                cannot be zero");
```

```
                State = ClassifiedAdState.PendingReview;
        }

        public UserId OwnerId { get; }
        public ClassifiedAdTitle Title { get; private set; }
        public ClassifiedAdText Text { get; private set; }
        public Price Price { get; private set; }
        public ClassifiedAdState State { get; private set; }
        public UserId ApprovedBy { get; private set; }

        public enum ClassifiedAdState
        {
            PendingReview,
            Active,
            Inactive,
            MarkedAsSold
        }
    }
}
```

In the new entity code, we have all properties to be typed as value objects, and we got one more property for the classified ad current state. In the beginning, it is set to `Inactive`, and when the ad is requested to be published, we change the state to `PendingReview`. However, we only do it when all the checks are satisfied.

To let the caller know if our entity is not ready to be published when some of those checks fail, we use our custom exception, which is implemented like this:

```
using System;

namespace Marketplace.Domain
{
    public class InvalidEntityStateException : Exception
    {
        public InvalidEntityStateException(object entity, string
        message)
            : base($"Entity {entity.GetType().Name} state change
            rejected, {message}")
        {
        }
    }
}
```

This method of checking constraints before executing the operation, in the operation method itself, has one disadvantage. If we now change the price to zero, it will go through, because `UpdatePrice` method is not checking the price value.

We could, of course, copy the price check to the `UpdatePrice` method too, but there might be more methods that need the same tests, and we will keep copying control blocks. It will lead to a situation when, if we need to change any of those rules, we need to go to numerous places to replace all of the checks; this is very error-prone.

To combine rules in one place, we can use techniques of contract programming. Part of contract programming can be seen in value objects since we evaluate pre-conditions for each parameter of the operation method. When we execute the operation without doing any additional checks, we will need to do a combined test (post-condition control). This check can be implemented in one place for the whole entity, and each operation will need to call it at the last line in the method.

For our classified ad entity, it could look like this:

```
namespace Marketplace.Domain
{
    public class ClassifiedAd
    {
        public ClassifiedAdId Id { get; }

        public ClassifiedAd(ClassifiedAdId id, UserId ownerId)
        {
            Id = id;
            OwnerId = ownerId;
            State = ClassifiedAdState.Inactive;
            EnsureValidState();
        }

        public void SetTitle(ClassifiedAdTitle title)
        {
            Title = title;
            EnsureValidState();
        }

        public void UpdateText(ClassifiedAdText text)
        {
            Text = text;
            EnsureValidState();
        }

        public void UpdatePrice(Price price)
        {
            Price = price;
            EnsureValidState();
        }

        public void RequestToPublish()
```

```
        {
            State = ClassifiedAdState.PendingReview;
            EnsureValidState();
        }

        protected override void EnsureValidState()
        {
            var valid =
                Id != null &&
                OwnerId != null &&
                (State switch
                {
                    ClassifiedAdState.PendingReview =>
                        Title != null
                        && Text != null
                        && Price?.Amount > 0,
                    ClassifiedAdState.Active =>
                        Title != null
                        && Text != null
                        && Price?.Amount > 0
                        && ApprovedBy != null,
                    _ => true
                });

            if (!valid)
                throw new InvalidEntityStateException(
                    this, $"Post-checks failed in state {State}");
        }

        public UserId OwnerId { get; }
        public ClassifiedAdTitle Title { get; private set; }
        public ClassifiedAdText Text { get; private set; }
        public Price Price1 { get; private set; }
        public ClassifiedAdState State { get; private set; }
        public UserId ApprovedBy { get; private set; }

        public enum ClassifiedAdState
        {
            PendingReview,
            Active,
            Inactive,
            MarkedAsSold
        }
    }
}
```

As you can see, we have added one method called `EnsureValidState` checking that, in any situation, the entity state is valid, and, if it is not valid, an exception will be thrown. When we call this method from any operation method, we can be sure that, no matter what we are trying to do, our entity will always be in a valid state or the caller will get an exception.

Also, we converted all `private` fields to public read-only properties. We need public properties to write tests, although we don't necessarily need to expose the internal entity state. To prevent setting values of these properties outside of operation methods, all properties have private setters, or no setters, for properties that are set in the constructor.

Now, let's write some tests to ensure that our constraints work:

```
using System;
using Marketplace.Domain;
using Xunit;

namespace Marketplace.Tests
{
    public class ClassifiedAd_Publish_Spec
    {
        private readonly ClassifiedAd _classifiedAd;
        public ClassifiedAd_Publish_Spec()
        {
            _classifiedAd = new ClassifiedAd(
                new ClassifiedAdId(Guid.NewGuid()),
                new UserId(Guid.NewGuid()));
        }

        [Fact]
        public void Can_publish_a_valid_ad()
        {
            _classifiedAd.SetTitle(
                ClassifiedAdTitle.FromString("Test ad"));
            _classifiedAd.UpdateText(
                ClassifiedAdText.FromString("Please buy my stuff"));
            _classifiedAd.UpdatePrice(
                Price.FromDecimal(100.10m, "EUR",
                new FakeCurrencyLookup()));
            _classifiedAd.RequestToPublish();

            Assert.Equal(ClassifiedAd.ClassifiedAdState.PendingReview,
                _classifiedAd.State);
        }

        [Fact]
        public void Cannot_publish_without_title()
```

```
{
    _classifiedAd.UpdateText(
        ClassifiedAdText.FromString("Please buy my stuff"));
    _classifiedAd.UpdatePrice(
        Price.FromDecimal(100.10m, "EUR",
            new FakeCurrencyLookup()));
    Assert.Throws<InvalidEntityStateException>(() =>
    _classifiedAd.RequestToPublish());
}

[Fact]
public void Cannot_publish_without_text()
{
    _classifiedAd.SetTitle(
        ClassifiedAdTitle.FromString("Test ad"));
    _classifiedAd.UpdatePrice(
        Price.FromDecimal(100.10m, "EUR",
            new FakeCurrencyLookup()));
    Assert.Throws<InvalidEntityStateException>(
        () => _classifiedAd.RequestToPublish());
}

[Fact]
public void Cannot_publish_without_price()
{
    _classifiedAd.SetTitle(
        ClassifiedAdTitle.FromString("Test ad"));
    _classifiedAd.UpdateText(
        ClassifiedAdText.FromString("Please buy my stuff"));
    Assert.Throws<InvalidEntityStateException>(
        () => _classifiedAd.RequestToPublish());
}

[Fact]
public void Cannot_publish_with_zero_price()
{
    _classifiedAd.SetTitle(
        ClassifiedAdTitle.FromString("Test ad"));
    _classifiedAd.UpdateText(
        ClassifiedAdText.FromString("Please buy my stuff"));
    _classifiedAd.UpdatePrice(
        Price.FromDecimal(0.0m, "EUR",
            new FakeCurrencyLookup()));
    Assert.Throws<InvalidEntityStateException>(
        () => _classifiedAd.RequestToPublish());
}
    }
}
```

This spec contains several tests for one operation (publish, or submit for review) with different pre-conditions. Here, we test a happy path when all necessary details are correctly set before the ad can be sent for review; we also test several negative cases when publishing is not allowed, due to missing mandatory information. Perhaps testing negative scenarios is even more essential, since it is straightforward to find out when the happy path does not work—your users will immediately complain. Testing negative scenarios prevents bugs in controlling entity invariants, which, in turn, prevents entities from becoming invalid.

By now, you might be wondering why we spent so much time talking about domain events and have not seen a single one in code? We will be discussing this in the next section.

Domain events in code

EventStorming allowed us to make useful domain discoveries. We gained some knowledge about the domain and managed to visualize it for shared understanding. Commands also appeared on the more detailed model. In this chapter, we learned how to create entities that protect themselves from executing invalid operations and never come to an invalid state. Operations on entities are performed by executing methods, which quite closely resemble commands that we discovered on our detailed model. So, this part is more or less clear, but events have never appeared in our code so far.

In fact, you can implement a system using DDD principles and patterns without having any domain events. It might sound strange after spending so much time working with them using sticky notes, but this is a fact. When we execute an entity method, it changes the entity state. This state change is an implicit event. For example, when our system executes the `RequestToPublish` method of the `ClassifiedAd` entity, it will set the entity `State` property to `ClassifiedAdState.PendingReview` value. Effectively, this can be translated to **classified ad sent to review**, and this is what we wrote on an orange sticky a while ago.

However, most of the time, making domain events first-class citizens in the domain model has excellent benefits. There are two primary use cases for domain events that are implemented explicitly as part of the domain model, listed as follows:

- Allowing one part of the system to inform other parts of the system about its state changes, using Ubiquitous Language, and state change details: we already discussed the idea of splitting the system into multiple pieces, and those pieces need to play well together by listening to each others' events and executing necessary operations. If a system is built in such a way that different parts of the system react to each others' changes, such a system is called a **reactive system**.
- Persisting domain events to get a full history of state changes inside the domain model: then, the state for any entity can be reconstructed by reading those events and reapplying them to the entity. This pattern is known as **Event Sourcing**, and we will spend a great deal of time discussing it in this book, especially in `Chapter 10`, *Event Sourcing*.

These two techniques can be combined, so when we persist domain events, we can also listen to everything that is being written in other parts of the system, and execute reactions to those events.

In this chapter, we will be looking at how we can bring domain events to code, and how our entity methods can raise them so we can use these events later.

Domain events as objects

Bringing domain events to code is easy. Each event is an object. It means that we can represent event types as classes or structs. Since we will need to serialize events later, and structs aren't playing nicely with serializers, we will implement domain events as classes.

We have the following basic operations on our `ClassifiedAd` entity:

- Create a new classified ad
- Set the ad title
- Update text
- Update price
- Publish the ad (send for review)

Each of those operations changes the state of our entity, and by doing this, raises an imaginary domain event. We have all those events on our sticky notes, shown as follows:

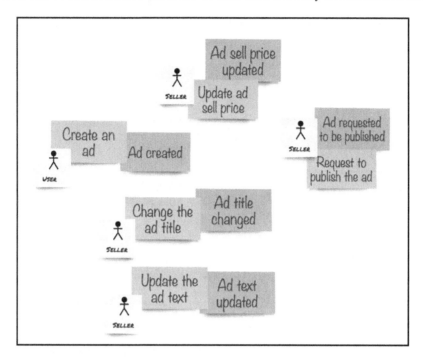

The full picture for the core business domain

Classes that represent events need to clearly describe events (what happened) and contain the necessary information that explains how the system state has changed. Usually, events are reactions to executions of commands. Therefore, data in events typically represent data in commands, and maybe some other details from the entity from which the event has been raised.

Let's create some domain event classes now. Bear in mind that this is our first ever implementation of domain events, and if you were reading about things like Event Sourcing, you might find it oversimplified, but this is intentional:

```
using System;

namespace Marketplace.Domain
{
    public static class Events
    {
        public class ClassifiedAdCreated
        {
```

```
            public Guid Id { get; set; }
            public Guid OwnerId { get; set; }
        }

        public class ClassifiedAdTitleChanged
        {
            public Guid Id { get; set; }
            public string Title { get; set; }
        }

        public class ClassifiedAdTextUpdated
        {
            public Guid Id { get; set; }
            public string AdText { get; set; }
        }

        public class ClassifiedAdPriceUpdated
        {
            public Guid Id { get; set; }
            public decimal Price { get; set; }
            public string CurrencyCode { get; set; }
        }

        public class ClassifiedAdSentForReview
        {
            public Guid Id { get; set; }
        }
    }
}
```

Event classes are wrapped inside the `Events` static class, which gives us some namespace.. Therefore, all properties in these classes are of primitive types. We do not use value objects in events. It is a significant thing to remember. The reason for only using primitive types in events is because domain events, as mentioned before, are often used *across* systems. Events can be seen as our system published contract. If we use Event Sourcing, and events are being persisted, we also cannot tolerate a situation where the rules in some value objects have changed. Furthermore, we cannot load our event anymore, because the data for the value object is now considered to be invalid. Of course, not using value objects in events mean that some more complex value objects need to be flattered. In our case, we extract values from the `Price` property to two properties of the `ClassifiedAdPriceUpdated`: `Price`, which represents the amount, and `CurrencyCode`.

You can see that each event has the `Id` property because it makes no sense to raise an event without knowing which entity it comes from. So, each operation needs to take care that the entity `id` is populated in the events that it raises.

Again, the most critical thing about domain events is to represent things that happened, and these things cannot be changed, because we have no time machine or TARDIS to erase or fix the past. Therefore, events should be as simple as possible so we can always load past events, and this should never fail.

Raising events

Now, let's see how domain events are being used in our entity. First, we need to raise events from our methods. To do this, we need some event list inside the entity so we can keep events that are being created. Otherwise, there is little point in creating event instances in the first place.

Since we expect this functionality of keeping events in some sort of a list inside the entity, we can move this to a base class for entities, which we didn't have before.

Let's create an abstract class and call it Entity:

```
using System.Collections.Generic;
using System.Linq;

namespace Marketplace.Framework
{
    public abstract class Entity
    {
        private readonly List<object> _events;

        protected Entity() => _events = new List<object>();

        protected void Raise(object @event) => _events.Add(@event);

        public IEnumerable<object> GetChanges() =>
        _events.AsEnumerable();

        public void ClearChanges() => _events.Clear();
    }
}
```

Since raised events will represent changes in the entity, methods that retrieve the list of events and clear this list are called GetChanges and ClearChanges.

The next step is to add this base class to our entity and start raising events from methods:

```
using Marketplace.Framework;

namespace Marketplace.Domain
```

```
{
    public class ClassifiedAd : Entity
    {
        public ClassifiedAdId Id { get; }

        public ClassifiedAd(ClassifiedAdId id, UserId ownerId)
        {
            Id = id;
            OwnerId = ownerId;
            State = ClassifiedAdState.Inactive;
            EnsureValidState();
            Raise(new Events.ClassifiedAdCreated
            {
                Id = id,
                OwnerId = ownerId
            });
        }

        public void SetTitle(ClassifiedAdTitle title)
        {
            Title = title;
            EnsureValidState();
            Raise(new Events.ClassifiedAdTitleChanged
            {
                Id = Id,
                Title = title
            });
        }

        public void UpdateText(ClassifiedAdText text)
        {
            Text = text;
            EnsureValidState();
            Raise(new Events.ClassifiedAdTextUpdated
            {
                Id = Id,
                AdText = text
            });
        }

        public void UpdatePrice(Price price)
        {
            Price = price;
            EnsureValidState();
            Raise(new Events.ClassifiedAdPriceUpdated
            {
                Id = Id,
                Price = Price.Amount,
```

```
                      CurrencyCode = Price.Currency.CurrencyCode
            });
        }

        public void RequestToPublish()
        {
            State = ClassifiedAdState.PendingReview;
            EnsureValidState();
            Raise(new Events.ClassidiedAdSentForReview{Id = Id});
        }

        // Rest of the entity code remains the same
    }
}
```

So now, if we imagine how our entity is used from the application service layer (which we will be discussing in detail later in this book), it could look like this:

```
public async Task Handle(RequestToPublish command)
{
    var entity = await _repository.Load<ClassifiedAd>(command.Id);
    entity.RequestToPublish();
    await _repository.Save(entity);

    foreach (var @event in entity.GetChanges())
    {
        await _bus.Publish(@event);
    }
}
```

This code is not production ready, as you could imagine, but serves the purpose of demonstrating how domain events can be used for integration between different parts of the system. If we publish events to some message bus, and other components in our system subscribe to those messages, they can execute reactive behavior, and make some changes in their domain models, or execute some particular actions, like sending emails, text messages, or real-time notifications. With modern single-page application frameworks that embrace client-side state management, you can even update information that your users currently have in their browsers, to enable real-time updates in web applications as well.

It is worth adding one small remark about the code that instantiates events. There we assign values of value objects to primitive types directly. It is done using the implicit conversion feature of C#, and the implementation looks like this:

```
using System;

namespace Marketplace.Domain
{
```

```
public class ClassifiedAdId
{
    private readonly Guid _value;

    public ClassifiedAdId(Guid value)
    {
        if (value == default)
            throw new ArgumentNullException(nameof(value),
                "Classified Ad id cannot be empty");
        _value = value;
    }

    public static implicit operator Guid(ClassifiedAdId self) =>
    self._value;
}
}
```

Implicit conversion allows us to simplify the assignments between entity properties and event properties significantly, although they are of incompatible types.

Events change state

If we move on to the idea of Event Sourcing, events represent the fact of state change. It means that an entity state cannot be changed without some interaction with a domain event. However, in our code so far, the fact of changing the system state and raising a domain event is completely separated. Let's see how we can change it.

First, we need to make some changes in the `Entity` base class:

```
using System.Collections.Generic;
using System.Linq;

namespace Marketplace.Framework
{
    public abstract class Entity
    {
        private readonly List<object> _events;

        protected Entity() => _events = new List<object>();

        protected void Apply(object @event)
        {
            When(@event);
            EnsureValidState();
            _events.Add(@event);
        }
```

```
protected abstract void When(object @event);

public IEnumerable<object> GetChanges()
    => _events.AsEnumerable();

public void ClearChanges() => _events.Clear();

protected abstract void EnsureValidState();
    }
}
```

We have renamed the `Raise` method to `Apply` since it will not only add events to the list of changes but physically apply the content of each event to the entity state. We do it by using the `When` method, which each entity needs to implement. The `Apply` method also calls the `EnsureValidState` method, which we previously had in the entity, but not in the base class. By doing this, we remove the need to call this method for each operation on the entity.

The next step would be to apply domain events and move all state changes to the `When` method:

```
using Marketplace.Framework;

namespace Marketplace.Domain
{
    public class ClassifiedAd : Entity
    {
        public ClassifiedAdId Id { get; private set; }
        public UserId OwnerId { get; private set; }
        public ClassifiedAdTitle Title { get; private set; }
        public ClassifiedAdText Text { get; private set; }
        public Price Price { get; private set; }
        public ClassifiedAdState State { get; private set; }
        public UserId ApprovedBy { get; private set; }

        public ClassifiedAd(ClassifiedAdId id, UserId ownerId) =>
            Apply(new Events.ClassifiedAdCreated
            {
                Id = id,
                OwnerId = ownerId
            });

        public void SetTitle(ClassifiedAdTitle title) =>
            Apply(new Events.ClassifiedAdTitleChanged
            {
                Id = Id,
                Title = title
```

```
    });

public void UpdateText(ClassifiedAdText text) =>
    Apply(new Events.ClassifiedAdTextUpdated
    {
        Id = Id,
        AdText = text
    });

public void UpdatePrice(Price price) =>
    Apply(new Events.ClassifiedAdPriceUpdated
    {
        Id = Id,
        Price = price.Amount,
        CurrencyCode = price.Currency.CurrencyCode
    });

public void RequestToPublish() =>
    Apply(new Events.ClassidiedAdSentForReview {Id = Id});

protected override void When(object @event)
{
    switch (@event)
    {
        case Events.ClassifiedAdCreated e:
            Id = new ClassifiedAdId(e.Id);
            OwnerId = new UserId(e.OwnerId);
            State = ClassifiedAdState.Inactive;
            break;
        case Events.ClassifiedAdTitleChanged e:
            Title = new ClassifiedAdTitle(e.Title);
            break;
        case Events.ClassifiedAdTextUpdated e:
            Text = new ClassifiedAdText(e.AdText);
            break;
        case Events.ClassifiedAdPriceUpdated e:
            Price = new Price(e.Price, e.CurrencyCode);
            break;
        case Events.ClassidiedAdSentForReview e:
            State = ClassifiedAdState.PendingReview;
            break;
    }
}

protected override void EnsureValidState()
{
    var valid =
        Id != null &&
```

```
                    OwnerId != null &&
                    (State switch
                    {
                        ClassifiedAdState.PendingReview =>
                            Title != null
                            && Text != null
                            && Price?.Amount > 0,
                        ClassifiedAdState.Active =>
                            Title != null
                            && Text != null
                            && Price?.Amount > 0
                            && ApprovedBy != null,
                        _ => true
                    });

            if (!valid)
                throw new InvalidEntityStateException(
                    this, $"Post-checks failed in state {State}");
        }


        public enum ClassifiedAdState
        {
            PendingReview,
            Active,
            Inactive,
            MarkedAsSold
        }
    }
}
```

There are two essential things that we changed in the entity class, listed as follows:

- All public methods to amend the entity state (operations) now apply to domain events. There are no state changes or validity checks left in those methods. As you remember, the validity contract method is now being called from the `Apply` method in the `Entity` base class.
- We have added a `When` method override, where the advanced pattern matching feature of C# 7.1 is being used to identify what kind of event is being applied, and how the entity state needs to be changed.

Hence, there are no changes in tests. If we execute all tests in the solution that have been created so far, they will all pass. It means that raising domain events and applying them to change the entity state can be considered as implementation details. Indeed, this is a style of working with domain events, typically used when DDD is applied with Event Sourcing, which we will be discussing later.

Please keep in mind that using DDD in general and domain events, in particular, does not imply using Event Sourcing, and vice versa. This book has more of a focus on Event Sourcing; therefore, this technique to change the state of the domain by applying events is presented quite early.

Some further changes are not that obvious but were required to make the whole thing work. If you look closely at the When method, entity properties that are still of value object types, use constructors for value objects instead of factory functions. It is because factory functions apply constraints and perform checks while constructing valid value objects. However, domain events represent something that already happened, so there is no point in checking these past facts for validity. If they were valid at the time, they should be just let through. Even if the logic in value object has changed, this should never have any effects on applying events with historical data.

To fix this, we needed to change value objects, so they have internal constructors instead of private ones. Also, checks are moved from constructors to factory functions, so constructors are now accepting any value. For the more complex Price object, we needed to add a constructor that does not require a currency lookup service. Even if the currency is not valid anymore, when we are trying to load some past event, it should get through. However, it does not change the use of factory functions. They still require the lookup service and will be using it as soon as we create new instances of the value objects in our application service layer. It will keep protecting us from executing commands that have some incorrect information, and therefore, can bring our model to an invalid state.

In the following, you can find changed value object for the classified ad text:

```
using Marketplace.Framework;

namespace Marketplace.Domain
{
    public class ClassifiedAdText : Value<ClassifiedAdText>
    {
        public string Value { get; }

        internal ClassifiedAdText(string text) => Value = text;
        public static ClassifiedAdText FromString(string text)
            => new ClassifiedAdText(text);
        public static implicit operator string(ClassifiedAdText text)
            => text.Value;
    }
}
```

Here is the full code for the value object that represents the ad title:

```csharp
using System;
using System.Text.RegularExpressions;
using Marketplace.Framework;

namespace Marketplace.Domain
{
    public class ClassifiedAdTitle : Value<ClassifiedAdTitle>
    {
        public static ClassifiedAdTitle FromString(string title)
        {
            CheckValidity(title);
            return new ClassifiedAdTitle(title);
        }

        public static ClassifiedAdTitle FromHtml(string htmlTitle)
        {
            var supportedTagsReplaced = htmlTitle
                .Replace("<i>", "*")
                .Replace("</i>", "*")
                .Replace("<b>", "**")
                .Replace("</b>", "**");

            var value = Regex.Replace(supportedTagsReplaced,
                "<.*?>", string.Empty);
            CheckValidity(value);

            return new ClassifiedAdTitle(value);
        }

        public string Value { get; }

        internal ClassifiedAdTitle(string value) => Value = value;

        public static implicit operator string(ClassifiedAdTitle title)
            => title.Value;

        private static void CheckValidity(string value)
        {
            if (value.Length > 100)
                throw new ArgumentOutOfRangeException(
                    "Title cannot be longer that 100 characters",
                    nameof(value));
        }
    }
}
```

Finally, the `Price` class, which is based on the `Money` class but has some additional rules in place:

```
using System;

namespace Marketplace.Domain
{
    public class Price : Money
    {
        private Price(
            decimal amount,
            string currencyCode,
            ICurrencyLookup currencyLookup
        ) : base(amount, currencyCode, currencyLookup)
        {
            if (amount < 0)
                throw new ArgumentException(
                    "Price cannot be negative",
                    nameof(amount));
        }

        internal Price(decimal amount, string currencyCode)
            : base(amount, new CurrencyDetails{CurrencyCode =
                currencyCode}) { }

        public static Price FromDecimal(decimal amount, string
        currency,
            ICurrencyLookup currencyLookup) =>
            new Price(amount, currency, currencyLookup);
    }
}
```

Again, although these changes might seem significant, we were not changing any domain logic and constraints. We have all existing tests intact, and they are still passing, so our refactoring was successful, and we managed to change implementation details while keeping the essence of our domain model intact.

Summary

In this chapter, we started to write a lot of code and learned the basics of implementing domain models in code. We looked at entities and value objects, what they are needed for, and how different they are. Explaining the power of value objects consumed a significant part of this chapter, but this topic is vital since value objects are often overlooked.

We used factory functions to create different ways of constructing value objects. A similar technique can be used to form valid entities, but we were not touching this topic just yet. We also used a domain service to make use of some external services inside our value object, while keeping the domain model itself clean from any external dependencies.

Constraints and invariants that play such an important role in keeping the state of the system valid at all times were also discussed, and we used different techniques to implement them.

Finally, we moved on to domain events and implemented some events that we previously only saw on orange stickies, directly in our code. Going forward, we learned how, from being a supportive tool, domain events could become the driver for state change in our model, and this lays a strong foundation for us before we move on to Event Sourcing.

In this chapter, we also wrote some tests. Writing tests and keeping them actual is crucial in any programming work, but when using DDD and being in an explorative mode inside the model, tests become one of the most important instruments to handle regression, and even express and document business rules, as we will see in the following chapters.

Since we started to move some of our sticky notes to code, in the next chapter, we will look at how to implement commands, and how commands are the glue between our domain model and the world outside it. In this state, we will learn how to make our model useful by letting people interact with it.

Acting with Commands 6

In the previous chapter, we went through the implementation process for a simple domain model. This model has one entity, and several value objects and domain services. The model represents just one area of our system, and we deliberately kept everything else out of scope. We discussed how the domain model project needs to be isolated from anything else, and how domain services can be part of the model although their implementation can be done in the application layer. Now, we are going to learn about putting our domain model in action. Hitherto, we have not been referencing the domain model from anywhere, which makes it rather useless. To start using the model in our application, we need to be able to call the model. In addition, we need to be able to persist all changes that happen in the model, so we do not lose the system state.

The following topics will be covered in this chapter:

- Application layer—the outer edge of the onion architecture
- Calling the domain model from the web API
- Persisting the domain model changes

Technical requirements

In addition to the technical requirements from Chapter 5, *Implementing the Model*, you need to install Docker, because we will be using containers to run necessary infrastructure components, such as databases. Docker is supported on all popular platforms, including Windows, macOS, and Linux. Please refer to the Docker installation documentation (https://docs.docker.com/install/) if you need to know more about how to install it.

Outside the domain model

We strive to keep our domain model intact from anything that is related to infrastructure, persistence, execution, and communication. This makes the domain model pure and keeps it focused on the business. However, we still need to create the whole system around it, keeping the domain model as the system core.

The whole world of runtime surrounds our domain model, and in this section, we are going to dissect all necessary components that are required to build a proper system and look at how these components need to be bound together, with each other and with the domain model.

Exposing the web API

Our system needs to have some visibility to users, and therefore, at some point, we will need to build a user interface. This topic is covered as we move on further, but right now we need to be able to expose our application in a way that the future UI can be built on top of it. We expect our system to have more than one UI potentially. Think about a **single-page web application (SPA)** and a mobile app. As a backend for both types of frontends, we need to build a web API. I would avoid the term REST API since it is much more than a simple web API and we aren't going to explore this topic in depth. Instead, we will concentrate on making some calls to our domain model via HTTP, to do something useful.

Let's start by creating an ASP.NET Web API controller, where we will put handlers for some of the HTTP endpoints. To do this, we need to add a class to our `Marketplace` project, because right now we will not be working inside the domain model, but outside it.

Before we add a controller, let's create a project folder called `Api`, to put all controllers and related services in one place. We will add different types of components to the application project later on, so it is better to keep things tidy from the beginning.

Public API contracts

To serve HTTP requests, we need more than just a controller. The controller needs to accept strongly typed requests, and the collection of those requests will be our public API and the models for those requests will be our contracts. Let's prepare a place where we'll put these models and create a folder called `Contracts`, in the application project.

Contracts are **data-transfer objects (DTOs)** and **plain-old C# objects (POCOs)**. It means that they have no logic, they only contain primitive types and do not require any tricks to be serialized and deserialized. Practically, you can add complex types to your DTOs just because some complex types are used in many contracts. An example of such a type could be the Address type.

Imagine we have the following contract class:

```
public class UpdateCustomerAddressDetails
{
    public string BillingStreet { get; set; }
    public string BillingCity { get; set; }
    public string BillingPostalCode { get; set; }
    public string BillingCountry { get; set; }
    public string DeliveryStreet { get; set; }
    public string DeliveryCity { get; set; }
    public string DeliveryPostalCode { get; set; }
    public string DeliveryCountry { get; set; }
}
```

It is very convenient to use the complex type instead of listing all properties for two addresses separately. After we add a new type called Address, our contract will be much more compact:

```
public class Address
{
    public string Street { get; set; }
    public string City { get; set; }
    public string PostalCode { get; set; }
    public string Country { get; set; }
}

public class UpdateCustomerAddressDetails
{
    public Address BillingAddress { get; set; }
    public Address DeliveryAddress { get; set; }
}
```

Be aware that complex types add compatibility issues since when you change the type, all contracts that use it will also change and this change will be implicit. Since you have no internal consumers of this contract, you will not be able to see whether the clients that use this contract will be affected. Such information can only be obtained by tests.

Speaking about changes, remember that everything you publish outside of your development machine is considered public. The public API is something that anyone who has appropriate permissions can use. Effectively, this means that you are not in control of who is using your API anymore. Therefore, any change in the published API can potentially break other parts of the system or other systems. Changes in public contracts need to be crafted with care since there are both non-breaking changes and breaking changes.

Some changes in POCO types are considered non-breaking, such as the following:

- Changing property type so any value of the type that was used before can be serialized to the new type. For example, we can change a property from being an integer to string, and it will be compatible.
- Adding a new property is also considered a non-breaking change. This is because when we try to deserialize an XML or JSON object that does not have this new property because the sender hasn't updated their contracts yet, most popular serializers will accept it and will use a default value if the value is not supplied.

Our software evolves, and of course, it is not always possible to make non-breaking changes. This means that we should be prepared to make breaking changes. We already discussed how the public API is something that is shared by default as soon as it is made public. Therefore, we need to ensure that when we make a breaking change, everyone who is using the old API will not get exceptions and will be able to work as before, at least for some time. This is done by **API versioning**. You probably have encountered different API versions for popular services such as GitHub or Twitter. For example, while I am writing this, the Twitter API documentation tells me to use this call to get the timeline of the tweet: GET `https://api.twitter.com/1.1/statuses/home_timeline.json`. As you can see, they have `1.1` as part of the URI, and it is their current stable API version. We could assume that they also have other versions and some of those older versions might still be operational and in use. So, in our API, we will also use versioned contracts although we don't expect many changes in the beginning.

We already know what operations we can do with our domain, so we can add some contracts to call these operations from the outside world. Let's create a file where we put our first contracts. We already have the `Contracts` folder, so we can create a new C# class file called `ClassifiedAds.cs` in this folder. After the file is in place, we can add our first contract there:

```
using System;

namespace Marketplace.Contracts
{
    public static class ClassifiedAds
```

```
    {
        public static class V1
        {
            public class Create
            {
                public Guid Id { get; set; }
                public Guid OwnerId { get; set; }
            }
        }
    }
}
```

Here, we use nested static classes, `ClassifiedAds` and `V1`, as a replacement for namespaces, so we can have more versions in one file when necessary. This method allows us to use static members import to keep code more concise.

What we have here is a *command*. I first mentioned *commands* in `Chapter 1`, *Why Domain-Driven Design?*, when we discussed CQRS. Commands allow users and other systems to execute actions in our domain model. When a command is successfully processed, the domain model state changes and new domain events are emitted. Now, when we have one command implemented in code, we need to accept this command coming from the outside world, and we'll use an HTTP endpoint for this.

HTTP endpoints

Since the most obvious communication method for APIs nowadays is using synchronous HTTP calls, we will start with this. We will be using the ASP.NET Web API. Therefore, we need to add a controller that will accept our commands. Let's add a file called `ClassifiedAdsCommandsApi.cs` to the `Api` folder of our executable project, make the class inherit from `Controller`, and add one `Post` method to handle the command that we added in the previous section:

```
using System.Threading.Tasks;
using Microsoft.AspNetCore.Mvc;

namespace Marketplace.Api
{
    [Route("/ad")]
    public class ClassifiedAdsCommandsApi : Controller
    {
        [HttpPost]
        public async Task<IActionResult> Post(
            Contracts.ClassifiedAds.V1.Create request)
        {
            // handle the request here
```

```
            return Ok();
        }
    }
}
```

We are not doing anything there yet. Instead, we are creating a web API that will accept commands from the outside world. We will add code that handles these commands later. Remember, this is our adapter for the HTTP infrastructure, which finds its place in the outermost layer of the onion architecture. That's we call this layer **the edge** because there is nothing outside of it, which we can consider a part of our app. The application can have multiple ways to communicate with the outside world, so if we added some other edge, such as messaging, we would expect for this new communication adapter to process the same commands.

Now, we need to add more code to the application startup to make the web API work. There are a few things we need to do to the Program class:

- Build the configuration.
- Configure the web host.
- Execute the web host.

To do these operations, we need the Program class to look like this:

```
using System.IO;
using Microsoft.AspNetCore.Hosting;
using Microsoft.Extensions.Configuration;
using Microsoft.Extensions.DependencyInjection;
using static System.Environment;
using static System.Reflection.Assembly;

namespace Marketplace
{
    public static class Program
    {
        static Program() =>
            CurrentDirectory =
Path.GetDirectoryName(GetEntryAssembly().Location);

        public static void Main(string[] args)
        {
            var configuration = BuildConfiguration(args);

            ConfigureWebHost(configuration).Build().Run();
        }
```

```
        private static IConfiguration BuildConfiguration(string[] args)
            => new ConfigurationBuilder()
                .SetBasePath(CurrentDirectory)
                .Build();

        private static IWebHostBuilder ConfigureWebHost(
            IConfiguration configuration)
            => new WebHostBuilder()
                .UseStartup<Startup>()
                .UseConfiguration(configuration)
                .ConfigureServices(services =>
                    services.AddSingleton(configuration))
                .UseContentRoot(CurrentDirectory)
                .UseKestrel();
    }
}
```

There is not much going on here. We ensure that our current directory is where the executable is located because this is where we also can find the configuration file. We then read the configuration, and from the configuration, we create the web host and start it. Right now, we have no configuration file and therefore no configuration, but we will be adding some later.

Now, we are using the `Startup` class to configure services, and it needs some attention as well. In the `Startup` class, we need to configure the web API so it can use our controller. In addition, we need an easy way to interact with the API without having any user interface yet. One nice and easy way is to use Swagger (`https://swagger.io/`) integration with the Web API. Before we can start using it, we need to add a Swagger Web API integration NuGet package, `Swashbuckle.AspNetCore`. With the new `.csproj` file format, the easiest way to do add the integration is probably by adding the package reference directly to the project file. Here, you can see the new content for the `Marketplace.csproj` file, and the changes are highlighted:

```xml
<Project Sdk="Microsoft.NET.Sdk.Web">
  <PropertyGroup>
    <TargetFramework>netcoreapp2.1</TargetFramework>
  </PropertyGroup>
  <ItemGroup>
    <PackageReference Include="Microsoft.AspNetCore.App" />
    <PackageReference Include="Swashbuckle.AspNetCore" Version="4.0.1" />
  </ItemGroup>
  <ItemGroup>
    <ProjectReference
Include="..\Marketplace.Domain\Marketplace.Domain.csproj" />
  </ItemGroup>
</Project>
```

The `Swashbuckle.AspNetCore` package might have a different version at the moment you are reading this book. Use the latest available version.

When you save the project file, your IDE will install the package and add the reference to your project.

Now, we can change the `Startup` class, so it registers web API internals, our controller, and all necessary Swagger generation. Also, we add an embedded version of the Swagger UI so we can test our API directly from the browser, without any additional software:

```csharp
using Microsoft.AspNetCore.Builder;
using Microsoft.AspNetCore.Hosting;
using Microsoft.Extensions.Configuration;
using Microsoft.Extensions.DependencyInjection;
using Swashbuckle.AspNetCore.Swagger;
using static System.Environment;
// ReSharper disable UnusedMember.Global

namespace Marketplace
{
    public class Startup
    {
        public Startup(IHostingEnvironment environment,
            IConfiguration configuration)
        {
            Environment = environment;
            Configuration = configuration;
        }

        private IConfiguration Configuration { get; }
        private IHostingEnvironment Environment { get; }

        public void ConfigureServices(IServiceCollection services)
        {
            services.AddMvc();
            services.AddSwaggerGen(c =>
                c.SwaggerDoc("v1",
                    new Info
                    {
                        Title = "ClassifiedAds",
                        Version = "v1"
                    }));
        }

        public void Configure(IApplicationBuilder app,
```

```
            IHostingEnvironment env)
    {
        if (env.IsDevelopment())
        {
            app.UseDeveloperExceptionPage();
        }

        app.UseMvcWithDefaultRoute();
        app.UseSwagger();
        app.UseSwaggerUI(c =>
            c.SwaggerEndpoint(
                "/swagger/v1/swagger.json",
                "ClassifiedAds v1"));
    }
  }
}
```

With everything in place now, we are ready to start the application for the first time. After pressing *F5*, you should see the following at the console:

```
Hosting environment: Development
Content root path: /home/alexey/github/ddd-book/Marketplace/bin/Debug/netcoreapp2.1
Now listening on:
Application started. Press Ctrl+C to shut down.
```

The application finally runs

Now, let's open the Swagger UI by going to `http://localhost:5000/swagger` in the browser. We should see one operation (**POST**), and when we expand it, the following should appear:

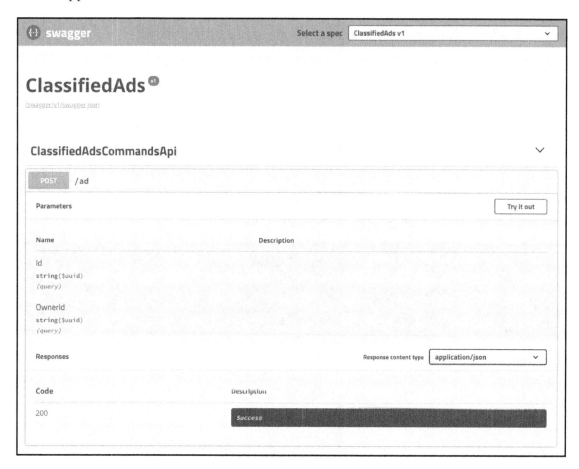

Swagger user interface for testing the API

You can click on the **Try it out** button and send some requests to the API, but it won't do anything because we always return the 200 OK response.

We completed all the necessary steps to expose a primitive web API endpoint, and have the bootstrap code to support it. We also created one API contract that represents the command to create a classified ad. It is time to make this command work.

Application layer

The edge—in our case, it is a simple web API—accepts requests from the outside world. The main job for our edge component is to accept some request, sent as a JSON document, XML document, message via RabbitMQ, or any other communication channel and serialization type; convert it to a command; and then ensure this command gets handled.

The edge can, of course, work directly with the domain model, but this would mean we accept the fact that we will always be working with one edge type only, with one communication protocol. Also, edge components are usually heavily dependent on the communication infrastructure—while this is fine for integration tests, creating unit tests for such components might be challenging.

To isolate the communication infrastructure from the actual request handling, we can introduce the application layer. In this layer, we need a component that will accept commands from the edge and use our domain model to handle these commands. Such a component is called **application service**.

If you refer to Chapter 4, *Designing the Model*, and look at the picture of the onion architecture, you will find application services between the infrastructure and the domain model. Application services have no dependency on the transport that is used to send commands from the outside.

However, the services need to have a way to load and store entities, because a typical operation of an application service would be to execute a command like this:

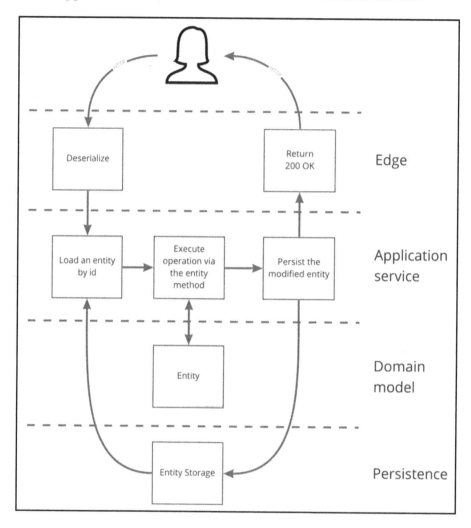

Typical interaction flow

There are a couple of exceptions in this flow. When the application service receives a command that requires creating a new entity, it won't load anything from the entity storage, since there is nothing to load yet. It will create the entity and save it to the entity store. Also, when handling a command requires deleting an entity, the application service will load the entity, but not necessarily save it back. It might just delete this entity from the store instead, but this very much depends on a model. For example, if the business requires keeping all the data, we might just mark the entity as deleted and then persist changes to the entity store.

Let's add a new application service class to our project and write some code. First, we need a new file in the `Api` folder of our executable web API project. Some might argue that application services aren't part of the API, but for now, we have only one edge and there is no real reason to separate them. The new filename would be `ClassifiedAdApplicationService.cs`, and it has the following code:

```
namespace Marketplace.Api
{
    public class ClassifiedAdsApplicationService
    {
        public void Handle(Contracts.ClassifiedAds.V1.Create command)
        {
            // we need to create a new Classified Ad here
        }
    }
}
```

Now, we need to call the application service from our API. We need to add the application serves as a dependency to our controller, and in the startup, we will register the dependency in the ASP.NET Core service locator. First, we do the registration. Since our application service class has no dependencies yet, we can use a singleton, so we add one line to the `ConfigureServices` method of the `Startup` class:

```
public void ConfigureServices(IServiceCollection services)
{
    services.AddSingleton(new ClassifiedAdsApplicationService());
    ...
}
```

When this is done, we can add the `ClassifiedAdsApplicationService` class as a dependency to the `ClassifiedAdsCommandsApi` controller and call the `Handle` method from our `Post` method:

```
using System.Threading.Tasks;
using Microsoft.AspNetCore.Mvc;

namespace Marketplace.Api
{
    [Route("/ad")]
    public class ClassifiedAdsCommandsApi : Controller
    {
        private readonly ClassifiedAdsApplicationService
_applicationService;

        public ClassifiedAdsCommandsApi(
            ClassifiedAdsApplicationService applicationService)
            => _applicationService = applicationService;

        [HttpPost]
        public async Task<IActionResult> Post(
            Contracts.ClassifiedAds.V1.Create request)
        {
            _applicationService.Handle(request);

            return Ok();
        }
    }
}
```

In the next section, we will dive into command handling, including saving entities to an entity store and retrieving them. We will add more commands and handlers for those commands too.

Handling commands

In the previous section, we created a simple web API and learned that the API is the *edge* of our application. The edge talks with the outside world and accepts requests via HTTP or another communication protocol. To execute these requests, we need an *application service* that works as an intermediary between edge components and the domain model. The application service is also responsible for persisting entities.

Going forward, we will learn more about handling commands and persistence. Also, we will discuss handling exceptions and checking whether incoming requests are valid.

The command handler pattern

There are several ways to handle commands in CQRS. One established pattern is to use command handlers. It is not specific to CQRS but it is being widely used because it is a very good fit. The command handler is a class that has one method to handle a single command type. For example, we might have a command handler such as this:

```
public class CreateClassifiedAdHandler :
    IHandleCommand<Contracts.ClassifiedAds.V1.Create>
{
    private readonly IEntityStore _store;

    public CreateClassifiedAdHandler(IEntityStore store)
        => _store = store;

    public Task Handle(Contracts.ClassifiedAds.V1.Create command)
    {
        var classifiedAd = new ClassifiedAd(
            new ClassifiedAdId(command.Id),
            new UserId(command.OwnerId));

        return _store.Save(classifiedAd);
    }
}
```

Two interfaces are used by the command handler earlier. The interfaces look like this:

```
public interface IHandleCommand<in T>
{
    Task Handle(T command);
}

public interface IEntityStore
{
    Task<T> Load<T>(string id);
    Task Save<T>(T entity);
}
```

Bear in mind that the IEntityStore interface is simplified and not all persistence methods can be represented by such an interface.

Make no mistake, I am not trying to seed the idea of generic repositories in your head. In fact, the entity store is not the exact math of the repository pattern. When the purpose of repositories is to mimic a collection of objects and hide the persistence, the entity store is a complete opposite. It does not represent a collection. It does exactly what it tells you about - persist one single object and retrieves it back. And while generic repositories are often considered as an anti-pattern, I wouldn't apply the same for the entity store interface.

We then can use this command handler in the API:

```
using System.Threading.Tasks;
using Marketplace.Contracts;
using Microsoft.AspNetCore.Mvc;
using static Marketplace.Contracts.ClassifiedAds;

namespace Marketplace.Api
{
    [Route("/ad")]
    public class ClassifiedAdsCommandsApi : Controller
    {
        private readonly IHandleCommand<V1.Create>
            _createAdCommandHandler;

        public ClassifiedAdsCommandsApi(
            IHandleCommand<V1.Create>
            createAdCommandHandler
        ) =>
            _createAdCommandHandler = createAdCommandHandler;

        [HttpPost]
        public Task Post(V1.Create request) =>
            _createAdCommandHandler.Handle(request);
    }
}
```

You can see here that we reference the command handler via the `IHandleCommand` interface. It gives us some freedom in choosing the implementation we want to use. To start with, we can register the implementation we already have:

```
services.AddSingleton<IEntityStore, RavenDbEntityStore>();
services.AddScoped<
    IHandleCommand<Contracts.ClassifiedAds.V1.Create>,
    CreateClassifiedAdHandler>();
```

Here, we register the `RavenDbEntityStore` class, which implements `IEntityStore`. We aren't going to look at the actual implementation here, but since `RavenDb` is the document database, such a class could be trivial to implement.

What we have done so far is very straightforward, but since we are using the `IHandleCommand<T>` interface in our API, we can do something more interesting. For example, we can create a generic command handler that retries failures:

```
public class RetryingCommandHandler<T> : IHandleCommand<T>
{
    static RetryPolicy _policy = Policy
        .Handle<InvalidOperationException>()
        .Retry();

    private IHandleCommand<T> _next;

    public RetryingCommandHandler(IHandleCommand<T> next)
        => _next = next;
    public Task Handle(T command)
        => _policy.ExecuteAsync(() => _next.Handle(command));
}
```

We just need to change the service registration to look like this:

```
services.AddScoped<IHandleCommand<V1.Create>>(c =>
    new RetryingCommandHandler<V1.Create>(
        new
CreateClassifiedAdHandler(c.GetService<RavenDbEntityStore>())));
```

Here, we wrap the actual command handler inside the generic retry handler. Since they both implement the same interface, we can build a pipeline using a composition of these classes. We can continue adding more elements to the chain, such as using a circuit breaker or a logger.

We can add more properties to the command class (remember the weak schema), but the only handler that we might want to change because of this would be the actual command handler. All transient handlers will remain unchanged because we are using the command type, which is a complex type, as a parameter, so the interface definition itself doesn't change.

The command handler pattern is compelling, and it adheres to the **Single Responsibility Principle (SRP)**. At the same time, each HTTP method in our API would require a separate command handler as a dependency. It is not a big deal if we have two or three methods, but we might have a little more than that. We might predict that we will have more than 10 methods in our classified ad web API, and an adequate number of command handlers, just by looking at the result of our EventStorming session. Command handlers need the entity store as a dependency, and since all web API controllers are instantiated per scope, all command handlers will be instantiated and injected as well, with all their dependencies. It is possible to mitigate the instantiation of a vast dependency tree by using factory delegates instead of dependencies per request, so each method would be able to instantiate its handler:

```
using System;
using System.Threading.Tasks;
using Marketplace.Contracts;
using Microsoft.AspNetCore.Mvc;
using static Marketplace.Contracts.ClassifiedAds;

namespace Marketplace.Api
{
    [Route("/ad")]
    public class ClassifiedAdsCommandsApi : Controller
    {
        private readonly Func<IHandleCommand<V1.Create>>
            _createAdCommandHandlerFactory;

        public ClassifiedAdsCommandsApi(
            Func<IHandleCommand<V1.Create>> createAdCommandHandlerFactory)
            => _createAdCommandHandlerFactory =
createAdCommandHandlerFactory;

        [HttpPost]
        public Task Post(V1.Create request) =>
            _createAdCommandHandlerFactory().Handle(request);
    }
}
```

This approach would require more advanced registration since we aren't using the actual type, but a delegate. Another solution might be to use Lazy<IHandleCommand<T>> as a dependency. Again, it will require more complex registration. The registration challenge might be resolved by using another dependency-injection container, such as Autofac, which supports automatic factory delegates and Lazy<T> out of the box.

In this book, we will not be using the command handler pattern, but instead, we will implement command handling using the application service. We already started to implement a simple service in this section and will continue in the next section. The command handler detour exists to bring a better overview of useful patterns since no pattern is good enough for all use cases.

Application service

In fact, how our application service will look and behave is very similar to a bunch of command handlers. A *classic* application service exposes some methods with multiple parameters, like this:

```
public interface IPaymentApplicationService
{
    Guid Authorize(
        string creditCardNumber,
        int expiryYear,
        int expiryMonth,
        int cvcCode,
        intcamount);
    void Capture(Guid authorizationId);
}
```

Using this kind of declaration is perfectly fine, except it doesn't play that well with the composition. It is not easy to add such an application service to a pipeline, where we have logging, retry policies, and so on. To make a pipeline, we need all our handlers to have compatible parameters, but these methods of IPaymentApplicationService just don't allow us to go that way. Every other call in the pipeline must have the same set of parameters, and as soon as we want to add one more parameter to any method, we are doomed to make numerous changes in multiple classes that form our pipeline. This is not something we'd like to do.

Alternatively, we can have one application service class that implements multiple IHandle<T> interfaces. This would work, but each command will then require a separate bootstrapping code, although we are adding the same elements to our pipeline:

```
services.AddScoped<IHandleCommand<V1.Create>>(c =>
    new RetryingCommandHandler<V1.Create>(
        new
CreateClassifiedAdHandler(c.GetService<RavenDbEntityStore>())));
services.AddScoped<IHandleCommand<V1.Create>>(c =>
    new RetryingCommandHandler<V1.Rename>(
        new
```

```
RenameClassifiedAdHandler(c.GetService<RavenDbEntityStore>())));
// more handlers need to be added with the same composition
```

Alternatively, we can generalize our application service to handle any type of command, and use the C# 7 advanced pattern-matching feature again (like we did with event handling). In this case, the application service signature would look like this:

```
public interface IApplicationService
{
    Task Handle(object command);
}
```

All our previous filters for the pipeline, such as the retry filter or the logging filter, can implement this simple interface. Since those classes don't need to get a hold of the command's content, everything will work just fine. Our classified ad service would then look like this:

```
using System;
using System.Threading.Tasks;
using Marketplace.Framework;
using static Marketplace.Contracts.ClassifiedAds;

namespace Marketplace.Api
{
    public class ClassifiedAdsApplicationService
        : IApplicationService
    {
        public async Task Handle(object command)
        {
            switch (command)
            {
                case V1.Create cmd:
                    // we need to create a new Classified Ad here
                    break;

                default:
                    throw new InvalidOperationException(
                        $"Command type {command.GetType().FullName} is
                        unknown");
            }
        }
    }
}
```

By implementing our application service like this, we will have a single dependency to handle for all of our API calls, and we keep the door open to compose a more complex command processing pipeline, just as we were able to do with individual command handlers.

Of course, the tradeoff here is that we have one class that handles several commands and some might see it as an SRP violation. At the same time, the level of cohesion for this class is high, and we will see more of it later in this chapter when we will adequately handle several commands and make calls to our application service from the edge.

Let's now add more commands and extend our application service and the HTTP edge accordingly.

First, we need to get back to our entity and check what actions we can command it to perform. These actions are as following:

1. Set the title.
2. Update the text.
3. Update the price.
4. Request to publish.

We can add four commands to execute these actions, since we could expect, based on our EventStorming sessions, that this is what our users would like to do.

The expanded commands list would look like this:

```
using System;

namespace Marketplace.Contracts
{
    public static class ClassifiedAds
    {
        public static class V1
        {
            public class Create
            {
                public Guid Id { get; set; }
                public Guid OwnerId { get; set; }
            }

            public class SetTitle
            {
                public Guid Id { get; set; }
                public string Title { get; set; }
            }
```

```
            public class UpdateText
            {
                public Guid Id { get; set; }
                public string Text { get; set; }
            }

            public class UpdatePrice
            {
                public Guid Id { get; set; }
                public decimal Price { get; set; }
                public string Currency { get; set; }
            }

            public class RequestToPublish
            {
                public Guid Id { get; set; }
            }
        }
    }
}
```

Each command needs to have the ID of the entity it is going to operate on. Other properties are command-specific.

Second, we can extend our edge to accept these commands as HTTP requests. The code for the new API version is as follows:

```
using System.Threading.Tasks;
using Marketplace.Contracts;
using Microsoft.AspNetCore.Mvc;
using static Marketplace.Contracts.ClassifiedAds;

namespace Marketplace.Api
{
    [Route("/ad")]
    public class ClassifiedAdsCommandsApi : Controller
    {
        private readonly ClassifiedAdsApplicationService
        _applicationService;

        public ClassifiedAdsCommandsApi(
            ClassifiedAdsApplicationService applicationService)
            => _applicationService = applicationService;

        [HttpPost]
        public async Task<IActionResult> Post(V1.Create request)
        {
            await _applicationService.Handle(request);
```

```
        return Ok();
    }

    [Route("name")]
    [HttpPut]
    public async Task<IActionResult> Put(V1.SetTitle request)
    {
        await _applicationService.Handle(request);
        return Ok();
    }

    [Route("text")]
    [HttpPut]
    public async Task<IActionResult> Put(V1.UpdateText request)
    {
        await _applicationService.Handle(request);
        return Ok();
    }

    [Route("price")]
    [HttpPut]
    public async Task<IActionResult> Put(V1.UpdatePrice request)
    {
        await _applicationService.Handle(request);
        return Ok();
    }

    [Route("publish")]
    [HttpPut]
    public async Task<IActionResult> Put(V1.RequestToPublish request)
    {
        await _applicationService.Handle(request);
        return Ok();
    }
}
}
```

You might already see some candidates for creating a useful abstraction or routine. You can probably also predict some issues with this code when it will run in production. The preceding edge code also violates an important principle that the API client needs to only sends valid commands to the command handler. In our code, there is nothing that does such checks. Don't worry; we will get back to the API code and solve some of those issues. For now, let's concentrate on the essential bits.

As you can see, our application service is expected to handle five commands. We need to take care that it does that. The new code for our application service would be the following:

```
using System;
using System.Threading.Tasks;
using Marketplace.Contracts;
using Marketplace.Domain;
using Marketplace.Framework;
using static Marketplace.Contracts.ClassifiedAds;

namespace Marketplace.Api
{
    public class ClassifiedAdsApplicationService
        : IApplicationService
    {
        private readonly IEntityStore _store;
        private ICurrencyLookup _currencyLookup;

        public ClassifiedAdsApplicationService(
            IEntityStore store, ICurrencyLookup currencyLookup)
        {
            _store = store;
            _currencyLookup = currencyLookup;
        }

        public async Task Handle(object command)
        {
            ClassifiedAd classifiedAd;
            switch (command)
            {
                case V1.Create cmd:
                    if (await
 _store.Exists<ClassifiedAd>(cmd.Id.ToString()))
                            throw new InvalidOperationException(
                                $"Entity with id {cmd.Id} already exists");

                    classifiedAd = new ClassifiedAd(
                        new ClassifiedAdId(cmd.Id),
                        new UserId(cmd.OwnerId));
```

```
                    await _store.Save(classifiedAd);
                    break;

            case V1.SetTitle cmd:
                    classifiedAd = await
_store.Load<ClassifiedAd>(cmd.Id.ToString());
                    if (classifiedAd == null)
                        throw new InvalidOperationException(
                            $"Entity with id {cmd.Id} cannot be found");

classifiedAd.SetTitle(ClassifiedAdTitle.FromString(cmd.Title));
                    await _store.Save(classifiedAd);
                    break;

            case V1.UpdateText cmd:
                    classifiedAd = await
_store.Load<ClassifiedAd>(cmd.Id.ToString());
                    if (classifiedAd == null)
                        throw new InvalidOperationException(
                            $"Entity with id {cmd.Id} cannot be found");

classifiedAd.UpdateText(ClassifiedAdText.FromString(cmd.Text));
                    await _store.Save(classifiedAd);
                    break;

            case V1.UpdatePrice cmd:
                    classifiedAd = await
_store.Load<ClassifiedAd>(cmd.Id.ToString());
                    if (classifiedAd == null)
                        throw new InvalidOperationException(
                            $"Entity with id {cmd.Id} cannot be found");

                    classifiedAd.UpdatePrice(
                        Price.FromDecimal(cmd.Price, cmd.Currency,
_currencyLookup));
                    await _store.Save(classifiedAd);
                    break;

            case V1.RequestToPublish cmd:
                    classifiedAd = await
_store.Load<ClassifiedAd>(cmd.Id.ToString());
                    if (classifiedAd == null)
                        throw new InvalidOperationException(
                            $"Entity with id {cmd.Id} cannot be found");

                    classifiedAd.RequestToPublish();
                    await _store.Save(classifiedAd);
                    break;
```

```
                    default:
                        throw new InvalidOperationException(
                            $"Command type {command.GetType().FullName} is
unknown");
                    }
                }
        }
    }
```

Here, we again use the `IEntityStore` abstraction. This interface is very simple:

```
using System.Threading.Tasks;

namespace Marketplace.Framework
{
    public interface IEntityStore
    {
        /// <summary>
        /// Loads an entity by id
        /// </summary>
        Task<T> Load<T>(string entityId) where T : Entity;

        /// <summary>
        /// Persists an entity
        /// </summary>
        Task Save<T>(T entity) where T : Entity;

        /// <summary>
        /// Check if entity with a given id already exists
        /// <typeparam name="T">Entity type</typeparam>
        Task<bool> Exists<T>(string entityId);
    }
}
```

We will be implementing this interface for different persistence types.

As you can see, handling the `Create` command looks different from handling all other commands. This is natural since when we create a new entity, we need to ensure it does not exist yet. When we handle operations on the existing entity, it works the other way around. In this case, we need to ensure that the entity exists, otherwise, we cannot perform the operation and must throw an exception.

Another thing worth mentioning is that the application service is responsible for translating primitive types, such as string or decimal, to value objects. The edge always uses serializable types that have no dependencies on the domain model. The application service, however, operates with domain concerns; it needs to tell our domain model what to do, and since our domain model prefers to receive data as value objects, the application service is then responsible for the conversion.

The code for handling commands for an existing entity looks very similar to handling updates for existing entities. In fact, only the line where we call the entity method is different. Therefore, we can significantly simplify the `Handle` method by using a straightforward generalization and replace the `switch` pattern-matching operator with the switch expression:

```
using System;
using System.Threading.Tasks;
using Marketplace.Domain;
using Marketplace.Framework;
using static Marketplace.Contracts.ClassifiedAds;

namespace Marketplace.Api
{
    public class ClassifiedAdsApplicationService
        : IApplicationService
    {
        private readonly IClassifiedAdRepository _repository;
        private readonly ICurrencyLookup _currencyLookup;

        public ClassifiedAdsApplicationService(
            IClassifiedAdRepository repository,
            ICurrencyLookup currencyLookup
        )
        {
            _repository = repository;
            _currencyLookup = currencyLookup;
        }

        public Task Handle(object command) =>
            command switch
            {
                V1.Create cmd =>
                    HandleCreate(cmd),
                V1.SetTitle cmd =>
                    HandleUpdate(
                        cmd.Id,
                        c => c.SetTitle(
                            ClassifiedAdTitle.FromString(cmd.Title)
```

```
                )
            ),
        V1.UpdateText cmd =>
            HandleUpdate(
                cmd.Id,
                c => c.UpdateText(
                    ClassifiedAdText.FromString(cmd.Text)
                )
            ),
        V1.UpdatePrice cmd =>
            HandleUpdate(
                cmd.Id,
                c => c.UpdatePrice(
                    Price.FromDecimal(
                        cmd.Price,
                        cmd.Currency,
                        _currencyLookup
                    )
                )
            ),
        V1.RequestToPublish cmd =>
            HandleUpdate(
                cmd.Id,
                c => c.RequestToPublish()
            ),
        _ => Task.CompletedTask
    };

private async Task HandleCreate(V1.Create cmd)
{
    if (await _repository.Exists(cmd.Id.ToString()))
        throw new InvalidOperationException(
            $"Entity with id {cmd.Id} already exists");

    var classifiedAd = new ClassifiedAd(
        new ClassifiedAdId(cmd.Id),
        new UserId(cmd.OwnerId)
    );

    await _repository.Save(classifiedAd);
}

private async Task HandleUpdate(
    Guid classifiedAdId,
    Action<ClassifiedAd> operation
)
{
    var classifiedAd = await _repository.Load(
```

```
                    classifiedAdId.ToString()
                );
                if (classifiedAd == null)
                    throw new InvalidOperationException(
                        $"Entity with id {classifiedAdId} cannot be found"
                    );

                operation(classifiedAd);

                await _repository.Save(classifiedAd);
            }
        }
    }
```

From the application service code, it becomes clear that the application service itself plays the vital role of an intermediary between the application edge and the domain model. An edge could be anything that communicates with the outside world. We used the HTTP API as an example, but it could also be a messaging interface or something entirely different. The important requirement for the edge would be the ability to accept commands, check them, and engage the application service to handle those commands.

When we handle a command, no matter whether we use multiple command handlers or single application service, the sequence of operations is usually very similar. A command handler needs to fetch a persisted entity from the entity store, call the domain model to do the work, and then persist changes. In our example, we only called one method of the entity, but this is not always the case. We will look deeper into this when we discuss the consistency and transactional boundaries in the next chapter.

Summary

In this chapter, we looked at how the intent of our users can be represented as commands that those users send to our system. We learned how these commands can be handled, looked at several examples of the command handler pattern, and then got to the application service.

We looked at API versioning; although it is not directly related to the book topic, the practice is too important to ignore. We will touch upon the versioning topic in `Chapter 10`, *Event Sourcing*.

Our application service grew throughout this chapter, and we used one of the latest features of C#, a gift from the functional world, called **advanced pattern matching**. We used this feature to simplify the application service interface, which ended up having just a single method. By doing this, we also enabled using a composition, yet another functional-style approach, to chain command handling with operational concerns, such as logging and retries. We will also look at how this can help us check the validity of commands.

In the next chapter, we will take a closer look at entity persistence. We will learn what types of consistency we need to deal with and how important it is to understand the consistency boundaries.

7
Consistency Boundary

In monolithic systems, everything seems to be fully consistent. To achieve consistency, a lot of logic is **outsourced** to the database engine and becomes implicit, hard to figure out at a glance, and hard to test. Database transactions are frequently used to ensure that multiple-state mutations are executed at once. If the data becomes inconsistent, that usually means failure, and that requires an extensive investigation to fix the issue.

Domain-Driven Design (DDD) means avoiding complex graphs of entities. Instead, developers need to find a minimal logical set of entities that belong together and therefore need to be updated together to ensure consistency. Such a group of entities is called an **aggregate**.

The following topics will be covered in this chapter:

- Command handling as a unit of work
- Consistency and transactions
- Aggregates and aggregate root patterns
- Constraints and invariants

Technical requirements

The code for this chapter can be found in the Chapter07 folder of the book repository on GitHub. Since we aren't using any infrastructure components yet (we will start using some in the next chapter), you still need nothing other than the IDE or code editor. The code in the repository represents the final version for the chapter, and if you want to follow along, you can use the previous chapter code as a starting point.

Domain model consistency

When it comes to modeling, we often hear that data models need to be at the center of any system. *If you want a good system, you need a good data model*. I have heard that saying countless times in my career as a software engineer. One of my colleagues once said this, and then added: "*I participated in a large project where we started with defining the data model, and, after eighteen months, the project was shut down because the model wasn't complete.*" Strangely, these two statements created no causal relationship for him, since the first statement was an axiom, and the project failure seemed to be caused by numerous reasons, but not by the fact that designing a single data model for complex systems is always a death march—many tables, directly and indirectly, connected to one another by foreign keys, an endless push for the third normal form to avoid data duplication that results in heavy queries to retrieve a meaningful set of data—these are the realities of taking this approach.

If we create a data model first and then try to create our code around it, it is very hard to understand why some rules are being enforced, why those columns in that table are mandatory, and why one table has a many-to-many relationship with another table. These relationships are also hard to test, and even if we have tests, we can only run them if we have a properly configured database with a pre-populated set of data, so our tests are also becoming database-oriented.

DDD advocates a different approach when the domain model is essentially detached from the persistence, and it is primarily designed to serve specific business rules. When we deal with domain models, we pursue different goals with the design. We need to encapsulate just enough information in our classes so we can ensure that our model keeps being consistent after any state transition. The kind of consistency we mean there is not the relational database consistency that can be **outsourced** to the database engine. Instead, we want to ensure that our objects cannot violate the rules that are defined by the business, and these rules need to be explicitly defined in code. Let's look at what kind of principles we can apply, and how we can define different types of consistency boundaries in a domain model-centric design approach.

Transaction boundaries

As we discussed before, commands express the intent of a user to do something with the system. It could be the case that command comes from another system or even from a timer, but it still expresses some intent. Before the command is handled, our domain model finds itself in a valid state. When the command is handled, the domain model should also be in a valid state. This can be a new state if the command handling resulted in an operation being executed, or the same state as before, if the command handling has failed.

Let's look at the code for handling commands that we created in the previous chapter:

```
private async Task HandleUpdate(Guid classifiedAdId, Action<ClassifiedAd>
operation)
{
    var classifiedAd = await _store.Load<ClassifiedAd>(
        classifiedAdId.ToString());
    if (classifiedAd == null)
        throw new InvalidOperationException(
            $"Entity with id {classifiedAdId} cannot be found");
    operation(classifiedAd);
    await _store.Save(classifiedAd);
}
```

This is a generic handler for any operation that does not create a new instance of the `ClassifiedAd` entity and doesn't remove an existing instance. The only reason we were able to generalize the command handling like this was because all the commands are handled in a similar fashion:

- Retrieve an entity from the store by means of the entity ID
- Execute an operation
- Commit changes back to the store

If the operation fails, or the store cannot find anything by a given ID, the handler will throw an exception.

For this chapter, the most important thing in the preceding code and in this list of steps that are performed when our application service is handling commands is that we execute an operation on *one single entity* only.

Let's look at why this is so, and, for this purpose, we need to reflect on a very common way of implementing business applications, where the database is the center of everything that the application does. We will use the e-commerce domain as an example since it is reasonably complex and the code won't interfere with our ongoing work with the `Marketplace` application.

If you have several year's experience of developing software in .NET, you might have seen many codebases with methods such as this:

```
[Route("/api/order/pay/credit/{orderId}")]
public async Task TakeOnCustomerCredit(int orderId)
{
    using (var context = new CommerceContext())
    using (context.Database.BeginTransaction())
    {
        var order = await context.Orders
            .Where(x => x.Id == orderId).FirstAsync();
        var amount = order.UnpaidAmount;
        var customer = order.Customer;
        if (customer.Credit < amount)
            throw new InvalidOperationException("Not enough credit");
        customer.Credit -= amount;
        order.PaidAmount += amount;
        order.UnpaidAmount -= amount;
        customer.TotalSpent += amount;
        if (customer.TotalSpent > CommerceConstants.PreferredLimit)
            customer.Preferred = true;
        order.IsPaid = order.UnpaidAmount == 0;
        await context.SaveChangesAsync();
    }
}
```

Here, the controller seems to be completing a single logical operation, and it might look like a command handling directly in the HTTP endpoint request-handling method. The operation seems to be isolated and concise. To be honest, during my career, I have seen much worse code, where one request of a user results in many unrelated database operations, but let's stick to this example since it seems quite reasonable at first. So, this code uses the **unit of work** pattern, and `DbContext` of the entity framework wrapped in the `using` block implements this pattern perfectly because it accumulates all changes in the database elements and commits those changes all at once when we call `context.SaveChangesAsync()`.

Let's look at the data model that is associated with this code:

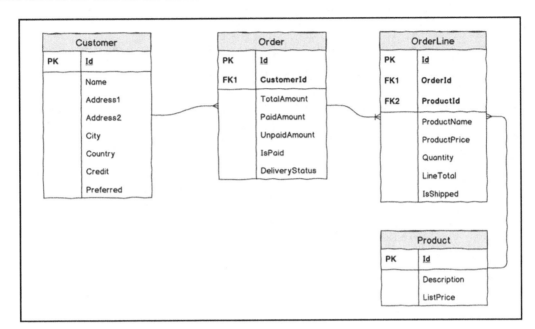

Simplified eCommerce data model

Of course, we could expect a lot more tables in the overall model. It could include things such as Product, Supplier, and Shipment. For our purposes, it is enough to have these four tables only. These tables all have relations to other tables, and those relations are all one-to-many (or zero-to-many). Our Entity Framework model uses an object reference between Order and Customer. This kind of reference is very popular when using ORM frameworks because it brings convenience to developers. We can access the Customer object that is associated with a particular order just by using the order.Customer property and modify any of the Customer properties as we wish, and this is exactly what the code does. It changes properties for both the order and the customer in one logical operation. This operation needs to either complete entirely, or fail. We cannot tolerate the fact that the customer's credit amount gets decreased but the order remains unpaid. Such behavior is typically associated with database transactions. A transaction is characterized by four principles, known as **ACID**:

- Atomicity
- Consistency
- Isolation
- Durability

For now, let's concentrate on atomicity. This characteristic means that all operations within a transaction must be complete or nothing happens at all, and it is often referred to as an **all-or-nothing** proposition.

In the preceding code, we can see that the transaction is wrapping the whole operation for paying an order using customer credit. This is correct, and what we are dealing with here is a **transactional boundary**. For that particular method, TakeOnCustomerCredit, the transactional boundary would include two tables—Customer and Order. If we imagine another operation on the same model, that could be something such as this:

```
public async Task ShipOrderLine(int orderLineId)
{
    using (var context = new CommerceContext())
    using (context.Database.BeginTransaction())
    {
        var orderLine = await context.OrderLines
            .Where(x => x.Id == orderLineId)
            .FirstAsync();
        orderLine.IsShipped = true;
        orderLine.Order.DeliveryStatus =
            orderLine.Order.OrderLines.All(x => x.IsShipped)
                ? DeliveryStatus.Shipped
                : DeliveryStatus.PartiallyShipped;
        await context.SaveChangesAsync();
    }
}
```

This method still uses the same model, and it has a few worrying concerns. But, for now, let's see what transaction boundary we are dealing with here. In this unit of work, we have records in Order and OrderLine tables changed in one transaction.

These two code snippets show that in *traditional* layered architecture, with no real domain model in place, transactional boundaries are being deliberately decided by any piece of code that performs changes in the database. The model itself does not enforce any kind of boundary. Two methods, which could even be located in one controller class, operate on two different transactional boundaries, although the Order table that both methods change will be a part of both transactions. It is quite easy to imagine that processing the remaining order payment on a customer's credit by calling the TakeOnCustomerCredit method could happen in parallel, with one order line being marked as shipped by the ShipOrderLine method:

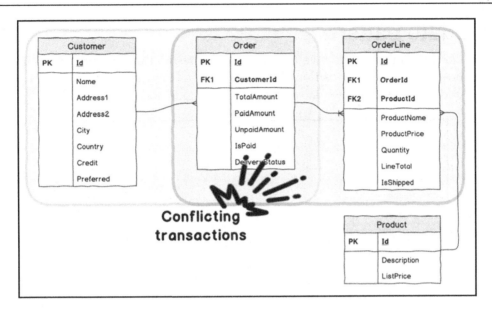

Updates for different reasons cause unjustified conflicting transactions

From the business logic point of view, these are two different operations, but because of the *consistency* part of ACID, one of these methods will fail. It would be very weird for users of this system to know that credit and payment processing is somehow related to shipment and delivery.

The reason for the appearance of this kind of model is quite clear. The very definition of the object-oriented approach in programming declares that objects in software programs represent objects in the real world.

Data models follow a similar approach. Very often, we see a system with one global data model that closely represents the model of the real world, covering all aspects of the domain that the system implements. It naturally results in large object graphs in code that reflect such a holistic data model. Nevertheless, DDD advocates another approach when we need to concentrate on modeling; only those aspects of the real-world models that are absolutely required to implement a set of use cases for the system. We already touched upon this essential aspect of the modeling in Chapter 4, *Designing the Model*.

Let's see what we can do to build our model in a way that we can define transactional boundaries such that different use cases will not conflict with one another when our software needs to execute operations on the same real-world objects that, however, can be represented by different objects in the software model, or even belong to different models.

Aggregate pattern

In the case of the data model that we were dealing with earlier in this chapter, we have one composition—Order is a composition of the OrderLine elements. You probably know how this model would look if we moved from a data model to a class diagram:

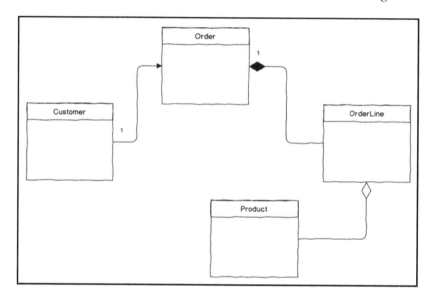

Aggregation in UML

In UML, composition implies that child elements cannot exist without their parent element. Indeed, having order lines that aren't linked to any order makes no sense. Such a composition as a whole forms a logical indivisible structure, although, inside this structure, we can find individual elements. For the outside world, an order includes its order lines and is seen as one thing, although the order can have many order lines. In DDD, such constructs are known as **aggregates**. Since we were using UML for a short while, it can create some confusion, because, in UML, aggregation means something else, and the closest analogy to a DDD aggregate is the UML concept of composition. Aggregates share the same propositions as UML compositions that the parent object consists of or owns all child objects, and when the parent object is removed, all child objects must be removed too, because it doesn't make sense for those objects to exist anymore. The parent object of an aggregate is called an **aggregate root**. Complex object graphs with a single parent could be visualized like a tree, where the parent object is where all the tree branches are growing from, so the root analogy makes perfect sense.

However, an aggregate is more than just a composition of classes. Aggregate boundaries also serve as transaction boundaries. For the purpose of this chapter, we will concentrate on two aspects of it—**atomicity** and **consistency**. As mentioned before, transactions imply the all-or-nothing principle of operations. An aggregate changes its state as a whole, no matter how the aggregate is persisted. If we use an ORM tool and our aggregate spans multiple database tables, all operations on those tables need to be wrapped in a database transaction. Furthermore, the consistency aspect requires an aggregate to ensure that the aggregate state is being validated across all operations that are executed on that aggregate. Hence, it is not a database or a code that is not part of the aggregate itself, such as an API controller or an application service. Unlike the preceding code, all these validity checks need to be a part of the aggregate code, and therefore they need to be implemented inside the domain model.

We already have quite a few characteristics of aggregates, so we can see how this pattern would apply to our preceding sample. If we start looking from the data model, we could suspect that `Order` and `OrderLine` form some sort of composition, since `OrderLine` records cannot exist without a parent `Order`. It applies both to atomicity and consistency. If we change the order status because one line of that order is marked as shipped—these changes need to be executed together; otherwise, the order state would become invalid—we might get an order with the status *pending* when one order line has already been marked as shipped. So, we would expect such an order to have a *partially delivered* status, and if that isn't the case, then our order state is not valid. Since we know that an order line is a child object, we don't really want to expose any operations on order lines directly from outside the domain model. It would make much more sense if the order lines are manipulated by the `Order` class itself. In this case, the `Order` class becomes our aggregate root, and it will have methods that change the state of its lines.

At the same time, an aggregate does not guarantee any consistency constraints that are external to the aggregate. For the relational data model, it would mean that we cannot have referential integrity between the table that is used to persist our aggregate root (`Order`) and anything that is outside the aggregate boundary.

If we make some changes in the data model to reflect the new insight, it would look like this:

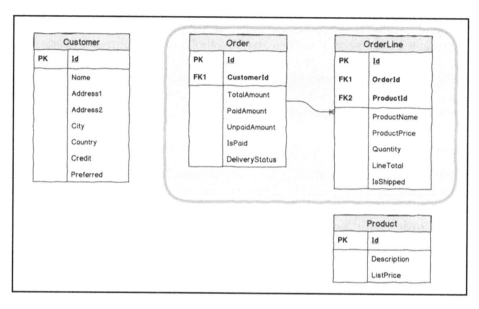

Removing references create explicit boundaries

Note that relations between `Order` and `Customer` tables and `OrderLine` and `Product` table are now gone, but we kept the reference fields—`CustomerId` and `ProductId`. We still need to know whether the customer has placed the order and what products we are selling. However, as regards the normal operation of our system, we don't need object references in ORM, and a lack of referential integrity that some developers might perceive as a negative side-effect of isolating the aggregate, in fact, gives us a new degree of freedom. For example, order lines need to stay intact if the product that was used for those lines goes out of sales and is then removed from the `Product` table. We won't discuss flags and other soft-delete methods since I am making a point of keeping these things separate.

Let's now take a look at how the code for the API controller would look:

```
public async Task ShipOrderLine(int orderId, int orderLineId)
{
    var order = await _orderRepository.Get(orderId);
    order.ShipOrderLine(orderLineId);
    await _orderRepository.Commit();
}
```

That's quite a change, isn't it? Of course, the logic has not disappeared; it has moved to the `Order` class itself:

```
public void ShipOrderLine(int orderLineId)
{
    var orderLine = OrderLines.First(x => x.Id == orderLineId);
    orderLine.IsShipped = true;
    DeliveryStatus =
        OrderLines.All(x => x.IsShipped)
            ? DeliveryStatus.Shipped
            : DeliveryStatus.PartiallyShipped;
}
```

As you can see, the accidental complexity of two-way object reference for order lines can now be removed. On the other hand, we have to change the API because we cannot just ask for an order line's ID. We need to know the order ID as well, because the order line's ID is internal to a given order, and we are using our aggregate root to access its child elements.

Of course, more complex operations would now require more work. How would we perform something such as what the `TakeOnCustomerCredit` method does? Since we do not have object relations between our `Customer` and `Order` objects, and we have decided that our aggregate is wrapping all about the `order` handling, but not `Customer`, we cannot complete one transaction on these two distinct objects. This might sound like an impossible task, and often, such dilemmas lead to workaround and shortcuts, and then the aggregate pattern is seen as something that gets in the way and needs to be ignored in one or two specific cases. In fact, we need to do quite the opposite. We have to go back to the modeling space to find out more about this problem.

Looking back at the method code, we can see that it does the following:

- Checks whether the customer has enough credit to cover what remains unpaid in relation to an order
- Decreases the customer's credit amount for the unpaid amount of the order
- Increases the order's paid amount
- Decreases the order's unpaid amount
- Sets the order status to *paid* if the unpaid amount is zero (for that code, it will always be true)
- Increases the customer's total spent amount by the payment amount
- Upgrades the customer to *preferred* status if this customer has spent over a certain threshold

That's quite a lot, and now we are going to use the power of aggregates to make more sense of the whole flow.

First, we need to check what does not belong here. The first candidate would be to evaluate the last two actions on the list: updating the total spent amount and upgrading the customer. It seems as if something has happened not only after taking a credit payment but also for the credit card, cash, and any other sorts of payments. Keeping the code here means that we need to either copy and paste it or have some shared code. None of these alternatives are really appealing. Most importantly, these two actions have no relation to the order processing. Imagine one of these actions failing. Such a failure should have no effect on the order processing.

Then, we need to check what we have to know and do in order to complete the operation. In our case, we must ensure that the remaining credit limit is higher or equal to the order unpaid amount. For our code to make a decision regarding whether to proceed with the payment on credit, we need to have the information about the available credit limit for the ordering customer. But these details are now out of our aggregate scope, so what can we do about it to ensure that an order cannot violate the consistency rule?

Here comes another aspect of emerging aggregate boundaries, where we need to evaluate the speed of change in objects that our system works with. The `Customer` object now contains some information that forms a customer profile—name, address, and so on. At the same time, it contains some financial details that potentially change for every order that we process. It is clear from our code that when we process orders, we do not have any rules that give a discount for customers that have their name starting with *A*, or their location in Belgium. We could imagine such a requirement due to logistics reasons, but it is not relevant to our example. Our conclusion should be that the customer profile information changes very rarely, while the remaining customer credit limit changes quite often. At the same time, information about the total allowed credit limit might still belong to the customer profile, and it changes rarely too. This means that we are dealing with two different aspects of customer details:

Customer profile	Customer running credit
Name, address, total credit limit	Available credit limit
Changes now and then	Changes for each credit order
No rules for order processing	Required for the consistency of order processing

We finally come to the conclusion that our *holistic* `Customer` object is not suitable for these different use cases. The solution for our model would be to move the information that is required to ensure order processing consistency and that the business rules need to be moved closer to the order processing logic. We can do this by splitting our `Customer` entity into two, each of which is responsible for its own set of use cases. We can even give the new entity a more explicit name: `CustomerCredit`, to express the specific use of this information. Our diagram would look like this:

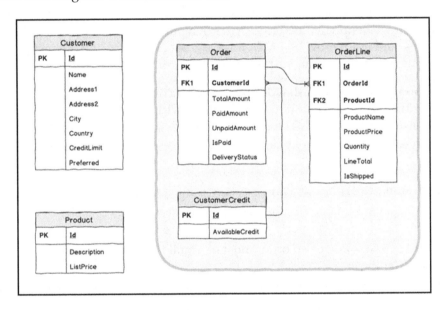

Moving all related concerns to one boundary

In fact, what we did here belongs more to finding linguistic and contextual boundaries, and this topic will be covered in more detail in `Chapter 9`, *CQRS - The Read Side*. For now, we will continue discussing the aggregate boundaries only.

Our new model looks better, but it has one issue—the aggregation has now shifted to the `CustomerCredit` entity, and it seems to become our aggregate root. From the relational consistency point of view, this is perfectly fine. From another point of view, it looks weird to process all orders by calling methods on the `CustomerCredit` entity. Another negative aspect is that the ownership of objects has also changed. Before, we had `Order`, which is responsible for its `OrderLine`. Now, we have `CustomerCredit`, which is responsible for everything. It looks as though if we remove the `CustomerCredit` object from the system, we also need to remove all of its orders. This is definitely not what we need. Customers come and go, but we definitely need to keep track of all our orders, including the completed ones, and not remove them. In this case, we clearly see the downside of having a larger aggregate with the dubious responsibility of the supportive entity.

It is also important to remember that despite having a constraint, we need to have enough credit to cover the order total before we can proceed with it, as the order itself can be valid even if this constraint is violated. The order has its own invariants—a set of unbreakable rules that guarantee the consistency of each order. Let's see what invariants the `Order` aggregate has:

- The sum of `PaidAmount` and `UnpaidAmount` should be equal to `TotalAmount`.
- `DeliveryStatus` of an order can only be set to `Delivered` if, for all order lines of the `IsShipped` property, this is set to `true`.
- The `TotalAmount` of an order must be equal to the sum of the `LineTotal` of all the order lines.
- For each order line, `LineTotal` must equal the `ProductPrice` multiplied by `Quantity`.

As you can see, there is nothing in these invariants that requires us to know the customer's available credit or any information about the product, and so on. So, for us to decide whether an order is consistent, it is sufficient to have the details pertaining to the order itself and all of its lines.

As regards ownership, it is also obvious that individual order lines cannot exist without the order they belong to.

Therefore, our final move would be to break the relationship between orders and customers, even for the more explicit `CustomerCredit` entity, while keeping the aggregation between `Order` and the `OrderLine` entities:

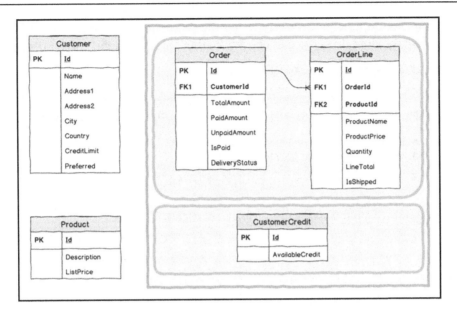

Making the boundaries smaller decrease transaction scopes

In this model, we have two aggregates inside an isolated part of the system. We know that these aggregates need to be inside the same contextual boundaries, but they need to be separated and form different transactional and consistency boundaries for the reason we discussed previously. Now, the question arises of how can we enforce our constraints if orders have no information about the available credit for the ordering customer, from inside the aggregate object graph. We will use the power of domain services to perform this check.

Inside our domain project, we can define an interface for such a domain service:

```
public interface ICustomerCreditService
{
    Task<bool> EnsureEnoughCredit(int customerId, decimal amount);
}
```

Notice that we have the `EnsureEnoughCredit` method that returns a Boolean value, instead of returning the available credit limit itself. By doing this, we enforce the utilization of the ubiquitous language and shift the credit limit check logic to the domain service. The service might, for example, decide that for preferred customers, we can allow an overdraft above the available limit. Of course, in such an instance, we'd also need to move the `Preferred` attribute to the `CustomerCredit` entity.

Then, we can use our application service to handle the `TakeOnCustomerCredit` command, where it will use the domain service to check whether this command can be processed:

```
public class OrderHandlingApplicationService
{
    private readonly IOrderRepository _orderRepository;
    private readonly ICustomerCreditService _customerCreditService;

    public OrderHandlingApplicationService(
        IOrderRepository orderRepository,
        ICustomerCreditService customerCreditService)
    {

        _orderRepository = orderRepository;
        _customerCreditService = customerCreditService;
    }

    public async Task Handle(TakeOnCustomerCredit command)
    {
        var order = await _orderRepository.Get(command.OrderId);
        var hasEnoughCredit =
            await _customerCreditService.EnsureEnoughCredit(
                command.CustomerId,
                order.UnpaidAmount);
        if (!hasEnoughCredit)
            throw new DomainException(
                $"Not enough credit for order {command.OrderId}");

        order.TakeOnCredit();
    }
}
```

I have to mention that moving the customer credit to a separate entity can cause situations when the credit amount goes below zero due to race conditions. When applying the credit limit change in a separate transaction, you might want to check if the operation results in the negative value and then decide what to do if the result is negative. One possible technique is to inform the account manager by email about the situation and let them resolve it with the customer. From a technical side, it is possible to create a compensating action to put the order on hold until the issue is resolved. Overall, those decisions should never be seen as technical. Talk to domain experts and ask them what solution would they prefer.

This approach moves some domain logic to the application service, and that might not be desirable in some cases. To solve this, we could use the double dispatch pattern and let the `Order` aggregate decide on the constraint. If we decide to use double dispatch, it would look like this:

```
public class Order : Aggregate<OrderId>
{
    public async Task TakeOnCredit(ICustomerCreditService
customerCreditService)
    {
        var hasEnoughCredit =
            await _customerCreditService.EnsureEnoughCredit(
                command.CustomerId,
                order.UnpaidAmount);
        if (!hasEnoughCredit)
            throw new DomainException(
                $"Not enough credit for order {command.OrderId}");

        // actual domain logic here
    }
}
```

Then, the application service will pass the dependency when calling the aggregate root method:

```
public async Task Handle(TakeOnCustomerCredit command)
{
    var order = await _orderRepository.Get(command.OrderId);
    await order.TakeOnCredit(_customerCreditService);
}
```

It might look as if we are creating a dependency between our domain model and the infrastructure since it is clear that the domain service needs to fetch the `CustomerCredit` entity to get the data. However, our `Order` aggregate root only gets the interface dependency, and, as you remember, the interface itself is defined inside the domain project. Its implementation is indeed located inside the application itself, but this is perfectly normal.

We have still not seen how our aggregate is protecting its invariants, but now it is time to get back to our `Marketplace` application and add some code there, based on what we have learned about aggregates so far. We also need to cover the aggregate persistence, since we already used the `IOrderRepository` interface that is responsible for getting the aggregate state from the database.

Protecting invariants

In Chapter 5, *Implementing the Model*, we went through using value objects to protect invalid values from even being used as parameters for entity constructors and methods. This technique allows us to move a lot of checks to value objects, provides nice encapsulation, and enables type safety. Then, when we create a new entity or execute some behavior using entity methods, we need to execute further checks. Since we can be quite sure that all parameters already contain valid individual values, we need to ensure that a given combination of parameters, the current entity state, and the executed behavior are not going to bring the entity to an invalid state.

Protecting the internal state from being invalid and, as a result, bringing the model into an inconsistent state, is one of the most important characteristics of aggregates. Aggregate invariants must be satisfied for each operation that triggers a state change; thus, we need to ensure that we control the aggregate state when calling any command method on the aggregate.

Let's look at what complex rules we have for our classified ad entity. To find such rules, we can use some sticky notes from our detailed EventStorming session in Chapter 3, *EventStorming*, and put them on a chart, as follows:

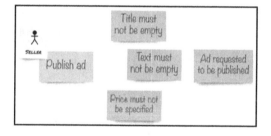

Business rules can prevent the command execution

Analyzing constraints for a command

We put the command to the left side, the event to the right side, and try to find out what could prevent our command from being executed in a way that it produces the desired outcome (the event). In our case here, we need to ensure that before an ad can be put to the review queue, it must have a non-empty title, text, and price.

We cannot put these checks combined with the value object, since before the ad is sent to review, it can have an empty title and text, and it can have no price. Only when a given command is being executed do we need to check whether these constraints are satisfied. It is what we can call an invariant for this entity—an ad that is in a pending review cannot have an empty title, empty text, or zero price.

There are at least two ways of ensuring that our entity never gets to an invalid state. The first and most obvious way is to add checks to the operation code. There is no way of requesting that the ad be published, so let's add it and make some changes related to the fact of using value objects for the entity state as well:

```csharp
namespace Marketplace.Domain
{
    public class ClassifiedAd
    {
        public ClassifiedAdId Id { get; }

        public ClassifiedAd(ClassifiedAdId id, UserId ownerId)
        {
            Id = id;
            OwnerId = ownerId;
            State = ClassifiedAdState.Inactive;
        }

        public void SetTitle(ClassifiedAdTitle title) => Title = title;

        public void UpdateText(ClassifiedAdText text) => Text = text;

        public void UpdatePrice(Price price) => Price = price;

        public void RequestToPublish()
        {
            if (Title == null)
                throw new InvalidEntityStateException(this,
                    "title cannot be empty");
            if (Text == null)
                throw new InvalidEntityStateException(this,
                    "text cannot be empty");
            if (Price?.Amount == 0)
                throw new InvalidEntityStateException(this,
                    "price cannot be zero");

            State = ClassifiedAdState.PendingReview;
        }

        public UserId OwnerId { get; }
        public ClassifiedAdTitle Title { get; private set; }
```

```
        public ClassifiedAdText Text { get; private set; }
        public Price Price { get; private set; }
        public ClassifiedAdState State { get; private set; }
        public UserId ApprovedBy { get; private set; }

        public enum ClassifiedAdState
        {
            PendingReview,
            Active,
            Inactive,
            MarkedAsSold
        }
    }
}
```

In the new entity code, we enforce the constraints that became visible from our detailed model, so the operation is only executed if all constraints are satisfied. To let the caller know if our entity is not ready to be published when some of those checks fail, we use our custom exception, which is implemented like this:

```
using System;

namespace Marketplace.Domain
{
    public class InvalidEntityStateException : Exception
    {
        public InvalidEntityStateException(object entity, string
        message)
            : base($"Entity {entity.GetType().Name}" +
              $"state change rejected, {message}")
        {
        }
    }
}
```

This method of checking constraints before executing the operation, in the operation method itself, has one disadvantage. If, now, we change the price to zero, it will go through, because the UpdatePrice method is not checking the price value. We could, of course, copy the price check to the UpdatePrice method too, but there might be more methods that need the same tests and we will keep copying the control blocks. This will lead to a situation where, if we need to change any of those rules, we need to go to numerous places to replace all of the checks. This approach is very error prone.

To combine rules in one place, we can use contract programming techniques. Part of contract programming can be seen in value objects, since we evaluate pre-conditions for each parameter of the operation method. When we execute the operation without doing any additional checks, we will need to do a combined test (post-condition control). This check can be implemented in one place for the whole entity, and each operation will need to call it at the last line in the method.

For our classified ad entity, it could look like this:

```
namespace Marketplace.Domain
{
    public class ClassifiedAd
    {
        public ClassifiedAdId Id { get; }

        public ClassifiedAd(ClassifiedAdId id, UserId ownerId)
        {
            Id = id;
            OwnerId = ownerId;
            State = ClassifiedAdState.Inactive;
            EnsureValidState();
        }

        public void SetTitle(ClassifiedAdTitle title)
        {
            Title = title;
            EnsureValidState();
        }

        public void UpdateText(ClassifiedAdText text)
        {
            Text = text;
            EnsureValidState();
        }

        public void UpdatePrice(Price price)
        {
            Price = price;
            EnsureValidState();
        }

        public void RequestToPublish()
        {
            State = ClassifiedAdState.PendingReview;
            EnsureValidState();
        }
```

```
            private void EnsureValidState()
            {
                var valid =
                    Id != null &&
                    OwnerId != null &&
                    (State switch
                    {
                        ClassifiedAdState.PendingReview =>
                            Title != null
                            && Text != null
                            && Price?.Amount > 0,
                        ClassifiedAdState.Active =>
                            Title != null
                            && Text != null
                            && Price?.Amount > 0
                            && ApprovedBy != null,
                        _ => true
                    });

                if (!valid)
                    throw new InvalidEntityStateException(
                        this, $"Post-checks failed in state {State}");
            }

            public UserId OwnerId { get; }
            public ClassifiedAdTitle Title { get; private set; }
            public ClassifiedAdText Text { get; private set; }
            public Price Price1 { get; private set; }
            public ClassifiedAdState State { get; private set; }
            public UserId ApprovedBy { get; private set; }

            public enum ClassifiedAdState
            {
                PendingReview,
                Active,
                Inactive,
                MarkedAsSold
            }
        }

    }
```

As you can see, we have added a method called EnsureValidState, which checks that in any situation, the entity state is valid, and if it is not valid, an exception will be thrown. When we call this method from any operation method, we can be sure that no matter what we are trying to do, our entity will always be in a valid state or the caller will get an exception.

Throwing an exception when the entity becomes invalid is the easiest way to prevent inconsistencies, but it has its downsides. The whole application needs to be able to handle such exceptions gracefully so the user gets properly informed.

The web API code for this chapter, for example, doesn't do it and expects all operations to be successfully executed. As a result, when we try executing commands that bring the entity to some incorrect state, will crash the API method and return the exception via HTTP. The web API code will be improved as we move along and we will start returning proper errors results from the API.

When using Event Sourcing one of the techniques to expose incorrect operations is to emit domain events like `PriceChangeDenied`, which include all values that the application tried to apply to an entity but failed. Using this method gives developers a powerful tool to find out why certain commands weren't executed and even potentially discover malicious behavior of the user.

Also, we converted all private fields to public read-only properties. We need public properties to write tests, although we don't necessarily need to expose the internal entity state. To prevent setting values of these properties outside operation methods, all properties have private setters, or no setters for properties that are set in the constructor.

Now, let's write some tests to ensure that our constraints work:

```
using System;
using Marketplace.Domain;
using Xunit;

namespace Marketplace.Tests
{
    public class ClassifiedAd_Publish_Spec
    {
        private readonly ClassifiedAd _classifiedAd;

        public ClassifiedAd_Publish_Spec()
        {
            _classifiedAd = new ClassifiedAd(
                new ClassifiedAdId(Guid.NewGuid()),
                new UserId(Guid.NewGuid()));
        }

        [Fact]
        public void Can_publish_a_valid_ad()
```

```
{
    _classifiedAd.SetTitle(
        ClassifiedAdTitle.FromString("Test ad"));
    _classifiedAd.UpdateText(
        ClassifiedAdText.FromString("Please buy my stuff"));
    _classifiedAd.UpdatePrice(
        Price.FromDecimal(100.10m, "EUR",
            new FakeCurrencyLookup()));
    _classifiedAd.RequestToPublish();

    Assert.Equal(
        ClassifiedAd.ClassifiedAdState.PendingReview,
        _classifiedAd.State);
}

[Fact]
public void Cannot_publish_without_title()
{
    _classifiedAd.UpdateText(
        ClassifiedAdText.FromString("Please buy my stuff"));
    _classifiedAd.UpdatePrice(
        Price.FromDecimal(100.10m, "EUR",
            new FakeCurrencyLookup()));
    Assert.Throws<InvalidEntityStateException>(
        () => _classifiedAd.RequestToPublish());
}

[Fact]
public void Cannot_publish_without_text()
{
    _classifiedAd.SetTitle(
        ClassifiedAdTitle.FromString("Test ad"));
    _classifiedAd.UpdatePrice(
        Price.FromDecimal(100.10m, "EUR",
            new FakeCurrencyLookup()));
    Assert.Throws<InvalidEntityStateException>(
        () => _classifiedAd.RequestToPublish());
}

[Fact]
public void Cannot_publish_without_price()
{
    _classifiedAd.SetTitle(
        ClassifiedAdTitle.FromString("Test ad"));
    _classifiedAd.UpdateText(
        ClassifiedAdText.FromString("Please buy my stuff"));
    Assert.Throws<InvalidEntityStateException>(
        () => _classifiedAd.RequestToPublish());
```

```
        }

        [Fact]
        public void Cannot_publish_with_zero_price()
        {
            _classifiedAd.SetTitle(
                ClassifiedAdTitle.FromString("Test ad"));
            _classifiedAd.UpdateText(
                ClassifiedAdText.FromString("Please buy my stuff"));
            _classifiedAd.UpdatePrice(
                Price.FromDecimal(0.0m, "EUR",
                    new FakeCurrencyLookup()));
            Assert.Throws<InvalidEntityStateException>(
                () => _classifiedAd.RequestToPublish());
        }
    }
}
```

This spec contains several tests for one operation (publish, or submit for review) with different pre-conditions. Here, we test a happy path when all necessary details are correctly set before the ad can be sent for review; we also test several negative cases when publishing is not allowed due to missing mandatory information. Perhaps testing negative scenarios is even more essential, since it is straightforward to find out when the happy path does not work—your users will immediately complain. Testing negative scenarios prevents bugs in controlling entity invariants, which, in turn, prevent entities from becoming invalid.

When we moved the entity state checks to one method, we effectively set up a holistic set of rules that need to be executed for each operation. This means that those rules aren't command-specific any more, and our EnsureValidState method has become a guardian for the entire object. It protects the invariants of our ClassifiedAd entity so it can never become invalid. The ability to protect its own invariants is one of the main aspects of the aggregate pattern. By executing each command for the ClassifiedAd entity within individual transactions, and by establishing invariant protection, we created our first aggregate.

Now, we have learned how to protect our entity from becoming invalid. But we expect more entities to appear in our application, and the code of the ClassifiedAd entity becomes quite verbose because we have to call the EnsureValidState method in each operation. Also, it is certainly possible to forget to put the call in an entity method and then get a chance to get the entity in an invalid state without getting any exceptions. However, this cannot possibly happen if we want to have a true aggregate, so let's see how we can use the power of events to ensure the state validity for all operations.

Enforcing the rules

Let's now examine how we execute operations on the entity:

- Call the entity method for operation (the CQS command)
- The method emits an event
- An event is then applied to the entity state to perform the state transition

So, if we want to ensure that all state transitions do not break our invariants, we can move the call to `EnsureValidState` to the `Apply` method. The need to protect its state only applies to the aggregate root entity because it must ensure that the whole aggregate state is correct, and not just its own state validity. Therefore, we can make a new base class for this special type of entity:

```
using System.Collections.Generic;
using System.Linq;

namespace Marketplace.Framework
{
    public abstract class AggregateRoot<TId>
        where TId : Value<TId>
    {
        public TId Id { get; protected set; }

        protected abstract void When(object @event);
        private readonly List<object> _changes;

        protected AggregateRoot() => _changes = new List<object>();

        protected void Apply(object @event)
        {
            When(@event);
            EnsureValidState();
            _changes.Add(@event);
        }

        public IEnumerable<object> GetChanges()
            => _changes.AsEnumerable();

        public void ClearChanges() => _changes.Clear();

        protected abstract void EnsureValidState();
    }
}
```

Here, we have renamed the _events collection to _changes to make the naming more explicit. We also added a call to EnsureValidState to the Apply method. This means that whenever we execute an operation that is supposed to change the aggregate root entity state, we apply a new event and the state changes in the When method. However, before adding the new event to the list of changes, we check whether the new state is valid and that no invariants are broken. If the new state violates the invariants, we throw an exception.

After we refactor our ClassifiedAd class to use the new base class, the code becomes simpler:

```
using Marketplace.Framework;
using static Marketplace.Domain.Events;

namespace Marketplace.Domain
{
    public class ClassifiedAd : Entity<ClassifiedAdId>
    {
        public ClassifiedAdId Id { get; private set; }
        public UserId OwnerId { get; private set; }
        public ClassifiedAdTitle Title { get; private set; }
        public ClassifiedAdText Text { get; private set; }
        public Price Price { get; private set; }
        public ClassifiedAdState State { get; private set; }
        public UserId ApprovedBy { get; private set; }

        public ClassifiedAd(ClassifiedAdId id, UserId ownerId) =>
            Apply(new ClassifiedAdCreated
            {
                Id = id,
                OwnerId = ownerId
            });

        public void SetTitle(ClassifiedAdTitle title) =>
            Apply(new ClassifiedAdTitleChanged
            {
                Id = Id,
                Title = title
            });

        public void UpdateText(ClassifiedAdText text) =>
            Apply(new ClassifiedAdTextUpdated
            {
                Id = Id,
                AdText = text
            });
```

```
public void UpdatePrice(Price price) =>
    Apply(new ClassifiedAdPriceUpdated
    {
        Id = Id,
        Price = price.Amount,
        CurrencyCode = price.Currency.CurrencyCode
    });

public void RequestToPublish() =>
    Apply(new ClassidiedAdSentForReview {Id = Id});

protected override void When(object @event)
{
    switch (@event)
    {
        case ClassifiedAdCreated e:
            Id = new ClassifiedAdId(e.Id);
            OwnerId = new UserId(e.OwnerId);
            State = ClassifiedAdState.Inactive;
            break;
        case ClassifiedAdTitleChanged e:
            Title = new ClassifiedAdTitle(e.Title);
            break;
        case ClassifiedAdTextUpdated e:
            Text = new ClassifiedAdText(e.AdText);
            break;
        case ClassifiedAdPriceUpdated e:
            Price = new Price(e.Price, e.CurrencyCode);
            break;
        case ClassidiedAdSentForReview _:
            State = ClassifiedAdState.PendingReview;
            break;
    }
}

protected override void EnsureValidState()
{
    var valid =
        Id != null &&
        OwnerId != null &&
        (State switch
        {
            ClassifiedAdState.PendingReview =>
                Title != null
                && Text != null
                && Price?.Amount > 0,
            ClassifiedAdState.Active =>
                Title != null
```

```
                        && Text != null
                        && Price?.Amount > 0
                        && ApprovedBy != null,
                    _ => true
                });

            if (!valid)
                throw new InvalidEntityStateException(
                    this, $"Post-checks failed in state {State}");
        }

        public enum ClassifiedAdState
        {
            PendingReview,
            Active,
            Inactive,
            MarkedAsSold
        }
    }
}
```

As you can see, all the conditions are now consolidated in one place, and no matter what we do, we cannot publish an ad that has no price or no text. Also, it is impossible to have a hidden bug in any other places of the application that could make an ad active and visible without being approved first. This technique to ensure the validity of the state is consistently very powerful, and it also improves the readability of our code by giving developers a clue as to where they can look when trying to figure out all the rules that an entity must adhere to.

Entities inside an aggregate

It might seem weird that we just added a base class called AggregateRoot and used it instead of the Entity class that we already had before. We could have just added new code to the Entity base class. However, this was done on purpose, because, as you might remember, aggregates can potentially form larger object graphs, and, in addition to the root entity, we might have several entities that will be the children of the root. We already discussed the ownership strategy, so when an aggregate is removed, the aggregate root and all its children are also removed from the system.

For all the child objects, we would be talking about value objects or entities, as the rule of the aggregate pattern is strict. None of those child objects should be referenced, accessed, or manipulated outside the aggregate boundary. All operations on an aggregate need to be performed by calling methods on the aggregate root. Also, accessing any child objects inside the aggregate needs to go via the aggregate root as well.

Let's illustrate this principle by adding an entity to our `ClassifiedAd` aggregate. One of our EventStorming sessions helped us to discover that we need pictures to be added to ads since, without pictures, people are really hesitant to buy anything. An ad can have multiple pictures, and we could think of these pictures as value objects because users cannot *change* images. They can either upload new ones or remove existing ones. However, it seems as if users need to be able to choose in what order those images appear and what image is shown in the search results, as the *main* image. We can solve this issue by using a value object called `ImageOrder`, which will be replaced each time the user changes the order of the pictures. But, even in this case, we would need to reference images somehow, using some sort of identity. It makes us certain that our future `Picture` objects will be entities so we can reference them by an identity inside the aggregate. If we do that, we do not need to have an `ImageOrder` object, since we can keep the ordering attribute inside the `Picture` object itself. So, our entity will have the option of a state change, and we need to handle that too.

We can use the `Entity` base class to create our new `Picture` class in the `Domain` project:

```
using System;
using System.Collections.Generic;
using Marketplace.Framework;

namespace Marketplace.Domain
{
    public class Picture : Entity<PictureId>
    {
        internal PictureSize Size { get; set; }
        internal Uri Location { get; set; }
        internal int Order { get; set; }

        protected override void When(object @event)
        {
        }
    }

    public class PictureId : Value<PictureId>
    {
        public PictureId(Guid value) => Value = value;

        public Guid Value { get; }
```

```
        }
    }
```

Here, we do not expect to hold the image itself inside the entity as a byte array. The physical image itself is not a concern for our domain. Within the domain model, we assume that all images are stored somewhere and we just need to have an image location (a URL to an external resource) to be connected to the classified ad.

We still need to remember that all operations are executed by calling the aggregate root, so we add an operation to the `ClassifiedAd` class:

```
public void AddPicture(Uri pictureUri, PictureSize size) =>
    Apply(new Events.PictureAddedToAClassifiedAd
    {
        PictureId = new Guid(),
        ClassifiedAdId = Id,
        Url = pictureUri.ToString(),
        Height = size.Height,
        Width = size.Width
    });
```

Of course, we need to create a class for the `PictureAddedToAClassifiedAd` event as well:

```
namespace Marketplace.Domain
{
    public static class Events
    {
        // all events are still here

        public class PictureAddedToAClassifiedAd
        {
            public Guid ClassifiedAdId { get; set; }
            public Guid PictureId { get; set; }
            public string Url { get; set; }
            public int Height { get; set; }
            public int Width { get; set; }
        }
    }
}
```

In the event class, `ClassifiedAdId` is the ID of our aggregate root. The picture ID is externally generated, and it will be sent to the application service by the client, but we will never use this ID to directly reference the picture from outside the aggregate boundaries. Also, we assume that pictures are always added to the end of the list, so we don't need to send the order number since it will be assigned by the aggregate logic.

We used two value objects as parameters for the AddPicture method. The System.Uri type is a .NET framework standard type, and we only need to define the PictureSize value object:

```
using System;
using Marketplace.Framework;

namespace Marketplace.Domain
{
    public class PictureSize : Value<PictureSize>
    {
        public int Width { get; internal set; }
        public int Height { get; internal set; }

        public PictureSize(int width, int height)
        {
            if (Width <= 0)
                throw new ArgumentOutOfRangeException(
                    nameof(width),
                    "Picture width must be a positive number");
            if (Height <= 0)
                throw new ArgumentOutOfRangeException(
                    nameof(height),
                    "Picture height must be a positive number");
            Width = width;
            Height = height;
        }

        internal PictureSize() { }
    }
}
```

Again, we use the power of value objects and ensure the validity of input values inside it, so we don't need to spread this logic everywhere. We still need an internal constructor that will allow us to create this object without validating values because we need to be able to unconditionally retrieve the existing object from the database, and we cannot rely on the idea that validation rules will not change over time.

Also here, throwing an exception is not the only way you can use to protect value objects from becoming invalid. One alternative way is to create a property IsValid for the value object but then you need to check it everywhere when using the value, probably in the application service. Another alternative is to create a special static object instance that would indicate an incorrect value. You can then check if the value you are trying to apply is valid or not. Although you'd need more code to implement both of those methods, you will avoid throwing exceptions. Remember that unlike Java, C# has no way to explicitly inform those who call your objects that the method can throw an exception. Therefore, some callers won't be considering wrapping the call in a try-catch block and the application can blow up at runtime.

Now, we have to change the aggregate state after we apply the new event to the aggregate root. We do this by adding a new case to our pattern matching case in the When method of the ClassifiedAd class:

```
protected override void When(object @event)
{
    switch (@event)
    {
        // previous cases as before, removed for brevity

        // picture
        case Events.PictureAddedToAClassifiedAd e:
            var newPicture = new Picture{
                Size = new PictureSize(e.Height, e.Width),
                Location = new Uri(e.Url),
                Order = Pictures.Max(x => x.Order) + 1
            };
            Pictures.Add(newPicture);
            break;
    }
}
```

As you might have noticed, we referenced a new property called Pictures. It is the list of entities that are held inside the aggregate, so they are child objects of our aggregate root. We declare it as a list. We also need to initialize the list in the aggregate root constructor, so we don't get a null reference exception when we don't have any pictures and try to add one:

```
public class ClassifiedAd : AggregateRoot<ClassifiedAdId>
{
    // existing code

    public ClassifiedAd(ClassifiedAdId id, UserId ownerId)
```

```
    {
        Pictures = new List<Picture>(); // <-- this is the new line
        Apply(new Events.ClassifiedAdCreated
        {
            Id = id,
            OwnerId = ownerId
        });
    }

    public List<Picture> Pictures { get; private set; }

    // existing code
}
```

This all seems fine, except it isn't. Our aggregate root performs the logic that belongs to the `Picture` entity itself. For now, it is just one operation, but we definitely expect at least the re-ordering functionality. The entity needs to be responsible for updating its own state, and since we do it using events, it needs to get the events that concern that entity. Notice that our `Picture` class implements the `When` method from the base class, but it is completely empty. We need to find a way to empower our entities to handle their own events. In addition, entities can have their own methods, so the aggregate root doesn't contain the logic that belongs to entities, and instead calls entity methods. When we add methods to an entity class, it will produce events to change the entity state. But those events can be of interest for the aggregate root as well, so we need to have some code that will traverse events from the entity level to the aggregate root level. Finally, we need events that are raised on the entity level to be added to the list of changes for the whole aggregate, and this list is maintained by the aggregate root. All those things require us to change the base classes, and that is what we are going to do now.

First, we add a new interface that both our entity base classes will implement. This interface has one method that applies domain events to an entity state (currently, we use the `When` method):

```
namespace Marketplace.Framework
{
    public interface IInternalEventHandler
    {
        void Handle(object @event);
    }
}
```

Then, we make a number of changes to the `AggregateRoot` base class. This will implement the new interface using a private explicit method. In addition, we add the `ApplyToEntity` method, which will allow us to push domain events to entities. This method does nothing when we pass `null` as the entity parameter because we plan to call it from the `When` method of the aggregate root and it should *never* fail. We will elaborate on why that is so in Chapter 8, *Aggregate Persistence*, when we'll talk about Event Sourcing. For now, we shall assume that our action method in the aggregate root will ensure that the child entity is present before producing an event that we will be propagating to the entity:

```csharp
using System.Collections.Generic;
using System.Linq;

namespace Marketplace.Framework
{
    public abstract class AggregateRoot<TId>
        : IInternalEventHandler where TId : Value<TId>
    {
        public TId Id { get; protected set; }

        protected abstract void When(object @event);
        private readonly List<object> _changes;

        protected AggregateRoot() => _changes = new List<object>();

        protected void Apply(object @event)
        {
            When(@event);
            EnsureValidState();
            _changes.Add(@event);
        }

        public IEnumerable<object> GetChanges()
            => _changes.AsEnumerable();

        public void ClearChanges() => _changes.Clear();

        protected abstract void EnsureValidState();

        protected void ApplyToEntity(
            IInternalEventHandler entity,
            object @event)
            => entity?.Handle(@event);

        void IInternalEventHandler.Handle(object @event)
            => When(@event);
    }
}
```

Finally, we need to change the `Entity` base class code in a way that it implements the new interface as well:

```
using System;

namespace Marketplace.Framework
{
    public abstract class Entity<TId>
        : IInternalEventHandler where TId : Value<TId>
    {
        private readonly Action<object> _applier;
        public TId Id { get; protected set; }

        protected Entity(Action<object> applier)
            => _applier = applier;

        protected abstract void When(object @event);

        protected void Apply(object @event)
        {
            When(@event);
            _applier(@event);
        }

        void IInternalEventHandler.Handle(object @event)
            => When(@event);
    }
}
```

We also added a constructor to this class that will accept an `applier` delegate. Since we always instantiate entities from the aggregate root, we will pass the `Apply` method of the root to all entities. Then, an entity will use double dispatch to inform the aggregate root of events that the entity will be producing. By doing this, we'll make sure that the aggregate root can also handle events from its child entities, that it calls the `EnsureValidState` method to ensure that there is no consistency violation within the aggregate boundaries, and that it adds new events to the single list of changes for the whole aggregate.

We use private methods to implement the new interface, so these methods will not be exposed when we use a class that is inherited from the `AggregateRoot` or `Entity` base classes, and this is exactly what we want.

So, our `Picture` entity now requires a little refactoring:

```
using System;
using Marketplace.Framework;

namespace Marketplace.Domain
{
    public class Picture : Entity<PictureId>
    {
        internal PictureSize Size { get; private set; }
        internal Uri Location { get; private set; }
        internal int Order { get; private set; }

        protected override void When(object @event)
        {
            switch (@event)
            {
                case Events.PictureAddedToAClassifiedAd e:
                    Id = new PictureId(e.PictureId);
                    Location = new Uri(e.Url);
                    Size = new PictureSize
                        { Height = e.Height, Width = e.Width};
                    Order = e.Order;
                    break;
            }
        }

        public Picture(Action<object> applier) : base(applier) { }
    }

    // the identity class code is still here
}
```

We changed two things:

- We added the constructor that accepts a reference to the `applier` delegate.
- We changed the `When` method, so it can now handle the creation of new pictures.

You perhaps noticed that the order is now coming from the event, so we need to add a new property to the event class. Currently, we don't use the `applier` delegate, because we have not added any operations to the entity yet, but we will be using it in the future. Also, it is important to stress that we are not using the public constructor for our `PictureSize` value object in the `When` method because the public constructor always applies business rules and can potentially fail, but it happens when we construct the value object in our application service before it even reaches the aggregate. In the `When` method, we need to process the event without checking those rules, because the `When` method should never fail.

Then, we can change the aggregate root code. First, we change the AddPicture method:

```
public void AddPicture(Uri pictureUri, PictureSize size) =>
    Apply(new Events.PictureAddedToAClassifiedAd
    {
        PictureId = new Guid(),
        ClassifiedAdId = Id,
        Url = pictureUri.ToString(),
        Height = size.Height,
        Width = size.Width,
        Order = Pictures.Max(x => x.Order)
    });
```

Then, we change the event handling in the When method (only changes are shown):

```
case Events.PictureAddedToAClassifiedAd e:
    var picture = new Picture(Apply);
    ApplyToEntity(picture, e);
    Pictures.Add(newPicture);
    break;
```

Let's now demonstrate how can we add some logic to the Picture entity and make sense of the applier delegate. One thing that can happen with an image is that it could be resized and we get new sizes. Out page, cannot be smaller than 800 x 600 pixels.

Again, we need to add a new event to our Events class:

```
public class ClassifiedAdPictureResized
{
    public Guid PictureId { get; set; }
    public int Height { get; set; }
    public int Width { get; set; }
}
```

Then, we need to add a ResizePicture method to the aggregate root. Since the command will get a picture id, we need to be able to find this picture in the list. To avoid spreading LINQ queries, we can add the following method to the ClassifiedAd class:

```
private Picture FindPicture(PictureId id)
    => Pictures.FirstOrDefault(x => x.Id == id);
```

Now, we can add the action method to the same class:

```
public void ResizePicture(PictureId pictureId, PictureSize newSize)
{
    var picture = FindPicture(pictureId);
    if (picture == null)
        throw new InvalidOperationException(
            "Cannot resize a picture that I don't have");
    picture.Resize(newSize);
}
```

When this is done, we can add a new `Resize` method to the `Picture` entity:

```
public void Resize(PictureSize newSize)
    => Apply(new Events.ClassifiedAdPictureResized
    {
        PictureId = Id.Value,
        Height = newSize.Width,
        Width = newSize.Width
    });
```

Then, we add some code to change the `Picture` state when the event is raised to the `When` method of the entity:

```
case Events.ClassifiedAdPictureResized e:
    Size = new PictureSize{Height = e.Height, Width = e.Width};
    break;
```

When we are done with these changes, we can add an additional invariant to our aggregate. We can define the picture size rule directly in each check inside the `EnsureValidState` method, but it will be quite verbose and not very clear from the language perspective. Instead, let's create a new extension method for the `Picture` entity, using a new `PictureRules` class:

```
namespace Marketplace.Domain
{
    public static class PictureRules
    {
        public static bool HasCorrectSize(this Picture picture)
            => picture != null
                && picture.Size.Width >= 800
                && picture.Size.Height >= 600;
    }
}
```

We use an extension method instead of putting this logic inside the entity itself because it is not really a rule for the entity. Perhaps the class name `PictureRules` is not very good and we need to fix it. On the other hand, we will never use the class name itself because it will only contain extension methods.

Let's change the invariant check code to include a new rule:

```
private Picture FirstPicture
    => Pictures.OrderBy(x => x.Order).FirstOrDefault();

protected override void EnsureValidState()
{
    var valid =
        Id != null &&
        OwnerId != null &&
        (State switch
        {
            ClassifiedAdState.PendingReview =>
                Title != null
                && Text != null
                && Price?.Amount > 0
                && FirstPicture.HasCorrectSize(),
            ClassifiedAdState.Active =>
                Title != null
                && Text != null
                && Price?.Amount > 0
                && FirstPicture.HasCorrectSize()
                && ApprovedBy != null,
            _ => true
        });

    if (!valid)
        throw new InvalidEntityStateException(
            this, $"Post-checks failed in state {State}");
}
```

You can see that we need one more piece of code to make things more explicit. Instead of using a LINQ expression in every call to find the *first* picture (we might need a better domain name for that too), we will use the `FirstPicture` property of the aggregate root. Now the check became less technical and more explicit in terms of the domain language. We might also create some more methods to enforce the language for other rules as well, and we will do this later throughout the course of this book.

Summary

In this chapter, we composed a few aggregates and performed operations on them via the aggregate root. We also evaluated possible persistence methods for aggregates and learned about the concept of the repository—a place where the aggregate state is stored.

Now, it is time to find a way to store our domain objects in a database and see our application working for the first time. In the next chapter, we will take a deep dive into the topic of aggregate persistence.

8
Aggregate Persistence

We have spent enough time discussing how to ensure domain model consistency with explicitly defined business rules. In this chapter, we will go further with persisting our aggregates to the database. Since our model is not being designed around any database, we might encounter issues when trying to get a complex object graph to be stored by using a database engine. That's because the database does not work with objects. Instead, relational databases are optimized to store data in tables that might have relations that use primary and foreign keys. Document databases store objects in machine-readable formats, like JSON, and are, by definition, able to persist complex object graphs as-is; however, we shouldn't fool ourselves, since there are still serious constraints about how these objects need to be organized so that the database client library can convert our objects to JSON and back. All these differences between having a domain object to persist on one side and a database engine with all its quirks and tweaks on the other side, will create challenges for developers.

In this chapter, we will cover the following topics:

- The repository pattern
- Impedance mismatch
- Using a document database for persistence
- Using a relational database for persistence

Technical requirements

The code for this chapter can be found in the `Chapter08` folder of the book repository on GitHub. There are three subfolders there. One is called `before`, and the code there can be used to follow the course of this chapter as it goes further with the persistence implementation. Two other folders, `ravendb` and `ef-core`, contain the final code that implements the aggregate persistence using the RavenDB document database and the Entity Framework Core and PostgreSQL.

You will need to use `docker-compose` to run the infrastructure. This implies that you need to have Docker installed, as well. Follow the Docker CE installation guidelines at `https://docs.docker.com/install/` and the Docker Compose installation guidelines at `https://docs.docker.com/compose/install/`.

If you have not run Docker on your machine before, or if you did it a while ago, you might need to log in using the `docker login` command. For that command, you need to have an account on Docker Hub, which you can create for free at `https://hub.docker.com`.

Aggregate persistence

Now that we have discussed in detail how complex object graphs with complex business rules can be implemented using the **aggregate** pattern, we need to look at how to enable persistence for the aggregates that we use in our system. In the previous chapter, we briefly looked at the **repository** pattern that allows us to abstract persistence from the domain. We also started implementing an implementation of the persistence layer by using the RavenDB document database, since it's easier to save complex objects as documents. However, we also learned that we will most likely face impedance mismatch when trying to comply with the requirements that a chosen persistence method might have for our objects, so that we can both save them to the database and retrieve them back.

Repository and units of work

Let's go back to the point where we used the repository pattern to persist our aggregates. As you will remember, the purpose of the repository pattern is to abstract aggregate persistence. That is exactly what we are going to do now. We still have the repository interface, and it looks like this:

```
public interface IClassifiedAdRepository
{
    Task<ClassifiedAd> Load(ClassifiedAdId id);
    Task Save(ClassifiedAd entity);
}
```

The repository pattern is one of the most debated patterns that exists, and to understand why that is, we need to get back to the definition. For example, this is how this pattern is defined in the *Patterns of Enterprise Application Architecture* book by Martin Fowler (extract taken from `https://martinfowler.com/eaaCatalog/repository.html`). It's recommended that you have a look at the definition given on that page.

The diagram that you can find on the web page that we mentioned earlier shows that a client can ask a repository to retrieve a set of objects that satisfy certain criteria. The client can also add and remove objects from the repository.

The debate about repositories generally involves the fact that in many cases, developers also implement a repository as a unit of work. In addition, it is quite common to see *generic repositories*, like this:

```
public interface IRepository<T>
{
    void GetById(int id); void Save(T);
    IEnumerable<T> Query(Func<T, bool> filter);
}
```

The `Query` method allows for sending a lambda expression to a typed repository, and the generic repository implementation will then send the query to the underlying ORM framework or document database API, without much thinking.

This approach makes people think that repositories are just unnecessary abstractions on top of ORM frameworks. Many argue that when developers send a free-form query and leave it to the ORM framework to translate this query to an SQL statement, it creates a sense of ignorance of the database technology for developers, and it rarely ends well. We cannot just ignore the database and send any query to it, because it can lead to performance issues, due to a lack of query optimization. For some document databases, this approach might not even work, because the database requires having a predefined index to execute queries. RavenDB can create automatic indexes based on any query, but it is not recommended, for performance reasons. For relational databases, using LINQ query translators via ORMs can lead to suboptimal queries that can severely impact not only the application performance, but the performance of the database server itself.

At the same time, if we decide not to have repositories, we might end up dealing with persistence when designing our domain model, and that should not be the case. A domain model exists on its own, and it is designed to deal with business rules and invariants, and not to deal with the database.

Eric Evans insists that querying repositories must happen by using predefined specifications and not by sending any queries. These specifications need to use the Ubiquitous Language to express the intent of a client to retrieve a set of objects from the repository.

For example, we must prefer using `IEnumerable<ClassifiedAd>`
`GetAdsPendingReview()` or `IEnumerable<ClassifiedAd>`
`Query(Specifications.GetAdsPendingReview)` over a generic call,
like `IEnumerable<ClassifiedAd> Query(x => x.State ==`
`ClassifiedAdState.PendingReview)`. One reason for it is to make queries more
expressive and use the domain language. Another reason is to let the repository decide how
to execute that particular query, since we have control over all queries that can be used by
the client. The last reason is that we put the query conditions inside the specification, or
inside the repository method, so we are free to change those rules if needed, and those rules
are only defined in one place.

So, if we spend less time arguing about repositories and more time understanding the
original definitions, we'll see that executing queries using a specification is not equal to
shoving queries to ORMs, but involves executing specific queries that are named following
the Ubiquitous Language and are optimized to work with the database that our application
intends to use.

Let's see how we can change our repository to be closer to the original definition. First, we
need to get rid of the `Save` method, since it is the repository client (our application service)
that will control the unit of work and will have a final say on whether changes need to be
committed to the database. Then, we add at least one query that we will need in the
application service when we check if an object already exists in the database:

```
using System.Threading.Tasks;

namespace Marketplace.Domain
{
    public interface IClassifiedAdRepository
    {
        Task<ClassifiedAd> Load(ClassifiedAdId id);

        Task Add(ClassifiedAd entity);
        Task<bool> Exists(ClassifiedAdId id);
    }
}
```

With this interface, we have no ability for the repository implementation to control
transactions, and that will become the responsibility of our application layer. We don't still
want our application service to be directly coupled to the persistence layer, following the
ports and adapters architecture.

Implementation for RavenDB

Now, let's start doing stuff with a real database; our first exercise will be using the RavenDB document database. This database was created with the NHibernate API in mind, but without the burden of object-relational mapping. It stores objects as JSON documents, supports transactions, and can handle queries on stored documents using quite complex filters. RavenDB is a commercial product, but it has a free license option, which is perfectly suitable to build a small application and put it into production.

 The choice of RavenDB for this book may not be obvious for some readers. Apparently, MongoDB would be a better choice in terms of popularity. Also, Azure Cosmos DB has the Mongo API and it makes the MongoDB driver more attractive to use in the sample app. At the same time, RavenDB has quite a lot of traction in the .NET community, and it also has a best-in-class web user interface that will be really helpful for seeing what is going on in the database as we move along with this chapter.

The choice of a document database is based on the fact that a document database has much less impedance mismatch as compared with relational databases, since document databases manipulate with objects, unlike relational databases, which deal with tables and relations.

We will start by implementing the repository interface with RavenDB persistence, in order to save and load individual aggregates.

To make things a bit more explicit, we can move the infrastructural parts, like database-specific classes, to a new folder in the `Marketplace` project, called `Infrastructure`.

Since we have already implemented our repository for RavenDB, we can start there. But now, we want to remove the `Save` method, because we want to remove the commit responsibility to the unit of work. Also, we can now move this file to the new `Infrastructure` folder. To implement the new repository interface, we need to make minor changes, so our code will look like this:

```
using System;
using System.Threading.Tasks;
using Marketplace.Domain;
using Raven.Client.Documents.Session;

namespace Marketplace.Infrastructure
{
    public class ClassifiedAdRepository : IClassifiedAdRepository
    {
        private readonly IAsyncDocumentSession _session;
```

```
public ClassifiedAdRepository(IAsyncDocumentSession session)
    => _session = session;

public Task Add(ClassifiedAd entity)
    => _session.StoreAsync(entity, EntityId(entity.Id));

public Task<bool> Exists(ClassifiedAdId id)
    => _session.Advanced.ExistsAsync(EntityId(id));

public Task<ClassifiedAd> Load(ClassifiedAdId id)
    => _session.LoadAsync<ClassifiedAd>(EntityId(id));

private static string EntityId(ClassifiedAdId id)
    => $"ClassifiedAd/{id.ToString()}";
    }
}
```

Here, we removed the `Save` method, and we now have the `Add` method that will only be used when we add new aggregates to the database. RavenDB uses the *session* not only to control the connection to the database, but also to track changes for objects that were added to the session by either calling the `Store` or `StoreAsync` methods for new objects or by loading existing objects from the database using the session. So, as soon as we use the `Load` or `Add` methods of our repository, the underlying session will track all changes that happen in these objects. In fact, the session itself represents the unit of work, since all changes that happened for all objects that are attached to the session will be committed to the database when we tell the session to commit changes as one transaction.

The ability to track and commit changes as a transaction is not an exclusive property of the RavenDB client library. For relational databases, **Entity Framework (EF)** and NHibernate allow for using the same technique. In particular, NHibernate also has an `ISession` interface with exactly the same abilities, since the RavenDB API was originally designed to resemble the NHibernate API quite closely. Also, the Marten (http://jasperfx.github.io/marten/) open source library that uses the native ability of PostgreSQL to work with document-like structures in JSONB fields has an implementation of a session that tracks changes in connected objects.

To complete the abstraction, we need to have an interface for the unit of work. We can start with something like this:

```
using System.Threading.Tasks;

namespace Marketplace.Framework
{
    public interface IUnitOfWork
    {
```

```
            Task Commit();
    }
}
```

The implementation of this interface will be quite trivial, since we are using the power of the RavenDB session to track changes in objects:

```csharp
using System.Threading.Tasks;
using Marketplace.Framework;
using Raven.Client.Documents.Session;

namespace Marketplace.Infrastructure
{
    public class RavenDbUnitOfWork : IUnitOfWork
    {
        private readonly IAsyncDocumentSession _session;

        public RavenDbUnitOfWork(IAsyncDocumentSession session)
            => _session = session;

        public Task Commit() => _session.SaveChangesAsync();
    }
}
```

In order to make it work with our application service, we need to make sure that the service gets both the repository and the unit of work interfaces in its constructor as parameters. The new code for `ClassifiedAdAplicationService` looks like this:

```csharp
using System;
using System.Threading.Tasks;
using Marketplace.Domain;
using Marketplace.Framework;
using static Marketplace.Contracts.ClassifiedAds;

namespace Marketplace.Api
{
    public class ClassifiedAdsApplicationService : IApplicationService
    {
        private readonly IClassifiedAdRepository _repository;
        private readonly IUnitOfWork _unitOfWork;
        private readonly ICurrencyLookup _currencyLookup;

        public ClassifiedAdsApplicationService(
            IClassifiedAdRepository repository, IUnitOfWork unitOfWork,
            ICurrencyLookup currencyLookup
        )
        {
            _repository = repository;
```

```
            _unitOfWork = unitOfWork;
            _currencyLookup = currencyLookup;
        }

        public Task Handle(object command) =>
            command switch
            {
                V1.Create cmd => HandleCreate(cmd),
                V1.SetTitle cmd =>
                    HandleUpdate(
                        cmd.Id,
                        c => c.SetTitle(
                            ClassifiedAdTitle.FromString(cmd.Title)
                        )
                    ),
                V1.UpdateText cmd =>
                    HandleUpdate(
                        cmd.Id,
                        c => c.UpdateText(
                            ClassifiedAdText.FromString(cmd.Text)
                        )
                    ),
                V1.UpdatePrice cmd =>
                    HandleUpdate(
                        cmd.Id,
                        c => c.UpdatePrice(
                            Price.FromDecimal(
                                cmd.Price, cmd.Currency,
                                _currencyLookup
                            )
                        )
                    ),
                V1.RequestToPublish cmd =>
                    HandleUpdate(
                        cmd.Id,
                        c => c.RequestToPublish()
                    )
            };

        private async Task HandleCreate(V1.Create cmd)
        {
            if (await _repository.Exists(cmd.Id.ToString()))
                throw new InvalidOperationException(
                    $"Entity with id {cmd.Id} already exists");

            var classifiedAd = new ClassifiedAd(
                new ClassifiedAdId(cmd.Id),
                new UserId(cmd.OwnerId)
```

```
        );

        await _repository.Add(classifiedAd);
        await _unitOfWork.Commit();
    }

    private async Task HandleUpdate(
        Guid classifiedAdId, Action<ClassifiedAd> operation)
    {
        var classifiedAd = await
        _repository.Load(classifiedAdId.ToString());
        if (classifiedAd == null)
            throw new InvalidOperationException(
                $"Entity with id {classifiedAdId} cannot be
                found");

        operation(classifiedAd);

        await _unitOfWork.Commit();
    }
  }
}
```

You can see that our application service gets three dependencies, instead of the two that it had before. We added the unit of work interface so that the service can decide when to commit changes to the database. It creates the challenge of rewriting our application startup code, so we add the missing dependency. One more issue awaits us there, because our unit of work commits using the document session that it gets as a dependency to itself. The repository also depends on the document session. You might remember that the document session tracks all changes in objects that are loaded or explicitly added to the session; that is what the repository does. But we do the commit in our unit of work, and it means that the repository and the unit of work that is used in the same instance of the application service must have *the same* document session.

That part is quite tricky if we decide to instantiate the dependency graph ourselves. For our application, we will use the ASP.NET (https://www.asp.net/) Core service collection to define dependencies. The service collection also works as a **dependency injection** container, so if we configure it properly, we get the dependencies right. The following startup code serves the purpose:

```
public void ConfigureServices(IServiceCollection services)
{
    var store = new DocumentStore
    {
        Urls = new[] {"http://localhost:8080"},
        Database = "Marketplace_Chapter8",
```

```
            Conventions =
            {
                FindIdentityProperty = m => m.Name == "_databaseId"
            }
        };
        store.Initialize();

        services.AddSingleton<ICurrencyLookup, FixedCurrencyLookup>();
        services.AddScoped(c => store.OpenAsyncSession());
        services.AddScoped<IUnitOfWork, RavenDbUnitOfWork>();
        services.AddScoped<IClassifiedAdRepository, ClassifiedAdRepository>();
        services.AddScoped<ClassifiedAdsApplicationService>();

        services.AddMvc();
        services.AddSwaggerGen(c =>
        {
            c.SwaggerDoc(
                "v1",
                new Info
                {
                    Title = "ClassifiedAds",
                    Version = "v1"
                });
        });
    }
```

This code is for the `Startup.cs` file in the `Marketplace` project. There, we register the document session using a factory delegate, `RavenDbUnitOfWork`, and `ClassifiedAdRepository` as scoped dependencies. Our application service is also registered as a scoped service. When we register any dependency as *scoped*, its lifetime will be limited by the lifetime of a single HTTP request. For our code, it means that only one document session will be instantiated for the request, and it will be used as a dependency for all other objects that are instantiated to handle the request. As a result, we will get one application service instance, one repository, and one unit of work. The last two will also get the same instance of the document session, and this is exactly what we want.

As a side note, I have to make it clear that the moment we encounter a strong need to have a dependency injection container to manage our dependencies and we cannot configure our dependencies manually, we need to notice that something is not going well with our code. In such a case, we need to reconsider the dependencies graph and try to simplify it so that we have less of a need, or no need, to use a container. In this particular case, we have no control over how ASP.NET Core instantiates the controller that it calls to handle HTTP requests. Therefore, we are forced to use the container. However, we will try to make the list of dependencies smaller to avoid injection hell and take back control of the request handling scope.

In the code for this chapter, you can also see that we have one helper method in the `ClassifiedAdCommandsApi` class, to handle HTTP requests by sending them to the application service and wrapping any exceptions that it might throw. We could have just used the developer error page provided by the web API; however, it contains a lot of HTML, and we are using Swagger, which won't render it and show the HTML source instead. It makes diagnostics harder, because we'd need to dig into a bunch of HTML tags to find the exception information and the stack trace. The method that is added is as follows:

```
private async Task<IActionResult> HandleRequest<T>(T request, Func<T, Task>
handler)
{
    try
    {
        Log.Debug("Handling HTTP request of type {type}",
        typeof(T).Name);
        await handler(request);
        return Ok();
    }
    catch (Exception e)
    {
        Log.Error("Error handling the request", e);
        return new BadRequestObjectResult(new {error = e.Message,
        stackTrace = e.StackTrace});
    }
}
```

Since we use the generic type argument here, we can send any request to this method, along with the application service `Handle` method as a delegate to handle the request. For example, the `Post` method in our controller now looks like this:

```
public ClassifiedAdsCommandsApi(
    ClassifiedAdsApplicationService applicationService)
    => _applicationService = applicationService;
```

You probably noticed that the `HandleRequest` method uses logging, as well. In this book, we use the `Serilog` open source logging library, which was the first library that provided structured logging to the .NET space and quickly became the most popular logging library for the .NET space.

Our initial stage of preparing to save our aggregate to RavenDB is complete. For the next step, we need to get RavenDB running, and the easiest way to do it is to use Docker Compose with the configuration file that is provided in the book repository for this chapter. The `docker-compose.yml` file contains instructions for Docker Compose to start two containers—one is RavenDB, and another one is PostgreSQL, which we will use later in this chapter, when we explore using relational databases to persist aggregates.

You should be able to run the `docker-compose up` command from the chapter folder in the Terminal window, and you will see something like this:

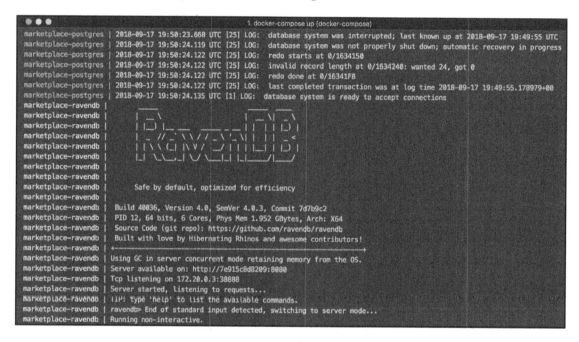

The Terminal output of the docker-compose command

If you have any issues when executing the command, please check the *Technical requirements* section for this chapter.

Remember that you can stop your `docker-compose` session by pressing *Ctrl + C* in the Terminal window where it runs, and in that case, the containers will be stopped. All data inside the containers will be kept, so when you use `docker-compose up` next time, you will see your databases again. If you use `docker-compose down`, the containers will be removed, and when you start them again, you will need to create the databases again. If you want to keep the data no matter what, consider specifying volumes in the `docker-compose.yml` file.

When you have RavenDB up and running for the first time, or any time the container gets recreated, you need to visit the database web UI by going to `http://localhost:8080` and accepting the license agreement. RavenDB is free to use for development and in small-scale production systems. When you accept the agreement, you will be redirected to the RavenDB Studio page:

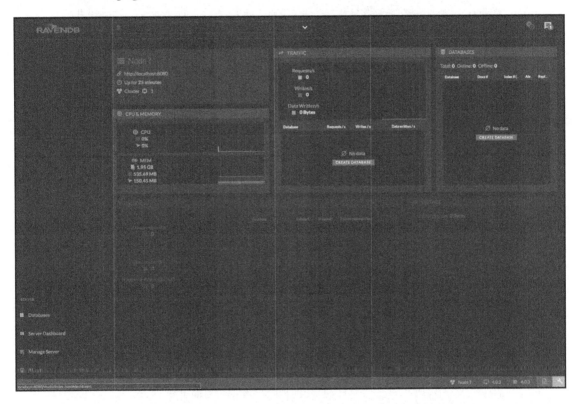

RavenDB user interface

Before we can save anything to RavenDB, we need to create a database. For this chapter, the database name in the sample application code is hardcoded to `Marketplace_Chapter8`. To create a new database, you can use the **CREATE DATABASE** button on the RavenDB Studio home page:

This button lets you create a new database

When you click on this button, you will get a popup where you can enter the database name and click on **Create**:

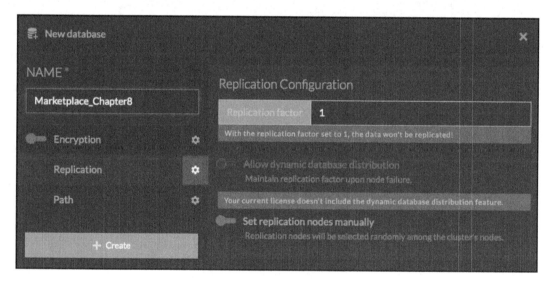

New database creation screen

Now, we can start our sample application. After the application starts, it produces output similar to this:

```
Hosting environment: Development
Content root path: ~/github/ddd-
book/chapter8/Marketplace/bin/Debug/netcoreapp2.2
```

```
Now listening on: http://localhost:5000
Application started. Press Ctrl+C to shut down.
```

By default, any ASP.NET Core application would start listening on
`http://localhost:5000`. There is no user interface in our app, but we have the Swagger
UI to send requests to the API added to the application configuration. Therefore, if you visit
the `http://localhost:5000/swagger/index.html` page, you will see all the API
endpoints that we have created so far:

Command API of the Swagger UI

Finally, we get very close to send commands to our application and see how it will work.
First things first; before doing any updates, we need to create our first aggregate. So, we can
click on the **POST** and then the **Try it out** button. We will get two fields to fill out with new
GUIDs, which can easily be generated by an online GUID generator, or a similar tool that is
available in JetBrains Rider or Visual Studio.

After entering two newly generated GUIDs into the parameter fields for a new POST request, you can press the **Execute** button, and after a short while, you will get a response:

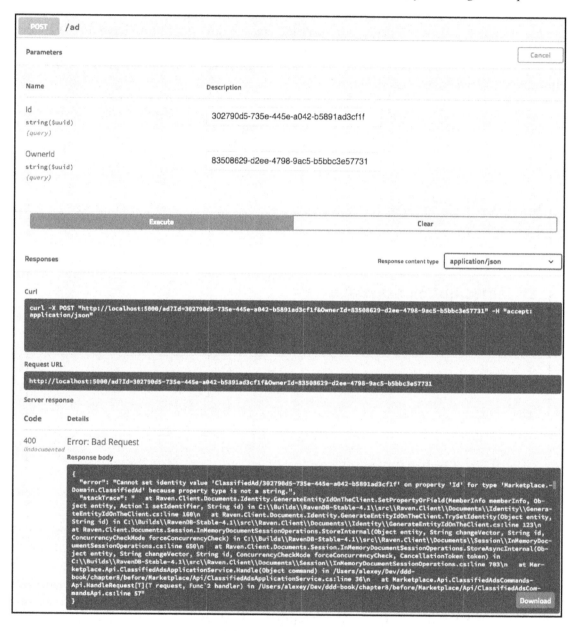

An exception is thrown when we try executing the command

But wait; we have an error! Let's look at what the error message tells us about what happened:

```
Cannot set identity value 'ClassifiedAd/302790d5-735e-445e-a042-
b5891ad3cf1f' on property 'Id' for type 'Marketplace.Domain.ClassifiedAd'
because property type is not a string.
```

Here, we have our first example of impedance mismatch. We have been modeling our domain classes without considering persistence and we have based all decisions on the structure of our classes only on the requirements for the domain. As soon as we started working with a database, although this database is document-based, and in theory, should persist any object we give it, the reality is a bit different. Now, we are forced to start adapting our domain classes in a way that they can be persisted. That is quite unfortunate, because ideally, we should keep our domain model implementation clean of any persistence concerns.

But, let's look at what we can do now. RavenDB requires any document that is being saved there to have an identity property or field of the type string. We are using the `ClassifiedAdId` value object type for the identity property. We explicitly tell RavenDB the object identity in our repository `Add` method, so it doesn't use the `Id` property for that. However, it failed to write the string value back to the `Id` field, because it is not the string. This can only be fixed by adding a new property or field with the type string to our aggregate class. RavenDB uses the name `Id` for the identity property, but we can configure conventions so that the database client API will use something else, instead.

We can start fixing the issue by adding a new `private` field to the `ClassifiedAd` class:

```
public class ClassifiedAd : AggregateRoot<ClassifiedAdId>
{
    // Properties to handle the persistence
    private string DbId
    {
        get => $"ClassifiedAd/{Id.Value}";
        set {}
    }
    // Aggregate state properties
```

It might seem weird that we don't use the property setter, but the database will read the `Id` property as an object, and we will get the value back. So, we can safely use the `Id` property for the `get` part, and `set` will only be used to keep the database happy.

We also need to explain to the database API that it needs to use this new property as the document identity. It is done by using conventions when we create the `DocumentStore` instance in `Startup.cs`:

```
var store = new DocumentStore
    {
        Urls = new[] {"http://localhost:8080"},
        Database = "Marketplace_Chapter8",
        Conventions =
        {
            FindIdentityProperty = x => x.Name == "DbId"
        }
    };
store.Initialize();
```

Now, let's start the application again and repeat the call from Swagger. We can use the same values, so if you kept the browser window open while changing the code, you can just execute the same request that previously generated an error. Now, the response is different:

Request URL	
http://localhost:5000/ad?Id=302790d5-735e-445e-a042-b5891ad3cf1f&OwnerId=83508629-d2ee-4798-9ac5-b5bbc3e57731	
Server response	
Code	**Details**
200	**Response headers**
	content-length: 0 date: Sat, 22 Sep 2018 12:53:40 GMT server: Kestrel

Getting 200 OK means everything worked

To confirm that our persistence code worked, we need to turn to the RavenDB Studio again, and if we open the database there, we will have one document that represents the state of the new aggregate:

The document is successfully stored

For the next step, we can execute one of the commands that perform state changes on an existing aggregate. To start, we can set the ad title by calling the /ad/name/ API endpoint with PUT. We need to use the same aggregate ID that we used for the POST call, since that's the only object we currently have in the system. In the following screenshot, you can see when the action has already been executed and the API has returned a 200 OK status:

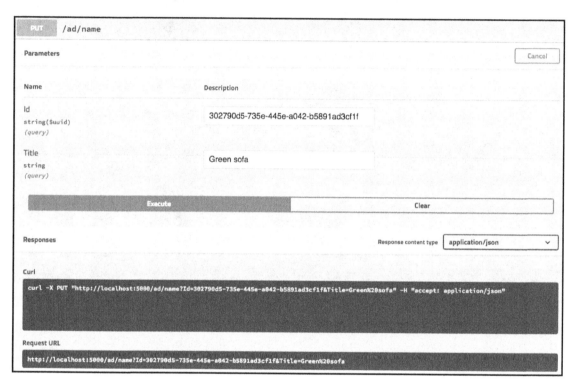

Successful execution of the update command

Let's check what happened with the document in RavenDB. If the document was still open in the Studio, you will see a small popup saying, **This document has been modified outside of the studio. Click here to refresh**. You can go on and click on the link so that the document gets refreshed and the new version shows up. Now, we can see that the document content has changed and the Title property has a proper value (further, I will only use the document content as JSON):

```
{
    "OwnerId": {
        "Value": "83508629-d2ee-4798-9ac5-b5bbc3e57731"
    },
    "Title": {
```

```
            "Value": "Green sofa"
        },
        "Text": null,
        "Price": null,
        "State": "Inactive",
        "ApprovedBy": null,
        "Pictures": [],
        "FirstPicture": null,
        "Id": {
            "Value": "302790d5-735e-445e-a042-b5891ad3cf1f"
        },
        "@metadata": {
            "@collection": "ClassifiedAds",
            "Raven-Clr-Type": "Marketplace.Domain.ClassifiedAd,
            Marketplace.Domain"
        }
    }
}
```

Now, let's try to call other endpoints. You can even try calling the same endpoint again, so that it tries to set the title to some other value. Surprisingly, this won't work. We can see the following error message:

```
Could not convert document ClassifiedAd/7b0a443f-
af9b-4f0d-8876-7896c9921cbc to entity of type
Marketplace.Domain.ClassifiedAd.ClassifiedAd
```

This message is not very informative, but what RavenDB is trying to tell us is that we have a serialization issue. Let's look at what the inner exception could tell us. The message here is as follows:

```
Unable to find a constructor to use for type
Marketplace.Domain.ClassifiedAd.ClassifiedAdTitle. A class should either
have a default constructor, one constructor with arguments or a constructor
marked with the JsonConstructor attribute. Path 'Title.Value'.
```

The issue here is that since we are only allowing our value objects to be created using factory methods in order to prevent the creation of value objects with invalid content. When we bypass the validation the serializer will not use it unless we put an [JsonConstructor] attribute on it. We definitely don't want to do that, because by doing so, our domain model will take a dependency on the Newtonsoft.Json library, which is a purely infrastructural concern. The only way to avoid this without compromising the purity of our domain project is to create a parameterless private constructor. It will allow us to keep the encapsulation and satisfy the serializer at the same time. This is yet another issue with a mismatch between the persistence layer and the domain layer.

Let's solve the issue by adding this line of code to the `ClassifiedAdTitle` class:

```
// Satisfy the serialization requirements
protected ClassifiedAdTitle() { }
```

Similar lines need to be added to all value object types, except for the identity types, because they already have public constructors with one parameter of `Guid`, and the serializer is happy to use it. After all these changes are done, all of the HTTP endpoints will start to work.

So, we can now conclude that the small changes that we made to overcome the impedance mismatch worked fine. You may have already noticed that all properties that have value object types are stored as a JSON object. This is a nice feature of any document database that can store and retrieve complex object graphs as one document.

It is possible to take a similar approach to implementing the persistence by using other types of document storage that support sessions and change tracking within a session. I already mentioned Marten earlier in this chapter. However, for other document databases, like MongoDB or Cosmos DB, you would need to step away from collection-style repositories and start committing updates from inside the repository, instead of using the unit of work. Such an approach might look as *not-by-the-book*, and because of that, developers sometimes feel guilty when implementing it. However, if we remember that an aggregate must be seen as a transactional boundary, there is no chance that you would need to update multiple objects within one transaction. If this rule is violated, then you might have a bigger issue than just having a `Save` method in your repository interface. But, when we only operate on one aggregate in the application service, the whole story with a separate unit of work starts to feel redundant. When our application services conform to the pattern of *load-act-save*, there might not be a practical reason to separate repositories from the unit of work. The application service will still be in charge of committing changes, but it can do it by calling the `_repository.Save()`, just as it calls `_unitOfWork.Commit()` in our code. We will look more closely at the repository pattern and its usefulness when we start discussing event-based persistence, in `Chapter 10`, *Event Sourcing*.

Implementation of Entity Framework Core

Although nowadays, developers have a wide choice of databases, in many cases, a relational database is still preferred. The reasons for this can be different, but the most popular ones include that some RDBMS databases, like Oracle or Microsoft SQL Server, are already used in the organization, and there are people available who can maintain it, or the development team itself has vast experience in working with relational databases. Of course, it often creates issues, due to the risk for domain models to quickly become data models, and the whole application would be built around the persistence.

Relational databases are also notorious for having a significant impedance mismatch. Although developers often tend to think that classes can be perfectly stored in tables, and relations between classes can be represented as foreign keys, that's not the whole picture. We will see this very soon, after the first iteration of the persistence implementation for our single aggregate is complete.

To overcome the impedance mismatch and make the persistence for relational databases more transparent for developers that work with objects, our industry invented a solution. Most of us are familiar with the **object-relational mappers (ORM)** that promise to transparently put objects into the database and retrieve them back. In the .NET space, in particular, we have two major ORM frameworks that are widely used. These frameworks are NHibernate and Entity Framework. NHibernate has a long history, and it was started as a clone of a popular Java ORM framework (Hibernate). For several years, NHibernate was the only ORM tool for the .NET space. Then, after a failed attempt from Microsoft to enter the ORM space with LINQ2SQL, the Entity Framework was born. Criticized by many for being slow, rigid, and not well designed, it nevertheless quickly became the tool of choice for many .NET developers, for the single reason that it was backed by Microsoft. Entity Framework also delivered the first visual designer tool that allowed for creating class models mapped to the persistence layer by drag and drop. After a few years of continuous improvement of the framework, Entity Framework gained a lot of adoption, and at some point, many considered NHibernate as dead. However, during the last couple of years, the NHibernate community has released version 4 with async/await support, and then version 5, with .NET Core support. The Entity Framework team has decided to step back and rethink the design, coming back with Entity Framework Core. This version is now being actively developed, and it is also included in the umbrella `Microsoft.AspNet.Core` NuGet package group, so it is directly available for all .NET Core applications.

Thanks to many members of the community that have an influence at Microsoft, like Julie Lerman, who dove deeply into DDD and its principles, and then provides a lot of valuable input for the Entity Framework team to improve their product in terms of mitigating the impedance mismatch, and support concepts like immutable value objects, out of the box. Therefore, I decided to include an example of how this framework can be used as a domain model persistence for relational databases, although this book is more oriented toward Event Sourcing.

The code for this part is available in the book's GitHub repository, in the folder `Chapter08/ef-core`.

We will be using the PostgreSQL database for this example, but the code can easily be converted for Microsoft SQL Server, since we won't be using any features that are specific to PostgreSQL. The `docker-compose.yml` file in the `ef-core` folder for this chapter will help you to start the database inside a container, just like we did with RavenDB. The initialization script will automatically be executed when the container is created. The script takes care of creating a database user and a new database called `Marketplace_Chapter8`, so you don't need to do anything before starting the application.

Now, let's see what we need to do to use a relational database to persist our aggregate. Since we already have the reference to the `Microsoft.AspNetCore.App` set of packages in our project, the Entity Framework Core itself is available to use straight away. We need to add a PostgreSQL driver package, called `Npgsql.EntityFrameworkCore.PostgreSQL`, to our project.

We need to tell the framework that it needs to map our `ClassifiedAd` class to the database. To do that, we need to create a new class, `ClassifiedAdDbContext`, in the Infrastructure folder of our `Marketplace` project. We will use the code-first approach and let the framework decide how the table will look and how to map the class `ClassifiedAd` properties to the table columns. Here is the first version of the class:

```
using Marketplace.Domain;
using Microsoft.AspNetCore.Builder;
using Microsoft.EntityFrameworkCore;
using Microsoft.EntityFrameworkCore.Metadata.Builders;
using Microsoft.Extensions.DependencyInjection;
using Microsoft.Extensions.Logging;

namespace Marketplace.Infrastructure
{
    public class ClassifiedAdDbContext : DbContext
    {
        private readonly ILoggerFactory _loggerFactory;
```

```
    public ClassifiedAdDbContext(
        DbContextOptions<ClassifiedAdDbContext> options,
        ILoggerFactory loggerFactory)
        : base(options) => _loggerFactory = loggerFactory;

    public DbSet<ClassifiedAd> ClassifiedAds { get; set; }

    protected override void OnConfiguring(
        DbContextOptionsBuilder optionsBuilder)
    {
        optionsBuilder.UseLoggerFactory(_loggerFactory);
        optionsBuilder.EnableSensitiveDataLogging();
    }

    protected override void OnModelCreating(ModelBuilder
    modelBuilder)
        => modelBuilder.ApplyConfiguration(
            new ClassifiedAdEntityTypeConfiguration());
}

public class ClassifiedAdEntityTypeConfiguration
    : IEntityTypeConfiguration<ClassifiedAd>
{
    public void Configure(EntityTypeBuilder<ClassifiedAd> builder)
        => builder.HasKey(x => x.ClassifiedAdId);
}

public static class AppBuilderDatabaseExtensions
{
    public static void EnsureDatabase(this IApplicationBuilder app)
    {
        var context = app.ApplicationServices
            .GetService<ClassifiedAdDbContext>();

        if (!context.Database.EnsureCreated())
            context.Database.Migrate();
    }
}
}
```

We don't do a lot here. By adding a property with the type DbSet<ClassifiedAd>, we tell the framework that it needs to map that class. Then, we also explain that the property ClassifiedAd.ClassifiedAdId should be used as the primary key. We didn't have this property before, but we already used something similar in the previous section for RavenDB, since the database needs to know what value is used as the entity identity, and it cannot be a value object.

Therefore, we also need to add this property to our aggregate. We want to encapsulate as much as we can, but since we need to have access to the property from the infrastructure configuration, we are forced to make it public, at least for getting its value. Unlike with RavenDB, we cannot specify the property by its name.

One more thing that we do in our `DbContext` implementation is tell Entity Framework Core to do logging, and also, to log sensitive data. It will be useful for debugging purposes, as it allows us to see what Entity Framework Core does behind the scenes, including all SQL statements and parameters. Remember that you should not use `EnableSensitiveDataLogging` in production, since it exposes all data, and it might result in some sensitive data becoming exposed via log files or the logging server.

There is one more class in the preceding code that implements an extension for the `IApplicationBuilder`. We will use this extension to create or migrate the necessary tables. This approach also isn't good for production, since you will probably want to do the migration separately.

So, we need to make the following changes in our aggregate class:

```
public class ClassifiedAd : AggregateRoot<ClassifiedAdId>
{
    // Properties to handle the persistence
    public Guid ClassifiedAdId { get; private set; }
    protected ClassifiedAd() { }

    ... more code here...

    protected override void When(object @event)
    {
        Picture picture;
        switch (@event)
        {
            case Events.ClassifiedAdCreated e:
                Id = new ClassifiedAdId(e.Id);
                OwnerId = new UserId(e.OwnerId);
                State = ClassifiedAdState.Inactive;
                // required for persistence
                ClassifiedAdId = e.Id;
                break;

    ... rest of the code ...
```

This would count as our first chance to address the impedance mismatch and to add one property, just to satisfy the persistence. For RavenDB, that was all we needed to do to get things rolling. Let's see if that's enough for EF Core.

As the next step, we need to have a new implementation of the unit of work. We will add a new class `EfUnitOfWork` to the `Infrastructure` namespace:

```
using System.Threading.Tasks;
using Marketplace.Framework;

namespace Marketplace.Infrastructure
{
    public class EfCoreUnitOfWork : IUnitOfWork
    {
        private readonly ClassifiedAdDbContext _dbContext;

        public EfCoreUnitOfWork(ClassifiedAdDbContext dbContext)
            => _dbContext = dbContext;

        public Task Commit() => _dbContext.SaveChangesAsync();
    }
}
```

Then, we will make the necessary changes in the repository class, `ClassifiedAdRepository`:

```
using System;
using System.Threading.Tasks;
using Marketplace.Domain;

namespace Marketplace.Infrastructure
{
    public class ClassifiedAdRepository : IClassifiedAdRepository
    {
        private readonly ClassifiedAdDbContext _dbContext;

        public ClassifiedAdRepository(ClassifiedAdDbContext dbContext)
            => _dbContext = dbContext;

        public Task Add(ClassifiedAd entity)
            => _dbContext.ClassifiedAds.AddAsync(entity);

        public async Task<bool> Exists(ClassifiedAdId id)
            => await _dbContext.ClassifiedAds.FindAsync(id.Value) !=
            null;

        public Task<ClassifiedAd> Load(ClassifiedAdId id)
            => _dbContext.ClassifiedAds.FindAsync(id.Value);
    }
}
```

As you can see, we are relying on `DbContext` to be instantiated per scope. In fact, `DbContext` is the Entity Framework implementation of the unit of work pattern, because it tracks all changes in objects that are attached to it during its lifetime and creates all necessary SQL statements to commit those changes to the database when we call `_dbContext.SaveChangesAsync()`.

The last part is the wiring. We need to change the `Startup.cs` file to tell the ASP.NET Core to use our context and register the database context in its IoC container. Certainly, we also need to register the new implementation of the unit of work. We do all of this in the `ConfigureServices` method, as follows:

```
public void ConfigureServices(IServiceCollection services)
{
    const string connectionString =
        "Host=localhost;Database=Marketplace_Chapter8;
        Username=ddd;Password=book";
    services
        .AddEntityFrameworkNpgsql()
        .AddDbContext<ClassifiedAdDbContext>(
            options => options.UseNpgsql(connectionString));

    services.AddSingleton<ICurrencyLookup, FixedCurrencyLookup>();
    services.AddScoped<IUnitOfWork, EfCoreUnitOfWork>();
    services.AddScoped<IClassifiedAdRepository, ClassifiedAdRepository>
    ();
    services.AddScoped<ClassifiedAdsApplicationService>();

    services.AddMvc();
    services.AddSwaggerGen(c =>
    {
        c.SwaggerDoc("v1",
            new Info
            {
                Title = "ClassifiedAds",
                Version = "v1"
            });
    });
}
```

Here, we also instructed Entity Framework Core to use PostgreSQL as the database and to use the hardcoded connection string. Remember that you should avoid hardcoding connection strings, as they must be part of the configuration. We use the simplified approach to have the connection string visible.

The last thing we need to do before starting the app is call our extension method to create or migrate the database objects. We do it in the `Configure` method of the `Startup` class:

```
public void Configure(IApplicationBuilder app, IHostingEnvironment env)
{
    app.EnsureDatabase();
    app.UseMvcWithDefaultRoute();
    app.UseSwagger();
    app.UseSwaggerUI(c =>
        c.SwaggerEndpoint("/swagger/v1/swagger.json", "ClassifiedAds
        v1"));
}
```

The changes that we have made more or less represent all the changes that we needed to do to use RavenDB for persistence. Ideally, everything should work now. Let's start the application and see what happens.

After pressing *F5*, we will see that the application doesn't start. Instead, it throws an exception immediately:
The entity type `ClassifiedAdId` requires a primary key to be defined.

That sounds weird, because `ClassifiedAdId` is not an entity. Here comes trouble. Entity Framework Core considers all object-to-object relations to be relationships between different entities. It wants to create a separate table to store the `ClassifiedAdId` object in it, but as an entity, it must have an identifier. Just about a couple of years ago, we'd be stuck right here, and the only way to overcome this limitation would be to use the **memento** pattern. The essence of this pattern is to be able to persist the object state and to be able to restore it later. Sometimes, it is referred to as **undo rollback**, but that is just a narrow use case for this pattern. Essentially, every object persistence method uses some implementation of the memento pattern.

In order to implement memento, we need to have a way to convert our complex object to something that can be persisted, like a text file, relational table, or JSON object. Upon any save operation, we'd need to manually convert the state of our aggregate to the memento, and when we retrieved the state back, a reverse operation would be required. However, today, we can solve this issue by telling Entity Framework Core that we are, in fact, dealing with value objects, and not work entities. In fact, the EF Core has implemented all of the pieces of the pattern for us. To use this feature, we need to add more code to the `ClassifiedAdEntityTypeConfiguration` class:

```
public class ClassifiedAdEntityTypeConfiguration :
IEntityTypeConfiguration<ClassifiedAd>
{
    public void Configure(EntityTypeBuilder<ClassifiedAd> builder)
    {
        builder.HasKey(x => x.ClassifiedAdId);
        builder.OwnsOne(x => x.Id);
        builder.OwnsOne(x => x.Price, p => p.OwnsOne(c => c.Currency));
        builder.OwnsOne(x => x.Text);
        builder.OwnsOne(x => x.Title);
        builder.OwnsOne(x => x.ApprovedBy);
        builder.OwnsOne(x => x.OwnerId);
    }
}
```

The `OwnsOne` method tells EF Core that it needs to persist the given property not as a separate entity in a separate table, but as a part of the same table. Since EF Core would only save the content of public properties, we need to expose the properties of our value objects for the `get` part. We still want encapsulation, so the setter remains private. This is what we need to add to the `PictureSize` value object code:

```
public class PictureSize : Value<PictureSize>
{
    public int Width { get; internal set; }
    public int Height { get; internal set; }

    internal PictureSize() { }

    ... rest of the code ...
```

EF Core also requires all objects that it persists to have either a constructor that accepts values for all properties, or a parameterless constructor. We use the second option, but we make the constructor internal, so no one can use it from outside of the `Domain` project.

Now, we also know that EF Core wants to know more about how to map objects to tables; it has also become clear that we need to map the `Picture` entity, as well. There, we want to keep objects persisted in a separate table. To do that, we need to add a new class `PictureEntityTypeConfiguration`. It can be added to the same `ClassifiedAdDbContext.cs` file:

```
public class PictureEntityTypeConfiguration :
IEntityTypeConfiguration<Picture>
{
    public void Configure(EntityTypeBuilder<Picture> builder)
    {
        builder.HasKey(x => x.PictureId);
        builder.OwnsOne(x => x.Id);
        builder.OwnsOne(x => x.ParentId);
        builder.OwnsOne(x => x.Size);
    }
}
```

Notice that we need to do the same trick with the picture ID that we did with the classified ad ID. I am not putting the code changes in the text for the sake of brevity, since all of the code can be found in the book repository for this chapter.

The `ClassifiedAdDbContext.OnModelCreating` now needs to include this additional mapping configuration, as well:

```
protected override void OnModelCreating(ModelBuilder modelBuilder)
{
    modelBuilder.ApplyConfiguration(new
    ClassifiedAdEntityTypeConfiguration());
    modelBuilder.ApplyConfiguration(new
    PictureEntityTypeConfiguration());
}
```

Now let's run the application again. This time, it start just fine; at first glance, all mappings seem to be correct. If we also look at the database (use the tool of your choice, like Database Explorer in Visual Studio or the Database tool window in Rider) we will see that two tables were created:

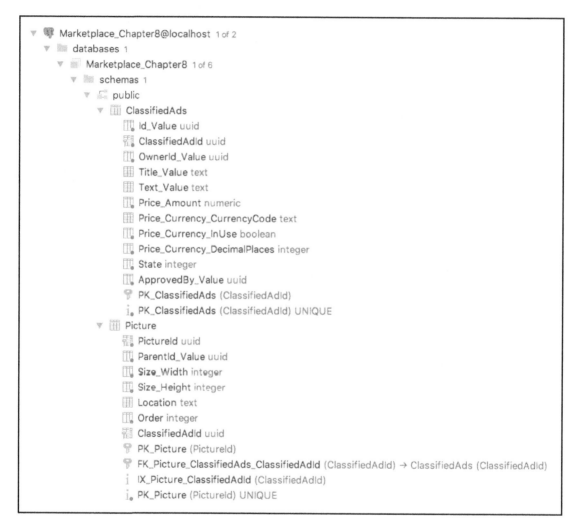

The database structure in the Visual Studio database explorer

As you can see, there are two tables for each entity type. Since the `Picture` entity is a part of the `ClassifiedAd` aggregate, we use the object-to-object relationship, and it was mapped as a foreign key in the database. For each value object, EF Core has created a set of columns to store all properties of each value object in the same table as the parent entity. So far, so good; now, we can try calling our API. You'd need two GUIDs to be filled out in Swagger, and after clicking on **Execute**, we will have quite a long wait. That's because EF Core initialization is implicit, and it is being called when we try to do anything with `DbContext` for the first time. Subsequent calls are processed faster, since the initialized model will be cached.

Let's look at what we got back from the HTTP call. This is not really surprising, it is an exception again. We are getting all the issues associated with the impedance mismatch, one by one! The new error message is as follows:

```
The entity of type 'ClassifiedAd' is sharing the table 'ClassifiedAds' with
entities of type 'ClassifiedAdText', but there is no entity of this type
with the same key value '{ClassifiedAdId: 302790d5-735e-445e-a042-
b5891ad3cf1f}' that has been marked as 'Added'.
```

This time, the error message is not really clear. In reality, what EF Core is telling us now is that it cannot handle value object properties of the `ClassifiedAd` object that are null. When we apply the `ClassifiedAdCreated` event in the `When` method, we only assign values to the properties that we have—the ID, and the owner ID.

There are a few ways to work around this limitation, and the most prominent one is to use instances of value objects that represent *no value*. In fact, this method also allows us to mitigate the risk of getting the null reference exception. We already touched upon the issue of null earlier in this book. Having specific *no value* instances for all our value objects would be similar to using the optional types that are commonly used in functional languages. In the following, you can see the code to implement such a value for the `ClassifiedAdTitle` class by adding a static property to it:

```
public static ClassifiedAdTitle NoTitle =
    new ClassifiedAdTitle();
```

When we have such properties in all value object types that can be empty (for example, `PictureSize` or `ClassifiedAdId` are always assigned, so we can skip these types), we need to assign empty values in the `When` method of the `ClassifiedAd` class for the `ClassifiedAdCreated` event handler:

```
protected override void When(object @event)
{
    Picture picture;
    switch (@event)
```

```
{
    case Events.ClassifiedAdCreated e:
        Id = new ClassifiedAdId(e.Id);
        OwnerId = new UserId(e.OwnerId);
        State = ClassifiedAdState.Inactive;
        Title = ClassifiedAdTitle.NoTitle;
        Text = ClassifiedAdText.NoText;
        Price = Price.NoPrice;
        ApprovedBy = UserId.NoUser;

        ClassifiedAdId = e.Id;
        break;

... rest of the code ...
```

With these changes complete, we can do the API call again, and now, it should work. On the console, we can see the following debug output:

```
[17:44:32 INF] Executed DbCommand (13ms)
[Parameters=[@p0='302790d5-735e-445e-a042-b5891ad3cf1f', @p1='2',
@p2='302790d5-735e-445e-a042-b5891ad3cf1f', @p3='', @p4='', @p5='',
@p6='0', @p7='False', @p8='-1', @p9='00000000-0000-0000-0000-000000000000',
@p10='83508629-d2ee-4798-9ac5-b5bbc3e57731'], CommandType='Text',
CommandTimeout='30']
 INSERT INTO "ClassifiedAds" ("ClassifiedAdId", "State", "Id_Value",
"Text_Value", "Title_Value", "Price_Currency_CurrencyCode",
"Price_Currency_DecimalPlaces", "Price_Currency_InUse", "Price_Amount",
"ApprovedBy_Value", "OwnerId_Value")
 VALUES (@p0, @p1, @p2, @p3, @p4, @p5, @p6, @p7, @p8, @p9, @p10);
```

We can also call the PUT method for /ad/title and get this debug output:

```
[17:46:48 INF] Executed DbCommand (5ms)
[Parameters=[@p1='302790d5-735e-445e-a042-b5891ad3cf1f', @p0='Green sofa'],
CommandType='Text', CommandTimeout='30']
 UPDATE "ClassifiedAds" SET "Title_Value" = @p0
 WHERE "ClassifiedAdId" = @p1;
```

We can also look at the content of the `ClassifiedAd` table and see that the values are indeed being assigned:

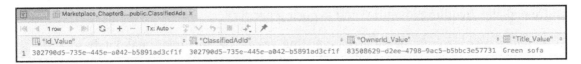

Updated data in the ClassifiedAd table

By now, we have managed to handle all the challenges that come from the mismatch between our domain model and the data model. This is not the only way to handle aggregate persistence using relational databases. Many developers prefer having the domain model and the data model completely separate. By doing that, they obtain more flexibility for changing the domain model without looking at persistence concerns all the time. However, such flexibility comes with the associated costs of overly increasing the complexity for the persistence layer, since the mappings between domain objects and data objects need to be handled manually. For larger applications, this approach might be preferred, because it also allows for tuning the data model to satisfy the performance needs of the underlying database. When we use the ORM framework to deal with our domain objects and persist them directly, we put a lot of trust in the framework capabilities to handle the data aspect properly. At the same time, EF Core is constantly improving to make database calls more optimal and to mitigate the impedance mismatch more transparently for developers. So far, we have been able to fix most of the issues by applying a more advanced configuration in the infrastructure configuration classes, and the changes in the domain model itself have not been that significant.

Summary

In this chapter, we dove deeply into the topic of aggregate persistence. You have seen many challenges that are associated with what is known as **impedance mismatch**, when we can clearly see that databases aren't exactly happy to persist complex object graphs as is due to specific requirements that different types of databases have. Also, you learned about using the repository pattern to abstract the persistence and keep both our domain model and the application service away from the database-related concerns.

You learned how to use RavenDB to persist our aggregate as a document, and what challenges we might encounter on this road. It became clear that document databases are, in general, more suitable for persisting complex objects, but some concerns still need to be addressed, like handling identities and exposing properties.

This chapter also covered the topic of persisting aggregates in a relational database. We used the Entity Framework Core with a PostgreSQL database to represent our aggregate as a set of tables with relations between them. Despite the significant improvements that the EF Core team has made during the last couple of years, persisting value objects is a particularly challenging subject, and we had to do quite a lot of configuration changes to make it work. However, the changes that we had to make in the domain model were not that dramatic, and we were still able to use value objects as-is, including the important characteristic of their immutability.

However, we haven't touched the topic of retrieving data from the database. Our API still only has endpoints to create new domain objects and perform state transitions in the existing object. In fact, we can only handle commands. You might wonder why we don't start adding more methods to our repository to fetch collections of aggregates based on some criteria or specification. That is one of the fallacies of persistence implementations that we see in many systems when trying to apply the principles of DDD. That's why I have dedicated the next chapter exclusively to queries. As you will see, it is not as straightforward, and there are some interesting things to discover ahead.

CQRS - The Read Side

9

In the previous chapter, we learned about persisting aggregates to different types of databases. However, we haven't looked at the topic of retrieving data from a database, except using the repository `Load` method to retrieve a single aggregate.

It is now time to get a hold on the data we managed to store in the database and add some `GET` endpoints to the API. For this book, I had no plans to show you how to build repositories with numerous `GetByThat` methods or, even worse, a generic repository that returns `IQueryable<T>`. That kind of approach, while it might seem attractive, removes the Ubiquitous Language from queries, since developers start to retrieve aggregates by filtering properties. For example, a query such as `_repository.Query(x => x.State == State.IsActive && x.Price.Amount > 100)` tells us very little about the intention of the query consumer. What does this filter mean for the business? We would never know unless we study every line of code that calls this query, and probably only then can we figure out its purpose. Also, free-filter queries open the Pandora's box of hitting the database server without any optimization. For relational databases, we end up with numerous heavy joins and unindexed queries. With document databases, we might even get failures if there are no automatic indexes supported by the database engine itself. RavenDB is clever enough to create automatic indexes when we execute a query for which the server has not built an index yet. While that is not a big issue during development, it will have a severe impact on production systems where the server deals with a significant number of documents.

So, in this book, we will be applying CQRS principles and separate commands from queries. Our repository is good enough to persist new aggregates and perform updates on existing aggregates when we execute commands. This means that our command side is fine. Now, we need to implement the query side, and we'll do it in a different way, without using repositories.

In this chapter, you will learn about the following topics:

- The read side of CQRS
- What are the read models?
- Using Ubiquitous Language for queries
- Implementing CQRS with one database

Technical requirements

The code for this chapter can be found in the Chapter09 folder of the book repository on GitHub. There are two subfolders there, ravendb and ef-core, containing the final code that implements the aggregate persistence and queries using the RavenDB document database, Entity Framework Core, and PostgreSQL. As a starting point, we'll be using the final code from Chapter 8, *Aggregate Persistence*.

You will need to use docker-compose to run the infrastructure. Check the requirements for the previous chapter if you have not completed the installation previously.

Adding user profiles

Before we start our journey to the read side of our application, we would benefit from adding some more concerns to the domain itself. So far, we have been concentrating on the core domain of classified ads. The core domain is what we should focus on when we create a new system. In our scenario so far, we have already made some progress implementing the core domain, and the team is now discussing what would be an absolute *must have* to add to the system before they start creating the prototypes.

You might remember that we have already partially addressed the concern of who owns the ad. We have the OwnerId property of the UserId type in the ClassifiedAd aggregate, but so far we haven't got the location where OwnerId comes from. Apparently, our system needs to have users that must register themselves before creating new ads. We need to know who they are and how to get in touch with them. So, as the bare minimum, we need to have their name and contact information, such as an email address and phone number. Most of the time, people don't like to show their real names in classified ads and prefer using nicknames instead, something that we call a **display name**. We must address this concern too.

After a short discussion on the EventStorming board, the team came up with something very basic to support these requirements. We don't care about the user registration process for the whole store; that is a complex topic by itself. It could potentially involve social media login, email and phone number confirmations, password requirements, and two-phase authentication. It is never a good idea to start implementing those features when you are building a new system. Oftentimes, developers fall into the **user registration** trap and spend weeks and months polishing the registration/login screen experience without any work being done on the core domain. Remember that the authentication domain is a generic supportive subdomain, and in most cases, it can be very useful to consider using a third-party system to handle these concerns.

Right now, all we need to do is to implement some basic functionality that will allow us to show the user information alongside the classified ad itself, both when we show a single ad on a page or a list of ads.

The following diagram shows what the team generated after a quick modeling session:

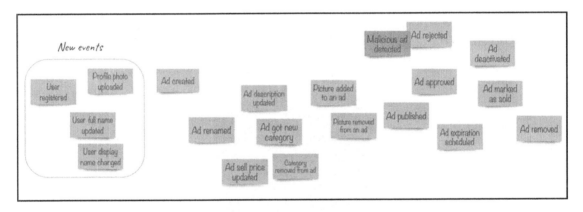

We can easily see that there is very little connection between the users and classified ads. In fact, we only need to have the user ID so that we can use it as the owner ID. Bearing that in mind, we can try implementing UserProfile as a new aggregate in our domain project. I'd urge you not to call this object User since it implies that the same object is used for authentication, and must, therefore, contain things such as password and social media login information. But we've already decided to keep it aside and resolve it later.

User profile domain concerns

First things first. The only thing we know for sure right now is that we have four different events to implement. We also know that we are adding a new aggregate to the same domain project that we already have. Since our aggregate will have a state, we'll probably need to create new value objects too.

Before adding new objects to the project, it would be a good idea to organize the project so that we get better visibility of its parts.

Domain project organization

We start by creating a new project folder called `ClassifiedAd` and moving existing relevant files over there. After that, we need to fix the namespace for all the files that we moved. The automatic refactoring feature of the IDE makes it quite easy. With ReSharper or Rider, you can just press *Alt + Enter* on the namespace name in the class and tell it to adjust the namespace accordingly. Then, we add a new folder for the `UserProfile` objects. It also makes sense to move all shared domain concerns, such as the `Exception` class, the `Money` class, and others, to the `Shared` folder. Now, the project structure changes to this:

Now we can start implementing those four new events. Let's add a new `Events` class to the `UserProfile` folder and write some code for those events, as follows:

```csharp
using System;

namespace Marketplace.Domain.UserProfile
{
    public static class Events
    {
        public class UserRegistered
        {
            public Guid UserId { get; set; }
            public string FullName { get; set; }
            public string DisplayName { get; set; }
        }

        public class ProfilePhotoUploaded
        {
            public Guid UserId { get; set; }
            public string PhotoUrl { get; set; }
        }

        public class UserFullNameUpdated
        {
            public Guid UserId { get; set; }
            public string FullName { get; set; }
        }

        public class UserDisplayNameUpdated
        {
            public Guid UserId { get; set; }
            public string DisplayName { get; set; }
        }
    }
}
```

We consciously keep other things, such as email addresses and telephone numbers, out of the version, since we don't need that information for anything that our application needs right now, but nothing will stop us from adding more events and more details to the domain model in the future.

Adding new value objects

For the next step, we add a new small aggregate called `UserProfile` to execute commands that will emit these events and perform the state transition for the aggregate. For the aggregate state, it is a good idea to implement value objects for the `DisplayName` and `FullName` state properties, so we will start with that.

The `FullName` class is rather trivial, and mostly repeats the code for the `ClassifiedAdTitle` class, as shown in the following code:

```
using System;
using Marketplace.Framework;

namespace Marketplace.Domain.UserProfile
{
    public class FullName : Value<FullName>
    {
        public string Value { get; }

        internal FullName(string fullName) => Value = fullName;

        public static FullName FromString(string fullName)
        {
            if (fullName.IsEmpty())
                throw new ArgumentNullException(nameof(fullName));
            return new FullName(fullName);
        }

        public static implicit operator string(FullName fullName)
            => fullName.Value;

        // Satisfy the serialization requirements
        protected FullName() { }
    }
}
```

I have added a small static class to hold extension methods for the `string` class, and currently, there is only one method there, called `IsEmpty`, which I use instead of `string.IsNullOrWhitespace`, so you can see that it is being used in the code for the `value` object.

Then we can implement the `DisplayName` class. It is not as straightforward, because, unlike the full name, the display name will be shown on public pages. We can definitely expect some malicious users to write things that we don't want to show on our website. While our ads will go through a review stage before getting published, user profiles will not be moderated. Normally, a user profile is shown in different places, such as discussions, review systems, and so on. Although we haven't started modeling these features just yet, we know our roadmap and the fact that we need to prevent users from putting malicious content in their public profiles.

One easy thing we can do is to automatically check whether the display name contains obscene words. There are openly accessible services out there that can help us. The implementation details won't be a part of the `Domain` project, since it is an infrastructural concern. Instead, we will create some abstractions for such a service so that we can check the text for profanity without coupling with the implementation. We already used a similar technique using the currency lookup domain service. Domain services, however, don't necessarily need to be implemented as interfaces. Another way of making a one-method domain service is by using delegates. The following code shows the profanity check domain service, which is declared as a delegate:

```
namespace Marketplace.Domain.Shared
{
    public delegate bool CheckTextForProfanity(string text);
}
```

I put the code in the `Shared/ContentModeration.cs` file. Now we need to implement the `DisplayName` value object and make use of the new domain service, as shown in the following code:

```
using System;
using Marketplace.Domain.Shared;
using Marketplace.Framework;

namespace Marketplace.Domain.UserProfile
{
    public class DisplayName : Value<DisplayName>
    {
        public string Value { get; }

        internal DisplayName(string displayName) => Value =
        displayName;

        public static DisplayName FromString(
            string displayName,
            CheckTextForProfanity hasProfanity)
        {
```

```
            if (displayName.IsEmpty())
                throw new ArgumentNullException(nameof(FullName));
            if (hasProfanity(displayName))
                throw new DomainExceptions.ProfanityFound(displayName);

            return new DisplayName(displayName);
        }

        public static implicit operator string(DisplayName displayName)
            => displayName.Value;
        // Satisfy the serialization requirements
        protected DisplayName() { }
    }
}
```

Here, you can see that the code will throw an exception of the ProfanityFound type if the delegate returns true, which would mean that the user is using bad language in the display name. I have moved all domain exceptions to one place in the Shared folder. The new code is located in the DomainExceptions.cs file and the code for this file is shown in the following code:

```
using System;

namespace Marketplace.Domain.Shared
{
    public static class DomainExceptions
    {
        public class InvalidEntityState : Exception
        {
            public InvalidEntityState(object entity, string message)
                : base($"Entity {entity.GetType().Name} state change
                rejected, {message}")
            { }
        }

        public class ProfanityFound : Exception
        {
            public ProfanityFound(string text)
                : base($"Profanity found in text: {text}")
            { }
        }
    }
}
```

We will be adding more exceptions to this file when necessary.

User profile aggregate root

It is now time to write the code for the `UserProfile` aggregate. We have built one aggregate before, so creating a new one will not be a big issue, especially considering that the user profile is a relatively simple object. The following is the code for the new `UserProfile.cs` file:

```csharp
using System;
using Marketplace.Framework;

namespace Marketplace.Domain.UserProfile
{
    public class UserProfile : AggregateRoot<UserId>
    {
        // Properties to handle the persistence
        private string DbId
        {
            get => $"UserProfile/{Id.Value}";
            set {}
        }
        // Aggregate state properties
        public FullName FullName { get; private set; }
        public DisplayName DisplayName { get; private set; }
        public string PhotoUrl { get; private set; }

        public UserProfile(UserId id, FullName fullName, DisplayName
        displayName)
            => Apply(new Events.UserRegistered
            {
                UserId = id,
                FullName = fullName,
                DisplayName = displayName
            });

        public void UpdateFullName(FullName fullName)
            => Apply(new Events.UserFullNameUpdated
            {
                UserId = Id,
                FullName = fullName
            });
        public void UpdateDisplayName(DisplayName displayName)
            => Apply(new Events.UserDisplayNameUpdated
            {
                UserId = Id,
                DisplayName = displayName
            });
        public void UpdateProfilePhoto(Uri photoUrl)
```

```
            => Apply(new Events.ProfilePhotoUploaded
            {
                UserId = Id,
                PhotoUrl = photoUrl.ToString()
            });
        protected override void When(object @event)
        {
            switch (@event)
            {
                case Events.UserRegistered e:
                    Id = new UserId(e.UserId);
                    FullName = new FullName(e.FullName);
                    DisplayName = new DisplayName(e.DisplayName);
                    break;
                case Events.UserFullNameUpdated e:
                    FullName = new FullName(e.FullName);
                    break;
                case Events.UserDisplayNameUpdated e:
                    DisplayName = new DisplayName(e.DisplayName);
                    break;
                case Events.ProfilePhotoUploaded e:
                    PhotoUrl = e.PhotoUrl;
                    break;
            }
        }

        protected override void EnsureValidState()
        {
        }
    }
}
```

The preceding code does nothing new compared to the `ClassifiedAd` aggregate root class code. We also use the same workaround to satisfy the database requirements for the identity property. Since we start with a RavenDB implementation, we need a string property to hold the document's identity.

As you can see, I used the `UserId` value object for the aggregate root ID. That's because, essentially, the profile identity must be the ID of the user. It required me to change the implementation of the `UserId` class by inheriting it from the `Value<UserId>` base class for value objects.

Finally, we need a repository interface so that our application service will know how to retrieve and persist the new entity. The interface is identical to the one we made for the ClassifiedAd entity, as you can see from the following code:

```
using System.Threading.Tasks;
using Marketplace.Domain.Shared;

namespace Marketplace.Domain.UserProfile
{
    public interface IUserProfileRepository
    {
        Task<UserProfile> Load(UserId id);

        Task Add(UserProfile entity);
        Task<bool> Exists(UserProfile id);
    }
}
```

Now we are done with the changes in our domain project. Let's continue by adding the user profile application service and the command API.

Application side for the user profile

It is time to look at our application project and check what we need to do to support the user profile feature. Before we start adding new classes, let's perform a similar project restructuring, making different core features differ visually in **Solution Explorer**. I don't want the application project to be structured according to infrastructure concerns either, but the current organization of the project implies just that, since we use the Api, Contracts, and Infrastructure folders. To do this, I have moved the ClassifiedAd concerns to a separate folder in the Marketplace project and created a new folder called UserProfile.

The project now looks different in the solution explorer, as you can see in the following screenshot:

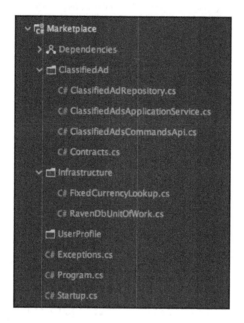

Now we have a place to add everything we need to support the new domain functionality. We start by adding commands to a new `UserProfile/Contracts.cs` file. We can understand what commands are needed by looking at the events since all those events, are user-driven. Look at the following code:

```
using System;

namespace Marketplace.UserProfile
{
    public class Contracts
    {
        public static class V1
        {
            public class RegisterUser
            {
                public Guid UserId { get; set; }
                public string FullName { get; set; }
                public string DisplayName { get; set; }
            }

            public class UpdateUserFullName
            {
```

```
                    public Guid UserId { get; set; }
                    public string FullName { get; set; }
                }

                public class UpdateUserDisplayName
                {
                    public Guid UserId { get; set; }
                    public string DisplayName { get; set; }
                }

                public class UpdateUserProfilePhoto
                {
                    public Guid UserId { get; set; }
                    public string PhotoUrl { get; set; }
                }
            }
        }
    }
```

By now, you might have noticed there is a mismatch between the name of the ProfilePhotoUploaded event, and our UpdateUserProfilePhoto command. We must keep the semantics clear as our application service will not handle the upload itself. Instead, it will receive a URL to a file that has already been uploaded. That is usually the case if we have a sophisticated UI that is able to perform file upload and additional operations, such as resizing and cropping in the browser. Alternatively, we can let the Web API controller deal with uploads. So, in fact, our command needs to represent what will happen in the domain—it will update the photograph URL rather than uploading the photograph itself. However, if you decide that your user profile application service needs to handle the upload too, the command name (and the corresponding event name) needs to be changed to reflect the nature of the action.

Let's start writing the new application service. This work is rather trivial if we use the ClassifiedAdApplicationService class as an example. I have ended up with the following code:

```
using System;
using System.Threading.Tasks;
using Marketplace.Domain.Shared;
using Marketplace.Domain.UserProfile;
using Marketplace.Framework;

namespace Marketplace.UserProfile
{
    public class UserProfileApplicationService : IApplicationService
    {
        private readonly IUserProfileRepository _repository;
```

```
private readonly IUnitOfWork _unitOfWork;
private readonly CheckTextForProfanity _checkText;

public UserProfileApplicationService(
    IUserProfileRepository repository, IUnitOfWork unitOfWork,
    CheckTextForProfanity checkText)
{
    _repository = repository;
    _unitOfWork = unitOfWork;
    _checkText = checkText;
}
public async Task Handle(object command)
{
    switch (command)
    {
        case Contracts.V1.RegisterUser cmd:
            if (await
            _repository.Exists(cmd.UserId.ToString()))
                throw new InvalidOperationException($"Entity
                with id {cmd.UserId} already exists");
            var userProfile = new
            Domain.UserProfile.UserProfile(
                new UserId(cmd.UserId),
                FullName.FromString(cmd.FullName),
                DisplayName.FromString(cmd.DisplayName,
                _checkText));
            await _repository.Add(userProfile);
            await _unitOfWork.Commit();
            break;

        case Contracts.V1.UpdateUserFullName cmd:
            await HandleUpdate(cmd.UserId,
                profile =>
    profile.UpdateFullName(FullName.FromString(cmd.FullName)));
            break;

        case Contracts.V1.UpdateUserDisplayName cmd:
            await HandleUpdate(cmd.UserId,
                profile => profile.UpdateDisplayName(
                    DisplayName.FromString(cmd.DisplayName,
                    _checkText)));
            break;

        case Contracts.V1.UpdateUserProfilePhoto cmd:
            await HandleUpdate(cmd.UserId,
                profile => profile.UpdateProfilePhoto(new
                Uri(cmd.PhotoUrl)));
            break;
```

```
            default:
                throw new InvalidOperationException(
                    $"Command type {command.GetType().FullName} is
                    unknown");
        }
    }
    private async Task HandleUpdate(Guid userProfileId,
    Action<Domain.UserProfile.UserProfile> operation)
    {
        var classifiedAd = await
        _repository.Load(userProfileId.ToString());
        if (classifiedAd == null)
            throw new InvalidOperationException($"Entity with id
            {userProfileId} cannot be found");

        operation(classifiedAd);

        await _unitOfWork.Commit();
    }
}
```

In this class, I have one dependency—`IUserProfileRepository`. You might already suspect that the repository implementation for the `UserProfile` entity would be almost the same as for `ClassifiedAd`, except that it will operate with another class type. You might think that you can use a generic repository. But we have already touched upon this topic, and you can either revisit it or read some articles on the internet that will invariably discourage you from using generic repositories; however, we can still either use the generic type as a dependency for our specific repository or we can inherit specific repositories from a generic one. Let's try the latter option and see what it looks like. I will add a new class to the `Infrastructure` folder for the application project, called `RavenDbRepository`, as shown in the following code:

```
using System;
using System.Threading.Tasks;
using Marketplace.Framework;
using Raven.Client.Documents.Session;

namespace Marketplace.Infrastructure
{
    public class RavenDbRepository<T, TId>
        where T : AggregateRoot<TId>
        where TId : Value<TId>
    {
        private readonly IAsyncDocumentSession _session;
        private readonly Func<TId, string> _entityId;
```

```
        public RavenDbRepository(
            IAsyncDocumentSession session,
            Func<TId, string> entityId)
        {
            _session = session;
            _entityId = entityId;
        }

        public Task Add(T entity)
            => _session.StoreAsync(entity, _entityId(entity.Id));

        public Task<bool> Exists(TId id)
            => _session.Advanced.ExistsAsync(_entityId(id));

        public Task<T> Load(TId id)
            => _session.LoadAsync<T>(_entityId(id));
    }
}
```

We still want to use specific repository interfaces and classes, but now we can implement UserProfileRepository (the file that needs to be added to the UserProfile folder of the Marketplace project) using the following code:

```
using Marketplace.Domain.Shared;
using Marketplace.Domain.UserProfile;
using Marketplace.Infrastructure;
using Raven.Client.Documents.Session;

namespace Marketplace.UserProfile
{
    public class UserProfileRepository
        : RavenDbRepository<Domain.UserProfile.UserProfile, UserId>,
        IUserProfileRepository
    {
        public UserProfileRepository(IAsyncDocumentSession session)
            : base(session, id => $"UserProfile/{id.Value.ToString()}") { }
    }
}
```

The same can be done to implement ClassifiedAdRepository, although the unchanged version will work as before. The final code for this chapter includes the simplified code.

It is time to implement the API controller class. If you look at the
`ClassifiedAdsCommandApi` class, you can see that we have a private method called
`HandleRequest` that helps us to simplify the request handling by calling the application
service using one line of code. The code for the new controller will be almost identical, so
we can reuse the request handler by creating a new static class in the `Infrastructure`
folder called `RequestHandler` with the following simple code:

```
using System;
using System.Threading.Tasks;
using Microsoft.AspNetCore.Mvc;
using Serilog;

namespace Marketplace.Infrastructure
{
    public static class RequestHandler
    {
        public static async Task<IActionResult> HandleRequest<T>(
            T request, Func<T, Task> handler, ILogger log)
        {
            try
            {
                log.Debug("Handling HTTP request of type {type}",
                typeof(T).Name);
                await handler(request);
                return new OkResult();
            }
            catch (Exception e)
            {
                log.Error(e, "Error handling the request");
                return new BadRequestObjectResult(new {error =
                e.Message, stackTrace = e.StackTrace});
            }
        }
    }
}
```

This generic method can now be used in both controllers. Let's look at what the new
controller would look like. I created a new `UserProfileCommandApi` class in the
`UserProfile` folder of the application project, as shown in the following code:

```
using System.Threading.Tasks;
using Marketplace.Infrastructure;
using Microsoft.AspNetCore.Mvc;
using Serilog;

namespace Marketplace.UserProfile
{
```

```
[Route("/profile")]
public class UserProfileCommandsApi : Controller
{
    private readonly UserProfileApplicationService
    _applicationService;
    private static readonly ILogger Log =
    Serilog.Log.ForContext<UserProfileCommandsApi>();

    public UserProfileCommandsApi(UserProfileApplicationService
    applicationService)
        => _applicationService = applicationService;

    [HttpPost]
    public Task<IActionResult> Post(Contracts.V1.RegisterUser
    request)
        => RequestHandler.HandleRequest(request,
        _applicationService.Handle, Log);
    [Route("fullname")]
    [HttpPut]
    public Task<IActionResult> Put(Contracts.V1.UpdateUserFullName
    request)
        => RequestHandler.HandleRequest(request,
        _applicationService.Handle, Log);
    [Route("displayname")]
    [HttpPut]
    public Task<IActionResult>
    Put(Contracts.V1.UpdateUserDisplayName request)
        => RequestHandler.HandleRequest(request,
        _applicationService.Handle, Log);
    [Route("photo")]
    [HttpPut]
    public Task<IActionResult>
    Put(Contracts.V1.UpdateUserProfilePhoto request)
        => RequestHandler.HandleRequest(request,
        _applicationService.Handle, Log);
    }
}
```

The classified ad controller can use `RequestHandler` in a similar fashion; the new implementation can be found in the chapter code.

We are almost done with all the changes, but one thing is still missing, and that is an implementation for the profanity check function. I will use PurgoMalum, a free web service to filter content and remove profanity, obscenity, and other things that we don't want to see on our public website.

The implementation is very simple, since all I need to do is call an HTTP endpoint with one argument. For that, I add one more class to the `Infrastructure` folder, called `PurgomalumClient`, as shown in the following code:

```
using System.Net.Http;
using System.Threading.Tasks;
using Microsoft.AspNetCore.WebUtilities;

namespace Marketplace.Infrastructure
{
    /// <summary>
    /// PurgoMalum is a simple, free, RESTful web service for filtering
    // and removing content of profanity, obscenity and other unwanted
    // text.
    /// Check http://www.purgomalum.com
    /// </summary>
    public class PurgomalumClient
    {
        private readonly HttpClient _httpClient;

        public PurgomalumClient() : this(new HttpClient()) { }
        public PurgomalumClient(HttpClient httpClient) => _httpClient =
        httpClient;

        public async Task<bool> CheckForProfanity(string text)
        {
            var result = await _httpClient.GetAsync(
                QueryHelpers.AddQueryString(
                    "https://www.purgomalum.com/service
                     /containsprofanity", "text", text));
            var value = await result.Content.ReadAsStringAsync();
            return bool.Parse(value);
        }
    }
}
```

For the final step, we need to do the wiring in the `Startup` class code. The only method we need to change is the `ConfigureServices` method. Here is the new code:

```
public void ConfigureServices(IServiceCollection services)
{
    var store = new DocumentStore
        {
            Urls = new[] {"http://localhost:8080"},
            Database = "Marketplace_Chapter9",
            Conventions =
            {
```

```
                    FindIdentityProperty = x => x.Name == "DbId"
            }
        };
    store.Initialize();

    var purgomalumClient = new PurgomalumClient();
    services.AddSingleton<ICurrencyLookup, FixedCurrencyLookup>();
    services.AddScoped(c => store.OpenAsyncSession());
    services.AddScoped<IUnitOfWork, RavenDbUnitOfWork>();
    services.AddScoped<IClassifiedAdRepository, ClassifiedAdRepository>
    ();
    services.AddScoped<IUserProfileRepository, UserProfileRepository>
    ();
    services.AddScoped<ClassifiedAdsApplicationService>();
    services.AddScoped(c =>
        new UserProfileApplicationService(
            c.GetService<IUserProfileRepository>(),
            c.GetService<IUnitOfWork>(),
            text => purgomalumClient.CheckForProfanity(text).
            GetAwaiter().GetResult()));

    services.AddMvc();
    services.AddSwaggerGen(c =>
    {
        c.SwaggerDoc("v1",
            new Info
            {
                Title = "ClassifiedAds",
                Version = "v1"
            });
    });
}
```

The registration of `UserProfileApplicationService` is a bit more complicated than `ClassifiedAdApplicationService`, since we are using a function, not an interface. In general, it is easier and cleaner to use delegates instead of interfaces with one method, but you'll need to deal with a bit more code when wiring things up.

Finally, you can run the app and try creating a new user profile, then change the full name or display name for the user. Try using some bad words for the display name to see the `ProfanityFound` exception in action. Remember to call `docker-compose up` from the `Chapter09/ravendb` folder of the chapter code repository before starting the app; otherwise, you won't have access to RavenDB.

And now that all these new things are in place and we have two nice aggregates in our system instead of just one, we can look at the query side of things.

The query side

So far, we have focused on state transitions in the system that are represented as events. When our domain model emits a new event, by definition, it means that we have put the system in a new state. State transitions are triggered by commands—that's why we have two APIs that are purposefully named `ClassifiedAdCommandApi` and `UserProfileCommandApi`. That shouldn't come as a surprise, since I have mentioned CQS and CQRS several times before in this book. Commands trigger methods of the aggregates, and following the CQS principle, none of those methods return anything, but instead change the system state. But no system can have only commands. Our users want to see something on the screen and it can't just be static texts and pictures. For our marketplace, the main purpose of the application is not that people can place classified ads in it; quite the opposite: we expect people to browse these ads, choose what they like, and make deals. This means that our system needs to deliver the information it possesses to the outside world so that it can be shown on the screen. Right at this moment, we can only see classified ads and user profiles that are stored in the database by looking at the database itself. Logically, what we need to do now is make this information available via some APIs.

CQRS and read-to-write mismatch

If you've studied other books about **Domain-Driven Design (DDD)** and done some work using DDD tactical patterns, including aggregate and repository, you might be wondering why I have not just included a couple of query methods in `ClassifiedAdRepository` and called it a day. Of course, I could have done that, but then I wouldn't have even started to write this book if I didn't have something else to discuss.

The point of repositories is that they are always dealing with aggregate state. As you might remember from the quote by Eric Evans in Chapter 8, *Aggregate Persistence*, the role of a repository is to represent aggregates that exist in the system in a way that looks like an in-memory collection of objects, hence the name of our two repositories so far—`ClassifiedAdRepository` and `UserProfileRepository`. This implies that the only details we can ever get from the repository are things that we have added to it. Since one repository handles the state of one aggregate—`ClassifiedAd`, for example—we can only query and retrieve classified ad details from the repository and nothing else. The issue here is that having only one aggregate in a bounded context (more about this in Chapter 12, *Bounded Context*) is a rare occurrence, and we are already dealing with two.

The information that we need to show is currently not represented on the EventStorming model. Again, that's because our big-picture model is more interested in how the system behaves, and what we show on the screen is not considered as behavior. However, as I just mentioned, that's still our core business, and we could think of something very obvious. If we go live and someone places an ad, they need to see how the ad appears to other users. The same screen is also needed when another user looks for something to buy and wants to check all the details—the ad title, description, and all available pictures, as well as the seller's information. Even if we haven't thought of the buying process just yet, that's the bare minimum that we definitely need. Also, people want to see all published ads. When the system gets more users and more ads are being published, we might consider showing ads per category. But when we are in the initial phase, showing all the ads with some search possibilities might be just fine.

All those screens that I have described are read models. These models might represent the state of a single aggregate, but in many cases, or in most cases, the information from several aggregates might be combined on one screen. For example, the screen for a single ad needs to have the information from both aggregate types that we currently have in the system. The screen that shows a list of published ads needs to display short versions of multiple aggregates, although just of a single type. While the latter case might be solved by adding a query method to the `IClassifiedAdRepository` interface, the first case would require something else. Oftentimes, when we have queries as part of repositories, we need to have some aggregation on the client side. Yet, returning a list of large object graphs (which is what repositories are supposed to do) too often is a far from optimal solution when we just need to show a couple of properties from each aggregate. Even worse, we might find ourselves in a situation when the object graph is too large and we start using those awkward ORM features of lazy loading that might work well in tests, but fail in the stateless world of the web simply because the session that we wanted to access in order to lazily load more data from is already gone by the time we try to ask it for more data.

All of these issues are effectively addressed by CQRS. The pattern postulates that there are almost no systems with an equal number of reads and writes. Most user-facing systems have a larger number of reads than writes. Think about the number of classified ads being created on Craigslist compared to the number of requests to retrieve and show them on someone's screen. The difference between them could be two orders of magnitude. Even so, most systems out there today struggle with scaling issues just because they ignore this simple fact. No database can be preoptimized for both reads and writes—you need to choose one. In the beginning, we all deal only with writes and try to optimize for them alone. RDBMS third-level normalization addresses exactly that—it shows the least amount of information that needs to be written to save space and avoid data duplication. When it comes to reads, though, third-level normalization doesn't work quite so well. We keep adding joins, one after another, to combine the information that we deliberately split when writing back together again. Soon, the number of reads overtakes the number of writes. Shortly after that, we see tens and hundreds of times more reads than writes, and this is where the trouble starts. There are, of course, other types of systems, such the world of the **internet of things** (**IoT**), high-frequency trading, and other business domains. In these cases, the amount of information that is being written to the database is by far greater than the amount of information that would ever need to be shown to anyone. Developers start to optimize for writes, decreasing the transaction time. This usually comes at the expense of removing indices and making the data flat. When it comes to reading, we start to see slow response times just because of this.

In essence, I am trying to make the point that when a developer is trying to address the concerns of either writes or reads to make them more efficient on the command side, the query side begins to suffer. It's also true the other way around. That's why CQRS was born. In this chapter, we will only look at the query side of things when using a single database. That might sound like a contradiction given what you just read, because, again, a database can rarely be optimized for both. But we need to start somewhere, and since optimization is the source of all evil, we'll start slowly. We will look at splitting read and writes into different types of storage when we get to Event Sourcing and projections in particular in Chapter 11, *Projections and Queries*. But for now, let's look at how we can perform more efficient reads from our existing storage without using repositories at all.

Queries and read models

When we were building our domain model, we needed to be careful taking dependencies so that the domain model stayed pure, free of any infrastructural concerns. Our goal was to provide a certain degree of freedom to implement the domain logic in a way that made sense from the point of view of the business, using Ubiquitous Language. We also defined repository interfaces as part of the domain model so that the application layer was able to implement these interfaces in order to enable aggregate persistence. Then, we defined commands as contracts that our application services could accept in order to perform operations on domain objects and potentially execute state transitions. Overall, the isolation and separation of concerns between the different parts of the command processing sequence are implemented according to the following diagram:

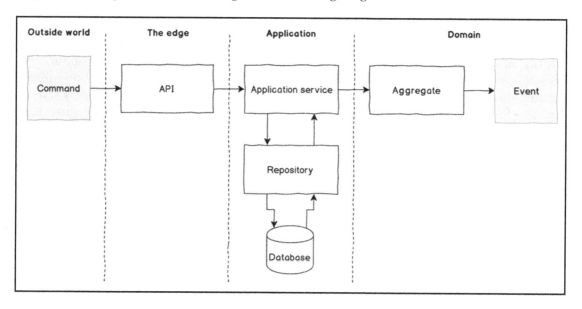

The typical command flow

When we need to query the data store where we put the state of our domain model using the repository, our goal changes. We don't need any business rules in queries; queries don't change the domain model state. But we definitely need to know how the repository implementation, which is implemented by our application, represents the state of our aggregate in the database. That makes queries a purely application-side concern. When we add an API to get something from our system, we need the API to only deal with persistence. The model that an API GET endpoint returns becomes our contract for the outside world. We don't need any other model either, such as the data model, to fetch the data; we can instead return what we got from the database directly as a response.

The flow for querying then becomes much simpler, and we can visualize it as shown in the following diagram:

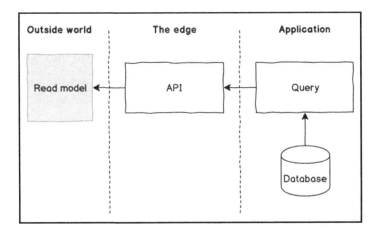

The typical query flow

What we see being returned by the API is the read model. We need to make our queries in a way that the read model can be retrieved from the database without any translation between different models—we return it as is. This allows us to simplify the way in which we obtain the data and return it to those who either need to show it on the screen or need it for any other imaginable purpose. That is, essentially, the whole idea behind the read side of CQRS. It is now time to write some code and show how it works.

Implementing queries

When implementing the read side, we don't need to touch anything in the domain model. We will concentrate our efforts on the application side. However, this doesn't mean that we need to forget about Ubiquitous Language. In the end, read models are part of the whole model anyway; we saw them during the EventStorming sessions as green sticky notes. Read models help people and other systems make decisions, based on the data they receive by executing our queries. Just as commands indicate the intent of external parties to run some operations on our domain, read models and queries express their intent to get something in return.

For example, for our `Marketplace` application, we would expect shoppers to browse through published ads. Ad owners need to see a list of their ads. Everyone needs to be able to open a single ad and see everything in it that is public, plus the owner's public details, such as their photo and display name. These are obvious queries and read models that we can start implementing. We already have all the data in the form of the state of multiple aggregates, and we just need to get it from the database in a form that is usable for those purposes I've listed.

Query API

We can start implementing queries by specifying read models and the API. We already have folders in our `Marketplace` project for different application features. It might seem logical to add queries there as well, until we remember that some read models combine data from different aggregates, such as classified ad details and the owner's profile information. Where do we place that kind of model and query? Well, there are some options, but I'd try to concentrate on the essence of the requested information. If we need to see a single ad, that's what we want to look at, mainly. Although we might also provide some owner details, the owner details are not the main things that we want to show. In the end, we query one single ad by its ID, and the user's profile information is derived from the ad details, such as the owner ID, so we can still quite clearly identify where to place those queries.

Since we have found several things that we want to return via the API, and all of those things are related to ads, we put the stuff there. Now we need to add two files to the `ClassifiedAd` folder of the `Marketplace` project—one is `ReadModels.cs` and the other one is `ClassifiedAdsQueryApi.cs`.

Based on the query requirements, let's define the read models first using the following code:

```
using System;

namespace Marketplace.ClassifiedAd
{
    public static class ReadModels
    {
        public class ClassifiedAdDetails
        {
            public Guid ClassifiedAdId { get; set; }
            public string Title { get; set; }
            public decimal Price { get; set; }
            public string CurrencyCode { get; set; }
            public string Description { get; set; }
```

```
        public string SellersDisplayName { get; set; }
        public string[] PhotoUrls { get; set; }
    }

    public class ClassifiedAdListItem
    {
        public Guid ClassifiedAdId { get; set; }
        public string Title { get; set; }
        public decimal Price { get; set; }
        public string CurrencyCode { get; set; }
        public string PhotoUrl { get; set; }
    }
  }
}
```

One way of implementing queries is to create a query service interface that will be used by the API. Then, we wire it to the database-specific implementation during startup. For our purposes, it could look like this:

```
public interface IClassifiedAdQueryService
{
    Task<IEnumerable<ClassifiedAdListItem>> GetPublishedAds(
        int page, int pageSize);
    Task<ClassifiedAdDetails> GetPublicClassifiedAd(
        Guid classifiedAdId);
    Task<IEnumerable<ClassifiedAdListItem>>
    GetClassifiedAdsOwnedBy(Guid userId, int page, int pageSize);
}
```

This approach has one disadvantage—all parameters are separated, and when we implement the API, we need to add all those parameters to the API method. If you decide to use something else for your edges, such as ServiceStack or a messaging framework, you will have to use typed requests and then expand the request properties to the query service method parameters. Should you need to change the parameters for some reason, you'd need to change the code in multiple places. This could also affect the UI. For example, if you use a **single-page application** (**SPA**) and the API is being called from the frontend JavaScript code, you'd probably abstract the API call in some kind of service that will need to change to add new parameters to the call.

The ServiceStack framework advocates a message-driven approach for the HTTP API for a reason. It makes the request typed and removes the need to have a long list of parameters for the API methods and all layers that communicate with the API. So, further on in the code, we'll use typed requests too, and therefore, typed queries. If we wanted to implement the query service with typed requests, it would look like this instead:

```
public interface IClassifiedAdQueryService
{
    Task<IEnumerable<ClassifiedAdListItem>>
    Query(GetPublishedClassifiedAds query);
    Task<ClassifiedAdDetails> Query(GetPublicClassifiedAd query);
    Task<IEnumerable<ClassifiedAdListItem>>
    Query(GetOwnersClassifiedAds query);
}
```

Here, we have several overloads of the `Query` method that all accept typed query requests. The type of query request defines what we expect to get back. We can also use the same types for the API. Let's implement these query contracts and the `ClassifiedAdQueryApi` class without using the query service just yet, as shown in the following code:

```
using System;

namespace Marketplace.ClassifiedAd
{
    public static class QueryModels
    {
        public class GetPublishedClassifiedAds
        {
            public int Page { get; set; }
            public int PageSize { get; set; }
        }

        public class GetOwnersClassifiedAd
        {
            public Guid OwnerId { get; set; }
            public int Page { get; set; }
            public int PageSize { get; set; }
        }

        public class GetPublicClassifiedAd
        {
            public Guid ClassifiedAdId { get; set; }
        }
    }
}
```

Here comes the API:

```
using System.Collections.Generic;
using System.Net;
using System.Threading.Tasks;
using Microsoft.AspNetCore.Mvc;

namespace Marketplace.ClassifiedAd
{
    [Route("/ad")]
    public class ClassifiedAdsQueryApi : Controller
    {
        [HttpGet]
        [Route("list")]
        public Task<IActionResult>
        Get(QueryModels.GetPublishedClassifiedAds request)
        {
        }

        [HttpGet]
        [Route("myads")]
        public Task<IActionResult>
        Get(QueryModels.GetOwnersClassifiedAd request)
        {
        }

        [HttpGet]
        [ProducesResponseType((int) HttpStatusCode.OK)]
        [ProducesResponseType((int) HttpStatusCode.NotFound)]
        public Task<IActionResult>
        Get(QueryModels.GetPublicClassifiedAd request)
        {
        }
    }
}
```

That looks pretty clean. We used both types of request and typed response. When we get one ad by its ID, we can return a 200 OK or a 404 Not Found response.

Now, let's get back to the query service. The big question that you might get about this is *why do I need an interface if I only have one implementation?* And this question is completely valid. Interfaces aren't meant to be used just to make it possible to mock dependencies for tests. Basically, if all you use an interface for is a test, you'll need to reconsider having that interface at all. Queries are especially relevant in this context because it makes little sense to test the API with a mocked query.

If you want to test your queries, and you know that they belong to the infrastructure and application, then what is the point of testing them without using the infrastructure? You end up only testing the serialization, and while this might be not that bad an idea, the main function of the queries will remain untested. Query tests really need to use the database they talk to.

After this important issue has been clarified, we can think about implementing queries closer to the database-level API. One way of doing this is by using extension methods. In the next two sections, we'll be using this approach to implement queries for RavenDB and Entity Framework and complete the API accordingly.

Queries with RavenDB

As we already know, the RavenDB client library allows us to store documents in the database using the document session interface. The document session interface represents a single, short-lived connection to the database. Usually, it is scoped per request, since the single request is our scope for the unit of work. It is not only valid for commands; we can also use the document session that is registered in the `Startup` class of our application in query endpoints.

In the following code, I try to implement one query to the database using extension methods for the `IAsyncDocumentSession` interface, which we register in the services container for the API:

```
using System.Collections.Generic;
using System.Linq;
using System.Reflection.Metadata.Ecma335;
using System.Threading.Tasks;
using Raven.Client.Documents;
using Raven.Client.Documents.Linq;
using Raven.Client.Documents.Session;
using static Marketplace.ClassifiedAd.ReadModels;
using static Marketplace.Domain.ClassifiedAd.ClassifiedAd;
namespace Marketplace.ClassifiedAd
{
    public static class Queries
    {
        public static Task<List<PublicClassifiedAdListItem>>
        Query(
            this IAsyncDocumentSession session,
            QueryModels.GetPublishedClassifiedAds query) =>
            session.Query<Domain.ClassifiedAd.ClassifiedAd>()
                .Where(x => x.State == ClassifiedAdState.Active)
                .Select(x => new PublicClassifiedAdListItem
```

```
            {
                ClassifiedAdId = x.Id.Value,
                Price = x.Price.Amount,
                Title = x.Title.Value,
                CurrencyCode = x.Price.Currency.CurrencyCode
            })
            .Skip(query.Page * query.PageSize)
            .Take(query.PageSize)
            .ToListAsync();
    }
}
```

The latest version of RavenDB supports inline projections, so all we need to do here is to run a normal query with `Where` and then project the complex `ClassifiedAd` aggregate state document to the read model object. Then, we need to apply the paging and call `ToListAsync` so that the query gets executed on the server.

With this one query ready to be used, we can call it from the API. I will comment out the API methods that currently have no queries that we can use. So, the API class would have one method, as shown in the following code:

```
using System;
using System.Threading.Tasks;
using Microsoft.AspNetCore.Mvc;
using Raven.Client.Documents.Session;
using Serilog;

namespace Marketplace.ClassifiedAd
{
    [Route("/ad")]
    public class ClassifiedAdsQueryApi : Controller
    {
        private readonly IAsyncDocumentSession _session;

        public ClassifiedAdsQueryApi(IAsyncDocumentSession session)
            => _session = session;

        [HttpGet]
        [Route("list")]
        public async Task<IActionResult>
        Get(QueryModels.GetPublishedClassifiedAds request)
        {
            try
            {
                var ads = await _session.Query(request);
                return Ok(ads);
            }
```

```
        catch (Exception e)
        {
            Log.Error(e, "Error handling the query");
            throw;
        }
    }
}
}
```

Since I already have some data in the database (one ad), I can now execute it using Swagger. I leave the page number as 0 and set the page size to 10, but the query returns nothing. That's because my classified ad is not published yet, so the query condition filters it out. I need to send the ad for review and then approve it using a new Guid for ApproverId. After doing this, I can see the read model that is returned from the API. The API can also be called directly in the browser by going to http://localhost:5000/ad/list?Page=0&PageSize=10, and the browser should show the following JSON:

```
[
    {
        classifiedAdId: "d338696a-342e-45cf-a02e-178dcb8e95f8",
        title: "Red sofa",
        price: 100,
        currencyCode: "EUR",
        photoUrl: null
    }
]
```

We want to add other queries now, but this would mean that we need to wrap all queries to this try/catch block. Let's see if we can follow the **DRY** (short for **don't repeat yourself**) principle and create a useful function to handle all queries. We already did this for commands that use the static RequestHandler class. I will add a new function here to handle queries too, as shown in the following code:

```
public static async Task<IActionResult> HandleQuery<TModel>(
    Func<Task<TModel>> query, ILogger log)
{
    try
    {
        return new OkObjectResult(await query());
    }
    catch (Exception e)
    {
        log.Error(e, "Error handling the query");
        return new BadRequestObjectResult(new
        {
```

```
                    error = e.Message, stackTrace = e.StackTrace
            });
        }
    }
```

Adding the next query that will allow us to get all classified ads for an owner by owner ID is quite trivial; we just need to change the condition and keep the read model projection from the document to the read model. To make methods a bit shorter, I've added the `PagedList` extension method, so the whole class now looks like the following:

```
using System.Collections.Generic;
using System.Threading.Tasks;
using Raven.Client.Documents;
using Raven.Client.Documents.Linq;
using Raven.Client.Documents.Queries;
using Raven.Client.Documents.Session;
using static Marketplace.ClassifiedAd.ReadModels;
using static Marketplace.Domain.ClassifiedAd.ClassifiedAd;

namespace Marketplace.ClassifiedAd
{
    public static class Queries
    {
        public static Task<List<PublicClassifiedAdListItem>> Query(
            this IAsyncDocumentSession session,
            QueryModels.GetPublishedClassifiedAds query
        ) =>
            session.Query<Domain.ClassifiedAd.ClassifiedAd>()
                .Where(x => x.State == ClassifiedAdState.Active)
                .Select(
                    x =>
                        new PublicClassifiedAdListItem
                        {
                            ClassifiedAdId = x.Id.Value,
                            Price = x.Price.Amount,
                            Title = x.Title.Value,
                            CurrencyCode =
                            x.Price.Currency.CurrencyCode
                        }
                )
                .PagedList(query.Page, query.PageSize);

        public static Task<List<PublicClassifiedAdListItem>> Query(
            this IAsyncDocumentSession session,
            QueryModels.GetOwnersClassifiedAd query
        )
            =>
                session.Query<Domain.ClassifiedAd.ClassifiedAd>()
```

```
                    .Where(x => x.OwnerId.Value == query.OwnerId)
                    .Select(
                        x =>
                            new PublicClassifiedAdListItem
                            {
                                ClassifiedAdId = x.Id.Value,
                                Price = x.Price.Amount,
                                Title = x.Title.Value,
                                CurrencyCode =
                                x.Price.Currency.CurrencyCode
                            }
                    )
                    .PagedList(query.Page, query.PageSize);

        public static Task<ClassifiedAdDetails> Query(
            this IAsyncDocumentSession session,
            QueryModels.GetPublicClassifiedAd query
        )
            => (from ad in session.Query<Domain.ClassifiedAd.
            ClassifiedAd>()
                where ad.Id.Value == query.ClassifiedAdId
                let user = RavenQuery
                    .Load<Domain.UserProfile.UserProfile>(
                        "UserProfile/" + ad.OwnerId.Value
                    )
                select new ClassifiedAdDetails
                {
                    ClassifiedAdId = ad.Id.Value,
                    Title = ad.Title.Value,
                    Description = ad.Text.Value,
                    Price = ad.Price.Amount,
                    CurrencyCode = ad.Price.Currency.CurrencyCode,
                    SellersDisplayName = user.DisplayName.Value
                }).SingleAsync();

        private static Task<List<T>> PagedList<T>(
            this IRavenQueryable<T> query, int page, int pageSize
        ) =>
            query
                .Skip(page * pageSize)
                .Take(pageSize)
                .ToListAsync();
    }
}
```

If we wanted to use LINQ-to-objects, we could also move the projection to a separate function. However, the query here is being sent to the server, and the server has no idea about our client-side code. Therefore, we need to repeat the projection code in each method.

Now I can add the API call and use the new `HandleQuery` function. Here is the code for the whole `ClassifiedAdQueryApi` class, which uses both queries:

```
using System.Threading.Tasks;
using Marketplace.Infrastructure;
using Microsoft.AspNetCore.Mvc;
using Raven.Client.Documents.Session;
using Serilog;

namespace Marketplace.ClassifiedAd
{
    [Route("/ad")]
    public class ClassifiedAdsQueryApi : Controller
    {
        private static ILogger _log =
        Log.ForContext<ClassifiedAdsQueryApi>();
        private readonly IAsyncDocumentSession _session;

        public ClassifiedAdsQueryApi(IAsyncDocumentSession session)
            => _session = session;

        [HttpGet]
        [Route("list")]
        public Task<IActionResult>
        Get(QueryModels.GetPublishedClassifiedAds request)
            => RequestHandler.HandleQuery(() =>
                _session.Query(request), _log);

        [HttpGet]
        [Route("myads")]
        public Task<IActionResult>
        Get(QueryModels.GetOwnersClassifiedAd request)
            => RequestHandler.HandleQuery(() =>
                _session.Query(request), _log);
    }
}
```

You can see that the methods for the API endpoint become just as concise as the command API methods, and all query logic is moved to the extension methods.

Finally, we get to the point where we need to create a query that will combine data from two different documents in one read model. To handle this scenario, RavenDB offers a feature of projections using a loaded document. Using this feature, we can load another document (`UserProfile`) using an ID that comes from the document that we query (`ClassifiedAd`).

The query looks a bit more complicated, but not much. Here we go (I only list the new function in the following code):

```
public static Task<ReadModels.ClassifiedAdDetails> Query(
    this IAsyncDocumentSession session,
    QueryModels.GetPublicClassifiedAd query)
    => (from ad in session.Query<Domain.ClassifiedAd.ClassifiedAd>()
        where ad.Id.Value == query.ClassifiedAdId
        let user = RavenQuery
            .Load<Domain.UserProfile.UserProfile>("UserProfile/" +
            ad.OwnerId.Value)
        select new ReadModels.ClassifiedAdDetails
        {
            ClassifiedAdId = ad.Id.Value,
            Title = ad.Title.Value,
            Description = ad.Text.Value,
            Price = ad.Price.Amount,
            CurrencyCode = ad.Price.Currency.CurrencyCode,
            SellersDisplayName = user.DisplayName.Value
        }).SingleAsync();
```

Now, we can complete the query API by adding one more method, just as short as the previous two, as shown in the following code:

```
[HttpGet]
public Task<IActionResult> Get(QueryModels.GetPublicClassifiedAd request)
    => RequestHandler.HandleQuery(() => _session.Query(request), _log);
```

The difference here is that we have no route because we want to get the resource by ID from the ad route itself. Now, I can start the application and go to `http://localhost:5000/ad?ClassifiedAdId=d338696a-342e-45cf-a02e-178dcb8e95f8` to see the following result:

```
{
    classifiedAdId: "d338696a-342e-45cf-a02e-178dcb8e95f8",
    title: "Red sofa",
    price: 100,
    currencyCode: "EUR",
    description: "Really good",
    sellersDisplayName: "prejudice",
    photoUrls: null
}
```

Please note that this GUID is the ad ID in my database; you might need to check the database to find out what you have used yourself. Some readers might also not be happy that the URL is not fully REST compliant, since it uses a query parameter instead of the route. I believe this would be an easy fix, but then you'd need to remove the query object and use parameters in the API method that map to the route parameter instead.

As you can see, we managed to make all the queries we wanted and keep them close to the underlying persistence. These queries can be called directly from the API, and our domain will remain untouched. We are also able to combine the data from two different aggregates in one read model, which we couldn't do using a repository because repositories always deal with the aggregate root only.

Our queries use the database features directly, without bringing any abstractions on top of `IAsyncDocumentSession`. Using extension methods also allows us to remove the need for interfaces, and our queries don't become any less testable because of that. We can quite easily write integrated tests that will directly use the database, so we can check how our queries work.

We also used query objects as our API contracts and as parameters for query methods. Similarly, by using read models, we were able to use the same objects as the query result and as the API call response, so we didn't need to make any useless mappings between models that live in different layers.

Queries with Entity Framework

Let's now see how we can do the same thing using SQL. You might be wondering if I really meant Entity Framework rather than SQL. In fact, I am not going to use any features of the Entity Framework itself, since the best way to implement the query side of CQRS with relational databases is to use SQL directly. We will get to one more issue that arises from using Entity Framework in a moment.

We did a lot of work in the previous section, where we created queries, read models, and API endpoints that used RavenDB. I won't go over all the steps that are the same. The following is a brief description of the stages that are exactly the same between these two implementations; you can use this list to just copy the relevant files over from one implementation to the other:

- The `UserProfile` aggregate and related value objects
- The command API and the application service for user profiles and classified ads
- The `ContentModeration` delegate

- Restructuring with feature folders
- Read models
- Query classes
- Both query APIs

Of course, we also need to copy a small change in the ClassifiedAd aggregate to handle the Publish command.

One more thing that I need to add to the Entity Framework-style project is UserProfileRepository. The interface it needs to implement is exactly the same as before. The repository implementation itself is the same as ClassifiedAdRepository, which we made in the previous chapter. Here we go:

```
using System;
using System.Threading.Tasks;
using Marketplace.Domain.Shared;
using Marketplace.Domain.UserProfile;
using Marketplace.Infrastructure;

namespace Marketplace.UserProfile
{
    public class UserProfileRepository : IUserProfileRepository,
    IDisposable
    {
        private readonly MarketplaceDbContext _dbContext;

        public UserProfileRepository(MarketplaceDbContext dbContext)
            => _dbContext = dbContext;

        public Task Add(Domain.UserProfile.UserProfile entity)
            => _dbContext.UserProfiles.AddAsync(entity);

        public async Task<bool> Exists(UserId id)
            => await _dbContext.UserProfiles.FindAsync(id.Value)
                != null;

        public Task<Domain.UserProfile.UserProfile> Load(UserId id)
            => _dbContext.UserProfiles.FindAsync(id.Value);

        public void Dispose() => _dbContext.Dispose();
    }
}
```

It looks like the only thing we need to do is to rename the existing `ClassifiedAdDbContext` to `MarketPlaceDbContext`, extend it with all the required configuration for the value objects, and then do the wiring. That was my first thought too. I added a new entity type configuration, as shown in the following code:

```
public class UserProfileEntityTypeConfiguration
    : IEntityTypeConfiguration<Domain.UserProfile.UserProfile>
{
    public void Configure(EntityTypeBuilder<Domain.UserProfile.UserProfile>
builder)
    {
        builder.HasKey(x => x.UserProfileId);
        builder.OwnsOne(x => x.Id);
        builder.OwnsOne(x => x.DisplayName);
        builder.OwnsOne(x => x.FullName);
    }
}
```

Note that, here, I have to use an extra property to hold the primitive value of the ID, just like we did for `ClassifiedAd` in Chapter 8, *Aggregate Persistence*.

Then, I could just add one more `DbSet`, as shown in the following code:

```
public DbSet<Domain.UserProfile.UserProfile> UserProfiles { get; set; }
```

Once that's done, I can change the `OnModelCreating` override, as follows:

```
protected override void OnModelCreating(ModelBuilder modelBuilder)
{
    modelBuilder.ApplyConfiguration(new
    ClassifiedAdEntityTypeConfiguration());
    modelBuilder.ApplyConfiguration(new
    PictureEntityTypeConfiguration());
    modelBuilder.ApplyConfiguration(new
    UserProfileEntityTypeConfiguration());
}
```

Now, we need to make use of it to change the wiring, as shown in the following code:

```
public void ConfigureServices(IServiceCollection services)
{
    const string connectionString =
        "Host=localhost;Database=Marketplace_Chapter9;
        Username=ddd;Password=book";
    services.AddEntityFrameworkNpgsql();
    services.AddPostgresDbContext<MarketPlaceDbContext>
    (connectionString);
```

```
        var purgomalumClient = new PurgomalumClient();

        services.AddSingleton<ICurrencyLookup, FixedCurrencyLookup>();
        services.AddScoped<IUnitOfWork, EfCoreUnitOfWork>();
        services.AddScoped<IClassifiedAdRepository, ClassifiedAdRepository>
        ();
        services.AddScoped<IUserProfileRepository, UserProfileRepository>
        ();
        services.AddScoped<ClassifiedAdsApplicationService>();
        services.AddScoped(c =>
            new UserProfileApplicationService(
                c.GetService<IUserProfileRepository>(),
                c.GetService<IUnitOfWork>(),
                text => purgomalumClient.CheckForProfanity(text)
                    .GetAwaiter().GetResult()));

        services.AddMvc();
        services.AddSwaggerGen(c =>
        {
            c.SwaggerDoc("v1",
                new Info
                {
                    Title = "ClassifiedAds",
                    Version = "v1"
                });
        });
    }
```

The preceding code uses the `AddPostgresDbContext` extension method; it just wraps what we had before. You can find the code in the chapter repository.

At this point, we can execute the application and create a new user profile, then use the same user ID to create a couple of classified ads, all using the command API.

The next step is to start implementing queries. As planned, we go for pure SQL. However, using SQL would require us to create additional contexts and have `DbSet` for each read model. That seems like overkill. Because of this, I will be using Dapper, a lightweight SQL to the object helper library. It adds a number of helpful extensions to the `SqlConnection` class, and we will be adding even more extensions, so that should be fine. So I added the Dapper package to the `Marketplace` project and did the wiring in the `Startup.ConfigureServices` method by adding this code. Now, the first query seems to be quite obvious, as you can see from the following code:

```
using System.Threading.Tasks;
using static Marketplace.ClassifiedAd.ReadModels;
using static Marketplace.Domain.ClassifiedAd.ClassifiedAd;
```

```
using static Marketplace.ClassifiedAd.QueryModels;
using Dapper;

namespace Marketplace.ClassifiedAd
{
    public static class Queries
    {
        public static Task<IEnumerable<PublicClassifiedAdListItem>>
        Query(
            this DbConnection connection,
            GetPublishedClassifiedAds query)
            => connection.QueryAsync<PublicClassifiedAdListItem>(
                "SELECT \"ClassifiedAdId\", \"Price_Amount\",
                \"Title_Value\" " +
                "FROM \"ClassifiedAds\" WHERE \"State\"=@State LIMIT
                @PageSize OFFSET @Offset",
                new
                {
                    State = (int)ClassifiedAdState.Active,
                    PageSize = query.PageSize,
                    Offset = Offset(query.Page, query.PageSize)
                });
```

The reason why I am not closing the connection is `DbConnection` is registered in the container as scoped, so it gets instantiated per request. Since we are using the connection once, it will be automatically disposed and, therefore, closed. You could, of course, close it explicitly.

However, if we try that, we get an empty result. If we check the database table to see what data is stored for an active classified ad, we can see that the `State` column for an active ad has a value of 2. At the same time, the `ClassifiedAdState` enum has the `Active` value on a second position. A weird thing in Entity Framework is, that it counts enum values from 1, while the `(int)` type case always counts from 0. We could, of course, use the static 2 value in the query, but it won't deliver any safety if we need to change the enum and reorder values. Reordering this enum would also be dangerous for the write side, since Entity Framework won't keep the right counter either. To fix this, let's add explicit `int` values to the enum instead of using the following code:

```
public enum ClassifiedAdState
{
    PendingReview = 1,
    Active = 2,
    Inactive = 3,
    MarkedAsSold = 4
}
```

After this change is made, we get a proper result. I have one active ad in the database, so I get one element in the JSON array, as shown in the following code:

```
[
  {
    "classifiedAdId": "556bc798-bacc-4bb8-a55b-50144add4f17",
    "title": "Green sofa",
    "price": 110,
    "currencyCode": null,
    "photoUrl": null
  }
]
```

So far, so good. Next, we can implement the `myads` route, which queries all classified ads for a specific user who owns those ads. The query is almost identical to the previous one; we just need to change the `WHERE` condition using the following code:

```
public static Task<IEnumerable<PublicClassifiedAdListItem>> Query(
    this DbConnection connection,
    GetOwnersClassifiedAd query) =>
    connection.QueryAsync<ReadModels.PublicClassifiedAdListItem>(
        "SELECT \"ClassifiedAdId\", \"Price_Amount\" price,
        \"Title_Value\" title " +
        "FROM \"ClassifiedAds\" WHERE \"OwnerId_Value\"=@OwnerId LIMIT
        @PageSize OFFSET @Offset",
            new
            {
                OwnerId = query.OwnerId,
                PageSize = query.PageSize,
                Offset = Offset(query.Page, query.PageSize)
            });
```

If I use the proper owner ID for an ad that I previously added to the system, I get exactly the same result as before. To demonstrate things a bit better, I added a new classified ad for the same owner ID and changed its title, but haven't published it. So, when I execute the `list` query, I still get the same result with a single ad. When I execute the `myads` query, I get the following two results instead:

```
[
  {
    "classifiedAdId": "556bc798-bacc-4bb8-a55b-50144add4f17",
    "title": "Green sofa",
    "price": 110,
    "currencyCode": null,
    "photoUrl": null
  },
  {
```

```
        "classifiedAdId": "21f750fa-5a24-405b-8aad-20935b5974ed",
        "title": "Not ready yet",
        "price": -1,
        "currencyCode": null,
        "photoUrl": null
    }
]
```

Here, we can see that the price property has –1 as a value, and that represents the Price.NoPrice value, which we can render in the UI accordingly when we have one.

The last query is a bit more complicated, since it requires a join. But since joins are very common SQL operations, it won't be hard to implement this query as well; we simply use the following code:

```
public static Task<ClassifiedAdDetails> Query(
    this DbConnection connection,
    GetPublicClassifiedAd query) =>
    connection.QuerySingleOrDefaultAsync<ClassifiedAdDetails>(
        "SELECT \"ClassifiedAdId\", \"Price_Amount\" price, " +
        "\"Title_Value\" title, " +
        "\"Text_Value\" description, \"DisplayName_Value\"
        sellersdisplayname " +
        "FROM \"ClassifiedAds\", \"UserProfiles\" " +
        "WHERE \"ClassifiedAdId\" = @Id AND
        \"OwnerId_Value\"=\"UserProfileId\"",
            new { Id = query.ClassifiedAdId });
```

Then, I can call the API using an existing classified ad ID and get the following result:

```
{
    "classifiedAdId": "556bc798-bacc-4bb8-a55b-50144add4f17",
    "title": "Green sofa",
    "price": 110,
    "currencyCode": null,
    "description": "Very nice sofa, almost as new",
    "sellersDisplayName": "prejudice",
    "photoUrls": null
}
```

Well, that's it! Queries seem to be much easier to implement than commands. By using direct access to the database engine itself without much of an abstraction, we can fully utilize the full power of the database. We need, however, to be aware of some quirks that the write-side persistence has created, such as enumeration issues and somewhat weird column titles for value objects, but in the end, it wasn't all that bad.

Interestingly enough, we didn't need to change anything at all in the query API classes between the two different implementations, except for using a different type for the database connection.

Summary

In this chapter, we finally got hold of the data that we put in the database. Now, our project contains several GET endpoints to retrieve the content of the underlying database. We used CQRS to create queries, which are completely separate from the models that we have in our domain. Certainly, we had to use aggregate types to query RavenDB, since these are the document types as well. This could be avoided by splitting the state model from the aggregate, but this is something you can explore yourself.

We embraced the power of native access to the database engine to do things that would otherwise be impossible or cumbersome to do if we'd just used repositories. That's because a repository type represents a collection of aggregates of a single type, and we would get in trouble if we needed to combine data from different aggregates in a single read model.

Read models allowed us to create objects that we can map to the database query result and return as is via the API without any additional mapping. Query objects nicely encapsulate all the parameters that we need to pass to the query itself. By using query objects, it is also easier to avoid signature conflicts if we need to send the same parameters to two different queries.

Using extension methods to build queries is a powerful pattern. You won't need interfaces and additional registrations just to get dependencies to the controller. If you are concerned about testing, bear in mind that queries should always be tested against the actual database. Therefore, there is no real need to use interfaces there; you can use these extension methods in your tests just like we used them in the controllers.

By adding a couple of helpful generic static methods, such as HandleCommand and HandleQuery, we decreased the number of lines in our controllers and removed all duplicated code. It is always a good idea to look for a helpful abstraction if you see repetition in your code; that would make your code cleaner and shorter, and the chance of making a mistake when copy-pasting the same code again and again would virtually disappear.

This is the last chapter in which we use traditional persistence on the write side of CQRS. All of the subsequent chapters will use Event Sourcing to persist aggregates, but we will still be using a variety of methods for read models by using projections.

10
Event Sourcing

You should already understand what domain events are, why they are important, and how to find and code them. Now, we will look into other uses for events. Hopefully, after reading this chapter, it will be clear why we need to use events to update the aggregate state. Before, we only used events inside our aggregates, and it might look a bit like overkill to raise those events and do the state transition separately, in the `When` method.

This time, you will learn how events can be used to persist the state of an object, instead of using traditional persistence mechanisms, such as SQL or a document database. That is not an easy thing to grasp, but the reward is satisfying. Using events to represent the system behavior and derive its state for any given moment in time has many advantages. Of course, silver bullets do not exist, and before deciding whether Event Sourcing is for you, it is essential that you understand the possible drawbacks.

We will continue developing our aggregates with more event handlers. Also, we will cover the concept of event streams and how streams relate to aggregates. We will use an event store to persist our aggregates in streams and load them back.

The following topics will be covered in this chapter:

- What is Event Sourcing?
- Why do we use Event Sourcing?
- The challenges and drawbacks of Event Sourcing
- Why Event Sourcing became popular in the DDD community
- Using the Event Store

Technical requirements

In this chapter, we will be using the Event Store (`https://eventstore.org`), which is an open source database.

The easiest way to run Event Store is to use Docker. We've used `docker-compose` in previous chapters, so it will be the same experience with the Event Store.

The code for this chapter contains a `docker-compose.yml` file that allows you to use Event Store by executing this command:

```
docker-compose up
```

Docker will pull the latest image from Docker Hub and start a named container. Two ports are mapped by this command from the container to your machine: `2113` and `1113`. Port `2113` is used to access Event Store via HTTP, and `1113` is used for TCP connections.

After the container starts, you can check its status by opening `http://localhost:2113` in your browser. You will get the following login prompt:

There, you need to enter the default credentials: admin as the username and changeit as the password. Then, click on the **Sign In** button, and the following screen should appear:

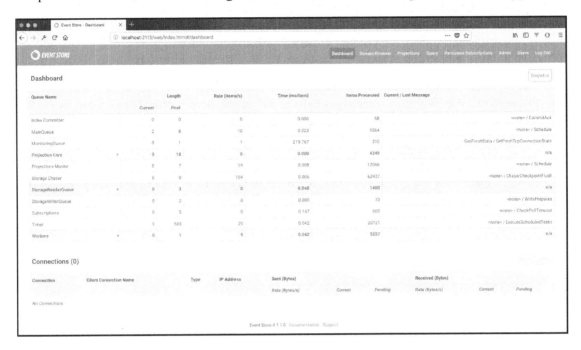

The product version and menu items might differ, depending on the latest version of Event Store.

Why Event Sourcing

In this section, we will not only discuss why one might want to use Event Sourcing—we will also look into the definition of this pattern and some history behind it. Like Greg Young often puts it, *"Event Sourcing is not new"*, and we will get into some history that should help you to understand the concept better.

After that, we will get into the *why* part. Armed with some knowledge about its history, it won't be very hard to understand why this way of storing data is becoming more popular.

By the end of this section, we will make it clear why one might not want to use Event Sourcing in their system, and what challenges are awaiting those who start using it for the first time.

Issues with state persistence

In the previous chapters, we used the term *domain event* many times. During the design phase, we used orange sticky notes to visualize domain events on the whiteboard. Later, during the implementation, we created classes for domain events. These classes translate things that happened in the system into something that the machine can read.

Each action in the domain model, represented as a method in aggregate, makes changes in the system state. We also made our aggregate to use events to describe these changes. When such a change is made, we then use the pattern-matching code to amend the aggregate state before it gets persisted to a database.

Now, let's suppose that we are not saving the aggregate state to the database, as we did in Chapter 8, *CQRS - The Read Side*. Instead, we will collect all new events that are generated when an action is executed. For example, in our code for the `ClassifiedAd` aggregate, we have an `UpdatePrice` method:

```
public void UpdatePrice(Price price) =>
    Apply(new Events.ClassifiedAdPriceUpdated
    {
        Id = Id,
        Price = price.Amount,
        CurrencyCode = price.Currency.CurrencyCode
    });
```

This method already creates a new event when we call it from our application service. We also have the `When` method for projecting events to the aggregate state, so when we call the `Apply` method, such as in the preceding code snippet, the aggregate state changes accordingly:

```
protected override void When(object @event)
{
    switch (@event)
    {
        // only a part of the When method is shown
        case Events.ClassifiedAdPriceUpdated e:
            Price = new Price(e.Price, e.CurrencyCode);
            break;
    }
}
```

So, if we look at how the aggregate state is changing over time, when we apply different events to it on a timeline, it will look like this:

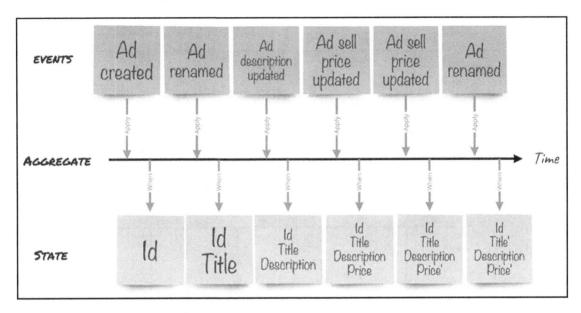

In the previous chapters, we were saving the aggregate state to the database by committing it to the repository for that aggregate type. Each time we needed to perform an operation of the aggregate, we would fetch its state back from the database by calling the `Get (int id)` method of the repository.

Each time we commit a new state, the previous state gets overwritten, so at any given moment, our database contains a snapshot of the system state, although there could have been many changes that made our system come to that state. We can visualize it using the timeline:

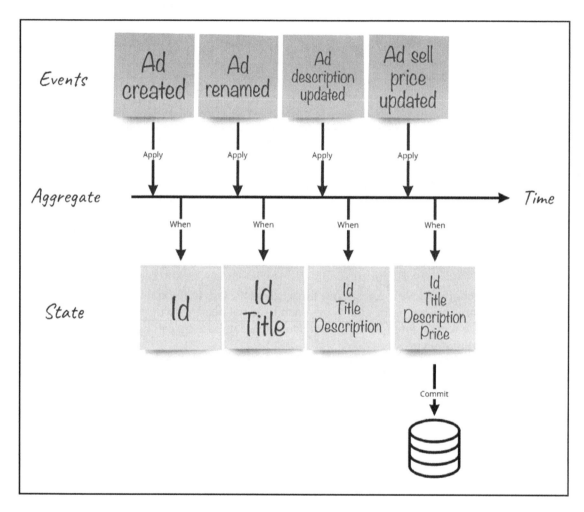

This is how executing any action on an aggregate will look:

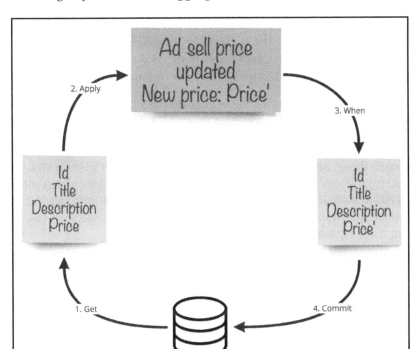

It works very well if we are only interested in the current state of things. We know the current sale price for a given classified ad. However, when the product owner says that we need to show a graph of the selling price history, we cannot do that. Another typical use case would be to only show those ads that had their price updated during the last couple of days. We can do this by adding the date of the last price update to our aggregate (just for the purpose of showing this new search result) but it will only work for new updates. It would mean that we cannot show the feature to our users before we collect enough data, since our persistence model is unable to provide us with any historical data.

As developers, we often encounter situations where we get some elements of a system in an unexpected or invalid state. Usually, we use log files to figure out what happened. When this approach fails, we start to interrogate the usual suspect—our users, who definitely did something wrong, something that they shouldn't have been even able to do. Of course, the users deny everything and say that they did nothing wrong, or did nothing at all; it happened **all by itself**.

Anyone who has found themselves in such a situation remembers the level of despair that is usually associated with an inability to find a cause. We end up dealing with the consequences, fixing the system state according to our best knowledge of how it should be corrected. Sometimes these issues exist for months, or even years, without developers being able to determine the cause of the problem. It is because they don't know the sequence of events that happened in the system, which led to this invalid state.

The importance of keeping a history of the events that led to a particular state is well described by Mathias Verraes in his blog post from 2014, *Domain-Driven Design is Linguistic* (`http://verraes.net/2014/01/domain-driven-design-is-linguistic/`).

As you would read there, having half a million Euros is the final system state. However, the preceding sequence of events might lead us to different conclusions about some other aspects of the system state that we did not consider before. If we want to add the emotional state or the level of happiness of our subjects to the system state, we won't be able to get this information if we haven't stored the history of events.

The issue of collecting the history of changes, for both reporting and debugging, can often be solved by introducing an artificial log of changes. Then, it would seem that all changes are being captured for future analysis. At the same time, there will be no direct relationship between event processing and records in the audit log. It could potentially lead to situations wherein some changes won't be recorded.

Another issue with only keeping the latest state is that to get any information about the system, we can only rely on those tables or documents that we use to persist our aggregates. Of course, if we have a CQRS system with two databases, we will be fetching the information from the read-side. But for those cases when we need to have a new screen in the system that contains data from different existing read models, the only thing we can do is make a complex query with joins to get the data we need. With time, it might diminish the advantages of using CQRS, because what we used to have optimized for reading is not tuned anymore, considering a bunch of new queries spanning across what looked like a perfectly clean model a while ago.

What is Event Sourcing?

We often need to see what behavior has triggered the state transition, and that is why we started using domain events. However, without having those events stored somewhere, to be used as the source of truth for the system state, we can never be sure that the behavior that we have recorded is precisely the one that brought our system to the state where it is now.

The principle of Event Sourcing is encoded in its name. It is quite simple. We already have an event generation in place in our code. So, instead of persisting the state of our aggregate, we save all new events to the database. When we fetch the aggregate from the database, instead of reading its state as one record in a table or document, we read all events that were saved before and call the `When` method for each of those events. By doing that, we get the aggregate state reconstructed from history.

Then, when we need to execute a command, we call a method of the aggregate, it generates new events, and we add those events to the list of events that are already in the database for that aggregate. It means that we never change or remove anything in the database; we only append new events.

We can visualize the execution of a single operation like this:

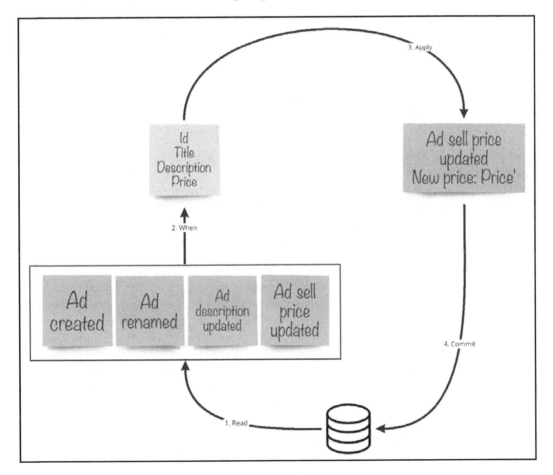

Notice that although reading the aggregate might look more complicated since we are doing two activities (reading and executing `When`), in the code, it seems the same. We need to put the code to do the whole `Get` into the persistence implementation, and it will allow us to keep the persistence implementation unchanged, at least for the reading part.

This approach addresses the issues of having historical data for different purposes—as an audit log, as a ledger, as a source for reports that need to get data from the past, and as a path that could help to find a trail that led the system to come into an invalid state.

One of the significant advantages of Event Sourcing is that it removes impedance mismatch. We were discussing this issue in `Chapter 7`, *Consistency Boundary,* when we talked about persisting aggregates to relational and document databases. Since using Event Sourcing we stop persisting object as-is entirely, the impedance mismatch just becomes irrelevant. Remember how complex the mapping between objects and databases could be? Being able to remove this burden from the software development process is a precious feature of using events to persist objects.

Event Sourcing around us

Although it might look like Event Sourcing is a new technique, it is not.

Back in 2007, Greg Young started the process of shaping Event Sourcing into the form that we have now. But, as Greg mentioned several times, we can trace similar techniques back to ancient Mesopotamia. The origins of writing are related to accounting, and cuneiform writing, the first known writing, was initially developed for accounting purposes. We know that from around 3500 BC, scribes recorded commercial transactions on clay tablets. Those tablets were then dried, making permanent, unchangeable records.

Accounting has changed a lot since Mesopotamian and Sumerian times. Nevertheless, modern principles of accounting are similar to Event Sourcing. Each operation in double-entry accounting is recorded at least twice—once on a debit account and once on a credit account. These two records form one operation. The sum of amounts within an operation must be zero. There is no concept of state for an account in the chart of accounts. The running balance is a sum of the starting balance and the amounts from any record on that account. So, to get the current balance, we need to read all the records for that account.

The same technique is used in many areas of finance. An example that we are all familiar with is banking. Bank accounts follow the same rule as accounts in bookkeeping. There is no *account balance* that is stored in a large SQL table that is called `Accounts`, in a field called `Balance`. It won't be possible for a bank to prove that the balance is correct in case of any disputes. The balance is therefore calculated by summing the amounts of all the transactions for that account. Of course, for a very intensively-used account, such sums would take too long to figure out. In this case, the bank makes an account snapshot once in a while. Most of us are familiar with the concept of the fiscal year. On one day, by the end of the fiscal year, all balances get fixed and all accounting is started anew, only transferring balances from the previous year.

In any case, there are two common principles of Event Sourcing that are observed in real-world applications, such as accounting and banking:

- Events are recorded for each operation, so an object state can be reconstructed by reading all those events
- Events cannot be changed or removed, because such an operation would undermine the whole concept of the audit log and make it invalid

For the purpose of corrections, accountants make new transactions that compensate for previously-entered operations that appeared to be incorrect. The same happens in banks. If you get an amount placed on your account by mistake, the bank will never **remove** the transaction, although it is wrong. You will see another transaction on your account, taking the same sum of money away from you. We can also see it happening when we get partial refunds. Instead of changing the sum of a transaction that is being partially refunded, we get a new transaction for the amount of the partial refund.

Event Sourced aggregates

Now, it is time to take a better look at how we can persist aggregates by saving the history of changes. In this section, we will discuss what event streams are and how we can use streams to persist aggregates to an event store and retrieve them. Of course, this implies that we will cover the topic of event stores, as well.

Event streams

So far, on all of the diagrams, we have seen events for only one aggregate. Of course, such a system is useless, and we need to find a way to store events for different aggregates, in order to make the system functional. The main requirement here would be that we need to be able to retrieve events for a single aggregate, preferably in one read. Of course, if there are thousands of events, we will need to split the read into multiple batches, but this is not in our scope right now. To achieve this ability to read events for only one aggregate, we need to write events with some metadata that indicates the aggregate identity. The second requirement is that events need to be read in the same strict order as they were written; and when we write changes as events to the database, these events need to be written in the exact order as we send them to the database.

Events that are coming to the system in a particular order form an event stream. For the purpose of Event Sourcing, the most comfortable solution would be to have a database that allows us to have one stream per aggregate. In this case, we will write to a known stream and read from it. The stream name will be a combination of the aggregate type and the aggregate identity; for example, for our `ClassifiedAd` aggregate with an ID of `e99460470a7b4133827d06f32dd4714e`, the stream name would be `ClassifiedAd-e99460470a7b4133827d06f32dd4714e`. An aggregate stream contains all events that happened during the aggregate life cycle. When we decide that we don't need the aggregate in the system, we can either remove the whole stream or write a final event, such as `ClassifiedAdRemoved`.

A critical feature of a database that we can use to persist events is to have a single stream with all events that have ever come to the system, in addition to individual streams. It won't be ideal, but we can deduce aggregate streams by controlling the stream ID metadata property, in case our database doesn't support separate streams natively. However, having a single stream that contains all events is absolutely necessary. Throughout the course of this book, we will reference this master stream as the `$all` stream, because this is what it is called in the Event Store, the database that we will use in our examples.

It is crucial to understand that we are referring to the same events when dealing with the `$all` stream and aggregate streams. You can see it in a way that all events are always present in the `$all` stream but in addition, there is an index that is put on top of these events. This index tells the system which individual stream an event belongs to.

The following diagram represents the $all stream with some events that are also indexed per aggregate stream:

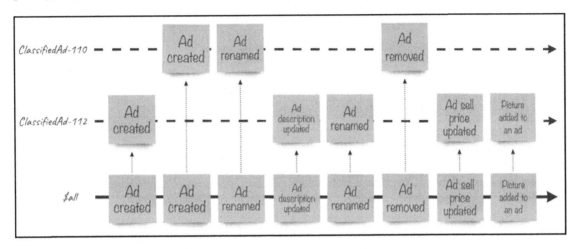

Aggregate streams and the $all stream

So far, we have been able to formulate the requirements for a database that we can use to persist our aggregate as streams of events. Now, we will look at concrete examples of such databases.

Event stores

In the preceding section, we discussed that in order to consider a database to be used as an event store, we need to ensure that this database can store events and metadata and put indexes on the metadata. We cannot put any indexes on events, because there is no single denominator for event objects; they are all different. Metadata, however, is structured in a known way. For example, the stream name must be present in the metadata for all events.

Such a definition could lead us to a conclusion that any database that supports querying events by stream ID can be used as an event store. This is true. Here, you can find examples of how different databases can be used as event stores:

Database	How to store events	How to read a single stream
RDBMS (SQL Server, PostgreSQL, and so on)	Use a single table; add one column for the stream name and one column for the event payload. One row is one event.	Select all rows where the stream name is what we want.
Document database (MongoDB, Azure Cosmos DB, RavenDB)	Use a document collection. Each document should have a metadata object and a field to store the payload. One document is one event.	Query all documents where the stream name (part of the metadata) is what we need.
Partitioned tables (Azure Table Storage, AWS DynamoDB)	Use a single table; add one field for the stream name (or ID) to be used as the partition key and another field as the row key (Azure) or sort key (DynamoDB). The third field will contain the event payload. One record is one event.	Query all records where the partition key is the name of the stream we are reading.
Specialized database (Event Store)	Native support for streams.	Read all events from a single stream.

Notice that for some relational databases, there are tools and libraries that can help to store events for Event Sourced systems. For example, the Marten framework (`http://jasperfx.github.io/marten/`) uses the native PostgreSQL feature to store unstructured data in JSONB-type columns and has an event store implementation based on that database. The SQL Stream Store (`https://github.com/SQLStreamStore/SQLStreamStore`) can also help you to use a variety of relational databases, including Microsoft SQL Server and PostgreSQL, as event stores. Both of these open source tools are actively being used in production systems around the world and have active communities behind them.

So far, we've been concentrating on persisting a single aggregate as an event stream and reading all events for a single aggregate from the database. However, this is not the only characteristic that we need to be looking at for an event store that we would be comfortable using. If you haven't noticed yet, we haven't touched the query part, when we need to read data for some aggregates, based on some criteria. Our primary requirement for an event store does not include the ability to query anything except events by the stream name. Definitely, a query such as `ClassifiedAdsPendingReview` wouldn't be possible, just because we would need to read all events (potentially millions) for all classified ads and then query in the memory. This is not a feasible approach for production, although it might be quite useful for prototyping. To solve this issue, we need to get back to CQRS, and this time, we need to use domain events to build our read models. In the case of an Event Sourced system, we will have to use a conventional database, SQL or NoSQL, which can be queried, to handle the query side of CQRS, and this query side can only be built from events. Thus, we need to have a reliable way to get real-time (or near real-time) updates about all new events from the event store to our read model builders. If we use traditional relational databases to store events, we almost inevitably turn to frequent polling. Some NoSQL databases, such as Azure Cosmos DB, RavenDB, and AWS DynamoDB, let us subscribe to the change stream and get information about all database operations. We will be using the term *subscription* when talking about this feature.

For all of the examples in this book, we will be using the Event Store (`https://eventstore.org`,) because it has years of experience building Event Sourced systems put into it by its creator, the *father* of CQRS and longtime advocate of Event Sourcing, Greg Young, the company behind this product and the open source developers community that keeps helping to make Event Store better. In addition, this product is free, and you only need to pay to get production-grade support. The Event Store has native support for store events, and it has transactional writes; we can subscribe to event streams to get all new (and existing) events from there, and so on.

Before going further, please ensure that you have completed the steps described in the *Technical requirements* section.

Event-oriented persistence

Now, we are going to write some code that will allow us to use events to persist our aggregates.

In Chapter 9, *CQRS - The Read Side*, we used repositories to store aggregates, but now, we will do something else. Appending events to a stream for the ClassifiedAd aggregate is no different from doing the same thing for the UserProfile aggregate. The specifics of repositories therefore disappear, and everything about persisting aggregates and retrieving them is done in exactly the same way. Consequently, we can use one interface, IAggregateStore, that will handle the persistence for any type of aggregate.

Now, let's start to implement some lower-level code to write events to Event Store streams and read them back. It will include serialization, paging, type handling, and optimistic concurrency.

 Throughout this chapter, we will be using the term **event store** when talking about a place where we can write events to streams and read them back. When we use the term Event Store, we will be referring to the product that you should have been able to execute by following the *Technical requirements* section.

Writing to Event Store

Before any read, there must be a write, so that is where we will start. Let's look at the Event Store API to write events to streams. The method that we would most likely use is this one:

```
Task<WriteResult> AppendToStreamAsync(string stream, long expectedVersion,
IEnumerable<EventData> events)
```

All of the parameters here are quite clear: a stream name and a list of events to be saved to the stream. Besides, we need to supply the aggregate version to handle optimistic concurrency. It will prevent overriding changes that someone else could have made in parallel by processing another command for the same aggregate. Event Store supports stream versioning out of the box, and we just need to supply the expected version when trying to save new events to the stream.

We will start to write the code by adding the following interface to the Marketplace.Framework project:

```
using System.Threading.Tasks;

namespace Marketplace.Framework
{
    public interface IAggregateStore
    {
        Task<bool> Exists<T, TId>(TId aggregateId);
        Task Save<T, TId>(T aggregate) where T : AggregateRoot<TId>;
        Task<T> Load<T, TId>(TId aggregateId)
```

```
            where T : AggregateRoot<TId>;
    }
}
```

You can compare it to the repository interfaces we used in `Chapter 8`, *Aggregate Persistence*, and you'll see that the new interface is some kind of a generic repository. Although we discussed why using generic repositories is usually not a good idea, in our case, it is perfectly acceptable, since all persistence aspects are handled in the same way for all aggregates.

The serialization code would require some external dependencies to be installed. In the preceding snippet, we used the `JsonConvert` class for serializing events to JSON. Therefore, we need to add the `Newtonsoft.Json` package to our `Marketplace.Framework` project. To get the Event Store API, we also need the `EventStore.ClientAPI.NetCore` package. We can either use the **Manage NuGet Packages** context menu on the project or run the following two commands in the Terminal window:

```
dotnet add Marketplace.Framework package Newtonsoft.Json
dotnet add Marketplace.Framework package EventStore.ClientAPI.NetCore
```

Now, we can start implementing this interface in a new class, `EsAggregateStore`, that we will add to the `Infrastructure` folder of the `Marketplace` project.

First, the stream name. At the beginning of this chapter, we already went through the concept of event streams, and since writing into one stream is a transaction, a stream becomes our transaction boundary, along with the aggregate boundary too. We will use the aggregate-per-stream strategy, and therefore, we can safely make the stream name derive from our aggregate name. But, what are the names of our aggregates? Well, we can start with the CRL type, such as `Marketplace.Domain.ClassifiedAd`. Then, we need to make those names unique. To do this, the obvious solution would be to add an aggregate ID. I want to cover two cases to create the stream ID: when we have an aggregate that needs to be persisted, and when we just have an ID of an aggregate that we want to load. To do that, I will add two methods to the `EsAggregateStore` class:

```
private static string GetStreamName<T, TId>(TId aggregateId)
    => $"{typeof(T).Name}-{aggregateId.ToString()}";

private static string GetStreamName<T, TId>(T aggregate)
    where T : AggregateRoot<TId>
    => $"{typeof(T).Name}-{aggregate.Id.ToString()}";
```

Looking further at the list of parameters for `AppendToStreamAsync`, the method doesn't accept `IEnumerable<object>`, but instead expects a collection of objects that have the `EventData` type. This class has the following public members:

```
public sealed class EventData
{
    public readonly Guid EventId;
    public readonly string Type;
    public readonly bool IsJson;
    public readonly byte[] Data;
    public readonly byte[] Metadata;
}
```

For us, it is important to understand that we need to save the event type as a string, so that we can deserialize the event back to an object of the event CLR type. We also have to convert the event object to a byte array when we save events, and convert a byte array to an object when we read events. So, for `Type`, we can again use the CLR type name of the event object. For the payload (`Data`), we can use whatever serialization is useful.

Nevertheless, Event Store has a nice UI that can show us the content of events, but it only does that if an event is serialized as JSON. This is exactly what the `IsJson` Boolean property is for. For the majority of applications, which doesn't require optimizing the performance by using more compact representations and a faster serialization process, such as protobuf, it is enough to use JSON, and that's what we are going to do.

Since we need to convert our objects to byte arrays and still use JSON, we can create a method that will help us in doing that:

```
private static byte[] Serialize(object data)
    => Encoding.UTF8.GetBytes(JsonConvert.SerializeObject(data));
```

Then, we need to think of how to get a list of new events from an aggregate and build a collection of `EventData` objects to represent those events.

From the very early versions of our application, we have the `GetChanges` method. First, we had it in the `Entity` base class, which we later renamed `AggregateRoot`. We can finally start using this method to get all new events that are generated as part of command execution. Here is the code that will get all changes from an aggregate and build a collection of `EventData` objects, just like we need for calling the `AppendToStreamAsync` method:

```
var changes = aggregate.GetChanges()
    .Select(@event => new EventData(
        eventId: Guid.NewGuid(),
        type: @event.GetType().Name,
```

```
    isJson: true,
    data: Serialize(@event),
    metadata: null));
```

In the preceding snippet, we specify the short event type name to be used as the event type in Event Store. It will be something like `ClassifiedAdRenamed`. But, when we start loading events back, we need to deserialize JSON strings back to concrete event types. The `Newtonsoft.Json` library won't understand the short-type; it needs to know the **fully-qualified class name (FQCN)**. If the events are defined in a different assembly, we also need to include the assembly information. If we use FQCN as an event type for Event Store, we will get quite an ugly picture in the Event Store UI, since it will be polluted with all that technical information about namespaces and assembly names. I don't like that, and therefore, I will still use the short-type name. However, we need a way to be able to tell the deserializer about the concrete event type. The best place to store any kind of technical information about the event is metadata, and that's what I am going to do. First, I will add a private nested class that we'll use for the event metadata:

```
private class EventMetadata
{
    public string ClrType { get; set; }
}
```

Now, I can modify the preceding code snippet to keep the FQCN with the event, as metadata:

```
var changes = aggregate.GetChanges()
    .Select(@event =>
        new EventData(
            eventId: Guid.NewGuid(),
            type: @event.GetType().Name,
            isJson: true,
            data: Serialize(@event),
            metadata: Serialize(new EventMetadata
                {ClrType = @event.GetType().AssemblyQualifiedName})
        ))
    .ToArray();
```

 Using the event CLR type name as the event name and the FQCN in the event metadata is a temporary solution. For production systems, I would recommend using the concept of a *type mapper*, which translates CLR types to strings and back. This method gives you some freedom to change namespaces if needed, without breaking the ability to deserialize events that were persisted in the past. I will not go into detail on using the type mapper, but you will find the working code in the repository for `Chapter 13`, *Splitting the System*.

Let's put this code into our new `EsAggregateStore` class:

```
using System;
using System.Linq;
using System.Text;
using System.Threading.Tasks;
using EventStore.ClientAPI;
using Newtonsoft.Json;

namespace Marketplace.Infrastructure
{
    public class EsAggregateStore : IAggregateStore
    {
        private readonly IEventStoreConnection _connection;

        public EsAggregateStore(IEventStoreConnection connection)
        {
            _connection = connection;
        }

        public async Task Save<T, TId>(T aggregate)
            where T : Aggregate<TId>
        {
            if (aggregate == null)
                throw new ArgumentNullException(nameof(aggregate));

            var changes = aggregate.GetChanges()
                .Select(@event =>
                    new EventData(
                        eventId: Guid.NewGuid(),
                        type: @event.GetType().Name,
                        isJson: true,
                        data: Serialize(@event),
                        metadata: Serialize(new EventMetadata
                            {ClrType =
                                @event.GetType().AssemblyQualifiedName})
                    ))
                .ToArray();

            if (!changes.Any()) return;

            var streamName = GetStreamName<T, TId>(aggregate);

            await _connection.AppendToStreamAsync(
                streamName,
                aggregate.Version,
                changes);
```

```
        aggregate.ClearChanges();
    }

    private static byte[] Serialize(object data)
        => Encoding.UTF8.GetBytes(
            JsonConvert.SerializeObject(data));

    private static string GetStreamName<T, TId>(TId aggregateId)
        => $"{typeof(T).Name}-{aggregateId.ToString()}";

    private static string GetStreamName<T, TId>(T aggregate)
        where T : Aggregate<TId>
        => $"{typeof(T).Name}-{aggregate.Id.ToString()}";
    }
}
```

The only thing that we have not touched upon previously is `IEventStoreConnection`. All reads and writes between our application and Event Store need to be executed on the open TCP connection to the Event Store cluster, which can also be a single-node cluster that we can create by running the Docker image. Our application will establish the connection when it starts, and we need to close the connection when the application stops. We will add this infrastructure code to our executable project.

Reading from Event Store

In our application service, the only command that doesn't require reading an aggregate before handling is the `CreateClassifiedAd` command. For all other actions, we need to read our aggregate first, and that's what we do by calling `_store.Load<ClassifiedAd>(id.ToString())`. While saving an aggregate to the store by collecting all changes and saving them to an event stream seems quite obvious, reading the aggregate back from the event stream is a little less trivial. Let's describe the steps to retrieve an aggregate from the event store:

1. Find out the stream name for an aggregate
2. Read all of the events from the aggregate stream
3. Loop through all of the events, and call the `When` handler for each of them

After we have done all these steps, we will recover all the history of a given aggregate and use the aggregate event handling rules to reapply all historical events to an empty aggregate object. By doing this, we will be bringing our aggregate to its latest state.

In the code, we will do all these steps in the `Load` method of the `EsAggregateStore` class:

```
public async Task<T> Load<T, TId>(TId aggregateId)
    where T : AggregateRoot<TId>
{
    if (aggregateId == null)
        throw new ArgumentNullException(nameof(aggregateId));

    var stream = GetStreamName<T, TId>(aggregateId);
    var aggregate = (T) Activator.CreateInstance(typeof(T), true);

    var page = await _connection.ReadStreamEventsForwardAsync(
        stream, 0, 1024, false);

    aggregate.Load(page.Events.Select(resolvedEvent =>
    {
        var meta = JsonConvert.DeserializeObject<EventMetadata>(
            Encoding.UTF8.GetString(resolvedEvent.Event.Metadata));
        var dataType = Type.GetType(meta.ClrType);
        var jsonData =
            Encoding.UTF8.GetString(resolvedEvent.Event.Data);
        var data = JsonConvert.DeserializeObject(jsonData, dataType);
        return data;
    }).ToArray());

    return aggregate;
}
```

Let's go through the `Load` method. In steps, it does the following:

1. Ensures that the aggregate ID parameter is not null
2. Gets the stream name for a given aggregate type
3. Creates a new instance of the aggregate type by using reflections
4. Reads events from the stream as a collection of `ResolvedEvent` objects
5. Deserializes those raw events to a collection of domain events
6. Calls the `Load` method of the empty aggregate instance to recover the aggregate state

There are a couple of things that need additional explanations.

First, we could have used the `new` constraint on the `T` generic type parameter, so we can instantiate an empty aggregate using a parameterless constructor. However, that would break encapsulation and force us to expose a public parameterless constructor, and we don't want that. Using reflections allows us to invoke the protected constructor that we already have in all our aggregate root types. You need to remember that this solution might cause performance issues if your system is dealing with loads of commands, and in such a case, an alternative solution is required. Exposing a public parameterless constructor could be an acceptable trade-off.

Secondly, we use a magic number, `1024`, to read what is called a **stream slice**, which is nothing more than a page. Your event streams can get bigger, and the Event Store doesn't allow us to read more than 4,096 events at once. For large streams, we would need to implement paging, but for this example, it is not necessary, since the life cycle of our aggregates don't assume having long streams.

The last thing is the missing `Load` method for the `AggregateRoot` abstract class. We didn't need this method, because we were not using Event Sourcing before. The `Load` method will complete the last step in the aggregate recovery sequence, looping through all events and calling the matching `When` for each of them. Let's see how we can implement this method in the `AggregateRoot` class:

```
public void Load(IEnumerable<object> history)
{
    foreach (var e in history)
    {
        When(e);
        Version++;
    }
}
```

As you can see, it is a very simple piece of code, and essentially, it represents what Event Sourcing is. We get a collection of events that we previously stored and then rebuild the state of our domain object from those events. The `When` method knows how to change the aggregate state for each event in the collection, so when we call it for each event from the history, we get our aggregate back to the last known state.

Notice that we also increase the `Version` property of the aggregate for each applied event, so we know what version our aggregate should have when we commit changes to the store. We discussed the aggregate version when talking about the optimistic concurrency. Unlike using state persistence, where we needed to have a property in our database for the aggregate version, we don't really store the version when we use events, because one event always increases the aggregate version by one, so we can just count events to get the current version.

One last thing that I need to use to finalize the implementation of the `IAggregateStore` interface is the `Exists` method. There is no simple way to ask Event Store whether a stream exists, but we can easily overcome this by trying to read a single event from a given stream:

```
public async Task<bool> Exists<T, TId>(TId aggregateId)
{
    var stream = GetStreamName<T, TId>(aggregateId);
    var result = await _connection.ReadEventAsync(stream, 1, false);
    return result.Status != EventReadStatus.NoStream;
}
```

By now, we should have a working implementation of the aggregate persistence that uses events.

The wiring infrastructure

To finish the work and make our application make use of all these changes, we need to write some initialization code for the Event Store connection, and also do the wiring for our application service so that it uses `EsAggregateStore`.

First, we need to configure our application by using the .NET Core configuration extensions. We will start by adding a simple `appsettings.json` configuration file. The content for this file, for now, will just be a connection string for Event Store that runs locally:

```
{
  "eventStore": {
    "connectionString": "ConnectTo=tcp://admin:changeit@localhost:1113;
     DefaultUserCredentials=admin:changeit;"
  }
}
```

Then, we need to read this configuration so that we will have access to these values. To do that, we will change the `BuildConfiguration` method of our `Program` class:

```
private static IConfiguration BuildConfiguration(string[] args)
    => new ConfigurationBuilder()
        .SetBasePath(CurrentDirectory)
        .AddJsonFile("appsettings.json", false, false)
        .Build();
```

For the settings file to be copied to the application output directory, we need to change its properties in the Marketplace.csproj file, to ensure that the project file has lines like these:

```
<ItemGroup>
  <Content Update="appsettings.json"
    CopyToOutputDirectory="Always"
    CopyToPublishDirectory="Always" />
</ItemGroup>
```

The connection to Event Store needs to open when our application starts and close when we shut down the application. To enable this, we will implement the Microsoft.Extensions.Hosting.IHostedService interface with a new class called HostedService. To do that, we will add a new file, called HostedService.cs, to our executable project:

```
using System.Threading;
using System.Threading.Tasks;
using EventStore.ClientAPI;
using Microsoft.Extensions.Hosting;

namespace Marketplace
{
    public class HostedService : IHostedService
    {
        private readonly IEventStoreConnection _esConnection;

        public HostedService(IEventStoreConnection esConnection)
        {
            _esConnection = esConnection;
        }

        public Task StartAsync(CancellationToken cancellationToken)
            => _esConnection.ConnectAsync();

        public Task StopAsync(CancellationToken cancellationToken)
        {
            _esConnection.Close();
            return Task.CompletedTask;
        }
    }
}
```

The final wiring takes place in the `Startup.cs` file, where we need to change the `ConfigureServices` method so it includes the Event Store connection and the `EsAggregateStore` registrations. Also, we need to register our `HostingService`, so that the web host knows that it needs to run something on startup and shutdown. The new version of the `Startup.ConfigureServices` method looks like this:

```
public void ConfigureServices(IServiceCollection services)
{
    var esConnection = EventStoreConnection.Create(
        Configuration["eventStore:connectionString"],
        ConnectionSettings.Create().KeepReconnecting(),
        Environment.ApplicationName);

    var store = new EsAggregateStore(esConnection);
    var purgomalumClient = new PurgomalumClient();

    services.AddSingleton(esConnection);
    services.AddSingleton<IAggregateStore>(store);

    services.AddSingleton(new ClassifiedAdsApplicationService(
        store, new FixedCurrencyLookup()));
    services.AddSingleton(new UserProfileApplicationService(
        store, t => purgomalumClient.CheckForProfanity(t)));

    services.AddSingleton<IHostedService, HostedService>();
    services.AddMvc();
    services.AddSwaggerGen(c =>
    {
        c.SwaggerDoc("v1",
            new Info
            {
                Title = "ClassifiedAds",
                Version = "v1"
            });
    });
}
```

Here, we created a new connection instance and registered it in the service collection as a singleton. It will then be injected into the `HostedService` constructor, and we will open it when the application starts. We will also change the registration for `IAggregateStore`, so that it takes our new `EsAggregateStore` class. Then, we will register `HostedService`.

We will also use `store` as a parameter for our application services. This parameter replaces the repositories we used before, so we need to change both application services, as well.

The aggregate store in application services

The changes required for application services are quite small. To make the work even more comfortable, I created a small extension for the `IApplicationService` interface that allows us to handle commands with one line of code. We already did it before, by using a private method `HandleUpdate` in each application service. Now, since we use the `IAggregateStore` interface instead of repositories, we can abstract that method, so that it has no dependencies on the specific infrastructure. Therefore, we can place it in the `Marketplace.Framework` project. Here is the code:

```
using System;
using System.Threading.Tasks;

namespace Marketplace.Framework
{
    public static class ApplicationServiceExtensions
    {
        public static async Task HandleUpdate<T, TId>(
            this IApplicationService service,
            IAggregateStore store, TId aggregateId,
            Action<T> operation)
            where T : AggregateRoot<TId>
        {
            var aggregate = await store.Load<T, TId>(aggregateId);
            if (aggregate == null)
                throw new InvalidOperationException(
                    $"Entity with id {aggregateId.ToString()} cannot be
                    found");

            operation(aggregate);
            await store.Save<T, TId>(aggregate);
        }
    }
}
```

Then, we need to replace the repository dependency in the application service classes to `IAggregateStore` and change all calls. The work is a bit boring, and I have done it all for you, so here is the new code for `ClassifiedAdApplicationService`:

```
using System;
using System.Threading.Tasks;
using Marketplace.Domain.ClassifiedAd;
```

```
using Marketplace.Domain.Shared;
using Marketplace.Framework;
using static Marketplace.ClassifiedAd.Contracts;

namespace Marketplace.ClassifiedAd
{
    public class ClassifiedAdsApplicationService : IApplicationService
    {
        private readonly ICurrencyLookup _currencyLookup;
        private readonly IAggregateStore _store;

        public ClassifiedAdsApplicationService(
            IAggregateStore store, ICurrencyLookup currencyLookup
        )
        {
            _currencyLookup = currencyLookup;
            _store = store;
        }

        public Task Handle(object command) =>
            command switch
            {
                V1.Create cmd =>
                    HandleCreate(cmd),
                V1.SetTitle cmd =>
                    HandleUpdate(
                        cmd.Id,
                        c => c.SetTitle(
                            ClassifiedAdTitle
                                .FromString(cmd.Title)
                        )
                    ),
                V1.UpdateText cmd =>
                    HandleUpdate(
                        cmd.Id,
                        c => c.UpdateText(
                            ClassifiedAdText
                                .FromString(cmd.Text)
                        )
                    ),
                V1.UpdatePrice cmd =>
                    HandleUpdate(
                        cmd.Id,
                        c => c.UpdatePrice(
                            Price.FromDecimal(
                                cmd.Price,
                                cmd.Currency,
                                _currencyLookup
```

```
                        )
                    )
                ),
            V1.RequestToPublish cmd =>
                HandleUpdate(
                    cmd.Id,
                    c => c.RequestToPublish()
                ),
            V1.Publish cmd =>
                HandleUpdate(
                    cmd.Id,
                    c => c.Publish(new UserId(cmd.ApprovedBy))
                ),
            _ => Task.CompletedTask
        };

    private async Task HandleCreate(V1.Create cmd)
    {
        if (await _store.Exists<Domain.ClassifiedAd.ClassifiedAd,
            ClassifiedAdId>(
            new ClassifiedAdId(cmd.Id)
        ))
            throw new InvalidOperationException(
                $"Entity with id {cmd.Id} already exists");

        var classifiedAd = new Domain.ClassifiedAd.ClassifiedAd(
            new ClassifiedAdId(cmd.Id),
            new UserId(cmd.OwnerId)
        );

        await _store.Save<Domain.ClassifiedAd.ClassifiedAd,
            ClassifiedAdId>(classifiedAd);
    }

    private Task HandleUpdate(
        Guid id,
        Action<Domain.ClassifiedAd.ClassifiedAd> update
    ) =>
        this.HandleUpdate(
            _store,
            new ClassifiedAdId(id),
            update
        );
    }
}
```

As you can see, the changes are quite small. We call _store.Save, and we don't need to commit, since we don't have an explicit unit of work, because we don't execute an operation on multiple aggregates at the same time, otherwise, we would break the rule of an aggregate in a transactional boundary, thereby not having a unit of work which isn't a problem. We also have no issues with detecting changes, since our changes are always represented as events, and we don't need any ORM magic to figure out what we need to update.

Following the same style, here is the new UserProfileApplicationService class:

```
using System;
using System.Threading.Tasks;
using Marketplace.Domain.Shared;
using Marketplace.Domain.UserProfile;
using Marketplace.Framework;
using static Marketplace.UserProfile.Contracts;

namespace Marketplace.UserProfile
{
    public class UserProfileApplicationService
        : IApplicationService
    {
        private readonly IAggregateStore _store;
        private readonly CheckTextForProfanity _checkText;

        public UserProfileApplicationService(
            IAggregateStore store,
            CheckTextForProfanity checkText
        )
        {
            _store = store;
            _checkText = checkText;
        }

        public Task Handle(object command) =>
            command switch
            {
                V1.RegisterUser cmd =>
                    HandleCreate(cmd),
                V1.UpdateUserFullName cmd =>
                    HandleUpdate(
                        cmd.UserId,
                        profile => profile.UpdateFullName(
                            FullName.FromString(cmd.FullName)
                        )
                    ),
                V1.UpdateUserDisplayName cmd =>
```

```
                    HandleUpdate(
                        cmd.UserId,
                        profile => profile.UpdateDisplayName(
                            DisplayName.FromString(
                                cmd.DisplayName,
                                _checkText
                            )
                        )
                    ),
                V1.UpdateUserProfilePhoto cmd =>
                    HandleUpdate(
                        cmd.UserId,
                        profile => profile
                            .UpdateProfilePhoto(
                                new Uri(cmd.PhotoUrl)
                            )
                    ),
                _ => Task.CompletedTask
            };

    private async Task HandleCreate(V1.RegisterUser cmd)
    {
        if (await _store
            .Exists<Domain.UserProfile.UserProfile, UserId>(
                new UserId(cmd.UserId)
            ))
            throw new InvalidOperationException(
                $"Entity with id {cmd.UserId} already exists"
            );

        var userProfile = new Domain.UserProfile.UserProfile(
            new UserId(cmd.UserId),
            FullName.FromString(cmd.FullName),
            DisplayName.FromString(cmd.DisplayName, _checkText)
        );

        await _store
            .Save<Domain.UserProfile.UserProfile, UserId>(
                userProfile
            );
    }

    private Task HandleUpdate(
        Guid id,
        Action<Domain.UserProfile.UserProfile> update
    ) =>
        this.HandleUpdate(
            _store,
```

```
                  new UserId(id),
                  update
              );
        }
    }
```

That's it; we don't need to do anything else to event-source our application! Let's see how it works now.

Running the event-sourced app

Finally, we can try things out and see how we can execute commands using our API, which remains unchanged from Chapter 9, *CQRS - The Read Side*. You might have noticed, however, that the query APIs and all code related to read models are not included in this chapter. That's because the read side of CQRS is vastly different from what we used for document and relational persistence.

When you start the app and visit the Swagger UI at http://localhost:5000, the screen that you will get is exactly the same as before. Of course, the Event Store must run at this time, either in a Docker container or as an executable. Running Event Store using docker-compose is described in the *Technical requirements* section. I used two new GUIDs as the new classified ad ID and owner ID, in order to create a new ad. So, I called the POST endpoint and got 200 OK as a result. Right after that, I executed the rename command by making the PUT request with the same ID and some text for the title. These operations are no different from what we were doing earlier.

Now, we can look at the result of those operations in our new store. To do that, we need to visit the Event Store web UI by going to http://localhost:2113 and log in by using the admin username and the changeit password. From there, we need to go to the **Stream Browser** page, and on the right-hand pane, there is a list of recently-changed streams. In this list, we can see the new stream for our new classified ad:

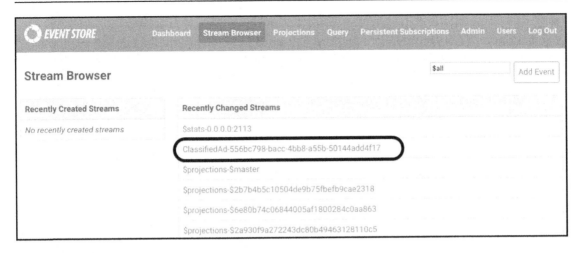

Here is our new aggregate stream

You can click on the stream name to see what the stream contains. Here is what I have:

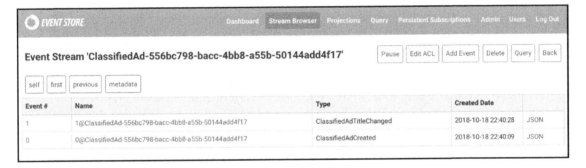

Two new events in the stream

Here, we can see two events that were added to the stream after I executed two commands. I can continue to run commands using the API until I get the ad published. When I look at the Event Store stream after that, I will see more events that were added to it:

More events are added if we execute more commands

That seems very nice. Each command triggers a state transition, but instead of overwriting the previous state with the new one, we can see the full history of changes, represented by events. For example, we can change the price several times, but we will always know about all the prices that the ad has had in the past.

Now, let's see what an event looks like. I will open event number **1**, which has the `ClassifiedAdTitleChanged` type, by clicking on the event name. Here is what I can see in the browser:

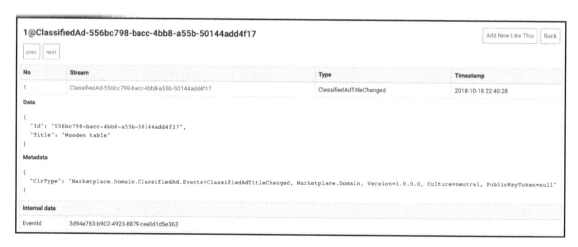

Event content as JSON

As you can see, the event data represents our domain event class—it has the aggregate ID and the title. The metadata only has one field that we decided to use for the purpose of deserialization—the FQCN of the event type. You can look at the content of other events to see what is stored there.

It might seem redundant to have the aggregate ID in each event, since the stream name already contains the ID, and to recover the aggregate state from events, we always read only one stream. We will see how this ID inside each event is used when we start building read models.

You can also execute some commands on the user profile command API to see the different type of aggregate to be stored in a stream with a different kind of name. Of course, it is possible to add more ads and users to the system now, and to see all those events coming into the Event Store.

Congratulations; we have just converted our application to using Event Sourcing instead of a more traditional persistence. As you may have noticed, we didn't need to make any changes to our domain objects to make it work. We can even remove the setters from aggregate and value-object properties, and make those properties private for better encapsulation. None of those changes will have any effect on how aggregates get stored and loaded using events. That's because for this type of persistence, the impedance mismatch is gone. All our events are simple, plain objects with properties that have primitive or simple types. It means that those domain events can easily be serialized, and that's the only thing we need to ensure in order for the Event Sourcing to work. By the way, it is not a requirement for Event Store to use JSON serialization. You can certainly use something such as protobuf. However, in such cases, you will lose the ability to check the content of events in the UI, since it only understands JSON. Hence, we used the `IsJson` property of the `EventData` class to tell Event Store that our events are, in fact, JSON strings. Event Store also has an integrated projection engine that uses JavaScript to execute operations on events inside the store in order to produce new events or to run queries. This feature also requires that events are stored in JSON, since this is the format that the JavaScript code can easily interpret. We will not be touching upon the projections topic in this chapter, but we'll go back to it in `Chapter 11`, *Projections and Queries*.

Summary

In this chapter, you got to use the feature of representing state transitions inside aggregates as events. I used that code style from the start intentionally, although I can imagine that it may have caused you some confusion. At the end of the day, why would you need to split each operation into `Apply` and `When`? Using that approach was necessary to prepare the readers for this chapter. Using domain events is a good practice, overall. Even if you don't use Event Sourcing, you should definitely consider using domain events to communicate updates between aggregates, and even between different Bounded Contexts, and using domain events for state transition makes it easy, because you will always have a list of changes as a collection of new events.

Since we had this collection ready, we only needed to figure out how to store those changes as-is, in an event stream that represents a single aggregate, and to also introduce the `Load` method to look through all events that we read from that stream to recover the aggregate state when we need to execute a new operation on it. That wasn't very hard. We used a bit of code to figure out how our infrastructure would work, and we needed to configure the serialization properly. We still kept the FQCN in the event metadata to be able to deserialize events back to C# objects, but we'll fix it in the future.

Event Store is a very efficient product when it comes to Event Sourcing and storing events in streams. Unlike Kafka, this product allows us to create millions of streams. Since our approach to store aggregates is to keep the events for each aggregate in a separate stream, this solution is perfectly suitable for us. If your company has issues, such as a limited number of pre-approved products used as databases, and you can't use Event Store just yet, you can look at libraries, such as SQL Stream Store (`https://github.com/SQLStreamStore/SQLStreamStore`), which implements an event store on a number of relational databases, including Microsoft SQL Server; or Marten (`http://jasperfx.github.io/marten/`), which uses the JSONB-type fields of PostgreSQL to implement both the document database and event store types of persistence.

In the next chapter, we will be looking at the challenges of querying the event-sourced system and solving these challenges by using separate read models and projections.

So far, you can see that Event Sourcing is not hard!

Further reading

There is not much literature about Event Sourcing available at the moment, but I can recommend watching a couple of talks by Greg Young, who coined the term CQRS and opened up Event Sourcing to the world:

- *A Decade of DDD, CQRS, Event Sourcing*, by Greg Young, DDD Europe 2016: `https://www.youtube.com/watch?v=LDW0QWie21s`
- *Event Sourcing*, Greg Young, GOTO Conference 2014: `https://www.youtube.com/watch?v=8JKjvY4etTY`

If you were already exploring this topic, you might have encountered some blog posts about the dark side of Event Sourcing, which mainly involves issues with event versions and eventual consistency. We'll be covering eventual consistency in the next chapter, and we'll learn even touch upon the versioning of events briefly; for more in-depth coverage of the event versions topic, refer to Greg's book:

- *Versioning in an Event Sourced System*, Greg Young, LeanPub 2017: `https://leanpub.com/esversioning`

Projections and Queries

11

In Chapter 9, *CQRS - The Read Side*, we changed our application to use events as the consistent aggregate storage. Instead of updating a snapshot of the state after handling a command, we can add new events to the stream that represents a single aggregate. We can then do a *left fold* on those events to reconstruct the aggregate state each time we load it again, before handling another command. In two lines of pseudo code, the essence of Event Sourcing can be represented as follows:

```
// Loading:
state = foreach(event in history: state = when(state, event))

// Command handling:
event = handle(state, command)
```

Here, `history` is what we load from the aggregate stream, `when` is the `AggregateRoot.When` method and `Handle` is one of the methods in the application service.

But, as I mentioned before, I removed all read models and the code associated with queries from the project for Chapter 9, *CQRS - The Read Side*. That's because queries in an event sourced system are done differently. In this chapter, we are going to look at exactly that. By the end of the chapter, we'll have the working solution that we already implemented in Chapter 10, *Event Sourcing*.

Throughout this chapter we are going to discuss the following topics:

- The issue of querying event streams
- What are projections?
- Projecting events to a document database
- Projecting events to a relational database
- Eventual consistency

Events and queries

One thing that I've heard many times when talking about event sourcing with developers who are new to this technique, is the claim that event sourcing is not suitable for reporting. Let's first define what reporting is. Normally, we think of it as the ability to retrieve the system state from the database on demand, using filters and grouping, with minimal latency. Relational databases are quite good for this purpose since this was the main reason that relational databases were invented in the first place. If you are old enough, you might remember a short period of hype around object databases (**ODBMSes**, short for **object-oriented database management system**) in the mid-1990s. What could be better than storing entire objects to a database, without taking care of the impedance mismatch? In a world that is largely dominated by different kinds of **relational database management systems (RDBMS)**, it is hard to digest the fact that the first object database for **Massachusetts General Hospital Utility Multi-Programming System (MUMPS or M)**, was created back in 1966. However, the first prototype of a relational database, System R by IBM, was only in the works from 1974, and the first generally-available RDBMS was created by Oracle, which was released in 1979. Exactly the same year, the M database by InterSystems came to light. Then, for decades, InterSystems became a major vendor of object databases and released Caché by the end of the 1990s, which was still based on many design ideas of MUMPS.

So, why haven't object databases dominated the world by now? There are a number of opinions about this, but one thing we can be certain about is that object databases weren't optimized to query substantial amounts of data. Indexes in such databases were either automatic or client-based, and couldn't possibly cope with larger datasets. Object databases handle writes perfectly well, but weren't really able to perform efficient queries. That said, I have to admit that I am not an expert in object databases and the opinion here could just be speculation. Of course, another obvious reason is that in the 20th century, disk space was a real issue. Third-level normalization of relational databases definitely helped to save precious space. Notice that the renaissance of document databases, which entertain similar ideas to object databases by storing the entire object graph as a single document, was only possible due to increasing computing power and cheaper storage when data duplication stopped being an issue.

The main reason for CQRS gaining momentum was the urge to handle reads and writes separately due to severe differences in optimization techniques for those much more distinct operations. For a third-level normalized relational database, writes are easy and reads are hard. Such a database schema can hardly cope with a significant transactional load, maintaining the ability to respond to complex queries at the same time.

The same issue also applies to systems that use events as the source of truth, by storing business-defined events in an append-only fashion. In such systems, as we discussed in `Chapter 10`, *Event Sourcing*, we don't have direct access to the system state. In order to get the current state of any object in the system, we must read all events from a stream that represents that particular object, and apply all events from that stream to an empty object to allow the events flow through the logic of state transitions. Basically, the object is being reborn every time we read it. Now, imagine that we need to run a query over a few thousand, or hundreds of thousands of such objects. This would mean that we probably need to load the whole system in memory before we can ask it for any information that spans across a dataset that contains more than one object. Such a system would certainly never work.

This is why CQRS is something that you can find in nearly every event-sourced system. Of course, there are systems that people call event-sourced, which continuously update the system state in an alternative database, for example, a relational database, at the same time as system-produced events. Sometimes, this happens in memory, or in one transaction if events are stored in the same database as the system state snapshot. In such a system, you usually find that events are, in fact, barely used for anything. Instead of loading an object from events, the application service would just get the latest object state from the snapshot database. It is a bit of a stretch to say that events are the source of truth in a system like this, as we won't be looking at this kind of scenario. At the same time, the techniques that you'll learn from this chapter might sound very similar to this, and I will do my best to explain the core differences.

Building read models from events

We are already familiar with read models from `Chapter 10`, *Event Sourcing*. We understand that the read-write model is common for many systems that we build, and sometimes it is beneficial to use different models to persist the system state and to retrieve data that we need to show on the screen or give away to other parties using the API. For event-sourced systems, we must use different models because, as previously discussed, event streams aren't optimized to retrieve the current state of the system and apply filters on it.

Therefore, we will need to create read models for our system somewhere else; for instance, in data storage that supports such queries with ease. Here, we are free to choose what we use. We could use a document database, a relational database, maybe even a filesystem, or a combination of all of the aforementioned methods. However, how can we build such read models? Well, we already defined that the state of our system is derived from all those events we store when any state transition occurs. This could give us the idea that we also need to use events to build read models. We will be using projections to derive the state of our read models from the stream of events that our system produces.

Projections

In relational algebra, a projection is a unary operation, written as $\Pi_{a_1,...a_n}(R)$, where R is a tuple, and $a_1, \cdots, a_n$ are the attribute names for R. When such an operation is executed, it returns a set that only includes the specified attributes, and all other attributes are discarded.

If this sounds too complicated, we can explicitly represent a projection as a SQL query. Consider a `People` table with the following structure and data:

Id	FirstName	LastName	City	Country
1	John	Smith	Bristol	United Kingdom
2	Jorrit	Bramsma	Eindhoven	The Netherlands
3	Jan Tore	Rosendal	Alta	Norway

If we execute the `SELECT FirstName, LastName FROM People` query, we effectively execute a projection. We specify two attributes to be included in the result set—`FirstName` and `LastName`, so that we get a result as follows:

FirstName	LastName
John	Smith
Jorrit	Bramsma
Jan Tore	Rosendal

All other attributes are discarded. Notice that we don't include any filtering in the query. Filtering is called **selection** and indeed, in most of the cases, a SQL query combines both projection and selection to produce a concise set of data that we are interested in. You will have already noticed that we used projections in `Chapter 10`, *Event Sourcing*, when we were retrieving a subset of attributes from a larger dataset of the whole system state, to be used for queries.

The process of building a piece of state from events is also called a **projection**, although we can't say that it operates on a single set where we choose a number of attributes that we want to project. However, we will need to project a subset of the whole event stream. Our read models also need to be updated as quickly as possible, but we only commit events to the store. It implies that we need to read all of these events as soon as they are committed, and project them. Usually, this is done either by polling the Event Store or by using a real-time subscription if the store supports it.

The process of building the read models from events using subscriptions and projections can be illustrated by the following diagram:

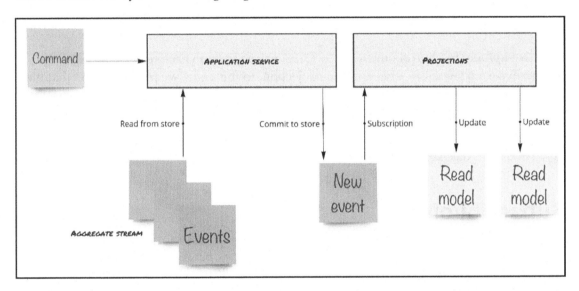

The command to read-model flow

When we execute a command, our aggregate is fully loaded from the aggregate stream by the application service. The aggregate then generates a new event (or several events) that represent the state transitions of the aggregate. Those events are committed to the store, so the store appends them to the end of the aggregate stream. A subscription receives these events and updates its read models.

This was the code from our aggregate class:

```
protected override void When(object @event)
{
    switch (@event)
    {
        case Events.UserRegistered e:
            Id = new UserId(e.UserId);
```

```
            FullName = new FullName(e.FullName);
            DisplayName = new DisplayName(e.DisplayName);
            break;
        case Events.UserFullNameUpdated e:
            FullName = new FullName(e.FullName);
            break;
        case Events.UserDisplayNameUpdated e:
            DisplayName = new DisplayName(e.DisplayName);
            break;
        case Events.ProfilePhotoUploaded e:
            PhotoUrl = e.PhotoUrl;
            break;
    }
}
```

Here, we update the state of our `UserProfile` aggregate with each new event. Now, it is time to make a confession—this is also a projection. In this code, we project events that the `When` method receives to update the properties of our `UserProfile` object. There's nothing more to say about projections and I can conclude the chapter!

Jokes aside, we still have work to do. First of all, we need to find out how our read-model projections will receive new events.

Subscriptions

Imagine our users are looking at a screen where they see the user interface for our marketplace. We already know how to let people execute operations. When a user does something, we send a `POST` or `PUT` request to the API. In turn, the API controller calls the application service and the command gets executed. The result of this would be either a `200 OK` response for a completed command or an error if something goes wrong. However, unlike a single-database system, where the data that we query is the same data on which we execute our commands, for an event-sourced application, this is not the case. Our read model is most probably located in a different database. This fact makes all of our queries eventually consistent. We will discuss this topic later in this book when we explore more advanced topics around event sourcing.

For now, we need to understand that our goal will be to minimize the time gap between the moment when an event is appended to the stream and the moment the read model gets updated. During the time between these two operations, the data that we show to the user is stale. Stale doesn't mean inconsistent, it is just not exactly up to date, and after a small delay, the query will eventually return more actual data. Mind the gap!

To minimize the time gap, we need to ensure that our projections receive new events in real time. Event Store can help here since it has a very nice subscriptions feature. There are two types of subscriptions in the Event Store—catch-up and persistent subscriptions, also known as **competing consumers**. The main difference is the **checkpoint** ownership. One more term for me to throw on you in this chapter!

A checkpoint is a specific position in the stream. As the projection has processed one event, it can store the checkpoint, so if the projection gets restarted, it will know where to start the processing and not project all events from the beginning of life. The concept of checkpoints is well-known in all systems that deal with real-time event processing, such as Kafka or Azure Event Hub.

If you decide to use some other product to store your events, you need to find out if it is possible to make real-time, or almost real-time subscriptions to the store and what you can use as the checkpoint. For example, you can use a SQL Server table to store events and use the auto-increment primary identity as the stream position. Then, you can continuously poll this table for new events and by doing that you will have a working subscription.

Checkpoints are unique to read models. I cited the code of the preceding `UserProfile.When` method and mentioned that it does what projections do as well. While that's true, for an aggregate instance, the `When` method is executed for all events of a single aggregate when we read the aggregate stream from the store before executing a command. Again, we read all the events from a single stream and call the `When` method for each event we get from the store. It's not hard. Projections, however, update their models continuously.

We could not allow ourselves to read all events from the whole store for each update, as this would defeat the purpose of having read models. Let's have a look at how read models listen to new events that come to the store:

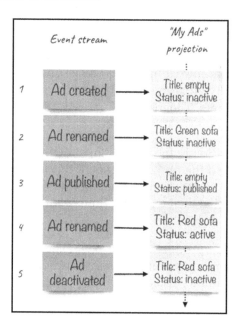

The read model is updated by new events

For example, if our **"My Ads" projection** gets an AdRenamed event and starts updating its read model, something happens—something such as a network failure, a database failure, or someone powering off the machine where the projection was running. Somehow, after the issue is fixed, the projection itself needs to figure out which position it needs to start reading events to continue updating its read model. For the case I just described, we need to keep the number **3** somewhere after we successfully projected the AdPublished event. So, when our service restarts and the projection kicks in, it needs to start reading event number **4**, ignoring everything that happened before. By storing this number, we are establishing a checkpoint. Our projection takes responsibility for keeping its own checkpoint somewhere. The checkpoint is only updated when a new event has been successfully projected, so we guarantee that each event is projected at least once.

There are two ways to store the checkpoint—via a client-based checkpoint or a server-based checkpoint. We can logically conclude that a client-based checkpoint is maintained and stored by the client (subscription), and when using a server-based variant, the Event Store is responsible for this instead.

 In Apache Kafka, the term *offset* is used for the same concept and, by default, the offset is maintained by the server.

A server-based checkpoint feature enables us to run multiple instances of the event consumer (a projection, in our case) and each consumer will get a portion of events. This concept is widely known in the messaging world. All message brokers support a similar pattern, which is called **competing consumers**. This pattern allows us to scale the process of handling messages (or events) easily, but the main issue here is that the order in which messages are processed cannot be guaranteed for competing consumers. That's easy to explain. Message-processing time cannot be fully predictable, as some glitches always happen in the network, and even on the machine where processes share computing and disk resources with other processes. As a result, the time needed to process one message can vary between different consumers, and even between identical messages for the same consumers. If we have multiple consumers that compete for messages, we will almost certainly get into a situation where one consumer has finished processing an event, E_n, while another consumer is still busy processing the E_{n+1} event. The free consumer then starts processing the E_{n+2} event before the processing of the E_{n+1} event has even finished. Clearly, there is no ordering guarantee here. For projections, processing events in order are absolutely crucial. If two renames are executed one after another, we want the second update to be applied to the read model after the first one, with no exceptions. It is, however, not necessary to use competing consumers when using server-maintained checkpoints. If you have one single subscriber for the persistent subscription, it will receive events in order.

When the client maintains their own checkpoint, things become easier and harder at the same time. If we control the checkpoint, we can easily reset or move it. For projections, this means that we can easily rebuild the read model by resetting the checkpoint and removing the existing data. This process is called **replay** and it is, in fact, one of the most powerful features of event sourcing. The harder part is that we need to store the checkpoint somewhere and update it every time the projection processes a new event. The best practice here is that the checkpoint is stored in the same place (that is, the database) as the read model itself. Remember about replay? If we kill the database where our read model is stored, the checkpoint will be gone at once; and, if we run the projection again, it will start processing events from the zero position and eventually, the read model will be rebuilt from the ground up!

So, in this book, we will use real-time subscriptions with checkpoints that are maintained by the client. In Event Store, such subscriptions are called **catch-up subscriptions**. Why catch-up? It's easy to guess. Remember replay? No, I am not repeating myself. In case we want or need to rebuild the read model and kill both its data and its checkpoint, the projection will subscribe to the stream of events, starting with the zero position. Until it processes all historical events, it will not be consuming any new events. Only when the projection eventually catches up with the end of the stream, will we be able to switch it to process new events in real time. Event Store does this automatically and that's why we call it a catch-up subscription. Using this type of subscription allows us to add new projections and build new read models, even for a system that is in production for quite some time and has a lot of events. Our new projection will catch-up on all those historical events, switch to real-time processing, and, from that moment on, our new read model will be usable.

Implementing projections

Now it is time to start writing some code. We will use the final code of `Chapter 9`, *CQRS - The Read Side,* as the starting point. The final code for this chapter is located in the GitHub repository, in the `Chapter11` folder.

We will go step by step and start by implementing one subscription just to see how subscriptions work in the Event Store. Then, we will create a few real read models using both RavenDB and PostgreSQL.

Catch-up subscriptions

In fact, to start making projections, we don't need any databases. I will show you a simple trick that allows you to go on with the initial development quickly, without any thoughts about the database engine that will be used to store read models. Very often, we don't really know what real life will bring us, and the database engine that we might have planned to use at the start might not be even suitable for the job we want to do. During the early stages of any project, the number of events we are working with is not significant, unless we want to put some synthetic tests on the system, or we are working with a high-frequency event-processing system. In our case, we deal with a rather simple classified ads website, so we don't expect a lot of events in the development environment and even in the system that we'd like to show to product owners and QA.

What can we do to keep things really simple? Well, if the source of truth for our system is in the Event Store, why do we need to persist read models somewhere? It would be perfectly fine to keep them in memory and rebuild each time our application starts. That's exactly what we are going to do.

First, I want to use the code for Chapter 9, *CQRS - The Read Side*, as the starting point. Remember, it has no queries and no read models. To bring these things in, I copy some code files from Chapter 10, *Event Sourcing*, and make minimal changes to minimize the work. So, I take only read models and queries from the ClassifiedAd folder of the main application project. Then, I remove some queries from the Queries file, because I only want to implement one to begin with. My new Queries class now looks like the following:

```
using System.Collections.Generic;
using System.Linq;

namespace Marketplace.ClassifiedAd
{
    public static class Queries
    {
        public static ReadModels.ClassifiedAdDetails Query(
            this IEnumerable<ReadModels.ClassifiedAdDetails> items,
            QueryModels.GetPublicClassifiedAd query)
                => items.FirstOrDefault(
                    x => x.ClassifiedAdId == query.ClassifiedAdId);
    }
}
```

You can see that I don't use any database connection here. Instead, the extension method is applied to a simple IEnumerable, so this implies that I will be using a collection of items in memory.

Then, I also need to remove API endpoints that won't be used and keep only one of them. Also, I need to replace the database connection with IEnumerable:

```
using System.Collections.Generic;
using Marketplace.Infrastructure;
using Microsoft.AspNetCore.Mvc;
using Serilog;

namespace Marketplace.ClassifiedAd
{
    [Route("/ad")]
    public class ClassifiedAdsQueryApi : Controller
    {
        private static ILogger _log =
            Log.ForContext<ClassifiedAdsQueryApi>();
```

```
private readonly IEnumerable<ReadModels.ClassifiedAdDetails>
_items;

public ClassifiedAdsQueryApi(
    IEnumerable <ReadModels.ClassifiedAdDetails> items) =>
    _items = items;

[HttpGet]
public IActionResult Get(
    QueryModels.GetPublicClassifiedAd request) =>
    RequestHandler.HandleQuery(() => _items.Query(request),
    _log);
    }
}
```

Notice that the `Get` method is not `async` anymore, because operations on collections are synchronous. Definitely, when we introduce some proper persistence, we would need to bring `async` back. Because of this change, I also need to change the `RequestHandler.HandleQuery` method so it will accept `Action` instead of `Func`, because we don't need to return `Task` for now:

```
public static IActionResult HandleQuery<TModel>(
    Func<TModel> query, ILogger log)
{
    try
    {
        return new OkObjectResult(query());
    }
    catch (Exception e)
    {
        log.Error(e, "Error handling the query");
        return new BadRequestObjectResult(new
        {
            error = e.Message, stackTrace = e.StackTrace
        });
    }
}
```

From `Chapter 9`, *CQRS - The Read Side*, we have the `EsAggregateStore` class. It has some code that helps us to deserialize a resolved event that comes from the Event Store. We also need to do the same operation in our projection. Therefore, I take this code out to an extension method for the `ResolvedEvent` class, so that we can use the same code in projections:

```
using System;
using System.Text;
using EventStore.ClientAPI;
```

```
using Newtonsoft.Json;

namespace Marketplace.Infrastructure
{
    public static class EventDeserializer
    {
        public static object Deserialzie(this ResolvedEvent
        resolvedEvent)
        {
            var meta = JsonConvert.DeserializeObject<EventMetadata>(
                Encoding.UTF8.GetString(resolvedEvent.Event.Metadata));
            var dataType = Type.GetType(meta.ClrType);
            var jsonData = Encoding.UTF8.GetString(
                resolvedEvent.Event.Data);
            var data = JsonConvert.DeserializeObject(
                jsonData, dataType);
            return data;
        }
    }
}
```

As you remember, we keep the **fully qualified class name (FQCN)** of the event class in the event metadata, and `EventDeserialzier` uses it to get our domain event back. I also remove this code from `EsAggregateStore` to avoid duplication, so the `Load` method will look as follows:

```
public async Task<T> Load<T, TId>(TId aggregateId)
    where T : AggregateRoot<TId>
{
    if (aggregateId == null)
        throw new ArgumentNullException(nameof(aggregateId));

    var stream = GetStreamName<T, TId>(aggregateId);
    var aggregate = (T) Activator.CreateInstance(typeof(T), true);

    var page = await _connection.ReadStreamEventsForwardAsync(
        stream, 0, 1024, false);

    aggregate.Load(page.Events.Select(resolvedEvent =>
        resolvedEvent.Deserialzie()).ToArray());

    return aggregate;
}
```

Now, let's do the actual subscription. It will live in a new class that I'll place in the `infrastructure` folder. It will be handling a single read model, so it is not generic in any way and doesn't really belong there. However, this solution is not permanent and we will make it better a bit later.

For this class, I need an instance of `IEventStoreConnection`, so that I can create a subscription to it. I also need a reference to the read models collection, so I can put items in it and change the properties of the existing items. The class will have two simple methods—`Start` and `Stop`. The `Start` method creates a new subscription. Events will immediately start coming in, so the connection must be started before I can subscribe to it. Here is the code for the `Start` method:

```
public void Start()
{
    var settings = new CatchUpSubscriptionSettings(2000, 500,
        Log.IsEnabled(LogEventLevel.Verbose),
        true, "try-out-subscription");

    _subscription = _connection.SubscribeToAllFrom(Position.Start,
        settings, EventAppeared);
}
```

There are some hard coded values here, which we will be reading from the application configuration later. The important line is where we subscribe. The method that I use is `SubscribeToAllFrom`. This method creates a subscription that will get all events that are persisted in the Event Store. The first parameter is where the subscription starts. Since our read model is not persisted and we will be rebuilding it from scratch every time the application starts, we must read it from the very beginning because that's why the parameter is getting `Position.Start`. The last parameter is a delegate, which will be called for each event that we receive from the subscription; we'll get back to it shortly.

The `Stop` method is very simple, it just stops the subscription, as follows:

```
public void Stop() => _subscription.Stop();
```

Now, let's create some code for the `EventAppeared` method. There, we will be building our read model, and, as I previously mentioned, the code will be handling the same domain events that we are handling in the `When` method of our aggregates, in a very similar fashion.

Before we can use advanced pattern-matching, we need to get the domain event from the `ResolvedEvent` class instance that our `EventAppeared` receives as a parameter. Here is the beginning of this method:

```
private Task EventAppeared(EventStoreCatchUpSubscription subscription,
ResolvedEvent resolvedEvent)
{
    var @event = resolvedEvent.Deserialzie();
    switch (@event)
    {
        case Events.ClassifiedAdCreated e:
            _items.Add(new ReadModels.ClassifiedAdDetails
            {
                ClassifiedAdId = e.Id
            });
            break;
        case Events.ClassifiedAdTitleChanged e:
            UpdateItem(e.Id, ad => ad.Title = e.Title);
            break;
    }

    return Task.CompletedTask;
}
```

The first line will get the domain event, then we use pattern-matching to make necessary changes in the read model. The first case will create a new read model for each new classified ad, and the second case will update the title.

This code is fine, but it won't work, because, as I mentioned before, when we subscribe using `SubscribeToAllFrom`, we will get all the events. These events are coming from the `$all` stream. But the Event Store uses events for its own internal operations, so we will also get many events of that kind. Luckily, we can easily identify events that we don't need by the value of the `resolvedEvent.Event.EventType` property. All technical events that have the `stat` event type start with the dollar ($) sign, so we can filter them out.

One last thing to note for this class is that I use the `UpdateItem` method to simplify updates for existing items.

Here is the full code for the `EsSubscription` class:

```
using System;
using System.Collections.Generic;
using System.Linq;
using System.Threading.Tasks;
using EventStore.ClientAPI;
using Marketplace.ClassifiedAd;
```

```csharp
using Marketplace.Domain.ClassifiedAd;
using Serilog.Events;
using ILogger = Serilog.ILogger;

namespace Marketplace.Infrastructure
{
    public class EsSubscription
    {
        private static readonly ILogger Log =
        Serilog.Log.ForContext<EsSubscription>();

        private readonly IEventStoreConnection _connection;
        private readonly IList<ReadModels.ClassifiedAdDetails> _items;
        private EventStoreAllCatchUpSubscription _subscription;

        public EsSubscription(IEventStoreConnection connection,
            IList<ReadModels.ClassifiedAdDetails> items)
        {
            _connection = connection;
            _items = items;
        }

        public void Start()
        {
            var settings = new CatchUpSubscriptionSettings(2000, 500,
                Log.IsEnabled(LogEventLevel.Verbose),
                true, "try-out-subscription");

            _subscription = _connection.SubscribeToAllFrom(
                Position.Start, settings, EventAppeared);
        }

        private Task EventAppeared(
            EventStoreCatchUpSubscription
            subscription, ResolvedEvent resolvedEvent)
        {
            if (resolvedEvent.Event.EventType.StartsWith("$"))
                return Task.CompletedTask;
            var @event = resolvedEvent.Deserialzie();
            Log.Debug("Projecting event {type}",
                @event.GetType().Name);

            switch (@event)
            {
                case Events.ClassifiedAdCreated e:
                    _items.Add(new ReadModels.ClassifiedAdDetails
                    {
                        ClassifiedAdId = e.Id
```

```
            });
            break;
        case Events.ClassifiedAdTitleChanged e:
            UpdateItem(e.Id, ad => ad.Title = e.Title);
            break;
        case Events.ClassifiedAdTextUpdated e:
            UpdateItem(e.Id, ad => ad.Description = e.AdText);
            break;
        case Events.ClassifiedAdPriceUpdated e:
            UpdateItem(e.Id, ad =>
            {
                ad.Price = e.Price;
                ad.CurrencyCode = e.CurrencyCode;
            });
            break;
    }

    return Task.CompletedTask;
}

private void UpdateItem(Guid id,
    Action<ReadModels.ClassifiedAdDetails> update)
{
    var item = _items.FirstOrDefault(
        x => x.ClassifiedAdId == id);
    if (item == null) return;

    update(item);
}

public void Stop() => _subscription.Stop();
}
}
```

Ideally, we'd need to wrap the deserialization call in a `try-catch` block, because we might get some events that we don't know about and it will cause our projection to break ungracefully. But again, we'll be making lots of changes in the code later on. Let's move on to the wiring part and try things out.

We must ensure that our subscription starts after the Event Store connection do indeed connect to the store. Right now, this operation happens in the HostedService class. Since it only handles the Event Store connection business, I will rename it to the EventStoreService. I also add the EsSubscription instance to its constructor, so we can start a subscription as soon as we connect. Here, you can see how this class looks after all those changes:

```
using System.Threading;
using System.Threading.Tasks;
using EventStore.ClientAPI;
using Marketplace.Infrastructure;
using Microsoft.Extensions.Hosting;

namespace Marketplace
{
    public class EventStoreService : IHostedService
    {
        private readonly IEventStoreConnection _esConnection;
        private readonly EsSubscription _subscription;

        public EventStoreService(
            IEventStoreConnection esConnection,
            EsSubscription subscription)
        {
            _esConnection = esConnection;
            _subscription = subscription;
        }

        public async Task StartAsync(
            CancellationToken cancellationToken)
        {
            await _esConnection.ConnectAsync();
            _subscription.Start();
        }

        public Task StopAsync(CancellationToken cancellationToken)
        {
            _subscription.Stop();
            _esConnection.Close();
            return Task.CompletedTask;
        }
    }
}
```

In the `Startup` class, I need to change the registrations and also create our fake storage instance (remember, that's just a collection). So, I change the code that registers the hosted service and add a couple of lines to that block of the `Startup.ConfigureServices` method:

```
var items = new List<ReadModels.ClassifiedAdDetails>();
services.AddSingleton<IEnumerable<ReadModels.ClassifiedAdDetails>>(items);

var subscription = new EsSubscription(esConnection, items);
services.AddSingleton<IHostedService>(
    new EventStoreService(esConnection, subscription));
```

We need to register the items collection, because our query API controller needs it to be injected by the service provider, as a constructor parameter.

One thing that we haven't done in Chapter 9, *CQRS - The Read Side,* is that despite us using Serilog for all of the logging, it was never initialized in the chapter code. We had nothing to log then really, but now it will be interesting to look at what we can log. So, I added a couple of lines at the beginning of the `Program.Main` method:

```
Log.Logger = new LoggerConfiguration()
    .MinimumLevel.Debug()
    .WriteTo.Console()
    .CreateLogger();
```

Well, this is it. Now, if you have the same `docker-compose` running since Chapter 9, *CQRS - The Read Side,* and have some data in it (you should have it if you followed along with the code of Chapter 9, *CQRS - The Read Side*), you can run the application and it will produce a kind of debug, as follows:

```
Hosting environment: Development
Content root path: /~/Dev/ddd-
book/chapter11/Marketplace/bin/Debug/netcoreapp2.1
Now listening on: http://localhost:5000
Application started. Press Ctrl+C to shut down.
[21:00:17 DBG] Projecting event ClassifiedAdCreated
[21:00:17 DBG] Projecting event ClassifiedAdTitleChanged
[21:00:17 DBG] Projecting event ClassifiedAdTextUpdated
[21:00:17 DBG] Projecting event ClassifiedAdPriceUpdated
[21:00:17 DBG] Projecting event ClassidiedAdSentForReview
[21:00:17 DBG] Projecting event ClassifiedAdPublished
[21:00:48 DBG] Projecting event ClassifiedAdCreated
[21:00:48 DBG] Projecting event ClassifiedAdTitleChanged
[21:00:48 DBG] Projecting event ClassifiedAdTextUpdated
[21:00:48 DBG] Projecting event ClassifiedAdPriceUpdated
[21:00:48 DBG] Projecting event ClassidiedAdSentForReview
```

```
[21:00:48 DBG] Projecting event ClassifiedAdPublished
[21:00:48 DBG] Projecting event ClassifiedAdCreated
[21:00:48 DBG] Projecting event ClassidiedAdSentForReview
[21:00:48 DBG] Projecting event ClassifiedAdTitleChanged
[21:00:48 DBG] Projecting event ClassifiedAdPublished
[21:00:48 DBG] Projecting event ClassifiedAdPriceUpdated
[21:00:48 DBG] Projecting event ClassifiedAdCreated
[21:00:48 DBG] Projecting event ClassifiedAdTextUpdated
```

If you were working with Chapter 10, *Event Sourcing*, code for a while and the Event Store was running for many days, you might notice some delay between events that belong to different classified ads. This is simply because all of those technical events are being continuously produced by Event Store and we get all of them. We ignore these events but we still need to read them, get to the application, check the name, and so on. This takes time. On the preceding debug output, you can see the delay of about 30 seconds, which means I let Event Store run 24/7 on my machine and it took me a while to work in Chapter 9, *CQRS - The Read Side*! We don't really want to have this delay and luckily, Event Store sets a small **time-to-live** (TTL) value on these technical events. This means that, in theory, most of them should be deleted. However, events that are marked for deletion, aren't being cleaned up until we execute a scavenge operation. That's because removing events in real time would have a significant performance impact. Scavenging can be started from the Event Store UI by going to **Admin**, where you can press the **Scavenge** button at the top-right corner of the screen. After I scavenged my local store, the delay decreased to six seconds. But make no mistake, this happens once only when you start the application. All new events will be projected instantly.

Now, we can test our GET query endpoint to see if the projection actually worked. I will use the classified ad that I previously created when working on Chapter 9, *CQRS - The Read Side*. Here is the query result in Swagger:

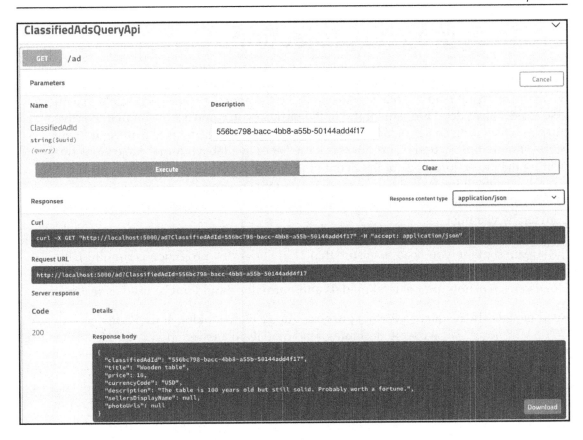

The query retrieves data from the real model

The first projection worked! However, we can see that we only projected the classified ad events, and therefore, the seller's display name is empty. We will be fixing it shortly.

Cross-aggregate projections

When people start doing event sourcing, one mistake that often happens is that developers try to get into the comfort zone of the persisted state of their aggregates as soon as they can. So, many interpret read models as a way to keep the aggregate state accessible in a queryable store. I have done the same thing in the past, so you can trust me on that. For the purpose of keeping an aggregate state in some database, I used a nice feature of Event Store—internal projections. You can check the list of available internal projections by visiting the Projections page of the Event Store web UI. One of those projections is `$by-category`, which links all events to special category streams. For example, `$ce-ClassifiedAd` will contain all events for the `ClassifiedAd` aggregate. You can inspect it yourself by visiting `http://localhost:2113/web/index.html#/streams/$ce-ClassifiedAd`. and check the stream content (you need to ensure that `$by-category` projection is running). By creating a subscription for this stream you can, for example, build an aggregate snapshot. However, snapshots are not read models and normally should not be used as real models.

Read models always serve a certain purpose. As we were looking at CQRS in Chapter 9, *CQRS - The Read Side,* we were designing read models to answer specific queries. Often, we need some information on the screen, and therefore, we make a read model to get all the required information using one single query. Without CQRS, we might need to call several queries that would retrieve the state of several different types of entities from repositories, and combine the information at the API backend to one single response DTO. This is a common strategy when we use a **Backend For Frontend** (BFF) approach. With CQRS, however, we are free to choose what information to query, as soon as the query only works with entities from a single database. We will look into more complex scenarios when our system becomes a composition of multiple autonomous subsystems when we go through the topics of bounded contexts and microservices.

Projecting events from two aggregates

Now, let's think about creating read models that are similar to what we had in Chapter 10, *Event Sourcing.* We have already started with one of them and as you have seen in the preceding Swagger screenshot, the seller name is empty in the response we get. That's because the only events we're handling in our projection are the `ClassifiedAd` events. However, our store contains all events for the whole application.

Since we use the `SubscribeFromAllFrom` method of the `IEventStoreConnection` interface, our projection will receive all events. We currently filter our system events, so we should get everything else, including events for the `UserProfile` aggregate. It seems simple to add one more `case` to the pattern-matching switch and handle the `UserDisplayNameUpdated` event to set the `ReadModels` property correctly. That seems legit, so when the owner updates their display name, our read model will get updated too.

One issue here is that we cannot give the `UpdateItem` method any ID. When the user updates their display name, this action is not associated with any classified ad. This means that we need to run a query and update all ads where the owner ID is the ID of the user who changed the name. This task is not hard, so we can add one more method, called `UpdateMultipleItems`, and give it a query and an operation to execute on each item that is returned by the query:

```
private void UpdateMultipleItems(
    Func<ReadModels.ClassifiedAdDetails, bool> query,
    Action<ReadModels.ClassifiedAdDetails> update)
{
    foreach (var item in _items.Where(query))
        update(item);
}
```

We can specify the action easily, but what should be the query? Our read model doesn't contain the owner ID! Well, we can easily fix this by adding an additional property to the read model, called `SellerId`, which we will assign from `OwnerId`. There is no way in our system to change the ad owner, so it is safe to do this assignment only when the ad is created.

The new code for the projection will be as follows:

```
private Task EventAppeared(EventStoreCatchUpSubscription subscription,
    ResolvedEvent resolvedEvent)
{
    if (resolvedEvent.Event.EventType.StartsWith("$"))
        return Task.CompletedTask;
    var @event = resolvedEvent.Deserialzie();
    Log.Debug("Projecting event {type}", @event.GetType().Name);

    switch (@event)
    {
        case Events.ClassifiedAdCreated e:
            _items.Add(new ReadModels.ClassifiedAdDetails
            {
                ClassifiedAdId = e.Id,
                SellerId = e.OwnerId
```

```
            });
            break;
        case Events.ClassifiedAdTitleChanged e:
            UpdateItem(e.Id, ad => ad.Title = e.Title);
            break;
        case Events.ClassifiedAdTextUpdated e:
            UpdateItem(e.Id, ad => ad.Description = e.AdText);
            break;
        case Events.ClassifiedAdPriceUpdated e:
            UpdateItem(e.Id, ad =>
            {
                ad.Price = e.Price;
                ad.CurrencyCode = e.CurrencyCode;
            });
            break;
        case Domain.UserProfile.Events.UserDisplayNameUpdated e:
            UpdateMultipleItems(x => x.SellerId == e.UserId,
                x => x.SellersDisplayName = e.DisplayName);
            break;
    }

    return Task.CompletedTask;
}
```

Of course, one thing to remember is how efficient the query will be on real storage. Since we are using a simple in-memory list, it is not an issue. In reality, one person would not have millions of classified ads, so the same query would work too, but we also need to remember that RavenDB only supports a limited number of operations per session, so an advanced technique might be needed if we expect to update thousands of items by this query.

Do you see another issue there? Of course, users don't really update their names that often. I don't actually remember changing my name since I was born. I do update some of my countless profiles on a number of online services that I use, but usually, I do this only once, especially when it comes to the name change. For our classified ad, the chance that the owner will update their name after the ad has been created and before it is removed is close to zero. So, what can we do?

Multiple projections per subscription

First, it seems that we need to build another projection that will handle events for the UserProfile aggregate and build a simple read model from them. We can use the same storage and keep everything in memory for now. Since we will have two projections, it makes sense to separate things and let our subscription handle multiple projections.

Since we will have one subscription that can handle multiple projections, we can rename our `EsSubscription` class to `ProjectionsManager`. It will need to accept projections as parameters and it is better to keep them in separate classes, so we need a simple interface. We can call it `IProjection` and place the file in the `Marketplace.Framework` project, as follows:

```
using System.Threading.Tasks;

namespace Marketplace.Framework
{
    public interface IProjection
    {
        Task Project(object @event);
    }
}
```

Then, we need to move the pattern-matching code to a new implementation of this interface. It is better to group projections together, so I created a folder in the `Marketplace` project, called `Projections`, and added a new `ClassifiedAdDetailsProjection` class there. After that, I moved the code from the `EsSubscription.EventAppeared` method to this new class:

```
using System;
using System.Collections.Generic;
using System.Linq;
using System.Threading.Tasks;
using Marketplace.Domain.ClassifiedAd;
using Marketplace.Framework;

namespace Marketplace.Projections
{
    public class ClassifiedAdDetailsProjection : IProjection
    {
        private List<ReadModels.ClassifiedAdDetails> _items;

        public ClassifiedAdDetailsProjection(List<ReadModels.
            ClassifiedAdDetails> items)
        {
            _items = items;
        }

        public Task Project(object @event)
        {
            switch (@event)
            {
                case Events.ClassifiedAdCreated e:
                    _items.Add(new ReadModels.ClassifiedAdDetails
```

```
                {
                    ClassifiedAdId = e.Id,
                    SellerId = e.OwnerId
                });
                break;
            case Events.ClassifiedAdTitleChanged e:
                UpdateItem(e.Id, ad => ad.Title = e.Title);
                break;
            case Events.ClassifiedAdTextUpdated e:
                UpdateItem(e.Id, ad => ad.Description = e.AdText);
                break;
            case Events.ClassifiedAdPriceUpdated e:
                UpdateItem(e.Id, ad =>
                {
                    ad.Price = e.Price;
                    ad.CurrencyCode = e.CurrencyCode;
                });
                break;
            case Domain.UserProfile.Events.UserDisplayNameUpdated
            e:

                UpdateMultipleItems(x => x.SellerId == e.UserId,
                    x => x.SellersDisplayName = e.DisplayName);
                break;
        }

        return Task.CompletedTask;
    }

    private void UpdateItem(Guid id,
        Action<ReadModels.ClassifiedAdDetails> update)
    {
        var item = _items.FirstOrDefault(
            x => x.ClassifiedAdId == id);
        if (item == null) return;

        update(item);
    }

    private void UpdateMultipleItems(
        Func<ReadModels.ClassifiedAdDetails, bool> query,
        Action<ReadModels.ClassifiedAdDetails> update)
    {
        foreach (var item in _items.Where(query))
            update(item);
    }
}
}
```

We also need a new projection that will build a read model for user details, so I created another implementation of the `IProjection` interface and called it `UserDetailsProjection`. It makes sense to also move the `ReadModels.cs` files to the `Projections` folder to keep things together. Here is the user details projection code:

```
using System;
using System.Collections.Generic;
using System.Linq;
using System.Threading.Tasks;
using Marketplace.Domain.UserProfile;
using Marketplace.Framework;

namespace Marketplace.Projections
{
    public class UserDetailsProjection : IProjection
    {
        List<ReadModels.UserDetails> _items;
        public UserDetailsProjection(
            List<ReadModels.UserDetails> items)
        {
            _items = items;
        }
        public Task Project(object @event)
        {
            switch (@event)
            {
                case Events.UserRegistered e:
                    _items.Add(new ReadModels.UserDetails
                    {
                        UserId = e.UserId,
                        DisplayName = e.DisplayName
                    });
                    break;
                case Events.UserDisplayNameUpdated e:
                    UpdateItem(e.UserId,
                        x => x.DisplayName = e.DisplayName);
                    break;
            }
            return Task.CompletedTask;
        }
        private void UpdateItem(Guid id,
            Action<ReadModels.UserDetails> update)
        {
            var item = _items.FirstOrDefault(x => x.UserId == id);
            if (item == null) return;

            update(item);
```

```
            }
        }
    }
```

Of course, we need to add a new read model class to the `ReadModels.cs` file, as follows:

```
using System;

namespace Marketplace.Projections
{
    public static class ReadModels
    {
        public class ClassifiedAdDetails
        {
            public Guid ClassifiedAdId { get; set; }
            public string Title { get; set; }
            public decimal Price { get; set; }
            public string CurrencyCode { get; set; }
            public string Description { get; set; }
            public Guid SellerId { get; set; }
            public string SellersDisplayName { get; set; }
            public string[] PhotoUrls { get; set; }
        }

        public class UserDetails
        {
            public Guid UserId { get; set; }
            public string DisplayName { get; set; }
        }
    }
}
```

Now, we need to finalize the projections manager so that it can accept multiple projections and call each of them when a new event appears. We want to be prepared for the future use of a real persistence store, so I want to keep all methods async, except `UpdateItem` and `UpdateItems`, which I can change later, as these are implementation details of individual projection classes. Here is the new `ProjectionManager` class code:

```
using System.Linq;
using System.Threading.Tasks;
using EventStore.ClientAPI;
using Marketplace.Framework;
using Serilog;
using Serilog.Events;

namespace Marketplace.Infrastructure
{
```

```
public class ProjectionManager
{
    private readonly IEventStoreConnection _connection;
    private readonly IProjection[] _projections;
    private EventStoreAllCatchUpSubscription _subscription;

    public ProjectionManager(IEventStoreConnection connection,
        params IProjection[] projections)
    {
        _connection = connection;
        _projections = projections;
    }

    public void Start()
    {
        var settings = new CatchUpSubscriptionSettings(2000, 500,
            Log.IsEnabled(LogEventLevel.Verbose),
            true, "try-out-subscription");
        _subscription = _connection.SubscribeToAllFrom(
            Position.Start, settings, EventAppeared);
    }

    public void Stop() => _subscription.Stop();

    private Task EventAppeared(EventStoreCatchUpSubscription _,
        ResolvedEvent resolvedEvent)
    {
        if (resolvedEvent.Event.EventType.StartsWith("$"))
            return Task.CompletedTask;
        var @event = resolvedEvent.Deserialzie();
        Log.Debug("Projecting event {type}",
            @event.GetType().Name);
        return Task.WhenAll(_projections.Select(
            x => x.Project(@event)));
    }
}
```

I want to keep logging all events that we project to see what is going on. In the last line of the EventAppeared method, you can see that we are collecting all of the tasks that project events for each projection and we want all these tasks to complete.

Next, we fix compilation errors in the EventStoreService class, so it uses ProjectionManager, instead of the removed (or renamed) EsSubscription class:

```
using System.Threading;
using System.Threading.Tasks;
using EventStore.ClientAPI;
```

```
using Marketplace.Infrastructure;
using Microsoft.Extensions.Hosting;

namespace Marketplace
{
    public class EventStoreService : IHostedService
    {
        private readonly IEventStoreConnection _esConnection;
        private readonly ProjectionManager _projectionManager;

        public EventStoreService(IEventStoreConnection esConnection,
            ProjectionManager projectionManager)
        {
            _esConnection = esConnection;
            _projectionManager = projectionManager;
        }

        public async Task StartAsync(
            CancellationToken cancellationToken)
        {
            await _esConnection.ConnectAsync();
            _projectionManager.Start();
        }

        public Task StopAsync(CancellationToken cancellationToken)
        {
            _projectionManager.Stop();
            _esConnection.Close();
            return Task.CompletedTask;
        }
    }
}
```

The final thing before we can start the app is to wire things up in Startup. We need one more collection, this time of the ReadModels.UserDetails, so we can use it in controllers and give it to the UserDetailsProjection constructor as a parameter:

```
var classifiedAdDetails = new List<ReadModels.ClassifiedAdDetails>();
services.AddSingleton<IEnumerable<ReadModels.ClassifiedAdDetails>>(classifi
edAdDetails);
var userDetails = new List<ReadModels.UserDetails>();
services.AddSingleton<IEnumerable<ReadModels.UserDetails>>(userDetails);

var projectionManager = new ProjectionManager(esConnection,
    new ClassifiedAdDetailsProjection(classifiedAdDetails),
    new UserDetailsProjection(userDetails));
```

This was some work, but now everything is done, I can finally press *F5* and see what happens. Well, nothing spectacular really; I only see the same events for an ad being projected again, but at least this part works as before. We see nothing new because I was cheating and created an ad without having any users in the system. Now I need to go back and create this user.

Event links and special streams

Assuming that we keep running `docker-compose` from `Chapter 10`, *Event Sourcing*, I can look up the owner ID of the only ad we have in the Event Store stream. The value I used there is `8dd8c5c6-6edb-4e42-ac9e-a232ea445b76`, so I can use the Swagger API for user profiles and create the following user:

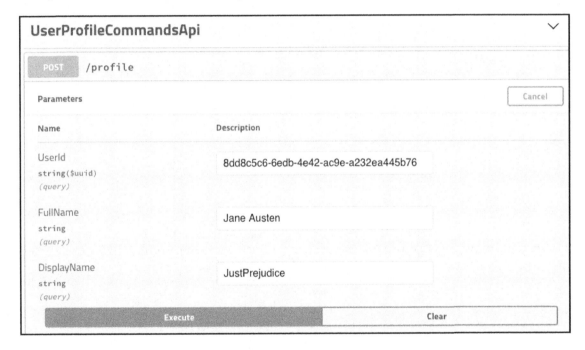

Creating a new user via the UserProfile API

I got a `200 OK` response and now I see more lines in the log, as follows:

```
[21:58:04 DBG] Projecting event UserRegistered
[21:58:04 DBG] Projecting event UserRegistered
[21:58:04 DBG] Projecting event UserRegistered
[21:58:04 DBG] Projecting event UserRegistered
```

Well, the new projection works, but why has this single event been projected four times? The mystery can be easily solved by looking at the `$all` stream that we used for our subscription:

Event Stream '$all'

| self | first | last | next | previous |

Event #	Name
74777	74777@$stats-0.0.0.0:2113
74776	74776@$stats-0.0.0.0:2113
74775	74775@$stats-0.0.0.0:2113
74774	74774@$stats-0.0.0.0:2113
735	735@$projections-$master
734	734@$projections-$master
733	733@$projections-$master
732	732@$projections-$master
0	0@$ce-UserProfile
0	0@$et-UserRegistered
0	0@$category-UserProfile
0	0@$$$ce-UserProfile
0	0@$$$category-UserProfile
0	0@$$$et-UserRegistered

Content of the $all stream

Here, you can see that several events were added to it. If we ignore system events, those of `0@$ce-UserProfile`, `0@$et-UserRegistered`, and so on look suspicious. These are linked events that were placed to different special streams by internal standard projections of Event Store. These internal projections are very helpful. For example, if you look at the `$ce-UserProfile` stream, you will find all events that were saved for all instances of the `UserProfile` aggregate. These `$ce` streams are known as category streams. Another stream type is the event type. For example, `$et-UserRegistered` contains all events of type `UserRegistered` from all other streams in the store.

However, we are subscribing to the `$all` stream and we don't need to get copies of a single event that is being linked to all those special streams. We could, of course, disable standard projections by going to the **Projection** tab of the Event Store UI and clicking the **Stop all** button, but that is not really a good way. Someone could come to our store later on and enable these projections again. But remember, these are linked events. We have a helpful parameter for the catch-up subscription, which is called `resolveLinkTos`, and we set it to `true`. Let's change it to `false` and see what happens. Here is the new code from the `ProjectionManager` class:

```
public void Start()
{
    var settings = new CatchUpSubscriptionSettings(2000, 500,
        Log.IsEnabled(LogEventLevel.Verbose),
        false, "try-out-subscription");
    _subscription = _connection.SubscribeToAllFrom(Position.Start,
        settings, EventAppeared);
}
```

If I run the application now, the input is much different:

```
[22:30:38 DBG] Projecting event ClassifiedAdCreated
[22:30:38 DBG] Projecting event ClassifiedAdTitleChanged
[22:30:38 DBG] Projecting event ClassifiedAdTextUpdated
[22:30:38 DBG] Projecting event ClassifiedAdPriceUpdated
[22:30:38 DBG] Projecting event ClassifiedAdSentForReview
[22:30:38 DBG] Projecting event ClassifiedAdPublished
[22:30:48 DBG] Projecting event UserRegistered
```

It appears that events for the `ClassifiedAd` aggregate were also projected multiple times before, for the same reason. Now the log makes much more sense, and each event is only projected once, as expected.

Enriching read models

At this moment, we have a collection that contains a single object of type `ReadModels.UserDetails` in memory. This object represents a single user, so we can find out what display name the user has if we have the user ID. This is helpful, but how can we use it to show the full details of our classified ad? There are two ways of doing this, considering that we are within a single-application boundary and use the same store (currently in memory) for all read models.

When developers start to deal with data that is spread across multiple data sources, the most obvious method that comes to their mind is to aggregate data on the edge. One of the most popular techniques is to build BFF. When the frontend needs to get some aggregated data, it sends one request to a single API endpoint at the backend, and the API itself calls different data sources and merges the data. This process can be illustrated by the following diagram:

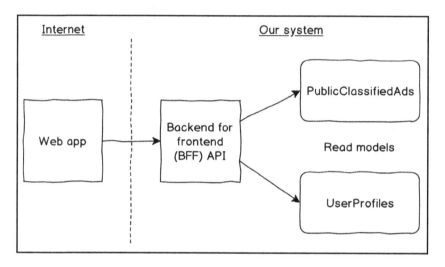

The BFF pattern

In the simplest scenario, we can just do one database call with some sort of join, since we have the knowledge about keys for both data elements that we need to query. In more complex situations, we might find ourselves dealing with remote calls to microservices that own the data we need and do the join in memory. There are quite a few concerns about this approach. When we start using remote calls, we expose our API endpoint to potential failures of any of the services it needs to call and all sorts of networking issues that might happen. Another important aspect is that we have to do the join each time the BFF API endpoint is called. If this particular set of data is being used frequently, we will get into a situation where we need to make potentially expensive joins, instead of using the power of read models to retrieve a preprocessed set of denormalized data that is targeted in that particular use case.

There are a few ways to get more data in the read model than it receives in events that the projection receives.

If we have the necessary data that our read model needs, in the same aggregate, we can add properties to the event that aren't necessary to convey the state transition. For example, if we need to build a read model that will contain a list of ads for one user (`MyClassifiedAds`), we would need to include the owner ID to all events that the projection would need to handle, such as `ClassifiedAdTitleChanged` or `ClassifiedAdTextUpdated`. This method is sometimes referred to as using **fat events**, which is the opposite of **slim events** that contain the minimal amount of data that is necessary to explain what happened. But this method won't work for a cross-aggregate read model, so it is not an option that we need to explore now.

We are going to implement two other methods that will allow us to get the data from other sources—querying from a projection and event up casting.

Querying from a projection

Currently, our main problem is that we don't have the name of the owner when our projection receives the `ClassifiedAdCreated` event. All other events for the classified ad aggregate don't have any effect on the owner, since the owner cannot be changed. We already handle the `UserDisplayNameUpdated` event in our projection, so we get the updated name if the ad owner decides to do such an update. To get the data we need, we will reach out to the `UserDetails` read model, using `OwnerId` from the event. The process would look like the following:

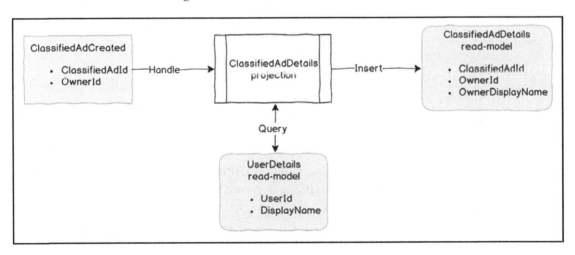

Enriching projections from another read model

Let's change our projection code to do this query. First of all, we don't have any knowledge about the other read model in the `ClassifiedAdDetailsProjection` class. This doesn't matter for now, as regardless of whether the data is stored in memory or in some database, we still need to get hold of it. A trivial way would be to give our projection a reference to the `UserDetails` storage and execute the query directly. But this approach, although very simple to implement, creates coupling between read models and projections. When such coupling is introduced, any future change will be harder to implement and testing will always be a challenge, since we always need to make sure that all storages are prepopulated with all the data we need.

A much more elegant and clean way is to give our projection an explicit way to retrieve `DisplayName` of a user for a given `UserId`. The easiest way to do this is by providing a delegate function so that we can add it as a parameter to the projection constructor:

```
public ClassifiedAdDetailsProjection(
    List<ReadModels.ClassifiedAdDetails> items,
    Func<Guid, string> getUserDisplayName)
{
    _items = items;
    _getUserDisplayName = getUserDisplayName;
}
```

Now, we can use this function to get the additional data we need for the read model, by adding the call to this function in the first `case` in the `ClassifiedAdDetailsProjection.Project` method:

```
case Events.ClassifiedAdCreated e:
    _items.Add(new ReadModels.ClassifiedAdDetails
    {
        ClassifiedAdId = e.Id,
        SellerId = e.OwnerId,
        SellersDisplayName = _getUserDisplayName(e.OwnerId)
    });
    break;
```

The last thing that we need to do is to complete the wiring, since the `Startup` class doesn't compile anymore. We need to change the projection constructor call to the following:

```
var projectionManager = new ProjectionManager(esConnection,
    new ClassifiedAdDetailsProjection(classifiedAdDetails,
        userId => userDetails.FirstOrDefault(
            x => x.UserId == userId)?.DisplayName),
```

That's all we needed to do, and now I can start the application and query the same endpoint as before to get the enriched result:

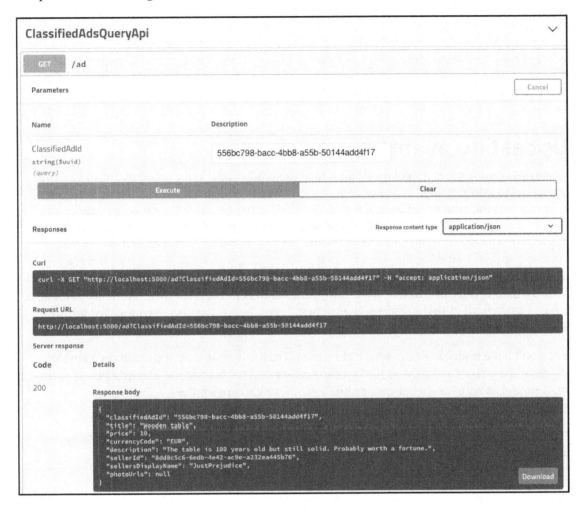

The query result shows all the data we need

You can see that the `sellersDisplayName` property in the response is correctly set to the value we want.

There are quite a few aspects that need to be taken care of when using queries in projections, mainly to ensure reliability. The main goal of such work is to ensure that projections never fail. When the data that you need to query is located in the same storage as the read model that you are updating, the speed of processing and reliability of the query should be on an acceptable level. You might still want to apply a retry policy on the whole projection to mitigate issues of transient networking failures and similar situations. However, you should really not try querying external data sources to get additional data. We will discuss how to solve situations like this when we talk about integration aspects.

Upcasting events

The most complex way to get more data into the read model is by using **event upcasting**. Basically, to implement this, we need to create a separate subscription to the Event Store that receives the slim event, gets the additional data from somewhere else, produces a new event with more data, and publishes it to a special stream. This stream could never be the aggregate stream since the new event is only needed to build a read model. We could choose a special name for the stream, such as `ClassifiedAd-Upcast`. Since the read model projection listens to the `$all` stream, it will receive and process these events as well. This method is only useful when the additional data is needed for different read models, so we can update all of them using one enriched event, hence we need to query for additional data only once.

We don't have many read models, but I can still demonstrate this approach on a single `ClassifiedAdDetails` event. Let's assume we need to include the owner's photo in the read model as soon as the ad gets published, so we can enrich the `ClassifiedAdPublished` event.

First, I need to add `SellersPhotoUrl` to the read model itself; it will be just a string, as follows:

```
public class ClassifiedAdDetails
{
    public Guid ClassifiedAdId { get; set; }
    public string Title { get; set; }
    public decimal Price { get; set; }
    public string CurrencyCode { get; set; }
    public string Description { get; set; }
    public Guid SellerId { get; set; }
    public string SellersDisplayName { get; set; }
    public string SellersPhotoUrl { get; set; }
    public string[] PhotoUrls { get; set; }
}
```

We also need to get the owner ID to the up caster, otherwise, it doesn't know which user it needs to ask for the photo. Here, we can use the fat event method and add the `OwnerId` property to our `ClassifiedAdPublished` event. After I've added the property, I need to change the `Publish` method of the `ClassifiedAd` aggregate, so it will populate this property from the aggregate state:

```
public void Publish(UserId userId) =>
    Apply(new Events.ClassifiedAdPublished
    {
        Id = Id,
        ApprovedBy = userId,
        OwnerId = OwnerId
    });
```

I also need to have the up casted event as a class, so I add it as follows:

```
public static class ClassifiedAdUpcastedEvents
{
    public static class V1
    {
        public class ClassifiedAdPublished
        {
            public Guid Id { get; set; }
            public Guid OwnerId { get; set; }
            public string SellersPhotoUrl { get; set; }
            public Guid ApprovedBy { get; set; }
        }
    }
}
```

We were saving events to the Event Store before and the code is located in the `EsAggregateStore` class. Now, we need this code again, so that we can create a useful extension to the `IEventStoreConnection` interface to make saving events more convenient:

```
using System;
using System.Linq;
using System.Text;
using System.Threading.Tasks;
using EventStore.ClientAPI;
using Newtonsoft.Json;

namespace Marketplace.Infrastructure
{
    public static class EventStoreExtensions
    {
        public static Task AppendEvents(
```

```
                    this IEventStoreConnection connection,
                    string streamName, long version,
                    params object[] events)
        {
            if (events == null || !events.Any()) return
                Task.CompletedTask;
            var preparedEvents = events
                .Select(@event =>
                    new EventData(
                        eventId: Guid.NewGuid(),
                        type: @event.GetType().Name,
                        isJson: true,
                        data: Serialize(@event),
                        metadata: Serialize(
                            new EventMetadata {ClrType =
                                @event.GetType().AssemblyQualifiedName})
                    ))
                .ToArray();
            return connection.AppendToStreamAsync(
                streamName,
                version,
                preparedEvents);
        }
        private static byte[] Serialize(object data)
            => Encoding.UTF8.GetBytes(
                JsonConvert.SerializeObject(data));
    }
}
```

Since this code is copied from the `EsAggregateStore` class, it would make sense to use this method there as well, and you can see the changed code in the GitHub repository.

Next, I need to create a new projection. I can call it `ClassifiedAdUpcasters` and put it to the `Projections` folder of the main project. The class needs to implement `IProjection` so that I can feed our `ProjectionManager` with it. In the `Project` method, I need to handle a single event; but for future use, I can still use the `switch` statement although it also has one `case`. In this `case`, I need to emit a new event to the upcasting stream, so I'd need to take `IEventStoreConnection` as a dependency. The code for the new class is shown as follows:

```
using System;
using System.Threading.Tasks;
using EventStore.ClientAPI;
using Marketplace.Framework;
using Marketplace.Infrastructure;
using static Marketplace.Domain.ClassifiedAd.Events;
using static Marketplace.Projections.ClassifiedAdUpcastedEvents;
```

```csharp
namespace Marketplace.Projections
{
    public class ClassifiedAdUpcasters : IProjection
    {
        private readonly IEventStoreConnection _eventStoreConnection;
        private readonly Func<Guid, string> _getUserPhoto;
        private const string StreamName = "UpcastedClassifiedAdEvents";

        public ClassifiedAdUpcasters(
            IEventStoreConnection eventStoreConnection,
            Func<Guid, string> getUserPhoto)
        {
            _eventStoreConnection = eventStoreConnection;
            _getUserPhoto = getUserPhoto;
        }

        public async Task Project(object @event)
        {
            switch (@event)
            {
                case ClassifiedAdPublished e:
                    var photoUrl = _getUserPhoto(e.OwnerId);
                    var newEvent = new V1.ClassifiedAdPublished
                    {
                        Id = e.Id,
                        OwnerId = e.OwnerId,
                        ApprovedBy = e.ApprovedBy,
                        SellersPhotoUrl = photoUrl
                    };
                    await _eventStoreConnection.AppendEvents(
                        StreamName,
                        ExpectedVersion.Any,
                        newEvent);
                    break;
            }
        }
    }

    public static class ClassifiedAdUpcastedEvents
    {
        public static class V1
        {
            public class ClassifiedAdPublished
            {
                public Guid Id { get; set; }
                public Guid OwnerId { get; set; }
                public string SellersPhotoUrl { get; set; }
                public Guid ApprovedBy { get; set; }
```

```
            }
        }
    }
}
```

As you can see in the code, I need to get a function that will allow the projection to get the user photo URL from somewhere. As soon as this projection received the `ClassifiedAdPublished` event, it will query the photo URL and emit a new, enriching event to the `UpcastedClassifiedAds` stream.

We also need to project the upcasted event in the `ClassifiedAdDetails` projection, so I add one more `case` to the `Project` method:

```
case V1.ClassifiedAdPublished e:
    UpdateItem(e.Id, ad => ad.SellersPhotoUrl = e.SellersPhotoUrl);
    break;
```

The last thing is the wiring, where I need to add this new projection to the projection manager, so it will include it in the subscription processing. So, I need to change the `Startup.cs` file, as follows:

```
var projectionManager = new ProjectionManager(esConnection,
    new ClassifiedAdDetailsProjection(classifiedAdDetails,
        userId => userDetails.FirstOrDefault(
            x => x.UserId == userId)?.DisplayName),
    new UserDetailsProjection(userDetails),
    new ClassifiedAdUpcasters(esConnection,
        userId => userDetails.FirstOrDefault(
            x => x.UserId == userId)?.PhotoUrl));
```

Here, you can see that I use `esConnection`, which has been instantiated before for the aggregate store, and the function to query the user photo URL from the `UserDetails` read model.

When everything is done, I can run the application again. In Swagger, I use the user profile command API to add the photo URL to the user, then use the classified ad command API to first request the ad to be published, and then publish it. Once I complete these operations via the API, I can go back to the query API and get the new details. The new result includes the photo URL, as expected:

```
{
    "classifiedAdId": "556bc798-bacc-4bb8-a55b-50144add4f17",
    "title": "Wooden table",
    "price": 10,
    "currencyCode": "EUR",
    "description": "The table is 100 years old but still solid. Probably
```

```
        worth a fortune.",
        "sellerId": "8dd8c5c6-6edb-4e42-ac9e-a232ea445b76",
        "sellersDisplayName": "JustPrejudice",
        "sellersPhotoUrl": "https://www.biography.com/.image/t_share
        /MTE1ODA0OTcxNTQ2ODcxMzA5/jane-austen-9192819-1-402.jpg",
        "photoUrls": null
    }
```

We can also look to the Event Store UI and check the content of the upcasted events stream by going to `http://localhost:2113/web/index.html#/streams/UpcastedClassifiedAdEvents`. The stream shows one event, and when I click on it, I see the following content:

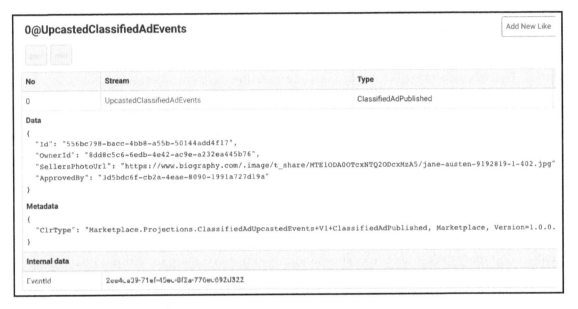

The consent of the upcasted event

Be aware that since we keep everything in memory, and our projections start from the very beginning of the `$all` stream each time the application starts, the up caster will handle the event again and will produce as many upcasted events as the number of times you run the application. The only way to avoid this is, of course, to store the stream position after we process each event. When we stop and start the application, we read the stored position and only start processing new events. We will dive into this in the next section.

Persistent storage

By now, we already have a few projections that build some useful read models that we can potentially use for the UI of our application. However, these read models aren't persistent and when we stop the app, everything disappears. Of course, read models are quickly rebuilt when we start the app again, and although it is a perfectly fine way to build read models at the beginning of the development cycle, this won't work for a production system. In addition, if we use upcasting, we will emit up cast events each time the app starts, since the upcasting subscription will process all events again. So, it is now time to persist our read models to a database.

Checkpoints

As we have seen before, our application reprocesses all events in all projections when we start it. That's because we give `Position.Start` as the initial position when we create a subscription in the `ProjectionManager` code. Since we want to store our read models in the database, we also need to start giving the subscription an actual position after processing events. This means that we also need to keep the position persisted somewhere. In different systems, such a position can be called differently. In event log systems, such as Kafka or Azure Event Hub, the term **offset** is used. Event Store uses the term **checkpoint** and this is what we are going to use in this book.

Ideally, we would keep the checkpoint in the same database as the read models for that subscription. For some database engines, it is even possible to wrap all read model updates and checkpoint updates into a single transaction, and that might be desirable. Using this method definitely makes the projection-handling code more complex, since a single transaction needs to pass through to all projections and to the checkpoint store.

We will be using RavenDB, and although it supports some sort of multi-document transactions, we won't be doing this to keep the code simpler. So, the first thing I need to do is to define an interface for the checkpoint store. For this, I add an `ICheckpointStore` file to the `Marketplace.Framework` project. The code is very simple; we only need a couple of methods, as follows:

```
using System.Threading.Tasks;
using EventStore.ClientAPI;

namespace Marketplace.Framework
{
    public interface ICheckpointStore
    {
        Task<Position> GetCheckpoint();
```

```
          Task StoreCheckpoint(Position checkpoint);
     }
}
```

Here, `Position` is the `struct` defined in the Event Store API, and we might want to try to avoid putting infrastructural dependencies in this project, but it will work for now.

We also need a document for RavenDB where the checkpoint will be stored. It needs to have an `Id` field of type string and the actual position:

```
using EventStore.ClientAPI;

namespace Marketplace.Infrastructure
{
    public class Checkpoint
    {
        public string Id { get; set; }
        public Position Position { get; set; }
    }
}
```

Next, we need to implement this interface. Since I plan to store everything in RavenDB, it would be logical to call the implementation, `RavenDbCheckpointStore`. I add this class to the `Marketplace` project in the `Infrastructure` folder:

```
using System;
using System.Threading.Tasks;
using EventStore.ClientAPI;
using Marketplace.Framework;
using Raven.Client.Documents.Session;

namespace Marketplace.Infrastructure
{
    public class RavenDbCheckpointStore : ICheckpointStore
    {
        private readonly Func<IAsyncDocumentSession> _getSession;
        private readonly string _checkpointName;

        public RavenDbCheckpointStore(
            Func<IAsyncDocumentSession> getSession,
            string checkpointName)
        {
            _getSession = getSession;
            _checkpointName = checkpointName;
        }

        public async Task<Position> GetCheckpoint()
```

```
    {
        using var session = _getSession();
        var checkpoint = await session
            .LoadAsync<Checkpoint>(_checkpointName);
        return checkpoint?.Position ?? Position.Start;
    }

    public async Task StoreCheckpoint(Position position)
    {
        using var session = _getSession();
        var checkpoint = await session
            .LoadAsync<Checkpoint>(_checkpointName);
        if (checkpoint == null)
        {
            checkpoint = new Checkpoint
            {
                Id = _checkpointName
            };
            await session.StoreAsync(checkpoint);
        }

        checkpoint.Position = position;
        await session.SaveChangesAsync();
    }
  }
}
```

Although the code is a bit long, it is not very complex. We need to give a session factory as a parameter for this class. We also need some sort of an identifier, in case we have multiple subscriptions. This checkpointName string will be used as the Checkpoint document ID.

In GetCheckpoint, we try to load the document, and if it doesn't exist, the method returns Position.Start, so that we can subscribe to the very beginning. It replicates the no-checkpoint situation and, in case you need to rebuild all read models from the ground up, you just need to remove this document, along with all documents for read models.

When we save the checkpoint, we must try loading one to see if it exists. If it does, we update it with the new position, otherwise, we store a new document.

The next thing is, of course, our `ProjectionManager`. It needs to be able to work with the checkpoint store. We don't need it to know about RavenDB since it is only needed for projections and the checkpoint store. But it needs to call the checkpoint store when making a subscription and to save the position after projecting each event. So, we need to add the `ICheckpointStore` parameter and call the two methods that this interface has, as follows:

```
using System.Linq;
using System.Threading.Tasks;
using EventStore.ClientAPI;
using Marketplace.Framework;
using Serilog;
using Serilog.Events;

namespace Marketplace.Infrastructure
{
    public class ProjectionManager
    {
        private readonly IEventStoreConnection _connection;
        private readonly ICheckpointStore _checkpointStore;
        private readonly IProjection[] _projections;
        private EventStoreAllCatchUpSubscription _subscription;

        public ProjectionManager(
            IEventStoreConnection connection,
            ICheckpointStore checkpointStore,
            params IProjection[] projections)
        {
            _connection = connection;
            _checkpointStore = checkpointStore;
            _projections = projections;
        }

        public async Task Start()
        {
            var settings = new CatchUpSubscriptionSettings(2000, 500,
                Log.IsEnabled(LogEventLevel.Verbose),
                false, "try-out-subscription");

            var position = await _checkpointStore.GetCheckpoint();
            _subscription = _connection.SubscribeToAllFrom(position,
                settings, EventAppeared);
        }

        public void Stop() => _subscription.Stop();

        private async Task EventAppeared(
            EventStoreCatchUpSubscription _,
```

```
                    ResolvedEvent resolvedEvent)
           {
               if (resolvedEvent.Event.EventType.StartsWith("$")) return;
               var @event = resolvedEvent.Deserialzie();
               Log.Debug("Projecting event {type}",
                   @event.GetType().Name);
               await Task.WhenAll(_projections.Select(
                   x => x.Project(@event)));

               await _checkpointStore.StoreCheckpoint(
                   resolvedEvent.OriginalPosition.Value);
           }
       }
   }
```

Persisting read models

Since we need RavenDb anyway, I used some code from Chapter 10, *Event Sourcing*, but
made it a little more advanced. I moved the initialization of the document store to a
separate method in the Startup class. The method will use the appsettings.json
configuration section instead of hard coded values. It will also create the database if it
doesn't exist, so we don't need to create it manually. It is not important for the content of
this chapter to know how the database is configured, you can check the code snippet of the
book to see how it is done. Check the settings file there as well, to see the configuration
structure.

After these changes are made, I need to change the Startup.ConfigureServices
method, so it calls the store initialization method. We need to have a document session
factory and also register IAsyncDocumentSession in the services collection since we'll
need it in the query API controller. Here are some of the changes in the registration:

```
var documentStore = ConfigureRavenDb(
    Configuration.GetSection("ravenDb"));

Func<IAsyncDocumentSession> getSession =
    () => documentStore.OpenAsyncSession();

services.AddTransient(c => getSession());
```

To make things simpler for individual projections, since they all will be using RavenDB for now, I created a simple base abstract class called `RavenDbProjecion`. It accepts the session factory for its constructor and contains a helpful method to execute updates on read model documents and that's why the class is a generic class, so we will use the read model class type as a generic parameter:

```
using System;
using System.Linq.Expressions;
using System.Threading.Tasks;
using Marketplace.Framework;
using Raven.Client.Documents;
using Raven.Client.Documents.Linq;
using Raven.Client.Documents.Session;

namespace Marketplace.Infrastructure
{
    public abstract class RavenDbProjection<T> : IProjection
    {
        protected RavenDbProjection(
            Func<IAsyncDocumentSession> getSession
        )
            => GetSession = getSession;

        protected Func<IAsyncDocumentSession> GetSession { get; }

        public abstract Task Project(object @event);

        protected Task Create(Func<Task<T>> model)
            => UsingSession(
                async session =>
                    await session.StoreAsync(await model())
            );

        protected Task UpdateOne(Guid id, Action<T> update)
            => UsingSession(
                session =>
                    UpdateItem(session, id, update)
            );

        protected Task UpdateWhere(
            Expression<Func<T, bool>> where,
            Action<T> update
        ) => UsingSession(
            session =>
                UpdateMultipleItems(
                    session, where, update
                )
```

```
    );

    private static async Task UpdateItem(
        IAsyncDocumentSession session, Guid id,
        Action<T> update
    )
    {
        var item = await session
            .LoadAsync<T>(id.ToString());

        if (item == null) return;

        update(item);
    }

    async Task UpdateMultipleItems(
        IAsyncDocumentSession session,
        Expression<Func<T, bool>> query, Action<T> update
    )
    {
        var items = await session
            .Query<T>()
            .Where(query)
            .ToListAsync();
        foreach (var item in items)
            update(item);
    }

    protected async Task UsingSession(
        Func<IAsyncDocumentSession, Task> operation
    )
    {
        using var session = GetSession();

        await operation(session);
        await session.SaveChangesAsync();
    }
    }
}
```

You have already seen `UpdateItem` and `UpdateMultipleItems`, which were implemented inside projection classes. Since the code is very similar, I was able to isolate it in the abstract class. I also made these methods private and made three methods with simpler signatures: `Create`, `UpdatedOne`, and `UpdateWhere`. Notice also the `UsingSession` method.

Since we are using the session factory, it will be our responsibility to dispose of it after use. To avoid the endless noise of the using statement in the projection code, we will be calling the UsingSession method that will do it for us. It also persists all changes that are done by the delegate that it calls before disposing of the session.

In order to save read models as documents to RavenDB, we must comply with the database engine conventions to make our life simpler. Therefore, we must change all identity properties to have the Id name and the type string (now we have Guid). In all places where type mismatches, I changed usages of Guid fields by calling ToString().

Now we are ready to convert the simplest projection to use RavenDB, and this will be the UserDetailsProjection. I changed it to inherit from the RavenDbProjection abstract class, so the helper method can go away. We need a constructor since it is required by the base class, but overall, the code is now smaller. The only real change was that I used those new helper methods to make the code simpler. Here is the new code:

```
using System;
using System.Threading.Tasks;
using Marketplace.Domain.UserProfile;
using Marketplace.Infrastructure;
using Raven.Client.Documents.Session;

namespace Marketplace.Projections
{
    public class UserDetailsProjection
        : RavenDbProjection<ReadModels.UserDetails>
    {
        public UserDetailsProjection(
            Func<IAsyncDocumentSession> getSession
        ) : base(getSession) { }

        public override Task Project(object @event) =>
            @event switch
            {
                Events.UserRegistered e =>
                    Create(
                        () => Task.FromResult(
                            new ReadModels.UserDetails
                            {
                                Id = e.UserId.ToString(),
                                DisplayName = e.DisplayName
                            }
                        )
                    ),
                Events.UserDisplayNameUpdated e =>
                    UpdateOne(
```

```
                                e.UserId,
                                x => x.DisplayName = e.DisplayName
                            ),
                        Events.ProfilePhotoUploaded e =>
                            UpdateOne(
                                e.UserId,
                                x => x.PhotoUrl = e.PhotoUrl
                            ),
                        _ => Task.CompletedTask
                };
        }
    }
```

Our second projection is more serious, so we need to make more changes, but still, the difference is not huge. We need to give it the session factory too, since it is required for the `RavenDbProjection` base class. An important change is that, since we can imagine the user display name query to be asynchronous, we need to change the delegate signature to return `Task<string>` instead of a string. All other changes are related to implementing updates by calling the `Update` and `UpdateWhere` methods of the base class. One thing to notice, in addition to this, is related to the asynchronous query of the user profile, so when we call the query, we need to await the call. Here is the full code:

```
using System;
using System.Linq.Expressions;
using System.Threading.Tasks;
using Marketplace.ClassifiedAd;
using Marketplace.Infrastructure;
using Raven.Client.Documents.Session;
using static Marketplace.Domain.ClassifiedAd.Events;
using static Marketplace.Domain.UserProfile.Events;
using static Marketplace.Projections.ClassifiedAdUpcastedEvents;
using static Marketplace.Projections.ReadModels;

namespace Marketplace.Projections
{
    public class ClassifiedAdDetailsProjection
        : RavenDbProjection<ClassifiedAdDetails>
    {
        private readonly Func<Guid, Task<string>>
            _getUserDisplayName;

        public ClassifiedAdDetailsProjection(
            Func<IAsyncDocumentSession> getSession,
            Func<Guid, Task<string>> getUserDisplayName
        )
            : base(getSession)
            => _getUserDisplayName = getUserDisplayName;
```

```
public override Task Project(object @event) =>
    @event switch
    {
        ClassifiedAdCreated e =>
            Create(async () =>
                new ClassifiedAdDetails
                {
                    Id = e.Id.ToString(),
                    SellerId = e.OwnerId,
                    SellersDisplayName =
                        await _getUserDisplayName(
                            e.OwnerId
                        )
                }
            ),
        ClassifiedAdTitleChanged e =>
            UpdateOne(e.Id, ad => ad.Title = e.Title),
        ClassifiedAdTextUpdated e =>
            UpdateOne(e.Id, ad => ad.Description = e.AdText),
        ClassifiedAdPriceUpdated e =>
            UpdateOne(
                e.Id,
                ad =>
                {
                    ad.Price = e.Price;
                    ad.CurrencyCode = e.CurrencyCode;
                }
            ),
        UserDisplayNameUpdated e =>
            UpdateWhere(
                x => x.SellerId == e.UserId,
                x => x.SellersDisplayName = e.DisplayName
            ),
        V1.ClassifiedAdPublished e =>
            UpdateOne(
                e.Id,
                ad => ad.SellersPhotoUrl = e.SellersPhotoUrl
            ),
        _ => Task.CompletedTask
    };
    }
}
```

The last projection is our up caster. Since it doesn't use RavenDB, there is no need to inherit it from the base class. The only change I needed to make there is to change the query delegate so that it will return `Task<string>`, and the query call needs to be awaited:

```
var photoUrl = await _getUserPhoto(e.OwnerId);
```

I won't be putting the full class code here, since the changes are minimal.

One thing to take care of is, of course, to create those queries in the `UserDetails` read model, since we won't be going to a simple `List`. To make the code a little simpler, I created a small class called `Queries` in the `ReadModels.UserDetails` namespace, with one method that will obtain the profile for a single user:

```
using System;
using System.Threading.Tasks;
using Raven.Client.Documents.Session;
using static Marketplace.Projections.ReadModels;

namespace Marketplace.UserProfile
{
    public static class Queries
    {
        public static Task<UserDetails> GetUserDetails(
            this Func<IAsyncDocumentSession> getSession,
            Guid id
        )
        {
            using var session = getSession();

            return session.LoadAsync<UserDetails>(id.ToString());
        }
    }
}
```

This is an extension method not to the session object itself, but to a session factory, since we must dispose of the session after calling this query. This will be different for controllers, since there, the service collection will give us a session as a transient dependency.

Wrapping up

All we need to do now is some wiring and make some small changes in the query API controller.

First, the `EventStoreService` class needs to await the call to `projectionManager.Start()`, since this method is now `async`. Then, we need to fix the query API controller, by making changes to the `Queries` extensions class to use the document session:

```
using System.Threading.Tasks;
using Raven.Client.Documents.Session;
using static Marketplace.ClassifiedAd.QueryModels;
using static Marketplace.Projections.ReadModels;

namespace Marketplace.ClassifiedAd
{
    public static class Queries
    {
        public static Task<ClassifiedAdDetails> Query(
            this IAsyncDocumentSession session,
            GetPublicClassifiedAd query
        ) =>
            session.LoadAsync<ClassifiedAdDetails>(
                query.ClassifiedAdId.ToString()
            );
    }
}
```

Since the query is now asynchronous, we need to prepare our `RequestHandler.HandleQuery` so that it can await the query, and also return `Task<IActionResult>` so the controller can be `async` as well:

```
public static async Task<IActionResult> HandleQuery<TModel>(
    Func<Task<TModel>> query, ILogger log)
{
    try
    {
        return new OkObjectResult(await query());
    }
    catch (Exception e)
    {
        log.Error(e, "Error handling the query");
        return new BadRequestObjectResult(
            new
            {
                error = e.Message, stackTrace = e.StackTrace
            });
    }
}
```

The last change for the API will be to fix the controller itself so that it can get the session injected as a dependency and become `async`:

```
using System.Threading.Tasks;
using Marketplace.Infrastructure;
using Microsoft.AspNetCore.Mvc;
using Raven.Client.Documents.Session;
using Serilog;

namespace Marketplace.ClassifiedAd
{
    [Route("/ad")]
    public class ClassifiedAdsQueryApi : Controller
    {
        private readonly IAsyncDocumentSession _session;
        private static ILogger _log =
        Log.ForContext<ClassifiedAdsQueryApi>();
        public ClassifiedAdsQueryApi(IAsyncDocumentSession session) =>
            _session = session;

        [HttpGet]
        public Task<IActionResult>
        Get(QueryModels.GetPublicClassifiedAd request)
            => RequestHandler.HandleQuery(() =>
                _session.Query(request), _log);
    }
}
```

The final thing to fix is the `Startup` class. I already mentioned the RavenDB initialization and the preceding registration code. We only need to make a few necessary changes to register our projection manager and all projections. Remember that we changed the query delegates to be async, so there are quite a few changes in the following lines of code:

```
var projectionManager = new ProjectionManager(esConnection,
    new RavenDbCheckpointStore(getSession, "readmodels"),
    new ClassifiedAdDetailsProjection(getSession,
        async userId => (await
        getSession.GetUserDetails(userId))?.DisplayName),
    new ClassifiedAdUpcasters(esConnection,
        async userId => (await
        getSession.GetUserDetails(userId))?.PhotoUrl),
        new UserDetailsProjection(getSession)));
```

First, we added the checkpoint store parameter. Then, we added the session factory as a parameter to two projections that use RavenDB. Finally, both queries became async and used the same session factory combined with our new query extension.

All is done, and it is now time to run the application and see what happens.

After I pressed *F5*, I saw messages in the log that the same events as we saw earlier are being projected. This is expected, since we started from scratch again. Now I can call the query API again to see that the result is just as I expected it to be. If I start the application again, it produces no logs from projections, since now we persisted the checkpoint and started the subscription from where we stopped. So, unless we start making new operations, we won't get new events. Our application will be processing all updates in real time from now on.

Let's see what have we got in the database. When I open the RavenDB Studio UI by going to `http://localhost:8080`, I see that the `Marketplace_Chapter11` database is present, so I can click on it and check the content. In the database, I found three documents in different collections, as follows:

Three collections in RavenDB

Two of these documents are our read models and one document is the checkpoint. Let's see what the `ClassifiedAdDetails` document contains. As expected, we got all the information that we were projecting from our events:

The read model as a RavenDB document

Now we can check what the checkpoint document contains. It has the ID of our checkpoint name and the JSON content is something like the following (you might have different values):

```
{
    "Position": {
        "CommitPosition": 48771203,
        "PreparePosition": 48771203
    },
    "@metadata": {
        "@collection": "Checkpoints",
        "Raven-Clr-Type": "Marketplace.Infrastructure.Checkpoint,
Marketplace"
    }
}
```

By this point, we have all read models properly stored in the database, so we can build more queries from it, just like we did in Chapter 9, *CQRS - The Read Side*.

Summary

In this chapter, we took CQRS to a whole new level and learned how to query data that we initially stored as streams of events. Since event streams are hard to query on demand, we need to build snapshots of data that we can show to our users. The power of event-sourced read models is that we can build virtually an unlimited number of use case-specific read models, with very precise sets of data. We could avoid things such as joins across object collections or tables, or even between remote services. We can remove all read models at once and rebuild them from scratch, using only events. If we somehow created our projection in a way that it showed the wrong data on screen, then we can quickly catch the bug and fix the read models by removing and rebuilding them.

Of course, everything has its trade-offs. Sometimes, we can't receive all the data that we need for a read model from the event that we project. However, we went through several techniques to avoid this limitation.

Still, we should remember that when the system grows, the number of events grows too, and building a new read model or rebuilding the one that existed before, but had a bug that we needed to fix and then build all records in the database again, may take a very long time. For systems with billions of events, it can take days or even weeks. There are ways to improve performance for projections, which I will mention later when we discuss the advanced topics of event sourcing. However, remember, by default, events are projected sequentially and the order is very important. So, the usual techniques that we apply in the messaging world, such as competing consumers for horizontal scaling, aren't directly applicable for projections. It is possible, however, to partition projections by splitting the `$all` stream into several streams by a given property. Event Store projections that are written in JavaScript and run directly on the server can be used for that purpose.

While we have gone through some quite advanced topics already, the last few chapters have been very technical. In `Chapter 13`, *Splitting the System*, we return to the concepts of **Domain-Driven Design (DDD)**, and will discuss the most important idea of DDD—that no complex system in the problem space can be implemented as a single system in the solution space. We will go on to the topic of bounded context and context mapping.

12
Bounded Context

So far, we have spent quite a lot of time working on our `Marketplace` system, as it will be a single application with one API and, possibly, one web UI that will talk to that API to serve its users. However, now it is time to take a step back and look at the big picture.

I've been writing software since the age of 15; so, as of writing this book, my experience in the industry is close to 30 years. Some systems that I've built have been replaced by something new and some are still very active, being developed further by other developers. Today, as I go along in the industry as a software architect and a consultant, I am involved in many hands-on activities, such as prototyping, modeling, and writing production code. Over the years, not only have I progressed as a developer so I write better-quality code, but I have also understood more about the foundational principles of building complex systems. This knowledge and experience allow me to be more successful with the companies I work for to create systems that will evolve and not need major rewrites in a couple of years.

One of the things that I believe made me a better developer and architect is the realization that systems can rarely be modeled as something singular and unbreakable, as a single unit. We already discussed the contextual nature of language in Chapter 2, *Language and Context*, and that hopefully led you to understand the importance of context.

During my career, I have seen many complex systems that were implemented as a single code base, with a single data model supporting it. In this chapter, we are going to look closer at this approach and, hopefully, I will convince you that it does not always work and there is a better way. We will spend some time discussing how the language context can be used to discover parts of the whole system that could be developed more efficiently with a good degree of isolation and autonomy.

In this chapter, you will learn:

- How linguistic boundaries can help identify system boundaries
- The definition of Bounded Context
- The benefits of splitting systems into parts
- Which factors need to be considered when context boundaries aren't clear

The single model trap

Let's take a look at how software usually starts its life, when developers first get their hands on keyboards and start writing code, hoping to build something useful. We will follow the usual progress that software companies (or IT departments) make while addressing the needs of their users, over the years they spent, working to make the software more useful, adding features and fixing issues. What I describe next is the usual evolutionary growth of software solutions that can be found everywhere. It is possible that some parts of the picture that I am going to paint will be recognizable to you and will resonate with your experience.

Starting small

We rarely find ourselves working for a company that has colossal plans to conquer the world with majestic software that solves a huge problem for humanity. Well, some businesses try but inevitably fail, and that's probably one of the well-learned lessons that people rarely forget. More often than not, businesses are trying to solve real problems that people are dealing with frequently. At least, that's what people that run the company believe. So, as a developer, you probably would work on a system with a reasonable scale, unless you work for a software giant such as Microsoft or SAP. But make no mistake, they started small as well, although most people forget that.

When a couple of developers start working on a system, everything works quite well because the team is small and the goal is hopefully quite clear. If the problem they are aiming to solve is real and the solution is viable, the company would probably start making some money rather quickly, after spending a year or two to build the first version of the software. By that time, the system would still be reasonably small and the number of people building it won't exceed a handful of engineers. Companies such as Uber, AirBnB, and GitHub all started that way.

In the beginning, everything is fine. Then, at some point, the system becomes quite large and the productivity starts to decrease due to the size of the system. One single data model is being changed for many different reasons, conflicting interests of multiple product owners of project managers that all have their own teams working on different parts of the system start to struggle with a growing number of conflicts. The coordination effort grows since different teams touch places in the systems that they didn't expect to, but they must in order to do their work. But often such changes interfere with other teams' work. Releases are being heavily coordinated and the effort of making a release sometimes exceeds the effort of creating features. The company never releases on Friday, because the risk is too high and people are almost certain that there are bugs that weren't caught during the testing phase, although the QA team is doing their best. Fixing bugs becomes a challenging and daunting task; by fixing one bug developers create two more.

Does this sound familiar to you? If not—you are very lucky, probably the company you work for is already doing DDD or something similar. For me, after spending decades in the industry, this is a very common situation. To be honest, I've never worked in a company that hasn't had those issues. So, how did such a small and concise system eventually become an unmanageable monster that developers don't dare touch?

Complexity, again

If you have some years of experience in the software development industry and have worked at one or more companies, you've probably worked on some production systems. Systems that are in production usually bring value to their users in one way or another. Such a system could be a product that people around the world use to solve their daily tasks, such as buying goods online or tracking their pets on a live map. Other systems are used internally to support company employees in what they do and by doing so, contributing indirectly to the value chain. That could be, for example, supply management, finance, billing, scheduling, or yield-management systems. Many companies develop their internal systems, which embrace the highest level of the domain knowledge that has been inherited by a long, successful history of a company's way of doing things over the years.

Usually, people need software to solve complex problems. Complex problems can rarely be solved by simple solutions; we spent a good deal of time discussing this matter in Chapter 1, *Why Domain-Driven Design?* and Chapter 2, *Language and Context*. One inevitable aspect of dealing with a complex system is that such systems grow over time. Engineers grasp more and more of the business insight and capture the ever-changing needs of their users in code. Unavoidably, such evolutionary progress leads to the ever-increasing complexity of the software, reflecting the complexity of business problems that the software is trying to address.

So, even if the original plan is to build a rather simple solution to fix one or two things that we think people struggle with in their daily work, hoping that they will thank us for it by buying our product, we find ourselves on a slippery slope from the start. Our users would never be fully satisfied. No one wants to pay continuously for something that doesn't evolve. So, unless you are building a simple, catchy game app for a smartphone, hoping for millions of users to pay you once, you are probably building software that evolves over time.

More often than not, we cannot create a model for our software that will be valid for many years. Our understanding of the domain changes, our ignorance decreases, and we learn more about our users and their wishes. Something that was clear three months ago is not as clear today, and the model that was perfectly fine last year is now an obstacle. But, do we keep spending the time to find a better model and refactor our code to reflect these new insights? Well, not always.

When the system is new and the market pressure is high, developers are being pushed to deliver new features instead. So, the software just grows, in the number of features, number of lines of code, number of database tables, and the relations between them. We have no time to take a break, take a deep breath, and look at the model to see whether it can be improved. I won't even mention the time to refactor the code for features that have already been delivered—what's done is done; the project manager would rarely understand the need to rewrite code that already works.

But that is not the worst part of it. As I mentioned before, nearly all systems start with a small code base. A small persistence model, or what we hear more often, the *data model*, comes along. We might not even have a class diagram, but most certainly someone spent time creating a relational model for the system, because relational databases are seen as the *default* choice to persist almost anything in this world, especially if you are working in a .NET space that is dominated by enterprises and companies that prefer using everything from Microsoft. So, SQL Server it is, most of the time.

New features lead to changes in the data model, new tables are added, new fields are added to the existing tables and before you realize, when you want to get anything from your database, you have to write a query with five inner joins because your DBA says that the database must be normalized and data duplication is evil. But some tables have so much data that you cannot just add a new field with a NOT NULL constraint, so you must add a couple of left outer joins as well. Of course, there are a couple of hundred stored procedures here and there, since it is faster that way and some people who worked here before you were better at writing SQL than C#. But stored procedures cannot be tested in isolation, and everything is tested on a copy of the production database. To add an insult to injury, there are no unit tests for the SQL code because the QA engineer will do regression tests manually anyway. Some stored procedures are so old that people prefer adding code at the end and don't dare touch the existing code for fear of breaking things because, well, there are no tests for stored procedures. Tables are well-known to be unavailable for the *find usages* feature of Visual Studio, so nobody really knows whether that particular table is being used for any query, although it occupies one gigabyte of the disk space that we tried to save by applying the third-level normalization to the database in the first place.

Maybe the picture I had drawn here is too dark, but I've seen it some many times during my decades of working in the industry that it is very hard for me to make it any softer. Does all or some of it sound familiar to you as well? So, where exactly did it go wrong? Surely, we can blame SQL databases for everything and try to change them to something fancier, but would we ever be sure that by doing such a thing we solve any of the aforementioned issues? At the end of the day, databases are just tools and like any other tool, it is used or misused.

Big ball of mud

What I described in the previous section is a pattern (or, more precisely, anti-pattern) known as *Big Ball of Mud*. The term was suggested by Brian Marick and then popularized by Brian Foote and Joseph Yoder in their paper called, unsurprisingly, *Big Ball of Mud*, published in 1997 (http://www.laputan.org/mud/).

Developers don't intentionally create software that later can be characterized by this awful term. We constantly work under pressure of the management, who want to get value from the software that we build and they see the value as new features. So, we don't really find time to improve the structure of our software. At least, this is the most common excuse that we give when someone asks us why the code is so convoluted and hard to maintain.

But, is it true? Is that the sole reason that exists for us to forget about the architecture and design? Certainly, the given reason is a valid one, but not the only one. What we tend to forget is that we don't really build systems. Such systems already exist and our software becomes part of some system.

Think about any kind of business. If you work for a bank, the bank is the system. It probably existed before without the software that is currently being used by the bank employees. Banks are interconnected and heavily regulated. They have customers with certain expectations about the reliability of the service provided by banks and the safety of their funds. This is just one of the countless examples that we can find around us.

Repeatedly, we make the same mistake of developing software that we see as a system on its own, ignoring the fact that it is just a part of something bigger, which is, in itself, a system. As I wrote before, software usually solves complex problems and therefore exists as a part of a larger landscape of some complex system. So, what is the system?

In the book *Thinking in Systems* by Donella H. Meadows, has defined system as an element set, which is interconnected. Such elements are organized in a coherent manner.

There are surprisingly many things we can learn from such a short definition; for now, let's concentrate on the fact that no system consists of just one part and the parts of the system are always interconnected, exchanging information between them, and that is something we often forget about. System parts are not classes, modules, database tables, or stored procedures. These are atoms of a certain system part. What we usually do is try to put too many parts in one box and call it a software system. Let's check one trivial example to illustrate the inevitable path that leads us to the big ball of mud.

Think about an e-commerce system that deals with customer orders. Obviously, we need somewhere to keep information about all the products we sell. Definitely, we must be able to place orders and follow the order cycle, from the moment an order is placed until it is delivered. We start small and create a simple model, such as this one:

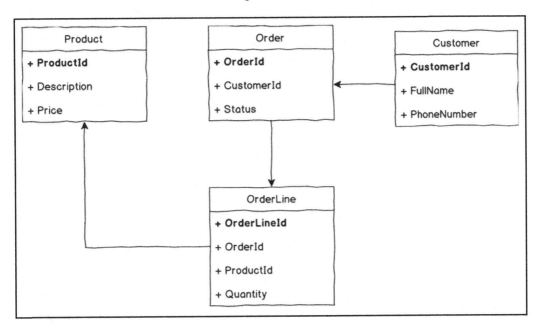

Simple e-commerce model

Of course, after a little while, we realize that the price on each order line cannot refer to the product price and must be fixed at the moment the line is created, so we implement that as well. Later, we get a requirement to keep the supplier information as well. Then, we must add a product image URL. When we start doing things for real, we must keep the stock-level information. Not long after that, we get a requirement to add the product-packaging information and the dimensions along with the weight, to be able to calculate shipping costs. Before we know it, our model looks quite a bit different:

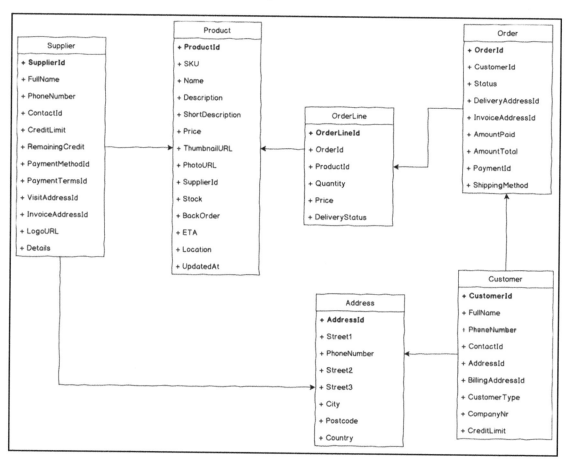

The model becomes larger with time

You might notice that the full model is certainly different since you can find references such as `PaymentMethodId`, `PaymentTermsId`, and `PaymentId`, which must point to some tables as well. But I think this is enough to show the essence of it.

My point here is that we can clearly see that a small original model uncontrollably grew, following the requirements coming from different directions, trying to satisfy all needs at once. You might notice one field of the `Product` table, called `UpdatedAt`. I haven't invented it but found it on a sample model, posted as the answer to some question on Stack Overflow. Now, let's imagine what the significance of the date we put in this field was. Was the name of the product updated on that date? Or the price? Or, perhaps, the stock level? All those changes have completely different reasons; however, we only have one field to keep the date and time of the change.

What is the danger of having a model such as this? At the end of the day, there are countless products that have such models in their backend and some of them are even quite successful. Not so much, I would say. Such companies and products usually thrive despite having such a model, not because of it. Let's see what happens when features are requested by different stakeholders:

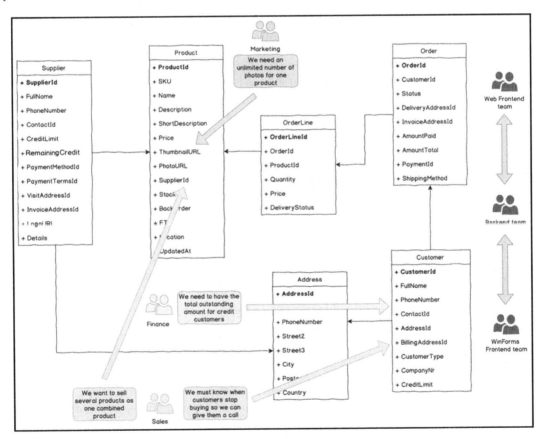

Coupling is not only for code. It applies to the whole organization.

The sales team is now interested in selling the product in packages. They tell us that it is quite simple—we just need to create *a special type of product* and a simple child-parent relationship. They don't really think about the supply chain but we currently have all this information in one place. If different components of this fictitious packaged product come from different suppliers, who will actually be *the* supplier for it? The stock level is even trickier, it seems like we must calculate on-demand?

The sales team also wants to have a tighter relationship with customers and give them a call when they stop buying from us. Maybe they have found another supplier and we can offer them a discount? To do that, we *simply* need to keep track of the running total of all sales for each customer and compare the numbers with our history. But, we don't have any history, so where do we get such data in the first place?

The finance team wants to see the total outstanding amount of customers who pay after they get the product, so-called **credit line customers**. If they are late with their payment, the finance department should decide different strategies for the debt collection, based on the amount. They see it as *just add another field* to the `Customer` table.

We also have to address the request of the marketing team. They want to improve sales by showing more photos of a product. Right now, we have only one and they want at least three; but ideally, they need an unlimited number of pictures for any product. So, we either need to *just add two more fields* to the `Product` table or add a new table for photos with the many-to-many relationship; but in the latter case, we'll have to deal with data migrations.

All those requests are potentially conflicting. We can clearly see that the same parts of the model will be touched when developers will be working on those new features. Let's add more damage to the picture and remember that we have three development teams. One team is only doing changes at the backend, two other teams are doing the frontend work—one for the web and the other for the legacy WinForm client.

The issue now is that we have three conflicting forces that push their requests through to developers, and in addition, we have three conflicting development teams working on the same parts of the model. It is hard to imagine that any of the frontend teams will be able to finish their work before the backend team will do the necessary changes to the database model and for all necessary layers if they have any.

Overall, we can see that the singular model for anything less trivial than a `Hello World` application would most probably lead to a big ball of mud. It might happen in a couple of months, but with a small team of good developers, a company might be happy with such a model for quite a while. But as soon as the business and the system grow, the mud monster will come and potentially do a lot of harm. At the very least, productivity will suffer. At most, the customers will get so annoyed by the lack of progress and the overall application performance that they will leave.

Structuring systems

I know I've been painting a somewhat horrifying picture so far now—when software undeniably slips toward becoming an unmanageable clew of spaghetti code. You might be wondering: what's the point if we end up in the land of horror anyway? When we find ourselves there, we can start fresh, and learn from the past to build a new, shiny, bright system, with the newest technology and everything will be fine again. We will get back to the big rewrite topic later on, but for now, let's think about why the new system would be better than the old one.

No matter whether we are planning to create a new software system or to refactor the old one, there is at least one thing we can do to ensure that we keep our software in good shape for quite a long time. We might not be able to use the most beloved programming language, the new, shiny silver-bullet framework, or a fancy new database, because our organization has certain constraints that are hard or impossible to fight against. These constraints rarely impose significant limitations on how we design our models. In the design of domain, models are where we can find the key to building better software.

In `Chapter 3`, *EventStorming*, we discussed domain models. We should remember that models don't represent the real world. Instead, models provide a simplified version of the real world that is relevant for building a particular piece of software. Throughout this book, we've learned to avoid giving more information and behavior to our models than was absolutely necessary in order to solve the specific problems that we are aiming to solve with our software.

But now we see that as the number of concerns for the software grows, the amount of required information in the model grows as well. At the same time, we clearly see that this information is put together into a single model deliberately by developers, who tend to enrich the domain object with unrelated properties. It usually happens because the domain object name seems to be the same across different domains, but developers don't realize this.

Now, we are going to look at how we can structure our software better, providing clear separation for concepts with similar names but different meanings. DDD offers the concept of *Bounded Context* to define such separation and we are going to look at how to find and define boundaries for such contexts.

Make no mistake, when I write about structuring the system, going away from a single model and introducing boundaries, this doesn't imply having multiple executables, using microservices, migration to Docker, and so on. Bringing sanity to domain models is the most important topic and we will touch upon the implementation details in the next chapter.

Linguistic boundaries

Remember that we talked about the *speed of change* when we were going through the aggregate design topic? So, you might wonder if we are going in circles right now. Indeed, we can clearly see that things such as the thumbnail URL or the photo URL of the product have nothing to do with the product price or stock level. The stock level might change every second if the product is popular and we have enough customers. The price might be dynamic as well, but we could expect it to be more stable. Photos, however, will probably never change, along with the weight and the packaging size. Keeping all this information in one aggregate is not something we'd embrace and we learned about this already.

Where, then, do we keep it? Do we create several aggregates, all called `Product`? Although that might sound weird, the answer could be *yes* if we can identify the boundaries where each of those aggregates will live. We must also talk to our domain experts and gain more insight, at least about the language. Some new discoveries could await us there, such as the inventory level is indeed being referred to as `Inventory` and not `Product`. But for some other areas, such as sales, marketing, and procurement, they may use the same term and mean different things. As we learned in `Chapter 2`, *Language and Context*, we can see the context is changing there.

When I see very common words such as `Customer`, `Person`, `Contact`, or `Order` scattered upon a large code base, an alarm bell goes off in my head. Here be dragons or, to be more specific, the big ball of mud. Developers of this system weren't cautious enough to dive deeper into the domain specifics to find what these terms mean in different parts of the business. If we look at the `Product` example in the previous diagram, we could see unrelated concepts placed in one object for no particular reason.

I can't stress enough how dangerous this approach is for the software and beyond. Think about a meeting you might have with two domain experts. One would be telling you about adding more pictures to the product to enrich the catalog. Another one is only interested in the delivery process and needs to have the product weight and packaging details to calculate the shipping costs. You might notice the difference in their language, and from such a conversation you might learn that the single model that you already have or plan to implement won't suit the business.

So, defining bounded contexts about the meaning of words, looking for particularities, and being eager to truly understand the context where these words are being used is the first and the most powerful method to find context boundaries:

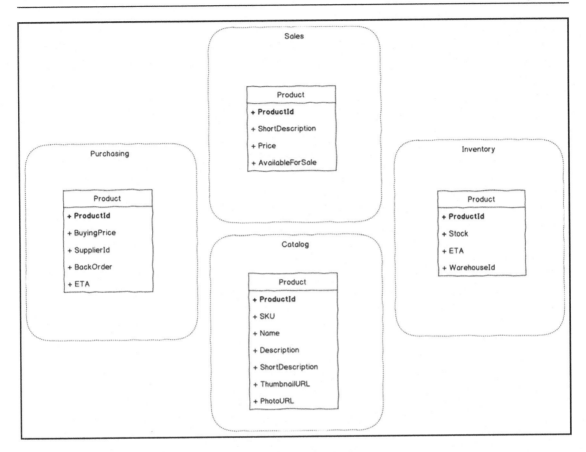

Words change meaning in a context

As you can see, one single term that is used in a different context with a different meaning can be modeled inside its own context with a concise meaning. Instead of a single object with unrelated properties, we now have several. Those new objects are much smaller and contain only the information that is relevant to the specific context. Making a change to an object in one context should have no effect on all other objects with the same name in other contexts, and it can be made freely by the developer that works with the context where these changes are being made, eliminating, or at least minimizing, the risk of introducing issues elsewhere. Naturally, this brings us to the next purpose and benefit of bounded contexts: the autonomy of development teams.

Another aspect of context boundaries is the extended *Tell, Don't Ask* principle. The original principle was formulated by Alec Sharp in his book *Smalltalk by Example*, published in 1997.

As you might have noticed from your own experience, there is a lot of code out there in production software that uses procedural style, even if it is written in an object-oriented language. Unfortunately, .NET-based projects suffer from this a lot, especially those that are written using WinForms and ASP.NET (`https://dotnet.microsoft.com/apps/aspnet`) WebForms. I've seen many applications where the business logic is concentrated inside the code—behind UI elements, scattered across numerous `OnClick` event handlers.

Better-designed software uses separate classes to implement business logic. The pattern that embraces the isolation of the business logic from the UI logic and the persistence is known as **multilayer architecture** or **n-tier architecture**. Wikipedia defines this term as a *client-server* type of architecture, but that is not exactly correct. You can have multiple layers without separating client and server code if the application is a desktop rich-client application or a web application with server-side rendering, where all actions cause a roundtrip to the server.

When we are looking for context boundaries, one of the indicators that can help in finding them is the availability of information that is needed to make decisions. When users (which could potentially include other systems) send commands to the domain model, the model itself must be able to handle this command without going to other parts of the system to fetch information. That might be confusing at the beginning because, at first glance, we might see that some commands require a lot of information that we considered to be located outside of the context where the command is executed. Let's take a look at the e-commerce example again:

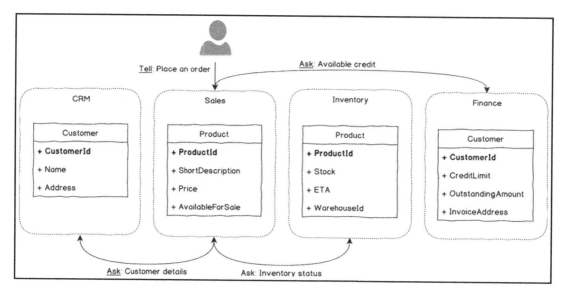

Several queries are needed to make a decision

When we tell the domain model of the `Sales` context to place an order, it seems to require a lot of information from other contexts to make decisions for the command's execution. This can create quite a lot of confusion, and if we follow our gut without thought, we would hardly resist the urge to put all the information from the whole system in one place. And, the big ball of mud strikes again.

In reality, we only need a fraction of the information from other contexts to make that decision. Besides, if we consider commands that affect that information, we could quite clearly see that none of them will be touching the sales context. For example, the inventory level is updated solely inside the `Inventory` context. The available credit limit for a customer is balanced between the agreed initial credit limit and the number of unpaid invoices. Contact details of the customer are updated in a completely independent fashion from anything else.

But, you might have noticed that there is still some level of information exchange. How does the inventory level change? How does the unpaid amount for the customer get updated? Surely, there are some actions that trigger those updates. We feel that somehow these triggers are linked to the order processing and that might even increase our certainty to put everything together, again.

But wait a minute. The inventory level doesn't necessarily decrease when the order is placed. We might need to clarify that with domain experts, but most certainly, the inventory only gets updated when the order is shipped and that's probably not handled by `Sales` but by the `Shipment` context instead. The same happens with the total outstanding amount—it probably only gets updated when we send an invoice for the order. That, in turn, might only happen when the order is shipped or even delivered. So, you can see that these links between contexts are not really that direct and straightforward. There is more logic involved that we might not even consider at first glance.

The topic of cross-context communication will be briefly touched upon in the next chapter, but even now I can tell you that it happens by the same *Tell, Don't Ask* principle. Contexts emit domain events after executing each command, as we learned in `Chapter 3`, *EventStorming*, and even implemented in the earlier chapters. We never used those events to share the information, but that's exactly how the necessary—and only the necessary—data gets across context boundaries. So, we might need to have some context-specific objects that we haven't originally considered. Let's look at the revised diagram of the `Place an order` command and the details needed to execute it:

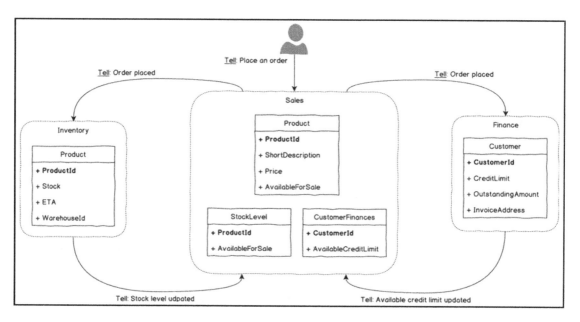

Tell-only flow

Here, you can see that there are no *ask* arrows anymore. All we do is *tell* others either to do something, or that something has been done.

There are two points that I would like to draw your attention to:

- You might wonder why the CRM context is not sharing any information with the `Sales` context. Don't we need customer details to place an order? Not exactly. We might need this information to know the customer's name and contact details to know where the order needs to be delivered. But none of those details is required to decide whether we can place the order. Of course, we might get more complicated requirements, when orders for certain delivery addresses cannot be placed, but that is something that needs to be clarified with domain experts and, clearly, some more domain knowledge is required to get such constraints into the system.

- I often hear complaints that keeping the information about the same physical entity in different contexts leads to data duplication. In the model shown in the previous diagram, that is not the case. The information we share is not exactly the same as the data we keep inside each context. For example, the number of product items available for sale doesn't necessarily replicate the current stock item. Some more complicated rules might be involved and the sales domain is kept happily ignorant to those rules, which are completely internal to the `Inventory` context. But then, some data will definitely be duplicated and that is a small price to pay to keep our models clean. There is no harm in keeping the same data in multiple places, the disk space is not a big issue these days.

But we definitely must ensure that keeping the information in sync is reliable, which is something we will be looking in the next chapter.

Team autonomy

If you ever used Kanban or at least learned about it, you probably remember that the holy grail of this methodology is to reduce **work in progress** (WIP). There is a lot you can learn from Kanban practitioners, but if you don't limit the WIP, you aren't doing Kanban. That, by the way, is why teams often fail when trying the methodology.

Originally, the idea of doing the work in small batches to eliminate queues and stocking up materials along the value creation stream comes from the manufacturing industry. You've probably heard of the *Toyota Way*, where Kanban originates from, or the **Theory of Constraints** (ToC) formulated by Eliyahu M. Goldratt. Although the philosophy of those methods comes from a rather different industry, where some of the aspects are drastically different from the software industry, I'd like to emphasize the following two principles that we can directly apply to our work in order to be more efficient in delivering business value: limiting work in progress and improving throughput.

Limiting work in progress

When a team or an individual developer is working on a list of things at the same time, completing any single item from the list would always take more time than if they were working solely on one thing. That happens, above all, due to the context switching, which I mentioned in `Chapter 2`, *Language and Context*. When we change our focus from one task to another, there will always be some time lost to bring our mind to the state when we can work on the new task efficiently. The more things we have unfinished, the more things that need to be remembered and then recovered—from memory and notes—when we go back to an unfinished task.

When teams that are working on a system that has a single model and single monolithic code base, those teams will have to coordinate with each other. Coordination might be required to prevent changes in share classes that are being changed for unrelated reasons. They might also need to ensure that before one team makes their changes, the other team does some prerequisite work. Data migration, regression testing, coordinated releases, and so on—we are quite familiar with those type of dependencies between teams.

But management rarely cares about such dependencies. If during the stand-up meeting, one team reports that they are waiting for another team to complete their work, their manager will ask them to do something else while they are waiting. When that happens, they get one more WIP item that cannot be completed right now, so they pull another item from the backlog and start working on it. That item might get some dependency as well and so the number of unfinished work snowballs. Teams start to blame each other for not delivering anything at all since they were all waiting for someone else.

What suffers most in these situations is the throughput.

Improving throughput

If there is a step in the delivery pipeline that is slow, the whole pipeline cannot produce more than this single step does. When teams work on a single codebase and a single model, they can have two major issues. First, there's the always-growing work in progress, as described in the previous paragraph. A constant need for coordination and continuous waiting leads to a lot of unfinished business. Some items from the *in progress* list will eventually be worked on again after the wait is over, but then comes the context switching. Sometimes, teams spend days or weeks picking up the work they put on hold a couple of months before. The time that is spent on the cross-team coordination—waiting for the others to complete the prerequisite job and to get back to the new context—is wasted. During that time, no value is produced but the money is spent as if the teams were doing something useful.

One more thing that could affect the throughput is a bottleneck. If all changes need to be done by two teams, no matter how fast or brilliant one team is, if the other team is slow or suffers from being understaffed of not skilled enough, the work will not be finished before the slowest of the two teams completes their part. Such a situation usually happens in organizations that split their teams not based on domain expertise or function, but on technological skill. A typical example would be the frontend team, the backend team, and the database team. You don't need to have all three, having just two of those will do enough damage to slow down the value chain tremendously. Before the database schema is changed, no work can be completed at the backend. Before the backend job took shape, at least in a form of the API contract (if the company is skilled enough to embrace contract-based development), the frontend team can do very little without having a risk of rewriting half of their code.

When teams are structured in this way, we can observe the worst example of Conway's law in real life.

Conway's law

Fifty years ago, in 1968, Melvin E. Conway published his paper called *How Do Committees Invent?* (`http://www.melconway.com/research/committees.html`). Perhaps the most cited part of that paper is the formulation of what we now call **Conway's law**, which states that if an organization designs a system, it will produce a design with a copy of that organization's communication structure.

I don't really want to overload you with details now but remember that this definition became so relevant that the 2017 edition of the DDD Europe conference had Conway's law as the main topic.

In the context of this chapter, my personal observations that how organizations structure their teams directly impacts the structure of their software, very much confirm the hypothesis of Mel Conway. I gave an example of technically-oriented teams because I experienced it during my career more than once. In one organization, I saw that the team that worked on a web part of the system user interface came so much in conflict with the team that was working on the rich-client for the same system, that they decided to create a separate domain model, backed by a separate database model, for them to use. That was done solely to avoid having blocking dependencies between those teams since they couldn't find a good way to coordinate. A lot of blood was spilled between those teams blaming each other, but in my view the situation was inevitable and there was no one to blame except the management that decided to structure teams like that.

Coordination between teams rarely works and most often leads to delays, tons of time spent on meetings and context switching. It also creates tensions between teams and create risks to slide into the blame-game. We can talk about *improving communication* for years and it won't improve the coordination even slightly.

Loose coupling, high alignment

I probably drowned you in the sea of problems that our industry suffers from on a large scale today. Let me bring some light to the picture and give you some clues as to how we can improve the situation.

As developers, we hear that we need to strive toward loose coupling and high cohesion in our code. Overall, the principle of one unit is responsible for one thing applies not only for classes in our code but also, for example, for services in the **service-oriented architecture (SOA)**. It also applies to the responsibilities of teams. Structuring teams around their technical proficiency are suboptimal. Let's look at how such teams might work when we have two distinct feature requests:

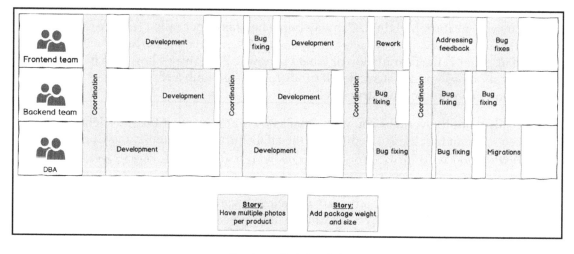

Flow when coordination is required

The flow shown in this diagram is greatly simplified, but you get the idea. All those white spots in between chunks of work that the teams are doing to complete those two stories are mostly wasted. That time could be spent on waiting, context switching, and small-scale coordination when developers from different teams need to agree on the sequence of work and issues discovered in the deliverables of other teams. In the end, there is not a single delivery done during the time frame, teams keep switching between tasks but the release is being constantly postponed.

If, however, teams are organized around business functions, or domains, the picture would be completely different:

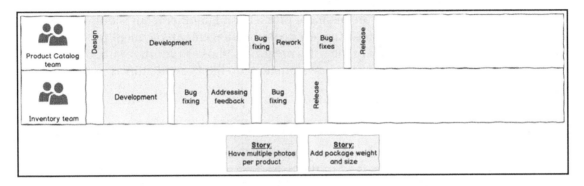

Flow without coordination

Don't be mistaken by the linear flow of work, since it is placed on a singular timeline. All these steps can be done in iterations, but iterations itself won't save you if teams require coordination.

Even if the amount of work is more or less the same, although it would probably be less due to a better focus and deeper domain knowledge, the coordination effort is gone along with context switching. Both teams are able to release independently and be ready to pick up new tasks.

Highly-aligned and loosely-coupled teams are one of the fundamental principles of the highly-praised Netflix culture, for example. One of the prerequisites to make such a structure even feasible is to have clear boundaries where each team operates. It doesn't mean, however, that teams must be assigned to work with a single bounded context. You might identify six contexts and have only three teams. In such a case, you need to look at the team size first. If each team has 10 members, maybe you want to have more teams that are smaller. Teams of five are fine in keeping the information-sharing tight and the feedback loop short.

But, there is no limitation to how many contexts one team can own. I can easily imagine a rather complex system that is being developed by a startup company that only has 10 engineers. They might identify that due to the complexity of the problem they are trying to solve, the system would need to be modeled with 10 bounded contexts. If they divide all developers into two teams of five, each team can handle multiple contexts. The most important aspect here is the ownership of the context, so teams should not share contexts. Transferring of the ownership is definitely possible, but it should be rare and complete so that after the transfer is complete, only one team owns the context.

The match between bounded contexts and teams can also give an indication of how many engineers the company might need. If the core business domain is properly identified, most probably all developers will work on the core domain With time it might happen that one team is solely engaged with the core business problem and another team is doing the work with all the supportive subdomains, such as account management, payment processing, and billing. When the complexity of the software grows, those supportive subdomains might be transferred to new teams. If a new core domain has been identified, some other team needs to take charge.

Geography

The last point that I would like to make in relation to Conway's law is the physical location of teams. It might come as a surprise, but this aspect is very important. Nowadays, more and more companies hire remote workers that work from home and also keep open offices on different parts of the planet. Keep in mind that such a distribution of the workforce, despite getting wider access to talent, also brings the burden of communication that is completely different for co-located teams and distributed teams.

If one bounded context is given to a team that contains members in different countries, or even worse, in different time zones, there will be a high level of risk involved. If engineers in such a team are experienced remote workers, it might be not a problem at all. But if people in that team are used to working in the office and suddenly they are asked to work together with someone that wakes up when they plan to go home, it might not work at all. So, it is a good idea to keep the geography consolidated if your company doesn't have much experience working with a remote workforce.

That shouldn't be seen as an obstacle to hire people in other countries and let them work remotely. But you might want to have several people that can sit in one place or at least live in one town, so they can communicate efficiently, meet regularly or even share one office, and call them a team. Such a team can easily take ownership of one or more of the bounded contexts of your software. The reduced burden of coordination and the high level of autonomy—those benefits of clearly defined bounded contexts will most certainly allow making even remote teams be much more successful and productive.

In fact, I believe that most of the failures that we hear about, when companies open remote offices and after some time declare the experience as a failure, are related to the fact that these companies weren't able to articulate the work they were giving to remote teams as bounded contexts. If teams are working on a shared code base, they must coordinate. They may make conflicting changes and all the burden and frustration that co-located teams are struggling with is multiplied by 10 when the teams are geographically distributed.

Summary

In this chapter, we finally started to use the term Bounded Context. It is often overlooked by people who started learning DDD. In Eric Evans's book, *Bounded Context*, it is explained in the strategic design part, which starts quite late in the book. A lot of useful patterns are introduced in that book before getting to the concept of Bounded Context and naturally, people start using what they know and sometimes find that to be enough.

But make no mistake, the power of DDD is not in aggregates and repositories. If you have a single model for a large, complex software system, having aggregates and repositories won't help you. When a large number of developers work with a single model, they suffer from an extensive need for coordination, conflicting changes, regression bugs, cognitive overload, and constant context switching. The fact that contexts aren't articulated properly in such a system doesn't remove them from existence. These contexts still exist as long as the business has people that are specialized in executing different business functions. Contexts lurk in a massive number of lines of code, numerous classes, and database tables that contain information about everything that happens. So, context switching is there, whether you like it or not.

As I first heard from Vaughn Vernon, DDD is a Ubiquitous Language developed within a Bounded Context. I like this definition a lot. It brings two of the most important principles of DDD into the spotlight. There is nothing more important than getting the language right, then finding linguistic boundaries for terms that are expressed by the same words but have a different meaning. And that would be the first obvious step toward finding the context boundaries.

Conway's law is something you must not ignore. If teams aren't structured by business capability and function, and instead are specialized by technical responsibility, even perfect Bounded Contexts won't help you. Only proper cross-functional teams that are organized around functional aspects of the system, that take ownership of one or more bounded contexts, will be able to work effectively and successfully. That is due to the fact that well-defined context boundaries bring the greatest level of autonomy to teams, as soon as no more than one team owns one bounded context. That doesn't imply that your organization must have as many teams as the number of identified bounded contexts. One team can probably handle more than one context, but not the other way around. High alignment and loose coupling are not only applicable for classes and services; these principles are fundamental for building successful teams that deliver.

Don't forget about the location of your colleagues. Distributed teams could work if they consist of people that have experience working remotely. But a remote team can take responsibility for one or more bounded contexts since they will not require a lot of coordination with other teams.

Other Books You May Enjoy

If you enjoyed this book, you may be interested in these other books by Packt:

Hands-On Object-Oriented Programming with C#
Raihan Taher

ISBN: 9781788296229

- Master OOP paradigm fundamentals
- Explore various types of exceptions
- Utilize C# language constructs efficiently
- Solve complex design problems by understanding OOP
- Understand how to work with databases using ADO.NET
- Understand the power of generics in C#
- Get insights into the popular version control system, Git
- Learn how to model and design your software

Hands-On Network Programming with C# and .NET Core
Sean Burns

ISBN: 9781789340761

- Understand the breadth of C#'s network programming utility classes
- Utilize network-layer architecture and organizational strategies
- Implement various communication and transport protocols within C#
- Discover hands-on examples of distributed application development
- Gain hands-on experience with asynchronous socket programming and streams
- Learn how C# and the .NET Core runtime interact with a hosting network
- Understand a full suite of network programming tools and features

Leave a review - let other readers know what you think

Please share your thoughts on this book with others by leaving a review on the site that you bought it from. If you purchased the book from Amazon, please leave us an honest review on this book's Amazon page. This is vital so that other potential readers can see and use your unbiased opinion to make purchasing decisions, we can understand what our customers think about our products, and our authors can see your feedback on the title that they have worked with Packt to create. It will only take a few minutes of your time, but is valuable to other potential customers, our authors, and Packt. Thank you!

Index

Made in the USA
Columbia, SC
12 March 2020